THE (

In the years following the Napoleonic Wars, a mysterious manuscript began to circulate among the dissatisfied noble elite of the Russian Empire. Entitled *The History of the Rus'*, it became one of the most influential historical texts of the modern era. Attributed to an eighteenth-century Orthodox archbishop, it described the heroic struggles of the Ukrainian Cossacks. Alexander Pushkin read the book as a manifestation of Russian national spirit, but Taras Shevchenko interpreted it as a quest for Ukrainian national liberation, and it would inspire thousands of Ukrainians to fight for the freedom of their homeland. Serhii Plokhy tells the fascinating story of the text's discovery and dissemination, unravelling the mystery of its authorship and tracing its subsequent impact on Russian and Ukrainian historical and literary imagination. In so doing, he brilliantly illuminates the relationship between history, myth, empire, and nationhood, from Napoleonic times to the fall of the Soviet Union.

SERHII PLOKHY is the Mykhailo Hrushevsky Professor of Ukrainian History at Harvard University. His previous publications include *Ukraine and Russia: Representations of the Past* (2008) and *The Origins of the Slavic Nations: Premodern Identities in Russia, Ukraine and Belarus* (2006).

NEW STUDIES IN EUROPEAN HISTORY

Edited by

PETER BALDWIN, *University of California, Los Angeles*
CHRISTOPHER CLARK, *University of Cambridge*
JAMES B. COLLINS, *Georgetown University*
MIA RODRÍGUEZ-SALGADO, *London School of Economics and Political Science*
LYNDAL ROPER, *University of Oxford*
TIMOTHY SNYDER, *Yale University*

The aim of this series in early modern and modern European history is to publish outstanding works of research, addressed to important themes across a wide geographical range, from southern and central Europe, to Scandinavia and Russia, from the time of the Renaissance to the Second World War. As it develops, the series will comprise focused works of wide contextual range and intellectual ambition.

A full list of titles published in the series can be found at:
www.cambridge.org/newstudiesineuropeanhistory

THE COSSACK MYTH

History and Nationhood in the Age of Empires

SERHII PLOKHY

CAMBRIDGE
UNIVERSITY PRESS

CAMBRIDGE
UNIVERSITY PRESS

University Printing House, Cambridge CB2 8BS, United Kingdom

Cambridge University Press is part of the University of Cambridge.

It furthers the University's mission by disseminating knowledge in the pursuit of education, learning and research at the highest international levels of excellence.

www.cambridge.org
Information on this title: www.cambridge.org/9781107449039

First published 2012
Reprinted 2013
First paperback edition 2014

A catalogue record for this publication is available from the British Library

Library of Congress Cataloguing in Publication data
Plokhy, Serhii, 1957–
The Cossack myth : history and nationhood in the age of empires / Serhii Plokhy.
pages cm. – (New studies in European history)
Includes bibliographical references and index.
ISBN 978-1-107-02210-2 (Hardback)
1. Ukraine–Historiography. 2. Istoriia Rusov. 3. Istoriia Rusov–Authorship. 4. Ukraine–History–Sources. 5. Cossacks–Ukraine–History–Sources. 6. Cossacks–Ukraine–Folklore. 7. Nationalism–Ukraine–History. 8. Ukraine–Relations–Russia. 9. Russia–Relations–Ukraine. 10. Imperialism–History. I. Title.
DK508.46.P55 2012
947.7′00491714–dc23
2012000083

ISBN 978-1-107-02210-2 Hardback
ISBN 978-1-107-44903-9 Paperback

For Olena

Contents

Figures

Maps

Note on transliteration and dates

In the text of this book, a simplified Library of Congress system is used to transliterate Ukrainian and Russian personal names and toponyms. The same system is applied in non-bibliographic references to persons and places in the footnotes. In bibliographic references, where the reader must be able to reconstruct Cyrillic spelling precisely from its Latin-alphabet transliteration, the full Library of Congress system (ligatures and breves omitted) is used. Toponyms are transliterated from the language of the country in which they are now located, with the notable exception of the Starodub region of the Russian Federation, which in the seventeenth and eighteenth centuries constituted part of the Ukrainian Hetmanate. In this particular case, both Ukrainian and Russian spellings are given on first mention. Pre-1918 dates in this book are given according to the Julian calendar, which in the nineteenth century lagged behind the Gregorian calendar by twelve days.

Map 1 The Hetmanate and surrounding territories in the 1750s.

Map 2 The Starodub regiment in the 1750s.

The Hetmanate as part
of imperial Russia, 1809

The Hetmanate

MOSCOW

KALUGA

MAHILIOŬ

TULA

MINSK

Orel

OREL

Dnieper

Desna

Chernihiv

Kursk

Voronezh

VOLHYNIA

CHERNIHIV

KURSK

VORONEZH

Zhytomyr

Kyiv

KHARKIV

POLTAVA

Kharkiv

KYIV

Poltava

PODILIA

KHARKIV

Katerynoslav

KATERYNOSLAV

BESSARABIA

KHERSON

TAURIDA

Odesa

Kherson

Sea of Azov

CRIMEA

CAUCASUS

Simferopol

Bahçesaray

Black   Sea

0   50   100   150   200 km

0   25   50   75   100   125 miles

Map 3 Imperial provinces: the Hetmanate as part of imperial Russia, 1809.

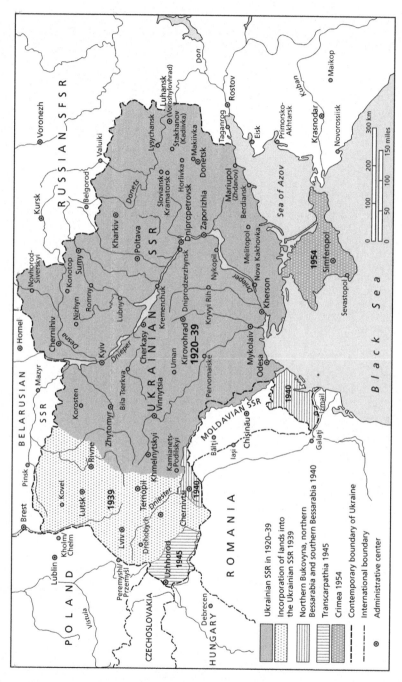

Map 4 Modern Ukraine.

Introduction

On the sunny morning of March 31, 1814, the citizens of Paris witnessed a scene that their city had not experienced in almost four hundred years. Armed foreigners poured into the streets and squares, making their way into the city through the Pantin Gate. A multinational army, some of its units dressed in uniforms never before seen in Western Europe, paraded in front of shocked and confused, but also amazed and occasionally amused Parisians. At the head of more than one thousand corps, consisting of Russian, German and Austrian troops, rode on his grey thoroughbred Alexander I, the Tsar of all the Russias, the liberator of Europe, and the conqueror of France. As he led the march through the streets of the French capital, Alexander was followed by his colorfully dressed Cossack guards, an object of interest and amazement to some citizens of Paris and a source of unease and concern to others.

On one side of Alexander rode the King of Prussia, on the other – the representative of the Habsburg emperor. Suddenly Alexander stopped his horse and declared to the surprised crowd: "I do not come as an enemy; I come to bring you peace and commerce!" His words were met with cheers. It was a moment of triumph of Russian arms and the Russian spirit that history had not seen before and would never see again. Joseph Stalin recalled Alexander's capture of Paris when he met President Harry Truman in Potsdam after the Second World War. In 1945, as in 1814, it seemed that a new era was dawning: Russia had repelled a brutal aggressor and emerged from the abyss of near defeat to bring liberation to the nations of Europe and peace and prosperity to the world. But there was a catch. On both occasions, Russia was eager to share with the world a commodity that it lacked itself. Freedom was in short supply in the Russian Empire and the Soviet Union, and victory abroad bore the seeds of future defeat at home.[1]

---

[1] Janet M. Hartley, *Alexander I* (London and New York, 1994), p. 124; Henri Troyat, *Alexander of Russia: Napoleon's Conqueror* (New York, 2003), pp. 187–206; Henry Kissinger, *Diplomacy* (New York, 1994), p. 398. On Napoleon's invasion of the Russian Empire and the campaigns of the

This book tells a story directly related to the growth and development of one of those seeds: the idea of the sovereignty and freedom of nations. The idea gained strength slowly but steadily throughout the nineteenth century, and in the wake of the First World War it brought about the disintegration of the Russian Empire. Few elements of Alexander's army of 1814 contributed more to unraveling the empire than the Cossacks. These colorfully dressed horsemen, who did not leave the French capital before introducing it to the concept of fast food – Parisian bistros have their origins in the Russian *bystro*, which means "fast" – were recruited from the steppe borderlands of the Russian Empire. Among those warriors were Cossacks of Ukraine or, in the official nomenclature of the time, Little Russia, who were particularly eager to join in the fighting and had high expectations of the war. Only a few decades earlier they had had an autonomous state with military units of their own. Now they had proved their loyalty to the empire and wanted it to recognize their service. The Cossacks did not expect the restoration of their state, but they hoped that their regiments would not be disbanded and that rank-and-file Cossacks who entered the imperial service would be exempt from peasant labor obligations. They were promised as much in 1812, when the state needed them to defend the empire. With the war won, the promises were forgotten.

By 1816 Cossack units in Ukraine had been dissolved, and the noble status of descendants of Cossack officers was again in question. Their special rights and privileges were taken away, and the conditions of their integration into the empire were demeaning. The Cossack conquerors of Paris found themselves victors abroad but vanquished at home. For the Cossacks of Ukraine this was a painful but not wholly alien experience. Their previous masters, the kings of Poland, had used them as cannon fodder for generations, luring them into state service in time of need and reneging on their promises thereafter. Back then, in the sixteenth and seventeenth centuries, the Cossack response was invariably the same: they would rise in revolt, starting bloody uprisings that claimed tens of thousands of victims, and shaking the foundations of the Polish state. The largest of those uprisings, led by Bohdan Khmelnytsky in 1648, inaugurated a lengthy period of wars that set the Polish-Lithuanian Commonwealth on the road to partition in the late eighteenth century. It also brought many Ukrainian Cossacks under the sovereignty of the

Russian imperial army in Europe in 1813–14, see Dominic Lieven, *Russia against Napoleon: The True Story of the Campaigns of War and Peace* (New York, 2010).

Russian tsars, who were astute enough to offer the Cossacks autonomy, which they had not enjoyed under the Polish kings.[2]

Now, with autonomy gone, the regiments disbanded, privileges under attack, and the noble status of officer families in question, the Cossacks were powerless to strike back in their usual manner. Their response was unconventional and at first largely ignored by the empire. A few years after the Napoleonic Wars, a mysterious manuscript began to circulate among the dissatisfied Ukrainian elite. It was a historical treatise called the *History of the Rus'*, in which the term *Rus'* referred to the Ukrainian Cossacks. They were presented as a nation separate from the Russians to the north. The manuscript told the history of the Cossacks in a manner befitting the hopes and expectations of the Romantic age: its narrative was replete with heroes and villains, as well as enthralling battle scenes, victories and defeats, and graphic depictions of bloody reprisals. The nation of Rus' emerged victorious from its numerous ordeals. It overthrew the Polish yoke and joined the Russian Empire of its own free will, responding to religious and ethnic affinity with the Muscovite tsar and his nation. But the new authorities mistreated the brave but naïve Cossacks, taking away their ancestral name of Rus' and appropriating it for themselves. The author of the treatise claimed that his purpose was to give the heroic Cossack nation the recognition it deserved. He achieved much more than that.[3]

For almost a quarter century the text existed only in manuscript, copied and recopied by descendants of the Cossack officer elite. It became one of the most influential – and, from the perspective of the Russian Empire, most destructive – historical texts of the modern era. The first Russian intellectual to fall under the spell of the *History* was Kondratii Ryleev, a veteran of the Napoleonic wars and a leading poet of the era. The manuscript inspired him to write one of the most impassioned poems of the nineteenth-century liberation movement, the "Confession" of Severyn Nalyvaiko, the leader of a late sixteenth-century Cossack revolt. The poem sent thousands of young Russians into unequal battle with their government. Alexander Pushkin was the next poet to be inspired by the *History*, and one of the first to publish excerpts from it. Nikolai Gogol, another literary genius of the era, was eager to follow suit: some

---

[2] For general surveys of Ukrainian history, see Orest Subtelny, *Ukraine: A History*, 4th edn. (Toronto, 2009) and Paul Robert Magocsi, *A History of Ukraine*, 2d edn. (Toronto, 2010).

[3] *Istoriia Rusov ili Maloi Rossii. Sochinenie Georgiia Koniskago, Arkhiepiskopa Beloruskago* (Moscow, 1846).

of the most impressive scenes of his novel *Taras Bul'ba* were based on the *History*. Despite his deep Ukrainian patriotism, Gogol, not unlike Pushkin before him, saw in the *History* a manifestation of Russian national spirit and imperial patriotism. A younger generation of Ukrainian intellectuals, led by the father of the modern Ukrainian nation, Taras Shevchenko, read the Cossack chronicle as a quest for national liberation. Thus interpreted, the *History*, which became known as the bible of the Ukrainian national movement, inspired thousands of Ukrainian patriots to fight for the freedom of their homeland.

The modern Ukrainian nation, which emerged from the ruins of the Russian Empire during the Revolution of 1917, employed the Cossack myth embodied in the *History of the Rus'* to legitimize its new state. In 1918 it revived the Cossack rank of hetman for its leader and chose for that office a descendant of one of the Cossack hetmans of the early eighteenth century. Independent Ukraine of the post-First World War era was soon crushed by the rising power of the Russian and Polish states, which divided the Ukrainian lands between themselves, but Cossack mythology survived the ordeal. Mykhailo Hrushevsky, Ukraine's greatest historian and the principal author of the Ukrainian national narrative, continued his research on Cossack history in Soviet Ukraine in the 1920s. His numerous students researched the history of Cossack statehood in Western Ukraine, which was under Polish rule during the interwar period. The Great Famine of 1933 and the accompanying persecution of the Ukrainian intelligentsia crushed the Ukrainian national revival in the USSR. Ironically enough, the outbreak of the Second World War and, in particular, the Soviet takeover of Western Ukraine and Western Belarus in September 1939 led to a revival of Cossack studies, which were considered useful for bolstering Soviet Ukrainian patriotism directed against Poland and, later, Nazi Germany.

The Cossack myth gained new legitimacy in Soviet Ukraine after the war under the aegis of the "friendship of peoples" paradigm. That paradigm stressed the accomplishments of the Cossack hetman Bohdan Khmelnytsky, who accepted the tsar's suzerainty over Ukraine in the mid seventeenth century. The Soviet authorities changed course once again in the early 1970s, banning further research on the subject because they saw the growing interest in the Cossack past as a manifestation of Ukranian nationalism. Their attempts to curb the dissemination of Cossack mythology were only partly successful. When in 1991 Ukraine reappeared on the political map of Europe, the new state was led to independence by activists deeply inspired by the *History of the Rus'*. Ivan Drach, the leader of *Rukh*, the largest pro-independence Ukrainian movement of the late 1980s and early 1990s, took it upon himself to translate the *History* into modern Ukrainian in the months leading up to independence. The Ukrainian referendum of December 1, 1991, put an end to the Russian Empire in its modern, Soviet incarnation. Few historical works contributed more to this global transformation than the *History of the Rus'*.[4]

This book examines how the history of Cossackdom as a social estate and an autonomous polity was transformed into a nation-building myth that helped split the monolith of Russian imperial identity and laid the foundations for the rise of the modern Ukrainian nation. It addresses this task by taking a close look at the origins of the *History of the Rus'*, by far the most important text in the formation of the Cossack myth and Ukrainian historical identity.

The most astonishing fact about the *History* is that scholars are still unable to agree even on the most basic facts about this seminal work, including the name of its author. The introduction to the *History* claims that it was written over a long period by several generations of Orthodox monks. It was then edited in the 1760s by Archbishop Heorhii Konysky of Mahiliou in Belarus. No one accepts that version today. Like Ossian's poetry in Britain, the *Manuscript of the Queen's Court* in the Czech lands, and the *Tale of Igor's Campaign* in Russia, the *History* was the product of an era of forgeries in which entrepreneurial intellectuals were busy producing birth certificates for their nations – the older, the better. While the Scots and the Czechs know the names of their mythmakers and venerate the memory of James Macpherson and Václav Hanka, the Russians and Ukrainians are still divided with regard to their storytellers. The claim that the *Tale of Igor's Campaign* is a well-written mystification is widely accepted in the West but vehemently rejected in Russia. The puzzle of the *History of the Rus'* is of a different nature. Few scholars accept the old notion that it was produced by Orthodox monks and their archbishop, but questions about the author, the time and place of the work's creation, and its intended message continue to haunt historians, literary scholars, and linguists almost two hundred years after the first appearance of the mysterious text.

In my search for the author of the *History of the Rus'*, I use the term "author" in the broadest possible terms, encompassing possible multiple authors and editors of the work. I bow to historiographic tradition in

---

[4] For the impact of the *History of the Rus'* on the development of Ukrainian national identity, see Parts I, II, and III of this book.

referring to that person, or group of persons, as "he." This implies no assumption that women were not involved, only the recognition that as of this writing we have no late eighteenth-century or early nineteenth-century historical works written by individual or collective female authors. The search for the author of the *History* constitutes the main story line of this book. Its two additional layers – a history of the Ukrainian Cossacks from the early sixteenth to the early nineteenth century and a history of the discovery, publication, and study of the *History* itself – serve to illuminate relations between history, myth, and nationhood from Napoleonic times to the present. By tracing the ways in which every new generation of students of the *History* reinterpreted the manuscript according to its own needs, fears, and models of its ever-changing national identity, I relate the search for the author of the *History* as a story of the search for modern Ukrainian and Russian identity. The book makes use of previously unknown archival sources, but its main conclusions are based on a textual analysis of the *History*, its sources, prototypes, and competitors. To make the results of my research accessible to readers not primarily interested in the details of intertextual relationships, I present my findings through the individual stories of scholars and potential authors of the *History*.

My main goal lies beyond the task of discovering the origins of a text that has mesmerized generations of scholars. In solving this particular puzzle, I attempt to put the *History* into its original political, ideological, and cultural context by establishing the time of its creation and identifying the circle of those involved in its production. I argue that the *History* was not a conscious manifesto of Russo-Ukrainian unity or of rising Ukrainian nationalism – the two opposing interpretations advanced by modern scholarship on the text – but an attempt on the part of the descendants of the Cossack officer elite to negotiate the best possible conditions for their incorporation into the empire. As the imperial authorities challenged the noble status of Cossack officeholders and liquidated the last vestiges of Cossack military organization, the Ukrainian nobility was eager to promote its historical achievements and prove that the descendants of the Cossack officers were equals of the Russian nobility. Indeed, the Ukrainian elite of the early nineteenth century claimed that the Cossacks were superior to the Russian nobles, as they were descendants of the Rus' tribes – the original founders of the Russian state and dynasty. The paradox that I highlight in my conclusions is that in contending for imperial elite status the creators of the Cossack myth laid the foundations for the rise of the new Ukrainian nation, leading to the demise of the all-Russian identity and the eventual collapse of the empire.

One of the most rewarding aspects of my research has been the fitting of my textual analysis and detective work into the broader context of the history of national mythologies. The dismantling of the "mythologized past," as Paul A. Cohen notes in his groundbreaking work on the events and historical image of the Boxer Uprising, "is seldom pain-free: it entails a loss, often irreversible, not unlike that resulting from death, that can be severely disturbing and may, because of this, be stubbornly resisted." Still, such dismantling is an extremely important task of history as an academic discipline. No less important is the study of historical myths and the process of mythmaking. In that regard, the story of the creation, dissemination, and reception of the *History of the Rus'* seems an ideal object of study. The *History of the Rus'* was a key text in the transformation of Cossackdom as a lived experience into a historical and national myth. No matter how idealized, inaccurate, and even fantastic the image of Cossack history presented in this text, it became an embodiment of "truth" about the past for generations of readers. As Cohen writes, "Once assertions about the past enter deeply into people's minds (and hearts), it is arguable that they acquire a truth of their own, even if this truth does not at all coincide with what actually happened at some point in past time. At the very least such assertions are true statements about what people *believe* and therefore must occupy a central place in any history of human consciousness."[5]

In my understanding of the term "myth," I follow the definition provided by George Schöpflin, a student of East European politics and coeditor of a collection of essays on *Myths and Nationhood*: "Myth is one of the ways in which collectives – in this context, more especially nations – establish and determine the foundations of their own being, their own system of morality and values. In this sense, therefore, myth is a set of beliefs, usually put forth as a narrative, held by a community about itself." According to Schöpflin, who in this case echoes numerous other scholars sharing an anthropological approach to the study of myth, "[i]t is the content of the myth that is important, not its accuracy as a historical account." The *History of the Rus'* seems to fit two of Schöpflin's nine categories of national mythology – the myths of military valor and ethnogenesis. By focusing on the heroic deeds of the Cossacks, the *History* provided the emerging Ukrainian nation with a story of its origins not as a social estate or a political entity but as an ethnic group of "native-born"

---

[5] Paul A. Cohen, *History in Three Keys: The Boxers as Event, Experience and Myth* (New York, 1997), pp. 211–12.

Rusians (that is, inhabitants of Rus'). I argue in this book that by doing so, the *History* helped replace the myth of all-Russian unity with that of Ukrainian historical and cultural uniqueness. It also turned the Cossack myth into one of the cornerstones of modern Ukrainian identity.[6]

My immediate point of departure in interpreting the *History of the Rus'* as an expression and embodiment of Cossack mythology has been John A. Armstrong's discussion of the role of the Cossack myth in Ukrainian nation-building. He defined myth as "the integrating phenomenon through which symbols of national identity acquire a coherent meaning." Also crucial to my interpretation of the role of the Cossack myth in the formation of Ukrainian national identity is Anthony D. Smith's observation that "myths, memories, symbols and values can often be adapted to new circumstances by being accorded new meanings and new functions." These broad definitions and general assumptions worked very well for me in the past, when I dealt with the evolution of premodern East Slavic identities and the uses and abuses of Cossack history in post-Soviet settings. Although they provided a good general framework for this study as well, in the course of my work I found, to my surprise, that I could no longer rely exclusively on the familiar literature about nations and nationalism that includes works by Benedict Anderson, Miroslav Hroch, Ernest Gellner, and Eric Hobsbawm.[7]

When I began work on this book, I expected that the traces of the *History*'s anonymous author would lead me to a group of dreamy intellectuals who contributed to Miroslav Hroch's "heritage-gathering" stage of nation-building without having a clear political goal in mind. My research led me in a different direction. The circle of "unusual suspects" discussed in this volume consisted of notables not only politically engaged

---

[6] George Schöpflin, "The Functions of Myth and a Taxonomy of Myths," in *Myths and Nationhood*, ed. Geoffrey Hosking and George Schöpflin (London, 1997), pp. 19–35. On the formation of Ukrainian national mythology, see Andrew Wilson, "Myths of National History in Belarus and Ukraine," in Hosking and Schöpflin, *Myths and Nationhood* pp. 182–97.

[7] John A. Armstrong, "Myth and History in the Evolution of Ukrainian Consciousness," in *Ukraine and Russia in Their Historical Encounter*, ed. Peter J. Potichnyj *et al.* (Edmonton, 1992), p. 133; Anthony D. Smith, *The Ethnic Origins of Nations* (Oxford and New York, 1986), p. 3. Cf. Serhii Plokhy, *Ukraine and Russia: Representations of the Past* (Toronto, 2008), p. 168; Plokhy, *The Origins of the Slavic Nations: Premodern Identities in Russia, Ukraine and Belarus* (Cambridge, 2006), p. 4. For the dominant "modernist" approaches to the study of nationalism, see Benedict Anderson, *Imagined Communities: Reflections on the Origins and Spread of Nationalism* (London, 2006); Miroslav Hroch, *Social Preconditions of National Revival in Europe* (New York, 2000); Ernest Gellner, *Nations and Nationalism* (Ithaca, N.Y., 2009); E. J. Hobsbawm, *Nations and Nationalism since 1780: Programme, Myth, Reality* (Cambridge, 1992); Gellner and Terence Ranger, eds., *The Invention of Tradition* (Cambridge, 1992).

at home but also well integrated into the empire. Individuals potentially responsible for the production of the *History* and definitely involved in its reading and dissemination included highly placed imperial officials who made their careers and fortunes by extending imperial boundaries and administering imperial borderlands. They received their education in the imperial capitals and sent their children to imperial institutions of higher learning, which turned them into Russian writers and poets. Why would such people produce, reproduce and disseminate a text that not only glorified the Cossack past but also promoted a separate Rus' nation and eventually contributed to the fall of the empire? In order to answer that question, I had to put the results of my research not only into the historiographic context of nationalism and national identities but also into that of the evolution of empires.

The last decade has seen a tremendous growth of interest in the history of empires and an explosion of literature on the relations between empires and nations. What I found particularly useful was the emphasis of this new research on the simple fact that national ideology did not develop in a vacuum but grew out of the political and ideological context of empires. While the early promoters of nations had specific political goals in mind, they did not necessarily regard nation and empire as irreconcilable political categories. In their recent global history of empires, Jane Burbank and Frederick Cooper note that the fathers of the American Revolution, like their counterparts in Haiti, "used imperial idioms and addressed imperial institutions" before they decided that the conflict was irresolvable and opted for secession. Nations did not replace empires overnight. They were conceived and formed within the boundaries defined by empires, and it is important to place the development of national ideas and mythologies into that historical context. "Once we get away from a nation-centered view of history and the assumption that history moves inexorably toward correspondence of one 'people' with one state," suggest Burbank and Cooper, "we can focus on longstanding debates over what democracy, citizenship and nationality actually meant and when, where, and to whom these notions applied – within empires, in interempire rivalries, in mobilizations against empires."[8]

---

[8] Jane Burbank and Frederick Cooper, *Empires in World History: Power and the Politics of Difference* (Princeton and Oxford, 2010), pp. 221, 245. For the recent literature on empires, see David Abernethy, *The Dynamics of Global Dominance: European Overseas Empires, 1415–1980* (New Haven, 2000); John Darwin, *After Tamerlane: The Global History of Empire since 1405* (London, 2008); Niall Ferguson, *Empire: The Rise and Demise of the British World Order and the Lessons for Global Power* (New York, 2003); Dominic Lieven, *Empire: The Russian Empire and its Rivals*

It is within this context of empire-defined historical, political, and intellectual space that I felt most comfortable placing my "suspects" and their ideas about history, politics, and the nation. There are a number of important specificities to be taken into account when examining relations between the elite of Ukrainian Cossack origin and the rulers of the Russian Empire in the eighteenth and nineteenth centuries. Unlike other social, religious, and ethnic groups in that empire (and many others), the descendants of the Cossacks were convinced – and the *History of the Rus'* offers the best evidence of that belief – that they were not conquered subjects but full participants in the ruling imperial nation, indeed, its most ancient, authentic, and central component. They considered themselves partners in the imperial undertaking and protested discrimination against them by the imperial center. The closest parallel to the Ukrainian/ Little Russian situation in the Russian Empire is the role played by the Scots in the formation and expansion of the British Empire, and I benefited enormously from the extensive literature on the role of literary texts in the formation of Scottish mythology and identity *vis-à-vis* the British Empire and the notion of "Britishness."[9]

Kenneth McNeil, one of the recent writers on the subject, points out the "unique historical conditions in Scotland that produced a professional elite, which assumed a central role in shaping British imperial attitudes while simultaneously feeling the increasing dominance of English political and cultural influences." Anyone familiar with the role played in the formation of the Russian Empire and Russian imperial identity in the eighteenth century by natives of Cossack Ukraine, from such heavyweights as Teofan Prokopovych and Oleksandr Bezborodko to the thousands of Ukrainian intellectuals, bureaucrats, and medical doctors (at one point, the latter made up more than two-thirds of all the empire's physicians), can recognize the parallels between Ukrainian and Scottish experiences of empire in that period. No less intriguing for a scholar of Russo-Ukrainian relations in their imperial context is McNeil's statement that the "ambivalence of the Scottish negotiation of the difference reflects

---

(London, 2001); Charles S. Maier, *Among Empires: American Ascendancy and its Predecessors* (Cambridge, Mass., 2007); Alexei Miller, *The Romanov Empire and Nationalism* (Budapest and New York, 2006).

[9] See, for example, Leith Davis, *Acts of Union: Scotland and the Literary Negotiation of the British Nation, 1707–1830* (Stanford, 1998); Stefan Thomas Hall, *The Role of Medieval Scottish Poetry in Creating Scottish Identity: "Textual Nationalism"* (Lewiston, N.Y., 2006); Katie Trumpener, *Bardic Nationalism: The Romantic Novel and the British Empire* (Princeton, 1997); Alok Yadav, *Before the Empire of English: Literature, Provinciality, and Nationalism in Eighteenth-Century Britain* (New York, 2004).

the anomalous condition of a minority culture seeking to transform itself into an imperial one." It is one of my conclusions that a similar ambivalence underlay the Cossack historical myth as formulated in the *History of the Rus'*.[10]

The Scottish and Czech parallels turned out to be exceptionally productive for interpreting the results of this study because they help place the *History of the Rus'* and the Cossack myth that it helped create and disseminate into the broader context of European mythmaking. The genre of national literary mystification, to which the *History of the Rus'* intimately belongs, found its best-known representatives in James Macpherson and Václav Hanka. The extensive literature on the literary forgeries of the era provides a useful framework for analyzing the origins and reception of the *History of the Rus'*. The demand for a national epic in the wake of a national disaster or defeat, the use of the imperial language in such an epic, the emphasis on the historical and cultural superiority of the defeated nation over its victors, the attribution of authorship to a long-deceased authoritative figure in order to authenticate the forged narrative and its message, the use of forgery to "restore" the lost national narrative and, finally, the political loyalty of the creators of such national mystifications to the empire – all these features typify the genre to which the *History of the Rus'* belongs.[11]

The focus of this book on the authorship of the *History of the Rus'* has influenced its narrative strategy and structure. It consists of seventeen chapters grouped in five parts. Part I, "The mystery," discusses the impact of the *History* on the Russian and Ukrainian historical imagination while

---

[10] Kenneth McNeil, *Scotland, Britain, Empire: Writing the Highlands, 1760–1860* (Columbus, Ohio, 2007), p. 14. On the parallels between Ukrainian and Scottish experience, see Stephen Velychenko, "Empire Loyalism and Minority Nationalism in Great Britain and Imperial Russia, 1707–1914: Institutions, Law and Nationality in Scotland and Ukraine," *Comparative Studies in Society and History* 39 (1997): 413–41. On the parallels between Walter Scott's writings and the portrayal of the Cossacks in Russian literature, see Judith Deutsch Kornblatt, *The Cossack Hero in Russian Literature: A Study in Cultural Mythology* (Madison, Wis., 1992) and Edyta M. Bojanowska, *Nikolai Gogol: Between Ukrainian and Russian Nationalism* (Cambridge, Mass., 2007).

[11] On historical forgeries and literary mystifications, see Nick Groom, *The Forger's Shadow: How Forgery Changed the Course of Literature* (Basingstoke and Oxford, 2002); Margaret Russett, *Fictions and Fakes: Forging Romantic Authenticity, 1760–1845* (Cambridge, 2006); K. K. Ruthven, *Faking Literature* (Cambridge, 2001); Susan Stewart, *Crimes of Writing: Problems in the Containment of Representation* (Durham, N.C., and London, 1994). On literary mystifications in Russia and Ukraine, see George G. Grabowicz, "National Poets and National Mystifications," in *Literární mystifikace, etnické mýty a jejich úloha při formování národního vědomí. Studie Slováckého muzea: Uherské Hradiště* 6 (2001): 7–24; Edward L. Keenan, *Josef Dobrovský and the Origins of the Igor' Tale* (Cambridge, Mass., 2004); Aleksei Tolochko, *"Istoriia Rossiiskaia" Vasiliia Tatishcheva: Istochniki i izvestiia* (Moscow, 2005).

telling the story of the discovery and publication of the manuscript – a source of unending questions and of a large body of evidence to be investigated. It also presents background information about the Cossacks and their state. Part II, "On a cold trail," considers previous attempts and failures to identify the elusive author of the *History*. It focuses on research by individual scholars and life stories of the "usual suspects" believed to have written the work. It also shows how the search for the author of the *History* was influenced by the scholars' own conceptions of their identity. As that identity changed, and scholars who adhered to populist ideals were replaced by those who valued the interests of the nation above all, so did candidates for authorship of the *History* and the understanding of its message.

The two central parts of the book (III and IV) are constructed around questions akin to those asked by detectives in criminal cases: when, where, and under what circumstances did the act of historiographic forgery take place; what was the motive; did the culprit act alone or have accomplices; and, finally, what was the identity of the mysterious perpetrator or perpetrators. Part III, "Pieces of a puzzle," establishes the geographic, social, and ideological context of the creation of the *History of the Rus'*. There I retire the files left to us by previous investigators. Using the evidence they collected, I go back to the source, the *History* itself, to investigate the time and place of its creation and the motives of its author. Part IV, "Unusual suspects," defines the immediate social and intellectual circle of the author of the *History of the Rus'*. With the time and place of the historiographic "crime" established, and the motives and methods of the mystification uncovered, it returns to the question of authorship by putting forward a "lineup" of new and unusual suspects. All of them were not only present at the right place and time but also had the appropriate background, education, connections, and intellectual capacity to commit the "crime of writing." Each new chapter serves as a stepping stone on the road to the virtual summit, where the answer to the big question – who was behind the creation of the *History of the Rus'* – is finally revealed. Part V, "A family circle," presents a considerable body of additional evidence to answer the questions posed in the introduction and early chapters of the book. This part not only establishes the circle behind the creation of the *History* but also addresses the much larger question of the political and social milieu in which the manuscript was produced. The conclusions put the *History* into the broad context of history, mythology, and nation-building on Europe's steppe frontier.

PART I

The mystery

CHAPTER I

A call for freedom

It was one of those white summer nights for which St. Petersburg is famous. The small crowd that gathered in the early hours of July 13, 1826 on the Holy Trinity Bridge across the Neva River and on the shore near the SS. Peter and Paul Fortress could clearly see the gruesome ritual taking place on the ramparts of the fortress. First, to the accompaniment of drumbeats, dozens of young and middle-aged men were led out of the fortress, most of them dressed in dirty and worn-out officers' uniforms. They were then divided into smaller groups and brought in front of the military detachments, summoned to the scene, in which they had once served and that some of them had led into battle. They listened calmly as the verdict of the court was read out, sentencing them to years of hard labor and exile. After the sentence was read, the convicts were brought to their knees and their sabers broken above their heads, signaling the revocation of their noble status, officer ranks, awards, and distinctions. Their epaulettes and military uniforms were burned in front of the fortress.

Once the ritual of "civic execution" was over and the convicts taken back inside the fortress, those gathered on the banks of the Neva could see guards escorting five more men in heavy chains out of the fortress gates. They led them to the gallows that had been hastily constructed on the riverbank. There was a pause as the executioners looked for benches on which to place the five men awaiting execution. They finally found some in the abandoned naval school nearby. What followed sent a chill through everyone who witnessed the scene, including the executioners themselves. As drums beat and the hangmen removed the benches and the floor of the scaffold from under the condemned men's feet, only two of them hung on their ropes, while the three in the middle fell into the ditch beneath the gallows. The ropes used to hang them proved too weak to carry the weight of their bodies and the chains around their ankles. There was a sigh of relief and astonishment among those present at the execution. Would the men be saved?

"God does not want them dead," said one of the guards, but the military governor of St. Petersburg, General Pavel Golenishchev-Kutuzov, ordered the survivors to be brought back to the scaffold and hanged again. The scenario of the execution had been written by Emperor Nicholas I himself, and the battle-scarred general, who had distinguished himself in the Battle of the Nations at Leipzig in 1813 and was then dispatched to St. Petersburg from Paris with the news of Napoleon's defeat, was determined to carry out the emperor's orders to the end. Nicholas had wanted the execution to be over by four o'clock in the morning: it was now close to five, with the sun up and the darkness all but gone, yet three convicts accused of high treason were still alive. Golenishchev-Kutuzov ordered his hangmen to hurry. The stunned and bloodied survivors, one of them barely able to walk, were led out again onto the hurriedly rebuilt scaffold. "It's an accursed land where they don't know how to plot, judge, or hang," one of them is alleged to have said. Another shouted at Golenishchev-Kutuzov: "Base lackey of a tyrant! Give the executioner your ornamental pins so that we don't die a third time!" The general was unmoved. By six o'clock the execution was finally over. The bodies of the five prisoners who believed that they had given their lives in the fight for freedom were removed from the scene. Next day their remains were transported to Goldai Island near St. Petersburg and buried in an unmarked grave.

The five men hanged that summer morning of 1826 on the banks of the Neva were the leaders of the Decembrist conspiracy, organized by veterans of the Napoleonic Wars who sought to change the political order of the Russian Empire. On December 14, 1825, seven months before the gruesome execution on the ramparts of the SS. Peter and Paul Fortress, a score of young, idealistic Russian officers had led their troops to the Senate Square in St. Petersburg with the hope of toppling the autocracy, abolishing serfdom, and convening a constitutional assembly. Their troops were surrounded by detachments loyal to the tsar and dispersed by artillery fire. A subsequent rising of the Chernihiv regiment in Ukraine was also suppressed. After a six-month investigation, the leaders of the two uprisings were hanged, participants and members of Decembrist circles exiled to Siberia or sent to wage war in the Caucasus. The revolt was crushed, plans for the radical restructuring of the empire (some of which included such drastic measures as the introduction of military dictatorship) dashed, and the autocracy emerged victorious. But the example of the five martyrs and the dream of freedom kindled by the leaders of the revolt would live on, inspiring future generations of rebels.[1]

The man who called General Golenishchev-Kutuzov a "base lackey of a tyrant" was a thirty-year-old retired officer and manager of the Russian-American Company in St. Petersburg, Kondratii Ryleev. He was the heart and soul of the Decembrist circle in St. Petersburg. It was in his apartment that the revolt was planned in the days leading up to December 14, 1825. A friend of Alexander Pushkin and an acclaimed poet in his own right, Ryleev inspired his friends and co-conspirators not only with his fiery poetry, in which he called on his readers to fight for freedom even at the cost of their lives, but also by his stoicism at the time of his execution. When a priest tried to console him, Ryleev took the priest's hand, put it on his chest and said, referring to his own heart: "Feel, Father, it's not beating any faster than before."[2]

Ryleev's friends believed that he had foreseen his own death when, a few months before the uprising, he published a short excerpt from a poetic novel on which he was working at the time. The poetic novel, titled *Nalyvaiko*, had as its main protagonist the leader of a late-sixteenth-century Cossack uprising in Ukraine. In the excerpt, titled "Nalyvaiko's Confession," Ryleev put the following words into the mouth of the Cossack leader as he faced execution:

> I know full well the direful fate
> Which must upon the patriot wait
> Who first dares rise against the foe
> And at the tyrant aim the blow.
> This is my destined fate – but say
> When, when has freedom won her way
> Without the blood of martyrs shed,
> When none for liberty had bled?
> My coming doom I feel and know,
> And bless the stroke which lays me low,
> And, father, now with joy I meet
> My death, to me such end is sweet.[3]

[1] "Kazn' dekabristov. Rasskazy sovremennikov," in *Russkii arkhiv* 2 (1881): 341–46; Nestor Kotliarevskii, *Ryleev* (St. Petersburg, 1908), pp. 186–91; "Dekabristy. Istoriia vosstaniia 14 dekabria 1825 goda na Senatskoi ploshchadi v Peterburge," www.patiks.ru/txt/3dekab77.shtml. On the Decembrist Revolt, see Anatole G. Mazour, *The First Russian Revolution, 1825: The Decembrist Movement* (Stanford, Calif., 1966).

[2] "Dekabristy. Istoriia vosstaniia 14 dekabria 1825 goda." On Ryleev, see Patrick O. Meara, *K. F. Ryleev: A Political Biography of the Decembrist Poet* (Princeton, N.J., 1984).

[3] K. F. Relaieff, *Voinarofskyi and Other Poems*, trans. T. Hart-Davies (Calcutta, 1879), p. 102.

When Ryleev first read this verse to his friend Mikhail Bestuzhev, who, along with his brother Nikolai, led the first rebel detachments to the Senate Square on December 14, 1825, Mikhail was shocked. According to the memoirs of Nikolai Bestuzhev, he told Ryleev: "Do you know what prediction you have written for yourself and for both of us?" Ryleev was fully aware of the significance of his words. "Do you really think that I hesitated even for a minute about my purpose?" he asked his friend. "Believe me that every day convinces me of the inevitability of my actions, of the coming death with which we must redeem our first effort on behalf of free Russia and, along with this, of the need for an example in order to awaken the sleeping Russians."[4]

Ryleev's verses inspired generations of revolutionaries and freethinkers in the Russian Empire. Among them were Vera Zasulich, a revolutionary assassin and one of the first Russian Marxists, and Mykhailo Drahomanov, an exile and the most influential Ukrainian political thinker of the nineteenth century. Drahomanov later recalled that in the mid 1850s, "*The Confession of Nalyvaiko* was copied in our secret notebooks along with the works of Shevchenko and was read with equal zeal." Ryleev himself drew inspiration from historical works, and in the last year before the uprising he was particularly fascinated by the history of the Ukrainian Cossacks.[5]

Kondratii Ryleev first became acquainted with Ukraine through his father, who served in Kyiv and even bought a house there that he bequeathed to his son. The young Ryleev's first encounter with the Cossack way of life took place after his return from the Napoleonic Wars. In February 1814 he joined the Russian army after graduating from a military college at the age of eighteen. With his artillery brigade, the young Ryleev marched through Poland, Germany, Switzerland, and France. In Dresden he was received at the court of the Russian ruler of Saxony, Nikolai Repnin, the future governor general of Little Russia, who was married to the granddaughter of the last hetman of Ukraine, Kyrylo Rozumovsky. Ryleev also spent some time in Paris. "I was infected with freethinking during the campaigns in France in 1814 and 1815," he testified after his arrest. Following the European campaigns, his detachment was brought back to the Russian Empire and stationed first in Lithuania and then in the vicinity of Ostrogozhsk (Ostrohozk), a town

---

[4] *Vospominaniia Bestuzhevykh* (Moscow and Leningrad, 1951), p. 7.
[5] Mykhailo Drahomanov, *Lysty na Naddniprians'ku Ukraïnu*, in Mykhailo Drahomanov and Borys Hrinchenko, *Dialohy pro ukraïns'ku natsional'nu spravu* (Kyiv, 1994), p. 160.

on the southern border of today's Russian Federation. Founded by Ukrainian Cossacks in the mid seventeenth century, Ostrogozhsk served as the headquarters of a Cossack territorial and military regiment until the 1760s. At the turn of the nineteenth century, for a short time, it was part of the imperial gubernia of Sloboda Ukraine. Its inhabitants preserved their Ukrainian customs and traditions well into the twentieth century.[6]

Ryleev spent close to three years in the vicinity of Ostrogozhsk, befriending local officers and becoming attached to the local culture. There he also found the love of his life, the daughter of a local nobleman. Natalia Teviashova came from a family of Cossack officers, with one of her ancestors serving as colonel of the Ostrogozhsk regiment in the early eighteenth century. After resigning from the military at the end of 1818 and eventually moving to St. Petersburg with his wife, Ryleev would come back to the region, to which he invariably referred as "Ukraine," in order to spend the summers in the company of his old friends. In December 1825, Ryleev wrote to Mykola Markevych, a descendant of a prominent Cossack family and a future historian of Ukraine: "I am a Russian, but I have spent three years in Ukraine: a short time for me, but sufficient to fall in love with that land and its fine inhabitants. Moreover, Ukraine has presented me with an uncommon, incomparable wife. My good Ukrainian lady has now been making me happy for six years, and so my attachment is complemented with the gratitude of my soul."[7]

Kondratii Ryleev did not forget his Ukrainian friends and acquaintances when he moved to St. Petersburg. In November 1820, having returned to the imperial capital after spending the summer in the Ostrogozhsk region, Ryleev published a letter in *Otechestvennye zapiski* (Fatherland Notes), a leading journal of the time, in which he praised his Ostrogozhsk friend Mikhail Bedraga, a retired officer of the Okhtyrka (Akhtyrka) hussar regiment. Established initially as a territorial and military unit of Ukrainian Cossacks in 1651, the Okhtyrka regiment was reformed into a hussar regiment in 1765 after the abolition of Cossack autonomy in the region. In 1814 the regiment entered Paris, where the Cossacks-turned-hussars used brown fabric that they requisitioned at a Capuchin convent to make new

---

[6] *Ibid.*, pp. 8–10; Kotliarevskii, *Ryleev*, pp. 21–24; B. T. Udodov, *K. F. Ryleev v Voronezhskom krae* (Voronezh, 1971), pp. 5–14.

[7] Kotliarevskii, *Ryleev*, pp. 24–29; K. F. Ryleev to Mykola Markevych, in *Literaturnoe nasledstvo*, ed. A. M. Egolin *et al.* (Moscow, 1954), vol. LIX, p. 153.

uniforms. These impressed Emperor Alexander I, who ordered that regimental uniforms be brown thereafter.[8]

Ryleev's letter was a follow-up to the note published in *Otechestvennye zapiski* by the legendary Russian poet Denis Davydov, an organizer of partisan warfare during the Napoleonic campaigns and the former commander of the Okhtyrka regiment. Davydov praised his former subordinate. Mikhail Bedraga came from the family of Major General Grigorii Bedraga. He was a dedicated and brave officer who served in the Okhtyrka regiment together with his two brothers from a very early age and fully demonstrated his outstanding qualities as a military commander during the Napoleonic Wars. Bedraga did not make it to Paris: having suffered a head wound in the famous Battle of Borodino (1812), he lived in isolation and obscurity on his family estate near Ostrogozhsk.

In a poem dedicated to Bedraga and written in the summer of 1821, Ryleev described conversations he had had with one of his Ostrogozhsk acquaintances, probably his father-in-law, Major Mikhail Teviashov. The subjects they discussed included the rebellion of the Greeks against Ottoman rule that was then under way in Morea, as well as the history of the Zaporozhian Sich, the Cossack stronghold below the Dnieper rapids, which served as a symbol of the struggle for Cossack freedom. It might be assumed that Ryleev had similar conversations with Bedraga. In a poem dedicated to his friend, Ryleev wrote:

> We talked of deeds of yore,
> Of freedom-loving Sich,
> Of peace and then of war,
> Till, surfeited with speech,
> To supper we would go.
> At table, as we dined,
> The major on occasion
> To argument inclined,
> Made bold by his libation.[9]

For Ryleev, the Ostrogozhsk Cossacks became champions of freedom and liberty inherited from their heroic past. The Cossack tradition never died out there, even among the peasants. "I do not consider it superfluous to say that peasant serfs were nowhere to be seen in the lands of Ostrogozhsk

---

[8] K. F. Ryleev, "Eshche o khrabrom M. G. Bedrage," in *Sochineniia i perepiska Kondratiia Fedorovicha Ryleeva*, 2nd edn. by his daughter, ed. P. A. Efremov (St. Petersburg, 1784), pp. 194–97; Aleksandr Mikhailenko, *I zhili druzhnoiu semeiu soldat, kornet i general* (Moscow, 2001), ch. 1–2.

[9] K. F. Ryleev, "Pustynia (K M. G. Bedrage)," in *Sochineniia i perepiska*, pp. 171–76.

until the end of the last century. The regimental lands that came into the possession of various officials of the Ostrogozhsk regiment were tilled by freemen or Cossacks," he wrote in one of his appeals to St. Petersburg authorities, advocating the return of economic freedom to the area, which suffered under difficult conditions. The tradition of Cossack freedom was indeed alive and well in the region. One of the local peasants who was ransomed out of serfdom with Ryleev's help later recalled that his grandfather, "taciturn, humble, and sensible when sober, once he had had something to drink ... was in the habit of holding forth on public affairs, recalling Cossackdom and the Hetman state; he was a harsh critic of the corruption of rural administration."[10]

Ryleev regarded Ostrogozhsk as a place where the tradition of freedom was passed on from fathers to sons and grandsons. It was a place where, as he wrote in his poem of 1823,

> Captive to the sound of glory,
> An aged man, from battles hoary,
> Inspired a seething generation
> To victory and liberation.[11]

The poem described a meeting at Ostrogozhsk in 1696 between Tsar Peter I and the Cossack hetman Ivan Mazepa – allies at the time, but later adversaries. In 1708 Mazepa led the Ukrainian Cossacks in revolt against Peter I and joined forces with the advancing army of King Charles XII of Sweden. The emperor declared Mazepa a traitor and had him anathematized by the Russian Orthodox Church. The anathema was repeated annually in churches throughout the empire.[12]

Ryleev did not shrink from engaging not only politically sensitive but plainly dangerous subjects. In the spring of 1823 Ryleev began work on a poetic novel, titled *Voinarovsky*, about Mazepa's revolt and its consequences. The protagonist was a young and idealistic nephew of Mazepa, Andrii Voinarovsky, who joined his uncle's rebellion against the tsar and followed him into emigration. He served as Charles XII's special representative in Istanbul. On his way from the Ottoman Empire to Sweden in

---

[10] K. F. Ryleev, "Ob Ostrogozhske," in *Sochineniia i perepiska*, pp. 193–94; Udodov, *K. F. Ryleev v Voronezhskom krae*, pp. 22–26, 67.
[11] K. F. Ryleev, "Petr Velikii v Ostrogozhske," in *Sochineniia i perepiska*, pp. 58–61.
[12] On Mazepa and his revolt, see Oleksander Ohloblyn, *Het'man Ivan Mazepa i ioho doba* (New York, Paris and Toronto, 1960); Orest Subtelny, ed., *On the Eve of Poltava: The Letters of Mazepa to Adam Sieniawski, 1704–1708* (New York, 1975); Subtelny, *The Mazepists: Ukrainian Separatism in the Early Eighteenth Century* (New York, 1981); Teodor Mackiw, *English Reports on Mazepa, Hetman of Ukraine and Prince of the Holy Roman Empire, 1687–1709* (New York, Munich, and Toronto, 1983).

October 1716, he was kidnapped by Russian agents and imprisoned in the
SS. Peter and Paul Fortress. He was then sent to Yakutsk in Eastern Siberia,
where he died after spending sixteen years in exile. *Voinarovsky* turned out
to be prophetic – if not for Ryleev himself, then for those of his colleagues
who were sent to Siberia after the suppression of the Decembrist Revolt.[13]

   The most controversial feature of the poetic novel was its portrayal of the
old Cossack hetman. Despite an introduction to the poem that followed
the tradition of Russian imperial historiography by casting Mazepa as a
self-seeking traitor, the hetman appeared in some scenes of the work as a
devoted patriot of his fatherland, ready to die for its freedom in the struggle
against tyranny. The introduction was written by Aleksandr Kornilovich
and the poem itself by Ryleev. Such was the image that Ryleev presented in
the episode where Voinarovsky recounts his first meeting with his uncle to
discuss rebellion against the tsar. Ryleev's Mazepa tells his young nephew:

> Under fate's hand, full well I know
> The step is bold, what may betide
> But future fortune can decide,
> Success may not attend the blow,
> Glory may gild my conquering name,
> Or foul disgrace may blast my fame,
> But I am firm, though o'er my land
> Fate threatening dark disaster stand.
> The hour is near, the strife at hand,
> On our side freedom's banners fly
> Ranged against ruthless tyranny.[14]

Excerpts from the poetic novel, followed by the complete work (with
significant omissions ordered by the vigilant censor), appeared in print in
1824 and 1825, and the reading public received the novel with enthusiasm.
Alexander Pushkin was among its admirers. But there were critical reac-
tions as well. In a private letter written in April 1825, Pavel Katenin,
another freethinker who had been exiled from St. Petersburg long before
the December 1825 uprising, wrote to an acquaintance: "These are all
copies of various works of Byron's in verse according to the new style;
what I find strangest of all is the thought of presenting the knave and
scoundrel Mazepa as a new Cato of some sort."[15]

---

[13] Liubomyr Vynar, *Andrii Voinarovs'kyi: istorychnyi narys* (Munich and Cleveland, 1962).

[14] Relaieff, *Voinarofskyi and Other Poems*, pp. 60–61; A. Kornilovich, "Zhizneopisanie Mazepy," in
Ryleev, *Sochineniia i perepiska*, pp. 91–96.

[15] K. F. Ryleev, "Pis'ma k A. S. Pushkinu," in *Sochineniia i perepiska*, pp. 203–6; Kotliarevskii, *Ryleev*,
pp. 54–55, 117–21; *Russkaia romanticheskaia poèma*, ed. Viktor Afanas'ev (Moscow, 1985), p. 113.

There was some truth in Katenin's treatment of Ryleev's new work as a reflection of Byron's literary style and sympathies. In the summer of 1819, Byron published his narrative poem *Mazeppa* to universal acclaim, instantly launching the eighteenth-century Cossack hetman on his posthumous career as a Romantic hero. Still, Ryleev was quite original both in his selection of his main protagonist, Voinarovsky (who was not even mentioned by Byron), and in his interpretation of the character of Mazepa, who emerged in Ryleev's work as a vehicle for the poet's expression of his own views on freedom and tyranny. Byron was only partly responsible for Ryleev's lenient treatment of Mazepa, or for the glorification of Cossack hetmans in general. Ryleev's subsequent poetry left no doubt in that regard.[16]

In 1821–23 Ryleev published a selection of poems under the title *Dumy*. They were inspired by the *Historical Songs* published in 1816 by Julian Ursyn Niemcewicz, a Polish poet and historian who was a strong supporter of the Polish Constitution of 1791 and served as a secretary to Tadeusz Kościuszko, the leader of the Polish uprising of 1794 against Russian rule. Ryleev knew Polish from his childhood, and Polish patriots, including Adam Mickiewicz, were welcome in Decembrist circles. Still, Ryleev was adamant that the Polish author's historical songs were not his only or primary inspiration. In the introduction to his collection of *Dumy* issued in 1825, he wrote: "The *duma* is an ancient inheritance from our southern brethren – our own native Russian invention. The Poles took it from us. To this day the Ukrainians sing *dumy* about their heroes – Doroshenko, Nechai, Sahaidachny, Palii – and the composition of one of them is attributed to Mazepa himself." The word *duma* is indeed the Ukrainian term for lyrical and epic songs of folk origin. Ryleev was probably familiar with the first collection of Ukrainian folk songs published by Nikolai Tsertelev in St. Petersburg in 1819 and knew the first work of modern Ukrainian literature, Ivan Kotliarevsky's *Eneïda*, a folk parody based on Virgil's *Aeneid* first published in St. Petersburg in 1798.[17]

There is reason to believe that sometime in 1824 Ryleev gained access to a new and fascinating source on the Cossack past. It was known to him and some of his friends as the Konysky History, and its authorship was attributed to the Orthodox archbishop of Mahilioŭ, Heorhii Konysky.

---

[16] On Mazepa as a Romantic hero, see H. F. Babinski, *The Mazeppa Legend in European Romanticism* (New York, 1974).

[17] K. F. Ryleev, "Dumy," in *Sochineniia i perepiska*, pp. 1–2; Drahomanov, *Lysty na Naddniprians'ku Ukraïnu*, p. 156.

The manuscript was not available to Ryleev in its entirety. The full text was hidden away in the Chernihiv area, far to the south of the imperial capital, in the libraries of the descendants of Cossack officers. But the excerpts of the mysterious manuscript that Ryleev was able to get his hands on ignited his romantic imagination. They opened up a world full of Cossack heroes. One of them, Severyn Nalyvaiko, was barely known not only in Western but even in Russian and Ukrainian historical writing until the 1820s. Nalyvaiko and his endeavors were allotted a mere two sentences in the first scholarly history of Ukraine, a two-volume work by Dmitrii Bantysh-Kamensky published in 1822. It was only the Konysky History that finally satisfied the interest of readers in the details of the Nalyvaiko affair. One might have assumed from the introduction to the work that those details came from the archives of Bohdan Khmelnytsky himself. The image of Nalyvaiko as a national hero came alive on the pages of the mysterious history, complete with a thorough account of his exploits and texts of his letters to the Polish king. Few images of fighters – indeed, martyrs – for the freedom of Rus' were as appealing to the early nineteenth-century mind as that of Nalyvaiko. Ryleev would turn Nalyvaiko into a symbol of Cossack freedom, courage, and patriotism.[18]

Severyn (Semerii) Nalyvaiko, who became a hero of the eighteenth-century Cossack chroniclers and made a spectacular career with the nineteenth-century Romantics, was a highly controversial figure in his own time. In 1593, as an officer in a Cossack troop employed by the Ukrainian prince Kostiantyn Ostrozky, Nalyvaiko helped defeat the revolt of another Cossack leader, Kryshtof Kosynsky. In the following year, by agreement with Ostrozky, Nalyvaiko took command of Cossack and peasant rebels, seeking to lead them away from his patron's estates and direct their rage and destructive power against his enemies. At the top of that list were two Orthodox bishops who negotiated a church union between the Orthodox metropolitanate on the territory of the Polish-Lithuanian Commonwealth and the pope of Rome at the time of the revolt. The Union of Brest became a reality in 1596, provoking strong opposition to what was regarded as a violation of the rights of the Orthodox Church and the entire nation of Rus', and turning Nalyvaiko, who was captured and executed by the Poles in 1597, into the first martyr for the cause.[19]

[18] Dmitrii Bantysh-Kamenskii, *Istoriia Maloi Rossii* (Moscow, 1822), vol. I, p. xxii.

[19] See Serhii Lep'iavko, *Kozats'ki viiny kintsia XVI stolittia v Ukraïni* (Chernihiv, 1996), pp. 170–72; Serhii Plokhy, *The Cossacks and Religion in Early Modern Ukraine* (Oxford and New York, 2001), pp. 33–36, 104–7.

It is hardly surprising that the Orthodox monks and Cossack authors who wrote the Rus' chronicles were most sympathetic to Nalyvaiko and his plight, but the historical data available to them was limited at best. The Konysky History, on the other hand, had plenty of material to play with. Ryleev borrowed details from the manuscript that he could find nowhere else, including references to Nalyvaiko's capital of Chyhyryn on the Tiasmyn River and the treatment of Colonel Hryhorii Loboda as Nalyvaiko's confidant. Those details were not entirely correct. Loboda, who was Nalyvaiko's rival, was executed by the Cossacks on suspicion of collaboration with the Poles. Chyhyryn, which is indeed located on the Tiasmyn River, did not become the Cossack capital until more than half a century after Nalyvaiko's death. But it is not so much the details of Ryleev's narrative, whatever their historical accuracy, as the ideological message embodied in Nalyvaiko as a historical and literary character that betrays Ryleev's reliance on the Konysky History in his treatment of the Cossack leader.

It was under the influence of the Konysky History that Ryleev portrayed Nalyvaiko not only as a man prepared to die defending the freedom of his nation but also as a promoter of equality and friendship among neighboring peoples:

> Cossacks were then the Pole's allies
> Bound each to each in equal ties,
> Such as free men would well beseem –
> Now all is vanished like a dream.
> Cossacks long since had learned to know
> How into tyrants friends may grow.[20]

The notion of an alliance of equals between Cossacks and Poles comes directly from the text of Nalyvaiko's letter to the king as it appears in the Konysky History. In his appeal, Nalyvaiko claims that the nation of Rus' was never conquered by the Kingdom of Poland or the Grand Duchy of Lithuania but "united voluntarily on rights and privileges equal and identical to theirs." Nalyvaiko goes on to argue that those rights had been violated in numerous ways, including the introduction of the church union. It was only after the defeat and execution of Nalyvaiko, according to the text of the Konysky History, that the Poles began to refer to the Orthodox as "schismatics" and lease Orthodox churches to Jews, who

---

[20] Relaieff, *Voinarofskyi and Other Poems*, p. 132.

were only too happy to turn that situation to their profit and charge the Orthodox exorbitant fees for the use of their own churches.[21]

The claim that Jews held the keys to Orthodox churches later became a rallying cry of those in the Russian Empire who stirred up anti-Semitic sentiments among its subjects. In his poetic play *Bogdan Khmelnitsky*, Ryleev used this theme to stress the oppression of the Cossacks by the Polish authorities prior to the uprising of 1648, which claimed tens of thousands of Ukrainian Jews as victims. In so doing, he revealed his acquaintance with another episode of the Konysky History – a description of the defeat of the Polish army at the hands of the Cossacks in the so-called "Night of Taras." This episode of the 1620s, like the Nalyvaiko revolt, was known to chroniclers only in general terms, but the Konysky History elaborated it in astonishing detail. Ryleev shared the distaste for Polish rule over Ukrainian lands manifested in the History. He regarded Nalyvaiko and Khmelnytsky as patriots who could not tolerate the oppression of their people by a tyrannical foreign power. For him the Cossacks, to whom he referred interchangeably as "Little Russians" and "Ukrainians," represented a freedom-loving but oppressed part of the Rus' nation.[22]

Few people were as grateful to Ryleev for his heroic portrayal of the Cossack past as the descendants of Cossack officer families in Ukraine. Mykola Markevych, who characterized himself in a letter to Ryleev as "a true citizen of my fatherland and a good Little Russian," wrote with regard to *Voinarovsky* and *Nalyvaiko*: "Accept my thanks and those of all compatriots known to me. Rest assured that our thanks are sincere; that we feel in our hearts the value of your works, which glorify you and our ancestors. The deeds of the great men of Little Russia are not yet lost to our sight; in many hearts the former strength of feeling and dedication to our homeland remains undiminished. You will find the spirit of [Hetman Pavlo] Polubotok still living among us. Accept our general thanks: you have done much, a great deal! You uplift the whole nation. Woe to him who seeks to oppress entire countries; who attempts to cover whole nations with contempt, and they repay him with contempt ... But glory to him who praises the greatness of the human soul, and whom whole nations should repay with gratitude. The *Confession of Nalyvaiko* is engraved in our hearts, and in mine as well."[23]

[21] *Istoriia Rusov ili Maloi Rossii. Sochinenie Georgiia Koniskago, Arkhiepiskopa Beloruskago* (Moscow, 1846), pp. 35–41.

[22] K. F. Ryleev, "Bogdan Khmel'nitskii," in *Sochineniia i perepiska*, pp. 145–52; *Istoriia Rusov*, pp. 51–52; Zenon Kohut, "The Khmelnytsky Uprising, the Image of Jews, and the Shaping of Ukrainian Historical Memory," *Jewish History* 17 (2003): 141–63.

[23] Quoted in Kotliarevskii, *Ryleev*, pp. 117–18.

Kondratii Ryleev drew inspiration for his freedom-loving poetry not only from the Cossack history. He was fascinated with the democratic tradition of the medieval republic of Novgorod and inspired by the Greek revolt of his own day against Ottoman rule. His thinking was nurtured by his reading of contemporary French, Polish, and Russian authors, and his ideas were shaped in discussions with people like the Bestuzhevs, Kornilovich, and Pushkin. Still, the Cossack past provided inspiration for his longest poetical works. He turned to the history of the Cossack revolts of the sixteenth and seventeenth centuries against Polish overlordship in order to make a case for revolt against the Russian autocracy. The young poet viewed the struggle against that government as a patriotic duty, and was prepared to follow the example of the Cossack heroes and die in battle for the freedom of his beloved fatherland. Images drawn from the Konysky History not only helped him articulate his dream of freedom but also foreshadowed his own fate.

Ryleev's last letter, written immediately before he was taken away by the executioners, was addressed to his wife. Like his most famous character, Severyn Nalyvaiko, Ryleev met his own death without regret and "blessed the stroke which laid him low." He wrote to his "good Ukrainian lady": "God and the Sovereign have decided my fate: I am to die, and die a shameful death. May His holy will be done! My dear mate, submit to the will of the Almighty as well, and He will comfort you. Pray to God for my soul. He will hear your prayers. Do not repine against Him or against the Sovereign: that would be both foolhardy and sinful. Is it for us to comprehend the inscrutable judgments of the One who passes understanding? I did not repine even once throughout the time of my imprisonment, and for that the Holy Spirit comforted me in wondrous fashion." He ended his letter with the following words: "Farewell! They are telling me to dress. May His holy will be done."[24]

---

[24] K. F. Ryleev, "Perepiska s zhenoiu iz kreposti," in *Sochineniia i perepiska*, pp. 300–1.

CHAPTER 2

The Cossack annals

What was the Konysky History on which Kondratii Ryleev relied in his writings about the history of the Cossacks, and where did he find it? Let us begin with the second part of the question, which can be answered quite briefly. The only direct reference to the manuscript comes from Ryleev's correspondence with his co-conspirator, a 33-year-old retired colonel, Aleksandr von Brigen. We find it in a letter that von Brigen wrote to Ryleev in the faraway Ukrainian village of Ponurivka (Ponurovka) on October 21, 1825, less than two months before the Decembrist Revolt.

A hero of the Battle of Borodino, for which he was awarded a golden saber, and a participant in the Russian campaigns against Napoleon in 1813–14, von Brigen retired from active service in 1819, citing health problems – he had suffered two serious wounds. In the summer and fall of 1825, he was visiting his father-in-law, Mykhailo Myklashevsky, a former senator and governor of a number of imperial provinces, including the Little Russian and Katerynoslav gubernias. Like Ryleev's beloved Ostrogozhsk, Myklashevsky's estate of Ponurivka is located on today's southern border of Russia. It was part of the Cossack settlements established around the town of Starodub, which served as the center of a Cossack administrative unit and military regiment until the 1760s. Several generations of Myklashevskys served in the regiment, with the owner of Ponurivka, Mykhailo Myklashevsky, becoming colonel of the Starodub carabineer regiment, established on the basis of the former Cossack unit.[1]

There was a secret aspect to von Brigen's trip to Ukraine. On Ryleev's request, he met in Kyiv with the future "dictator" of the Decembrist revolt, Prince Sergei Trubetskoi, to inform him about the conflict that

---

[1] "Brigen, fon-der Aleksandr Fedorovich," in *Alfavit dekabristov*, Virtual'nyi muzei dekabristov, ed. A. Samal' http://decemb.hobby.ru/index.shtml?alphavit/alf_b; Oleksander Ohloblyn, "Mykhailo Myklashevs'kyi," in *Liudy staroï Ukraïny* (Munich, 1959), pp. 150–67; D. R. Poklonskii, "Miklashevskii Mikhail Pavlovich," in *Starodubskaia starina, XI–XIX vv. Istoricheskie ocherki*, vol. II (Klintsy, 2002), p. 243ff.

had taken place in St. Petersburg regarding plans to assassinate Emperor Alexander I. But in his letter of October 21, 1825, von Brigen made no allusion to his secret mission to Kyiv, focusing instead on the subject that seemed to interest both him and Ryleev in equal measure – the history of the Ukrainian Cossacks. "Having carried out your request, esteemed Kondratii Fedorovich," wrote Brigen, "I am sending you herewith an extract copied from the Konysky History." In June 1825, as von Brigen left St. Petersburg for Ukraine, Ryleev apparently discussed with him not only the assassination of the emperor and the exile of the imperial family but also his literary plans. Ryleev was continuing work on *Nalyvaiko*, writing parts of a new poetic drama about Bohdan Khmelnytsky, and planning a new poetic novel about Ivan Mazepa. He needed additional sources on Ukrainian history. It would appear that the Konysky History mentioned by Brigen was among the manuscripts that the poet had consulted previously but did not have in his possession. Ryleev asked his friend to copy an excerpt from that work once he reached his father-in-law's estate. Von Brigen was glad to oblige.[2]

Von Brigen's letter to Ryleev is one of the first references to the manuscript that later became known under the title *History of the Rus' or Little Russia, written by Archbishop Heorhii Konysky of Belarus.* Heorhii Konysky was probably the best-known Orthodox bishop of the late eighteenth century. He was born into a Cossack officer family in the Ukrainian town of Nizhyn in 1717. As an eleven-year-old boy he came to Kyiv to study at the [Peter] Mohyla Academy, at that time the leading educational institution in the Russian Empire. He excelled in his studies, becoming a professor and eventually president of the academy before being appointed in 1755 to serve as bishop of Mahiliou, a Belarusian town then in the Polish-Lithuanian Commonwealth. There Konysky assumed responsibility for Orthodox parishes in a country where Orthodoxy was under attack. The more intrusive were Russian policies in the Commonwealth, by then weak and dependent on the support of foreign powers, the harder was the line taken by the Polish Catholic elites against the Orthodox, whom they regarded as St. Petersburg's "fifth column." Konysky became the target of numerous humiliations and physical attacks by the Catholic majority. After barely surviving one of them, he traveled to the Russian Empire to demand action from Catherine II, the German-born empress who had just been elevated to the Russian throne and was eager to show

---

[2] V. I. Maslov, *Literaturnaia deiatel'nost' K. F. Ryleeva* (Kyiv, 1912), appendix, pp. 97–98; A. F. Brigen, *Pis'ma. Istoricheskie sochineniia* (Irkutsk, 1986), pp. 96–98.

her devotion to Orthodoxy. Konysky's lobbying on behalf of the Commonwealth Orthodox (he spent years in St. Petersburg making his case before going back to Mahiliou) played an important role in the events leading up to the First Partition of Poland, which made Mahiliou a Russian town in 1772. A celebrated preacher, theologian, and defender of imperial Orthodoxy, Konysky died in Mahiliou in February 1795, a few months before the third and last partition of Poland wiped that state off the map of Europe.[3]

Konysky's numerous writings on theological topics were published during his lifetime. The manuscript of the *History of the Rus'* allowed one to suggest that there was more to Konysky than met the public eye. It appeared that he was also involved in writing history, and not history of any kind, but of a caliber that could fire the imagination of freethinkers conspiring to kill the emperor himself and change the political order of the empire. The introduction to the *History* explained Konysky's role in producing the text. The archbishop, claimed the introduction, had edited the text of the work, which he sent to Hryhorii Poletyka, a former student of his at the Kyivan Academy. Poletyka, also a native of Ukraine, represented the Ukrainian nobility at the Legislative Assembly convened by Catherine II in 1767 to reform Russian laws in the spirit of the Enlightenment. He was seeking a "history of the fatherland" to promote his work in the assembly and got one from his former professor. Konysky allegedly had sent its text to Poletyka "with archpastoral assurances that it has been known for many years to discerning men of the cathedral monastery of Mahiliou, who have obtained necessary information from learned men of the Kyivan Academy and various prominent monasteries of Little Russia, especially those in which Yurii Khmelnytsky, the former Little Russian hetman, resided as a monk, leaving in them many notes and papers of his father, Hetman Zynovii Khmelnytsky, as well as actual journals of national monuments and deeds, and, moreover, that it has again been revised and corrected by him."[4]

The reader gained the impression that he or she was dealing with a chronicle compiled in ancient monasteries whose authors had had access to documents of the mid seventeenth century – the times of the Khmelnytsky Uprising. Given that the Legislative Commission was

---

[3] *Istoriia Rusov ili Maloi Rossii. Sochinenie Georgiia Koniskago, Arkhiepiskopa Beloruskago* (Moscow, 1846). On Konysky, see M. V. Kashuba, *Heorhii Konys'kyi: svitohliad ta vikhy zhyttia* (Kyiv, 1999).

[4] *Istoriia Rusov*, p. ii.

convoked in 1767 and dissolved in 1768, Konysky must have sent the History to Poletyka around that time. The reference to the papers of Hetman Bohdan Khmelnytsky (referred to by his first baptismal name, Zynovii) and his son, Yurii, who indeed became a monk after serving for some time as hetman of Ukraine, indicated that the main value of the history lay in its presentation of the events of Ukrainian and, more specifically, Cossack history. This impression was strengthened by the reference to the expertise of professors of the Kyivan Academy and the involvement of Konysky himself.

The text of the *History* confirmed all these claims. It ended with a description of the events of 1769, suggesting that a few paragraphs may have been added to its text after it left Konysky's hands, but that for the most part the account given in the text and the story told in its introduction were mutually corroborative. Despite its main title, *History of the Rus'* – the term *Rusy* was often employed to denote the Eastern Slavs in general – the book did indeed focus on Ukraine, a fact reflected in its subtitle. In the latter part of the nineteenth century, the term "Little Russia" became coterminous with "Ukraine." Throughout the eighteenth century and the early decades of the nineteenth, however, "Little Russia" had been largely limited to the Ukrainian lands on the Left Bank of the Dnieper (Dnipro) River. That was the territory of the Hetmanate, an autonomous Cossack state that existed for more than a century until its abolition by Catherine II in the 1760s. It received its name from the title of the Cossack leaders, who were known as hetmans.

The *History of the Rus'*, which so excited Aleksandr von Brigen and Kondratii Ryleev in 1825, was first and foremost a history of the Cossacks of Ukraine. The Ukrainian Cossack Host came into being south of Kyiv, along the middle and lower reaches of the Dnieper River, in the course of the sixteenth century. By the mid seventeenth century the Dnieper Cossacks had created a polity of their own and shifted the balance of power in the region by siding with Muscovy against their former masters – the kings of Poland.

Cossackdom was a product of the Eurasian frontier, where steppe and settled area, farmers and nomads, Christianity and Islam came together during late medieval and early modern times to create a unique culture. The Cossacks emerged as a distinct social stratum on the margins of the Eurasian steppelands in the late fifteenth and early sixteenth centuries. The term "Cossack" means freeman, guard, and freebooter in the Turkic languages of the area, and the first Cossacks were of Turkic rather than Slavic stock. These were nomadic warriors engaged in acts of steppe piracy on their own initiative, not on orders of their superiors: khans and leaders of local tribes. By the late fifteenth and early sixteenth centuries, the situation had changed. The Ottoman sultan and his officials began to complain to the rulers of the Kingdom of Poland, the Grand Duchy of Lithuania, and the Tsardom of Muscovy, whose lands bordered on the Black Sea steppes, that Ottoman subjects were being harassed by Slavic Cossack formations. The Polish, Lithuanian, and Muscovite authorities denied responsibility for the actions of the steppe riff-raff, responding to the sultan that the Cossacks came from all states and nations and were under no one's jurisdiction.[5]

The Ottomans continued to complain, resorting to threats and occasionally organizing special expeditions to deal with this new breed of Cossacks, who not only attacked merchants in the southern steppes but also embarked on seagoing expeditions, attacking Ottoman ships on the Black Sea and the Sea of Azov and pillaging coastal settlements, including the suburbs of Istanbul, the capital of the Ottoman Empire. In 1621 the young Ottoman sultan Osman II led his army into the Black Sea steppes and besieged the fortress of Khotyn on the border between Moldavia and the Polish-Lithuanian Commonwealth. Among other things, he intended to punish the Polish king for Cossack expeditions of previous years. The Polish forces defeated the invader with the help of a Cossack army of twenty thousand. Defeated and humiliated, Osman II returned to Istanbul, only to be assassinated by his courtiers for bringing disgrace on the empire. The Cossacks continued their seagoing expeditions.

If the Cossacks were a headache for Istanbul, they were double the problem in Cracow, Warsaw, Vilnius, and Moscow. In the course of the sixteenth and seventeenth centuries, Cossack settlements emerged along the entire perimeter of the Eurasian steppe. Normally the individual settlements would be organized in larger formations, known as Cossack hosts, which chose as their bases the lower reaches of south-flowing rivers in the region. There were Dnieper Cossacks, Don Cossacks, Volga and Yaik Cossacks and, finally, Siberian Cossacks. The first to organize themselves were the Dnieper or Ukrainian Cossacks. Borderland officials first of the Grand Duchy of Lithuania and then of the Kingdom of Poland (which joined in the Union of Lublin of 1569 to form the

---

[5] On the history of the Eurasian steppe frontier, see Michael Khodarkovsky, *Russia's Steppe Frontier: The Making of a Colonial Empire, 1500–1800* (Bloomington and Indianapolis, 2002); John LeDonne, *The Grand Strategy of the Russian Empire, 1650–1831* (Oxford, 2003); Brian Boeck, *Imperial Boundaries: Cossack Communities and Empire-Building in the Age of Peter the Great* (Cambridge, 2009); Shane O'Rourke, *The Cossacks* (Manchester, 2008).

Polish-Lithuanian Commonwealth) tried to control the Cossacks and often served as their commanders. Prince Dmytro Vyshnevetsky, who served both the Grand Duke of Lithuania and Ivan the Terrible of Moscow, and who died in Ottoman captivity according to legend, was also the founder of the first Cossack stronghold (*sich*) beyond the Dnieper rapids, on the lower reaches of the river.

The Cossacks combined their freebooting with fishing, hunting, and foraging. They later turned to farming as they began to cultivate land taken from the nomads and protected it against them. They refused to pay taxes and recognized no state jurisdiction, relying on the principles of military democracy and direct representation. The Cossack council elected, deposed, and punished Cossack officials. This Cossack way of life was more of a threat to the governments of the Cossacks' home countries than their freebooting expeditions, which provoked Ottoman displeasure, rage, and retaliation. Cossackdom attracted thousands of new recruits from the ranks of the local peasantry and townspeople, undermining the existing social order, increasing social tensions, and setting off uprisings. These would occasionally turn into full-fledged peasant wars that claimed tens of thousands of victims among the upper classes and non-Orthodox minorities in the region – principally Catholics and Jews.

Severyn Nalyvaiko, whose plight was described in the *History of the Rus'* and immortalized by Kondratii Ryleev, was the leader of one of the first Ukrainian Cossack uprisings, which took place in 1594–95. The first major Cossack revolt (1591–93) was led by another Cossack chieftain, Kryshtof Kosynsky (Krzysztof Kosiński). There was a decisive reason why Nalyvaiko and not Kosynsky made such a spectacular career in the popular imagination of a later era. Kosynsky was suspected by later historians to be a Polish noble who ended up among the Cossacks, while Nalyvaiko was an Orthodox Ukrainian or Ruthenian, in the nomenclature of the time. Nalyvaiko's troops not only rebelled against the authorities and pillaged noble estates but also turned their arms against initiators of the church union – an attempt to place the Orthodox Church in the Polish-Lithuanian Commonwealth under the jurisdiction of the pope. Captured and executed by the royal authorities, Nalyvaiko was an ideal candidate for representation not only as a Cossack hero who fought in defense of Cossack freedoms but also as a martyr for faith and nation.

The suppression of the Kosynsky and Nalyvaiko uprisings established some semblance of order in the borderlands but did not stop the growth of Cossack power in the region. The royal authorities increased the Cossack register, putting more well-to-do Cossacks on the government payroll in order to police the rank and file. Cossack involvement in the Time of Troubles in Muscovy, where Cossacks staffed the armies of both the False Dmitriis pretending to the throne, worked to the benefit of the Polish government, which later sent its standing army to Moscow in 1610 and occupied the city. The royal court also benefited from the support of the twenty-thousand-strong Cossack army during Osman II's siege of the fortress of Khotyn in 1621. While the Commonwealth found itself in possession of a large army that cost the treasury next to nothing, the political burden of that army on the Commonwealth proved enormous.

Petro Konashevych-Sahaidachny, the Cossack leader at Khotyn, took the Orthodox Church, persecuted by the Commonwealth authorities, under his protection. After the Union of Brest, royal officials prohibited the consecration of new Orthodox bishops, and by 1620 the church was almost leaderless. In that year Patriarch Theophanes of Jerusalem was making his way back from Moscow, and Sahaidachny convinced him to consecrate a new Orthodox hierarchy despite the king's direct prohibition. This gave the Cossacks a distinctly new legitimacy. From now on they would fight not only for their own rights and privileges but also in defense of the persecuted Orthodox Church and the wronged Ruthenian nation. There was one more problem with allowing the Cossacks to become so powerful and so indispensable for the protection of the Commonwealth. Once the Cossack army had been recruited, it was almost impossible to disperse it. Peasants and townsfolk turned Cossack when war was in the offing, demanded Cossack privileges, including the payment of salary and exclusion from the jurisdiction of local officials, refused to pay taxes, and took part in foreign expeditions that antagonized neighboring states. In 1625, a few years after Khotyn, the Commonwealth sent its army against the Cossacks, forcing them to disperse. The registered or official Cossack Host was limited to six thousand, which left at least fourteen thousand Cossacks off the government payroll. The peace did not last very long.

In 1630 the Cossacks rose again. This time their leader was one Taras Fedorovych, a baptized Tatar who made a spectacular career in the Cossack Host. He called on the Cossacks and the border population to rise against Polish oppression, inspiring a Ukrainian jacquerie. Led by Fedorovych, the Cossacks and rebel peasants defeated the Polish army and forced the authorities to increase the registered Cossack Host to eight thousand, but the price was Fedorovych's head. When the Polish authorities demanded his extradition, Fedorovych and his loyalists had no choice but to leave the Host, joining Muscovy in its war against the Polish-Lithuanian

Commonwealth. Fedorovych's heroic and tragic story inspired the author of the *History of the Rus'* and scores of Romantic writers after him, who referred to the Cossack chieftain as "Taras Triasylo." The disappearance of Taras Fedorovych from the scene did little to allay Cossack dissatisfaction with what they considered an encroachment on their rights: the royal authorities built the fortress of Kodak on the lower Dnieper to cut them off from the Black Sea and stop their seagoing expeditions. It did not help much. A new wave of Cossack revolts shook the Dnieper region in the late 1630s. They were led by Pavlo But and Yakiv Ostrianytsia, another hero of the *History of the Rus'*. The rebels were defeated, the Cossack register again reduced to six thousand, and Polish officers appointed to serve as Cossack colonels in order to stop the Cossacks from ever rising again.

The Cossack problem appeared to have been resolved, and the "golden peace," as Polish authors called it, was at hand. So it seemed on the surface. The Kodak fortress beyond the rapids was rebuilt after being destroyed by the Cossacks and made their seagoing expeditions much more difficult. Now, instead of going south, the Cossacks went west to offer their mercenary services to European rulers embroiled in the Thirty Years' War. But peace in the borderlands was short-lived. Under the apparent calm, forces were gathering that would shake the Commonwealth to its foundations and lead to the creation of a Cossack state. As Cossack detachments fought in Europe and engaged in seagoing expeditions against the Ottomans (they circumvented the Kodak fortress, making their way to the Black Sea via the Sea of Azov), Polish and Ruthenian magnates moved into lands recently colonized by the Cossacks, taking away the holdings of the Cossack elite. Peasants fleeing enserfment, which was an integral part of the magnates' manorial economy, swelled the ranks of the unregistered Cossacks. Only a spark was needed to set off the next revolt.[6]

It came unexpectedly from the very top of the Cossack hierarchy. Bohdan Khmelnytsky, the one-time chancellor of the Cossack Host (the highest office a Cossack could attain under the new regulations), was the very embodiment of the new Polish order in Ukraine. An alumnus of an Orthodox school and a Catholic college, a veteran of Cossack

---

[6] On the early history of the Cossacks, see Mykhailo Hrushevsky, *History of Ukraine-Rus'*, vol. VII, trans. Bohdan Strumiński (Edmonton and Toronto, 1999); Alexander Baran and George Gajecky, *The Cossacks in the Thirty Years War*, 2 vols. (Rome, 1969–83); Linda Gordon, *Cossack Rebellions: Social Turmoil in the Sixteenth-Century Ukraine* (Albany, N.Y., 1983); Serhii Plokhy, *The Cossacks and Religion in Early Modern Ukraine* (Oxford and New York, 2001), pp. 16–175.

participation in the Polish-Ottoman wars and a sometime captive of
the Ottomans, a loyal Cossack officer during the Cossack revolts of the
late 1630s, a commander of Cossack troops in France in the early 1640s,
and one of the Cossack representatives at talks with the Polish king,
Khmelnytsky was in his fifties, a time to retire from military service
and reflect on one's life, when he unexpectedly emerged as the leader
of the largest Cossack revolt ever to take place. In his own mind, he
had no choice but to rebel. In 1647, when his long and loyal service to
the Commonwealth was to come to its dignified conclusion, he was
suddenly imprisoned and robbed of his possessions, while his father's
estate and, reportedly, his wife were taken away from him by the servitor
of a Polish magnate who was augmenting his landholdings in the area.
Khmelnytsky escaped from prison in early 1648 and, accompanied
by a small group of supporters, fled to the Sich beyond the Dnieper
rapids. There he was proclaimed the Cossack hetman – commander-in-
chief – a word that the Cossacks borrowed from the Poles, who in turn
took it from the Germans by Slavicizing the term *Hauptmann*.
What followed was the most explosive and successful Cossack uprising
in history.

Khmelnytsky secured himself behind the lines by making an alliance
with the Crimean khan and enlisting the feared Tatar cavalry as part of his
forces – a crossing of religious and cultural boundaries that shocked
the Commonwealth and ensured the Cossack victories of the next two
years. The registered Cossacks soon joined Khmelnytsky, and the Polish
standing army was wiped out in two battles in May 1648. The Polish
commanders found themselves in Crimean captivity. The Commonwealth was defenseless, but Khmelnytsky was not sure what to do with
his unexpected victory. He stayed in the Dnieper region, forming his new
insurgent army, and sent emissaries throughout Ukraine and Belarus to
rouse the people to rebellion. Rebellion it was. Driven by an overwhelming desire for freedom from serfdom, vengeance on their masters, and
religious fanaticism, the Cossacks, peasants, and townsfolk turned on the
Polish nobles and Jewish settlers who had come to the region as part of the
magnate manorial economy. The result was a massacre of both groups,
with Jews much less able to defend themselves against the uprising than
the Polish landlords. The Jews were faced with the alternatives of con-
verting to Christianity or losing their lives. One way or another, Jewish
communities in Dnieper Ukraine were wiped out for generations to
come. Khmelnytsky and his Cossack veterans did not take part in the
massacres, but the hetman later raised the Jewish theme – the claim that

the Poles had allowed the Jews to lord it over the Orthodox Ruthenians – as justification of the Cossack revolt in the eyes of Christian Europe.

The popular uprising allowed Khmelnytsky to take control of most of Ukraine. In the fall of 1648, with the help of the peasant rebels, Khmelnytsky's Cossack army defeated the forces levied by the Commonwealth nobility. By the end of that year, Cossack troops were besieging Lviv and Zamość, making their way into Polish ethnic territory. Khmelnytsky then turned back and staged a triumphal entry into Kyiv, the ancient capital of the Rus' princes. He was met there by the patriarch of Jerusalem and hailed as the Moses of the Ruthenian nation. A year after escaping from a Polish prison, he told Polish emissaries who came to Kyiv to treat for peace that he was the sovereign of Rus' and that the Poles should confine themselves to the lands beyond the Vistula. In the following year the combined Cossack-Tatar forces faced a new Polish army led by the king himself. The Poles were on the verge of defeat and the king about to be captured when the Crimean khan intervened, preventing a Polish defeat and maintaining a balance of power in the region, where he did not want either of the contending forces to emerge victorious. Khmelnytsky had to retreat. Under the terms of the Treaty of Zboriv (1649), the Cossacks created an autonomous state of their own in three eastern provinces of the Commonwealth, collectively known at the time as Ukraine – the palatinates of Kyiv, Chernihiv, and Bratslav. Khmelnytsky also had the right to increase his Cossack register to forty thousand men.

The Zboriv treaty established legal foundations for the continuing existence of a separate Cossack polity known to history as the Hetmanate, but it did not put an end to Polish-Cossack hostilities. The war resumed in 1651, with the pendulum swinging in favor of the Polish side. This was followed by another Cossack victory in 1652 and an indecisive battle in 1653. Neither side was in a position to deal a death blow to the other. At this point Khmelnytsky, who had lost his elder son in battle, made one more dramatic shift in foreign policy, replacing the Crimean khan as his ally with the Orthodox tsar of Muscovy. Agreement with the Muscovites was reached in January 1654 at a Cossack council in the town of Pereiaslav. Tsar Aleksei Romanov agreed to take the Hetmanate under his protection, recognizing the hetman's authority in Ukraine and expanding the Cossack register to sixty thousand. The only restriction placed on the hetman's powers by the agreement of 1654 pertained to foreign relations: the hetman was to inform the tsar of communications received from other sovereigns. Decades later, Khmelnytsky's successors would regard the agreement as a golden charter of Cossack liberties. At the time, Khmelnytsky saw it as an alliance of convenience and a temporary limitation on his own powers, justified by the tsar's immediate dispatch of Muscovite troops to fight the Cossacks' Polish arch-enemies.

Within the first year of the alliance, the Muscovites captured Vilnius, while the Cossacks returned to the gates of Lviv. Clearly, the gamble had paid off for Khmelnytsky. But Muscovite–Cossack relations soured when the tsar decided to conclude a peace treaty with the Poles. Taking advantage of Polish defeats at the hands of the tsarist and Cossack armies, King Charles X of Sweden invaded the Polish-Lithuanian Commonwealth from the north. To prevent the seemingly inevitable collapse of the Commonwealth, Aleksei Romanov stopped fighting and negotiated a peace with the Poles, leaving Khmelnytsky in the lurch. The hetman ordered his Cossack army to continue fighting in alliance with the Protestant ruler of Transylvania, Ferenc Rákóczi, and the tsar's arch-enemy, Charles X. When Khmelnytsky died in the summer of 1657, the Cossack-Muscovite alliance was all but defunct.[7]

That alliance was broken under Khmelnytsky's successor, Hetman Ivan Vyhovsky, whom the author of the *History of the Rus'* considered an ethnic Pole and treated with great contempt. Unlike Khmelnytsky, Vyhovsky had had little to do with Cossackdom before the uprising of 1648. A descendant of a noble Orthodox family, he began his career as a lawyer and developed a reputation as an effective bureaucrat before he joined the Commonwealth army and was captured by the Tatars in one of the first battles of May 1648. According to legend, Khmelnytsky found him among the Tatar captives, exchanged him for a horse, and appointed him chancellor. As the Cossack Host became a polity with its own territory, Vyhovsky turned his originally not very influential position into the second most powerful office of state, making himself Khmelnytsky's closest collaborator. He brought to that office not only his bureaucratic and diplomatic talents but also a Polish education and the traditional inclinations of the Ruthenian Orthodox nobility, whose animosity toward the Polish state, with its highly developed noble democracy, was never as strong as it was among the Cossacks, and whose attitude toward Muscovy was never as positive as that of certain leaders of the Cossack army. These traditions helped Vyhovsky carry out what Khmelnytsky did not have

[7] On the Khmelnytsky Uprising, see Mykhailo Hrushevsky, *History of Ukraine-Rus'*, vols. VIII–IX, trans. Marta D. Olynyk (Edmonton and Toronto, 2002–10); Frank E. Sysyn, *Between Poland and the Ukraine: The Dilemma of Adam Kysil* (Cambridge, Mass., 1986); Sysyn, "The Khmelnytsky Uprising and Ukrainian Nation-Building," *Journal of Ukrainian Studies* 17, nos. 1–2 (Summer–Winter 1992): 141–70; Plokhy, *The Cossacks and Religion*, pp. 176–333.

time to accomplish – to break the union with Muscovy and change the course of the Cossack ship of state in the uncertain political waters of Eastern Europe. They also made him suspect to the established Cossack elite, which never fully trusted this smooth lawyer, too immersed in Polish culture for its liking.

After Khmelnytsky's death Vyhovsky was elected hetman of the Cossack Host with Moscow's blessing, but he regarded his relations with the tsar as contractual. When Vyhovsky discovered that Moscow was conspiring against him with rivals among the Cossack colonels, he negotiated a new deal with the Polish-Lithuanian Commonwealth. The Union of Hadiach, concluded between Cossack and Commonwealth negotiators in the fall of 1658, proclaimed the creation of a new Commonwealth in which the Grand Duchy of Rus', led by a hetman and a knighted Cossack elite, was to acquire rights equal to those of the autonomous Grand Duchy of Lithuania, which had joined the Kingdom of Poland in the Union of Lublin (1569). Muscovy reacted by sending an army of twenty-five thousand to Ukraine. Faced with an imminent threat to his rule and bereft of effective allies, Vyhovsky repeated Khmelnytsky's maneuver of 1648, allying himself with the Crimean khan. The joint Cossack-Tatar forces annihilated the Muscovite army at the Battle of Konotop in June 1659. The enemy was defeated, and the dream cherished by generations of Ruthenian nobles – the creation of an autonomous Ruthenian state within the Commonwealth – seemed within reach. But that idea did not sit well with the Cossack rank and file: the Union of Hadiach, which was never approved in its entirety by the Polish Diet, discriminated against the Cossacks to the benefit of the nobility. Moreover, it drastically reduced the prerogatives of the hetman, the Host, and the Cossack social estate as compared with Khmelnytsky's agreement of 1654 with the tsar. Identified with the Union of Hadiach, Vyhovsky was soon forced to resign in the face of a new Cossack rebellion supported by Muscovy and directed against him. The Ruthenian nobility's dream vanished into Polish exile along with Vyhovsky.

Vyhovsky's successor was Bohdan Khmelnytsky's younger son, Yurii, whom the author of the *History of the Rus'* treated with great sympathy. It was allegedly from Yurii's archive that sources dealing with Bohdan's hetmancy made it into the *History*. The young Khmelnytsky assumed the hetman's office in September 1659. He had first been elected to that office by his father's supporters at the age of seventeen, in August 1657, immediately after Bohdan's death. But the election results were soon reversed by a vote of larger Cossack councils, which made Vyhovsky

Yurii's regent and then full-fledged hetman. Now the "justice" of the first election was restored, and the nineteen-year-old youth, who possessed none of the charisma, skill, or experience of his father, became the official leader of the army and the state. Although Yurii was elected by a Cossack council with Moscow's strong support, he would soon follow his predecessor by turning against Muscovy, for the tsar's officials continued to encroach on the hetman's rights and the sovereignty of the Cossack state, which they never recognized. In November 1660 Yurii Khmelnytsky switched sides, joining the Polish king and dealing the Muscovite army another major defeat.

Moscow responded by sponsoring the election of a new hetman on the Left Bank of the Dnieper, which bordered on Muscovite territory. The Cossack state was effectively divided, and there began a long period of fratricidal struggle that pitched Right-Bank Cossacks fighting on the Polish side against Left-Bank Cossacks fighting on the Muscovite side. This chapter of Ukrainian history, known as the Ruin, led to the devastation of a significant part of the Cossack state and the depopulation of Right-Bank Ukraine. Not cut out to be the ruler of a rebel polity, Yurii Khmelnytsky became a pawn of neighboring powers and a symbol of the fiasco of Cossack politics. In utter desperation, Yurii resigned his office in 1663 and took monastic vows. Not convinced of his intention to abandon politics, the Poles imprisoned him in the Marienburg Fortress. After his release in 1667, Yurii lived in one of the Ukrainian monasteries but then re-entered the political arena. He reclaimed the hetmancy and ruled part of Ukraine from 1677 to 1681 with the help of the Ottomans, contributing to the devastation and depopulation of his realm. He was executed by his Ottoman masters in 1685 after refusing to follow their orders. Bohdan Khmelnytsky's last male descendant was now dead, as was the idea of a Cossack dynasty and an independent Cossack state. The ruin of Ukraine had reached its nadir.

Cossackdom was wiped out on Right Bank of the Dnieper, where its leaders vacillated between loyalty to the Polish king and the Ottoman sultan, but it survived, though in diminished form and with much less strength, on the Muscovite-controlled Left Bank. Moscow was able to ensure its rule not only by playing off one hetman against another and removing unreliable Cossack leaders from office but also by giving more rights to the Cossack Host than either the Poles or the Ottomans were prepared to do in their realms. The tsars also allocated sufficient military resources to the area to give the population a degree of security unknown in other parts of the former Cossack polity. During the last decades of the seventeenth century the Cossack officers, the rank and file, and the population at large moved in large numbers to Left-Bank Ukraine in order to find protection and a degree of stability under the rule of the Muscovite tsars. The Hetmanate, a significantly reduced Cossack state now limited to the Left Bank of the Dnieper, experienced a political, economic, and cultural revival in the last two decades of the seventeenth century and the early years of the eighteenth. The Kyivan Academy, founded in 1632 by Metropolitan Peter Mohyla, renewed its activity; old churches and monasteries were restored and new ones built; and hetmans and Cossack officers began to construct impressive public buildings and private villas on an unprecedented scale.[8]

The new prosperity was closely associated with the name of Ivan Mazepa, a native of Right-Bank Ukraine who began his career at the court of the Polish king, continued it in the service of the Right-Bank Hetman Petro Doroshenko, and then switched sides, joining the Left-Bank Hetman Ivan Samoilovych and restarting his career in the Cossack Host under the auspices of the Muscovite tsars. The story of Mazepa's youthful love for the wife of a Polish noble, in which he was punished for adultery by being tied to a horse that eventually brought him half-dead to the Cossacks, inspired Voltaire, Byron, and Pushkin and made Mazepa a darling of European romanticism. The author of the *History of the Rus'* regarded Mazepa as a promoter of Ukrainian independence, but he also believed that, like Vyhovsky before him, Mazepa was an ethnic Pole and thus an exemplar of sophistication, duplicity, and canniness. Indeed, it was through numerous manifestations of unwavering loyalty to Tsar Peter I that Mazepa ensured the longevity of his rule in Ukraine and attained heights of power unmatched by any of his predecessors, short of Bohdan Khmelnytsky himself. It all came to an end one autumn day in 1708. As the hitherto invincible armies of Charles XII of Sweden approached the Hetmanate and Peter I refused to send troops to protect his Cossack dependency, Mazepa concluded that the Muscovite protectorate was defunct and joined the advancing Swedes.

---

[8] On Ivan Vyhovsky's rule and the period of the Ruin in Ukrainian history, see Andrzej Kaminski, "The Cossack Experiment in *Szlachta* Democracy in the Polish-Lithuanian Commonwealth: The Hadiach (*Hadziacz*) Union," *Harvard Ukrainian Studies* 1, no. 2 (June 1977): 178–97; Kaminski, *Republic vs. Autocracy: Poland-Lithuania and Russia, 1686–97* (Cambridge, Mass., 1994); David A. Frick, "The Circulation of Information about Ivan Vyhovs'kyj," *Harvard Ukrainian Studies* 17, nos. 3–4 (December 1993): 251–78; Brian L. Davies, *Warfare, State and Society on the Black Sea Steppe, 1500–1700* (London and New York, 2007), pp. 115–87; Serhii Plokhy, *The Origins of the Slavic Nations: Premodern Identities in Russia, Ukraine and Belarus* (Cambridge, 2006), pp. 32–38.

The tsar, previously unable to spare even a single soldier for the defense of Ukraine, now proclaimed Mazepa a modern-day Judas and sent a large army to punish the traitor and repel the invader. The tsar's troops captured the hetman's capital of Baturyn, burned it down, and massacred the inhabitants. By means of terror and massive propaganda that promised the restoration of Cossack freedoms to those officers who had joined Mazepa, the tsar regained the loyalty of the Hetmanate's army and the population. In June 1709 his forces prevailed at the Battle of Poltava. The Swedish army, already weakened by the harsh winter of 1708 and decimated by disease, now found itself without Cossack support and facing rebellion on the part of the local population. The tsar's victory at Poltava became a turning point in European history, heralding the decline of Sweden and the rise of Muscovy/Russia as a superpower. But nowhere was the outcome of the battle more dramatic than in the Cossack Hetmanate.

Peter I was careful at first not to spurn the Cossack elite, and after Mazepa's defection in the fall of 1708 he allowed the election of a new hetman, Ivan Skoropadsky. After Skoropadsky's death in 1721, however, no new election of a hetman was allowed, and Peter appointed a Russian-dominated committee, the Little Russian College, to rule over the Hetmanate, violating the rights and privileges of the Cossack Host to a degree unthinkable before Poltava. The Cossack elite complained but did not dare to rebel. The officers turned to history, recalling the glorious days of Bohdan Khmelnytsky and the privileges promised by the tsars back in 1654. They wanted the office of hetman restored, and they got their way after the death of Peter. In 1727 they elected as their new hetman a former supporter of Mazepa, Colonel Danylo Apostol, born in 1654. This fact of the new hetman's biography linked two epochs of Cossack history, but there was much more symbolism than substance in the coincidence. The new hetman had few of the prerogatives reserved to his famous predecessor, and when he died in 1734 the hetman's office was abolished once again. The incorporation of the Hetmanate into the Russian Empire proceeded apace.

Some Cossack chroniclers considered the year 1734 to mark the terminus of Cossack history, but the hetman's office was restored yet again in 1750. This time it was done not only to satisfy the Cossack officers' aspirations but also to advance the career of a parvenu with good connections at the court of St. Petersburg. Empress Elizabeth, a daughter of Peter I, fell in love with and secretly married a court singer, Oleksii Rozum, the son of a Cossack from the Hetmanate. Rozum was born in 1709, the year of Poltava. At court he changed his name to the Russian-sounding Aleksei

Razumovsky, which suggested noble origin. Oleksii Rozumovsky, who played an important role in Elizabeth's ascent to the throne in 1741, became a count and a field marshal; among other things, he promoted the career of his younger brother, Kyrylo Rozumovsky (Kirill Razumovsky). At the age of eighteen the younger Rozumovsky became president of the Russian Academy of Sciences, and four years later he was hetman of Ukraine. He rebuilt Mazepa's capital, Baturyn, and restored to the Hetmanate some of the rights of autonomy taken away in previous decades. If Yurii Khmelnytsky came to stand for the disasters of Cossackdom under Polish kings and Ottoman sultans, Kyrylo Rozumovsky symbolized its success under the Russian emperors. A Cossack hetman was now president of the Academy of Sciences and all but a member of the imperial family. Beneath the appearances, however, little remained of the hetmans' former independence and the autonomy of their realm. Rozumovsky would soon learn this the hard way.

In 1762, the 34-year-old Kyrylo Rozumovsky helped bring to the throne a German-born empress who became known as Catherine II. Her right to rule the empire was more than questionable, as her husband, Peter III, was removed by means of a coup and died under suspicious circumstances a few days later. Other possible candidates, such as the illegitimate daughter of Oleksii Rozumovsky and Empress Elizabeth, were sought out in Italy and brought back to St. Petersburg to die in captivity. As one of the leading participants in the coup, Kyrylo Rozumovsky expected gratitude in the form of more rights for the Hetmanate and a hereditary hetmancy for his family. He was to discover that the new empress would have none of it. Raised on Enlightenment ideals and believing in universal rules and values, she set her mind to bringing order, centralization, and the rule of law to Russia, with little regard for the particular rights and privileges of autonomous units of the empire. In November 1764 Rozumovsky was recalled to St. Petersburg and forced to resign. The office of hetman was abolished once and for all. In the course of two decades the empress managed to integrate the Ukrainian Cossack lands into the empire. She destroyed the Zaporozhian Sich, an autonomous Cossack entity beyond the Dnieper rapids; abolished the autonomous status of the Hetmanate, which was divided into a number of imperial provinces ruled directly from St. Petersburg; disbanded Cossack regiments; and introduced serfdom into the former hetman state.

As Catherine did away with Cossack autonomy, she did her best to incorporate the Cossack elite into the imperial service. A Cossack officer, Petro (Petr) Zavadovsky (1739–1812), became one of the favorites of the new empress and spearheaded educational reform in the empire from the 1780s, becoming the first Russian minister of education at the beginning of the nineteenth century. Colonel Oleksandr (Alexander) Bezborodko of the Kyiv Cossack Regiment made an even more spectacular career, rising from secretary to the empress to become Grand Chancellor of the empire and the architect of its foreign policy. He was behind many Russian initiatives against the traditional enemies of the Ukrainian Cossacks – the Ottomans and the Poles. The peace treaties with the Porte that brought the northern Black Sea region and the Crimea under Russian control and the arrangements with Austria and Prussia that resulted in the partitions of Poland and the abolition of the Polish state bear the hallmarks of Bezborodko's diplomatic efforts. If Cossack officers like Bezborodko helped extend the imperial borders into the former Polish-Lithuanian Commonwealth, natives of the Hetmanate like Archbishop Heorhii Konysky of Mahilioŭ helped propagate imperial Orthodoxy in the newly acquired territories.

Not all the Ukrainian Cossacks were willing or able to follow in the footsteps of the Rozumovskys, Bezborodko, and Konysky. Most of the petty Cossack officers and their descendants were regarded with contempt by the imperial authorities, and their claims to noble status based on service in Cossack formations were questioned or even rejected. Hryhorii Poletyka, a native of the Hetmanate who made a bureaucratic career in St. Petersburg, served as a defender of his homeland's rights and privileges on Catherine's Legislative Commission in the 1760s. But after little more than a year the commission was dismissed, and the battle for Cossack rights was relegated to the sphere of petitions to the imperial authorities, bureaucratic intrigues, and historical writings. As in the times following the first abolition of the hetmancy by Peter I, Cossack intellectuals of the late eighteenth and early nineteenth centuries turned to history to defend the privileges bestowed on their forefathers by Polish kings and Russian tsars. Their preoccupation with the past coincided with the new importance attributed to the historical imagination in the dawning age of Romanticism and heightened interest in the origins of nations.[9]

[9] On the decline and liquidation of the Hetmanate, see Orest Subtelny, *The Mazepists: Ukrainian Separatism in the Early Eighteenth Century* (New York, 1981); Zenon E. Kohut, *Russian Centralism and Ukrainian Autonomy: Imperial Absorption of the Hetmanate, 1760s–1830s* (Cambridge, Mass., 1988); David Saunders, *The Ukrainian Impact on Russian Culture, 1750–1850* (Edmonton, 1985), pp. 15–144; Plokhy, *The Origins of the Slavic Nations*, pp. 343–53; Frank E. Sysyn, "The Image of Russia in Early Eighteenth-Century Ukraine: Hryhorii Hrabianka's *Diistvie*," in *Russische und ukrainische Geschichte*, ed. Robert O. Crummey, Holm Sundhaussen, and Ricarda Vulpius, vols. XVI–XVIII (Wiesbaden, 2001), pp. 243–50.

The *History of the Rus'*, whose origins were traced by its producers not only to Konysky but also to Poletyka, became the expression of the response of the Cossack officers and their descendants to political and cultural change in the Hetmanate and in the empire as a whole. As things turned out, that response resonated exceptionally well not only in the former Cossack lands but also in the imperial capitals. In October 1825, Colonel Aleksandr von Brigen was so impressed with the *History of the Rus'* found on his father-in-law's estate that he was thinking about "a critical edition of Konysky, which contains a great deal that is fine and unknown to Karamzin himself." The reference was to the official historiographer of the Russian Empire, Nikolai Karamzin, whose multivolume *History of the Russian State*, the first scholarly history of Russia, began to appear in print in 1818. In the *History of the Rus'*, von Brigen was finding what he could not glean from the official history of his country.[10]

The planned critical edition never materialized. On December 14, guards regiments led by von Brigen's co-conspirators marched to the Senate in downtown St. Petersburg. Their revolt was crushed, its leaders arrested. The authorities hunted for co-conspirators throughout the empire. As news of the uprising reached Ukraine, Sergei Muravev-Apostol, a descendant of the eighteenth-century Cossack hetman Danylo Apostol, and his fellow officer Mikhail Bestuzhev-Riumin initiated a revolt of officers and soldiers of the Chernihiv regiment, stationed south of Kyiv. The revolt began on December 27, 1825. By January 3, 1826 it had been crushed by troops loyal to the government. Aleksandr von Brigen, still residing on his father-in-law's estate of Ponurivka, decided that the time had come to leave the empire. Together with his wife, Sofiia Myklashevska, he embarked on his westward journey but had to turn back when Sofiia fell ill. On January 10, 1826 the discoverer of the *History of the Rus'* was arrested in the village of Berezivka near Starodub. He was sent under guard to St. Petersburg and joined his co-conspirators in the cells of the SS. Peter and Paul Fortress. In July 1826 the former colonel found himself among the lucky ones whose "public execution" on the ramparts of the fortress ended with breaking sabers above their heads and burning their uniforms and epaulettes.

Von Brigen was sentenced to two years of hard labor in Siberia. The sentence was commuted to one year, but von Brigen was not allowed to

---

[10] Maslov, *Literaturnaia deiatel'nost' K. F. Ryleeva*, appendix, pp. 97–98; Brigen, *Pis'ma. Istoricheskie sochineniia*, pp. 96–98.

return to the European part of the empire until after the death of Nicholas I in 1855. Only then was the hero of Borodino and the European campaigns again permitted to wear his commemorative medal of the war of 1812 with Napoleon and the military cross for service in the Battle of Kulm (August 1813). Until then, a scar identified in a police report as visible on von Brigen's face from a wound received during the Battle of Kulm was the only indication of his martial heroism to those who met the Siberian exile. By that time, von Brigen's family life was in shambles – he married another woman in Siberia – and many of his plans and dreams remained unrealized. In the summer of 1857, when von Brigen finally managed to visit his former wife's estate, where he had been arrested more than thirty years earlier, the *History of the Rus'* that he then considered for publication had already been in print for more than a decade. Before its appearance in Moscow in 1846, the book had made a spectacular career in manuscript form, copied and recopied by scores of devotees of Ukrainian history. It influenced historical and political discourse in the Russian Empire to a degree unmatched by any other manuscript of its kind. Von Brigen and Ryleev were only the first to appreciate its appeal and importance.[11]

---

[11] Brigen, *Pis'ma. Istoricheskie sochineniia*, pp. 376–77; "Brigen, fon-der Aleksandr Fedorovich," in *Alfavit dekabristov*.

CHAPTER 3

The birth of the myth

"The air suddenly grew colder: they could feel the vicinity of the Dnieper," wrote Nikolai Gogol, describing the approach of his most famous character, Taras Bulba, and his two sons to Ukraine's largest and most famous river. "And there it gleamed afar distinguishable on the horizon as a dark bend. It sent forth cold waves, spreading nearer, nearer and finally seeming to embrace half of the entire surface of the earth." Travelers attempting to reach Kyiv from the left bank of the river on April 5, 1847 must have had similar impressions. That spring the melting snow caused floods, and the Dnieper, which is quite wide near Kyiv under normal circumstances, had swollen and become even wider.[1]

Among those making the crossing that spring day was a modestly dressed man carrying all his earthly belongings in a small suitcase. His name was Taras Shevchenko. Born a serf in a country where serfs made up more than a third of the population, the 34-year-old Shevchenko could consider himself lucky. Very early in life he had shown talent as an artist and was bought out of serfdom with the help of some of the most prominent figures on the Russian cultural scene. A renowned Russian artist, Karl Briullov, painted and auctioned off a portrait of one of the best-known literary figures in the empire, the poet Vasilii Zhukovsky. The auction brought in enough money to buy the young man's freedom. Shevchenko turned out to be not only a talented artist but also an outstanding poet. The publication of his first collection of poems, *Kobzar* (The Minstrel, 1840), made him famous. Written in Ukrainian, the poems laid the foundations for the development of modern Ukrainian literature and, many would add, the Ukrainian nation itself. In 1845 Shevchenko, by that time a graduate of the St. Petersburg Academy of Arts, returned to his native land, where he was employed by the Kyiv Archeographic Commission to travel the country, drawing and painting

---

[1] Nikolai Vasilevich Gogol, *Taras Bulba and Other Stories* (Whitefish, Mont., 2004), p. 22.

Ukraine's architectural monuments. Now, having spent close to a year on the road, the artist was on his way to Kyiv to attend a friend's wedding and take up a teaching position at Kyiv University.[2]

The future could not have looked brighter for Shevchenko when he boarded the Dnieper ferry on that spring day in 1847. However, what happened when the ferry finally reached the other shore not only took him by surprise but also crushed his dreams. As the ferry docked, a policeman boarded it. He had a lazy eye, and it was not clear where he was looking at any given moment. But the passengers soon grasped that he had found his quarry. As the policeman spotted Shevchenko and announced that he was placing him under arrest, one of the passengers recognized the modestly dressed man as Ukraine's best-known poet. He approached Shevchenko and offered to throw his suitcase into the river, thereby ridding him of what might be incriminating evidence. Shevchenko refused. This would prove a major error with regard to his own fate but a boon to his country's literature.[3]

When the police opened the suitcase, they found three guns, drawings, and a collection of papers. It was not the guns but the papers that gave rise to official concerns. Next day the Kyiv governor informed the head of the Third Department, the tsar's secret police in St. Petersburg, of Shevchenko's arrest: "Yesterday, on his return from the Chernihiv gubernia, that artist was detained at the entrance to the city of Kyiv and brought directly to me. Discovered among his papers was a manuscript book with Little Russian poems of his own composition, many of them offensive and criminal in content. Hence I considered it my duty to deliver both those poems and all others found in Shevchenko's possession, as well as his personal correspondence, to the Third Department of His Imperial Majesty's Own Chancery." The suspect was sent to the imperial capital under the escort of two local policemen. The case was of such importance that it had to be investigated in St. Petersburg, not in provincial Kyiv.[4]

The papers found in Shevchenko's suitcase were part of the evidence that condemned him to ten years of military service as a private, returning him to serfdom in all but name, for it was serfs who, along with state

[2] On Shevchenko's life and work, see George Grabowicz, *The Poet as Mythmaker: A Study of Symbolic Meaning in Taras Ševčenko* (Cambridge, Mass., 1982); Pavlo Zaitsev, *Taras Shevchenko: A Life*, ed. and trans. George S. N. Luckyj (Toronto, 1988).

[3] Mikhail Chalyi, *Zhizn' i proizvedeniia Tarasa Shevchenka: svod materialov dlia ego biografii s portretom* (Kyiv, 1882), pp. 62–63; N. Belozerskii, "Taras Grigor'evich Shevchenko po vospominaniiam raznykh lits," *Kievskaia starina*, no. 10 (1882): 72–73.

[4] *Kyrylo-Mefodiïvs'ke tovarystvo*, 3 vols. (Kyiv, 1990), II: 198.

peasants, manned the lower ranks of the imperial army. Tsar Nicholas I ordered him to be kept "under the strictest surveillance, forbidden to write or paint." Shevchenko found these conditions especially painful. "If I had been a monster or a vampire, even then a more horrible torture could not have been devised for me," he wrote later about his sentence. The severity of the punishment was directly linked to Shevchenko's serf origins and the personal attack on the tsar and the tsarina in the poems found in his possession. Particularly damaging was the "evidence" discovered in the poem "Son" (A Dream). It depicted Shevchenko's imaginary flight across the Russian Empire, allowing him to juxtapose images of the tsar's court with those of his beloved Ukraine, which the poet believed to be suffering under the tsarist regime.

Unlike Ryleev and the Decembrists, Shevchenko did not contemplate killing the emperor, but he took a particularly harsh attitude toward the imperial couple, especially the tsar's consort, Empress Aleksandra Fedorovna, born Frederica Louise Charlotte Wilhelmina of Prussia. An object of the tsar's love and affection, Aleksandra was sickly and looked much older than her years. She was exceptionally thin, suffered from nervous twitching, and convulsively shook her head. The Marquis de Custine, a French aristocrat who visited Russia and met with the empress in 1839, believed that she had "never recovered from the anguish she had to undergo on the day of her accession to the throne." The reference was to the Decembrist Uprising, which was crushed by Nicholas I as he succeeded his brother, Alexander I.[5]

Shevchenko took no prisoners in his attack on the imperial masters, calling the empress a "dried up mushroom" and concluding his description of her with the ironic exclamation, "So that's the goddess?!" Shevchenko's attack on the monarchy was not limited to living members of the ruling dynasty. Among the targets of his satire were Emperor Peter I and Empress Catherine II, Russia's most famous rulers of the previous century. "The FIRST one racked my country dear," wrote Shevchenko about Peter. Referring to Catherine, he added: "The SECOND gave the final blow/That brought my land to utter woe./Ah, hangmen both, voracious beasts!/Upon our folk have been your feasts,/To the last shred. What token fond/Went with you to the world beyond?/Such heaviness oppressed my head/As if in those two words I read/All history of our Ukraine." The poem was written in St. Petersburg in July 1844.

[5] Marquis de Custine, *Empire of the Tsar: A Journey through Eternal Russia*, foreword by Daniel J. Boorstin; introduction by George F. Kennan (New York, 1989), pp. 137–38.

In February and March 1847, before embarking on his trip to Kyiv, Shevchenko made his final changes to its text. The poem would serve to incriminate not only Shevchenko but also friends of his who read and kept copies of earlier versions.[6]

What "history of Ukraine" did Shevchenko have in mind? A reading of "A Dream" leaves no doubt that much of the historical data and at least some of his inspiration came from the *History of the Rus'*. Shevchenko first encountered the mysterious manuscript around 1840. From that time on, his poetry was replete with images of the *History*'s heroes, including the hetmans Severyn Nalyvaiko and Yakiv Ostrianytsia – incarnations of sacrifice and suffering for the sake of Shevchenko's homeland. The *History*'s influence on "A Dream" becomes particularly apparent in his depiction of the fate of the acting hetman Pavlo Polubotok, who was jailed by Peter I and died in captivity in the St. Petersburg fortress of SS. Peter and Paul in 1724. The Ukrainian historian Mykola Markevych wrote in 1825 to Kondratii Ryleev that the spirit of Polubotok still lived among the elite of the former Hetmanate. The *History of the Rus'* was vivid proof of that. According to its author, Polubotok delivered a speech before Peter accusing him of violating Cossack rights and privileges and saying that God alone could resolve his dispute with the tsar. The hetman allegedly told the all-powerful emperor that the Cossacks had been "forced to dig trenches and canals and drain impassable marshes, fertilizing all this with the corpses of our dead, who have fallen by the thousands from oppressive burdens, hunger, and climate." He was referring to the use of Cossack regiments for the construction of the tsar's new capital, St. Petersburg.[7]

Taras Shevchenko retold the *History*'s account of Peter and Paul by making Polubotok say the following words:

> O greedy and voracious Tsar!
> O wicked ruler that you are,
> O serpent that all earth should shun,
> What have you to my Cossacks done?
> For you have glutted all these swamps
> With noble bones! To feed your pomps,

---

[6] *The Poetical Works of Taras Shevchenko: The Kobzar*, trans. C. H. Andrusyshen and Watson Kirkconnell (Toronto, 1964), pp. 170–73; cf. Taras Shevchenko, *Zibrannia tvoriv u shesty tomakh* (Kyiv, 2003), 1: 272–75.

[7] Shevchenko, *Zibrannia tvoriv*, 1: 274–75; *Istoriia Rusov ili Maloi Rosii. Sochinenie Georgiia Koniskago, Arkhiepiskopa Beloruskago* (Moscow, 1846) pp. 229–30; Mykhailo Vozniak, *Psevdo-Konys'kyi i Psevdo-Poletyka (Istoriia Rusov u literaturi ta nautsi)* (Lviv and Kyiv, 1939), pp. 29–31.

You reared your shining capital
On tortured corpses of them all,
And in a gloomy dungeon cell,
Me, their free hetman, by a hell
Of utter hunger you have slain,
A martyr to our sad Ukraine![8]

Like Kondratii Ryleev before him, Shevchenko found a call for freedom in the *History*, but he also discerned something that never occurred to Ryleev – a call to arms in defense of the Ukrainian nation against its oppressors, the Russian tsars and nobles. It was Shevchenko's interpretation that captivated readers of his day and turned the manuscript into the bible of the Ukrainian movement. His verses inspired hundreds, thousands, and eventually hundreds of thousands of Ukrainians to struggle for their national rights. Many came to revere him not only as a martyr but also as a national prophet, the father of a modern nation not yet born at the time of his arrest in the spring of 1847. But was Shevchenko right in his reading of the *History*?

Taras Shevchenko was not the first writer to follow in Ryleev's footsteps and turn to the *History of the Rus'* in search of historical data and artistic inspiration. He was preceded by two great contemporaries, Alexander Pushkin and Nikolai Gogol, whose readings of the *History* were also quite different from Ryleev's.

Alexander Pushkin, by far the best-known Russian poet of the nineteenth century and the founder of modern Russian literature, was fascinated with the mysterious manuscript. "Many passages in the 'History of Little Russia' are pictures drawn by the brush of a great painter," he wrote, referring to the *History of the Rus'*. In 1836 Pushkin published long excerpts from the manuscript in his journal, *Sovremennik* (The Contemporary). He hoped that the entire manuscript would appear in print before long. "As a historian, Heorhii Konysky has not yet received his due, for a well-wrought madrigal sometimes brings greater fame than a truly sublime creation, rarely intelligible to avid connoisseurs of the human mind and hardly accessible to most readers . . . Let us hope that this great historian of Little Russia will also ultimately find a publisher of equal merit." At the time Pushkin wrote these words, he was a recognized leader of the Russian literary world, and his assessment of the *History* had a major impact on intellectuals all over the Russian Empire.[9]

---

[8] *The Poetical Works of Taras Shevchenko*, p. 174; cf. Shevchenko, *Zibrannia tvoriv*, I: 275–76.
[9] Aleksandr Pushkin, "Sobranie sochinenii Georgiia Konisskogo, arkhiepiskopa Belorusskogo," in *Polnoe sobranie sochinenii*, 12 vols. (Moscow, 1949), XII: 12–19.

Born in Moscow to a noble family, Pushkin underwent a profound ideological metamorphosis in the course of his short life. An alumnus of an elite lyceum for noble youth and a close friend of many future Decembrists, he had fallen out of favor with the authorities by 1820, the year of the publication of his first long poem, *Ruslan and Liudmila.* He was regarded by the court as a dangerous freethinker and forced to spend much of the next decade in exile, first in the Caucasus, then in southern Ukraine and Moldavia, and later at his mother's estate of Mikhailovskoe in northwestern Russia. It was there that Pushkin received news of the Decembrist Uprising, led by some of his personal friends, including Kondratii Ryleev. Pushkin initially decided to go to the capital but then turned back and burned incriminating papers and poetic manuscripts. Some believe that Pushkin the freethinker also perished in those flames. In the following year he wrote to the tsar, asking pardon and promising loyalty in return. A meeting between the tsar and the poet took place in early September 1826, a few months after the execution of the Decembrists. Nicholas I reinstated Pushkin's freedom of movement but also told the poet that henceforth he would be his personal censor. Some scholars argue that that there were two Pushkins, one before the Decembrist Uprising of 1825 and another after it.[10]

A point on which the post-1825 Pushkin and the Russian tsar seemed to be in complete agreement was their devotion to the empire. The Polish Uprising of 1830 turned Pushkin into an ardent defender of Russian rule in the western borderlands acquired by Catherine II a few decades earlier. The former promoter of freedom and admirer of liberal values wrote a number of poems attacking the West for its support of the Polish rebels. The most famous of those poems, written in 1831, was titled "To the Maligners of Russia" and intended as a response to speeches delivered in the French parliament in support of the Polish cause. In another poem, "The Anniversary of Borodino" written on the occasion of the Russian capture of Praga, a suburb of rebellious Warsaw in August 1831, Pushkin expressed his concern about the future of Russian possessions in the west, including not only Poland but also Ukrainian lands annexed to Muscovy in the times of Bohdan Khmelnytsky: "Where shall we shift the line of

---

[10] On Pushkin's political views, see T. J. Binyon, *Pushkin: A Biography* (New York, 2003); Yuri Druzhnikov, *Prisoner of Russia: Alexander Pushkin and the Political Uses of Nationalism* (New Brunswick, N.J., 1999).

forts?/Beyond the Buh, to the Vorskla, to the Estuary?/Whose will Volhynia be?/And Bohdan's legacy?"[11]

In the midst of the Polish uprising, Pushkin decided to write a history of Cossack Ukraine or, in the parlance of the time, Little Russia. He drafted an outline of the history and began writing the text. In the opinion of Boris Modzalevsky, one of the best students of Pushkin's life and literary work, the poet's periodization of Ukrainian history came not from the writings of Mikhail Karamzin or Dmitrii Bantysh-Kamensky, the author of the three-volume *History of Little Russia*, but from the *History of the Rus'*. Although Pushkin drafted his outline in Russian, he began writing the text in French, apparently intending it for a Western audience. In July 1831 Pushkin submitted his outline to Count Aleksandr Benkendorf, the head of the Third Department (the tsar's secret police), who took over the role of Pushkin's personal censor from Nicholas I. The projected history was supposed to become part of the state-sponsored effort to counter Western propaganda and refute Polish claims to Ukraine. The uprising was soon crushed, and the history project lost its topicality. Its outline, along with Pushkin's later publications, allows one to suggest that the poet regarded the author of the *History of the Rus'* as a fellow defender of the Russian Empire. For him the manuscript was not only a well-written work of history but also an indictment of Poland and the Catholic Church for their brutal rule over part of the Rus' lands in the not so distant past. That indictment now provided moral justification for the suppression of the Polish revolt.[12]

Pushkin's first encounter with the *History of the Rus'* took place in 1829, soon after the publication of his epic poem *Poltava*. That work, devoted to Peter's victory over Charles XII and his Cossack allies in 1709, is often interpreted as Pushkin's response to what he saw as Byron's idealization of the "traitorous" Hetman Ivan Mazepa. Byron's poem *Mazeppa* (1818) highlighted the love story of the young Mazepa, turning him into a literary symbol of the new Romantic age. Kondratii Ryleev treated Mazepa with barely concealed sympathy in his *Voinarovsky*, and Pushkin resolved to give a different, much more negative treatment of the Cossack hetman. In the preface to *Poltava*, composed in January 1829, Pushkin wrote: "Mazepa is one of the most outstanding figures of that epoch.

---

[11] Pushkin, "Borodinskaia godovshchina," in *Polnoe sobranie sochinenii* (Moscow, 1948), III: 273–75, here 274.

[12] Pushkin, "Ocherk istorii Ukrainy," in *Polnoe sobranie sochinenii* (Moscow, 1949), XII: 196–98, 422; B. L. Modzalevskii, commentary on Pushkin, "Ocherk istorii Ukrainy," in Pushkin, *Polnoe sobranie sochinenii v 10-ti tomakh* (Moscow, 1958), VIII: 557–58.

Some writers wanted to make him a hero of liberty, a new Bohdan Khmelnytsky. History presents him as an ambitious individual given over to perfidy and evil deeds ... a traitor to Peter before his victory and a traitor to Charles after his defeat: his memory, consigned by the church to anathema, also cannot escape the curse of humankind." Pushkin did not mention Ryleev by name, but most scholars are now agreed that the reference was indeed to Ryleev and his *Voinarovsky*. This was a major change in Pushkin's attitude to the work of his executed friend. Before the Decembrist revolt, Pushkin liked *Voinarovsky* and told Ryleev so.[13]

Poltava got mixed reviews. Some of Pushkin's critics attacked him for departing from Byron's image of Mazepa, others for his lack of historical accuracy and invention of episodes that had never taken place. But there was at least one reviewer prepared to vouch for Pushkin's fidelity to the historical record. Mykhailo Maksymovych, a professor of botany at Moscow University and later the first rector of Kyiv University, soon published an article: "On Pushkin's Poem *Poltava* from the Historical Viewpoint." There he defended Pushkin's presentation of historical facts by referring to "oral accounts more trustworthy than others." The reference was to the *History of the Rus'*, where Maksymovych found confirmation of Pushkin's claim that Mazepa had rebelled against the tsar to avenge the humiliation he suffered when the tsar seized him by the moustache at a banquet.[14]

By 1831, Pushkin himself was turning to the *History of the Rus'* to defend the accuracy of his depiction of the moustache episode. The "proof," however, came from a different part of the *History* – the section on the Khmelnytsky Uprising. In an article entitled "Objections to Critics of *Poltava*," Pushkin wrote: "Mazepa acts in my poem exactly as he did in history, and his speeches explain his historical character. It has been remarked to me that Mazepa is too rancorous in my work; that a Little Russian hetman is not a student and would not want to take revenge for a slap in the face or for having his moustache pulled. Once again, this is history refuted by literary criticism: once again, *although I know it, I do not*

[13] Pushkin, "Poltava," in *Polnoe sobranie sochinenii v 10-ti tomakh* (Moscow, 1959), III: 449–50; K. F. Ryleev, "Pis'ma k A. S. Pushkinu," in *Sochineniia i perepiska Kondratiia Fedorovicha Ryleeva*, 2nd edn. by his daughter, ed. P. A. Efremov (St. Petersburg, 1784), pp. 203–6.

[14] Mikhail Maksimovich, "O poème Pushkina *Poltava* v istoricheskom otnoshenii," *Atenei*, no. 6 (1829): 507–15. On Maksymovych, see Viktor Korotkyi and Serhii Bilen'kyi, *Mykhailo Maksymovych ta osvitni praktyky na Pravoberezhnii Ukraïni v pershii polovyni XIX stolittia* (Kyiv, 1999); Nadiia Boiko, *Mykhailo Maksymovych – naviky z ridnym kraiem* (Cherkasy, 2004); Mykola Korpaniuk, *Slovo i dukh Ukraïny kniazhoï ta kozats'koï doby (Mykhailo Maksymovych – doslidnyk davn'oukraïns'koï literatury)* (Cherkasy, 2004).

believe it! Mazepa, educated in Europe at a time when notions of nobiliary honor were at their strongest – Mazepa might long have remembered the Muscovite tsar's insult and taken revenge on him when the opportunity presented itself. His whole character – secretive, cruel, single-minded – is in that trait. Pulling a Pole or a Cossack by the moustache was the same as seizing a Russian by the beard. One recalls that for all the offenses Khmelnytsky suffered from Czapliński, he was compensated, by verdict of the Commonwealth, with the shaven moustache of his enemy (see the Konysky Chronicle)."[15]

In the first volume of *Sovremennik*, the journal he founded in 1836, partly in the hope of improving his financial situation, Pushkin included two excerpts from the *History* as part of his review of a recently published collection of Heorhii Konysky's works. Although the *History of the Rus'* was routinely called the "Konysky History" long before Pushkin, he was the first to make a written attribution of its authorship to the archbishop of Mahilioŭ. "Heorhii wrote it for reasons of state," asserted Pushkin. "When Empress Catherine established a commission to draft a new law code, a deputy of the Little Russian nobility, Andrii Hryhorovych Pole-tyka, turned to Heorhii as a man well versed in the ancient laws and resolutions of that land, justly considering that the history of the people alone could explain its true needs. He set about his weighty task and accomplished it with astonishing success, combining the poetic freshness of the chronicle with the criticism imperative in history." Pushkin explained away inaccuracies in the *History* by stressing Konysky's patriot-ism and strong anti-Catholicism. "Bold and conscientious in his testi-mony, Konysky is not without a measure of involuntary passion," wrote Pushkin. "Hatred of Catholic superstition and of the repressions that he himself so actively opposed resounds in his eloquent narration. Love of his homeland often takes him beyond the bounds of strict justice."[16]

Pushkin saw Konysky as his own predecessor – a Russian patriot and zealot of Orthodoxy who wrote his history to meet the needs of the Russian Empire. In preparing the excerpts for publication, Pushkin rendered all references to the Rus' people and the Rus' church as references to the Russian people and religion. In the aftermath of the Polish upris-ing, the imperial government launched a major campaign to russify its western borderlands, abolish the Uniate Church, and treat both Poles and

---

[15] Pushkin, "Vozrazheniia kritikam Poltavy," in *Polnoe sobranie sochinenii* (Moscow, 1949), XI: 164–65.
[16] Pushkin, "Sobranie sochinenii Georgiia Konisskogo, Arkhiepiskopa Belorusskogo," in *Polnoe sobranie sochinenii*, XII: 12–24.

Jews as enemies. The two excerpts of the *History* that Pushkin selected for publication had very strong anti-Polish, anti-Catholic, and anti-Jewish overtones. The first dealt with the introduction of the church union at the Council of Brest (1596), while the second described the Polish authorities' execution of Hetman Ostrianytsia and his comrades, leaders of the Cossack uprising of 1638–39 in Ukraine. The Poles were Pushkin's main target. One of the excerpts contained the following passage: "Poles with large complements of staff were dispatched to all Little Russian administrative and judicial offices; the towns were taken over by Polish garrisons, and other settlements by their troops; they were empowered to do to the Russian people whatever they wanted and could think up, and they carried out that order with interest: anything that licentious, arrogant, and drunken humanity could conceive, they inflicted on the unfortunate Russian people with no pangs of conscience – pillage, rape of women and even children, beatings, torture, and murder exceeded the bounds of the most unenlightened barbarians."[17]

If Ryleev saw the Cossacks depicted in the *History of the Rus'* as predecessors of his own struggle against autocracy, Pushkin, writing after the defeat of the Decembrist Uprising of 1825, regarded them as allies in strengthening imperial rule over the western borderlands, fighters against Catholicism and Western oppression, and symbols of true Russian and Orthodox spirit. The Cossack myth introduced into Russian literature in the 1820s with the help of the *History of the Rus'* as an appeal against autocracy and in support of a constitutional republican order and liberal values was transformed in the next generation into a vehicle for strengthening autocracy, crushing republicanism, and promoting the imperial agenda in the borderlands. Even so, its evolution was far from over.

Pushkin's interest in the *History* was picked up by his younger colleague Nikolai Gogol, who came up with his own version of the Cossack myth. Like Ryleev and Pushkin, Gogol found the *History of the Rus'* a source of inspiration and a repository of historical episodes and images on which he could draw for his own work. Nikolai Gogol was born Mykola Hohol in 1809 in the Poltava region of Ukraine to a noble family with deep Cossack roots. In 1821, at the age of twelve, Mykola was sent to the Bezborodko Lyceum in Nizhyn, the first secular institution of higher learning in the former Hetmanate. It was founded by Count Illia Bezborodko in memory of (and, in part, with funds inherited from) his elder brother, the

----

[17] *Ibid.*, pp. 21–24.

chancellor of the Russian Empire, Prince Oleksandr Bezborodko. After eight years at the lyceum, the nineteen-year-old Gogol followed in the footsteps of the Bezborodko brothers and left Ukraine to conquer St. Petersburg. His obsession, however, was the pursuit of literary fame, not of imperial power. In the capital the young Gogol found a prevailing interest in Ukraine and things Ukrainian, heightened by the Polish uprising of 1830. The educated Russian public saw in Kyiv and Ukraine not only the cradle of the Russian dynasty, religion, and nation, but also part of the Russian heritage that had to be protected against the threat of the Polish insurrection. Ukraine emerged in the Russian imagination as an ultimate Romantic utopia, a land populated by epic heroes engaged in life-and-death struggles with the enemies of Russia. Gogol drew on this interest in and fascination with Cossack and Ukrainian themes.[18]

In the spring of 1829 Gogol began writing his Ukrainian tales, based largely on folklore sources supplied by his mother. They would be published two years later under the title *Evenings on a Farm near Dikanka*, bringing their author renown throughout the empire. In 1830 we see him working on a historical novel titled *Get'man*. Its main character was a beloved hero of the *History of the Rus'*, Hetman Ostrianytsia. While the author of the *History* turned the Cossack leader Yakiv Ostrianyn into Hetman Stepan Ostrianytsia, Gogol transformed him into Taras Ostrianytsia. The novel begins with an episode directly influenced by Gogol's reading of the *History*: Ostrianytsia appears on the scene to save an old Cossack from persecution by a Pole and a Jew for unpaid taxes. He saves the Jew from popular wrath and humiliates the Polish officer by tearing off part of his moustache – an episode inspired by the passage of the *History* that Pushkin cited in defense of his *Poltava*.[19]

Gogol never finished *Get'man*. It is believed that he abandoned work on the novel to begin writing *Taras Bul'ba*. The new novel was closely linked to its unfinished predecessor, and the *History of the Rus'* remained one of Gogol's foremost historical sources. *Taras Bul'ba* was completed in 1834 and first published a year later. Gogol reworked it in 1842, adding

[18] On Gogol and his place in Russian and Ukrainian literature, see Edyta Bojanowska, *Nikolai Gogol between Ukrainian and Russian Nationalism* (Cambridge, Mass., 2007); Richard Peace, *The Enigma of Gogol: An Examination of the Writings of N. V. Gogol and Their Place in the Russian Literary Tradition* (Cambridge, 2009).

[19] Nikolai Gogol, "Get'man," in *Polnoe sobranie sochinenii v 14-ti tomakh* (Moscow, 1937–52), III: 277–323; V. I. Matsapura, "Nezavershennyi roman Gogolia 'Get'man': osobennosti poètiki, problema konteksta," *Hoholeznavchi studiï: Zbirnyk naukovykh prats'*, vol. XVII (Nizhyn, 2008), pp. 26–42; Bojanowska, *Nikolai Gogol*, pp. 157–60.

new scenes but not altering the main story line. The main characters are the Cossack colonel Taras Bulba and his two sons, Ostap and Andrii. The Cossack uprising of 1638–39, led by Hetman Ostrianytsia, serves as the background to the story, which culminates with the capture and execution by the Polish authorities of Taras's elder son, Ostap. Generations of readers of the short novel and viewers of its six movie adaptations, the first of which was produced in 1909, were shocked and moved by the scene, which features an exchange of last words between the father, beholding the sufferings of his Cossack son, and the son, who calls on his father without knowing that he is present in the crowd.

"Ostap endured the torture like a giant," wrote Gogol. "Not a cry, not a groan, was heard. Even when they began to break the bones in his hands and feet, when, amid the death-like stillness of the crowd, the horrible cracking was audible to the most distant spectators; when even his tormentors turned aside their eyes, nothing like a groan escaped his lips, nor did his face quiver. Taras stood in the crowd with bowed head; and, raising his eyes proudly at that moment, he said, approvingly, 'Well done, boy! well done!' But when they took him to the last deadly tortures, it seemed as though his strength were failing. He cast his eyes around. O God! all strangers, all unknown faces! If only some of his relatives had been present at his death! He would not have cared to hear the sobs and anguish of his poor, weak mother, nor the unreasoning cries of a wife, tearing her hair and beating her white breast; but he would have liked to see a strong man who might refresh him with a word of wisdom, and cheer his end. And his strength failed him, and he cried in the weakness of his soul, 'Father! where are you? do you hear?' 'I hear!' rang through the universal silence, and those thousands of people shuddered in concert."[20]

The inspiration for this scene, as well as for the following passage, in which Gogol describes the revenge of Taras and his victories over the Polish army led by Mikołaj Potocki, came directly from the *History of the Rus'*. Gogol was clearly impressed by the scene of Ostrianytsia's execution that Pushkin later published in *Sovremennik*. The passage read as follows: "The place of execution was full of people, soldiers, and torturers with their instruments. Hetman Ostrianytsia, General Quartermaster Surmylo, and Colonels Nedryhailo, Boiun, and Ryndych were broken on the wheel, and, as their arms and legs were incessantly broken, their veins were stretched across the wheel until they expired." As in the *History of the Rus'*, so in *Taras Bul'ba* the execution takes place in Warsaw. Gogol also

---

[20] Gogol, *Taras Bulba and Other Stories*, pp. 109–10.

borrowed the *History*'s account of the execution of a Cossack hetman by burning him alive in a copper barrel called a "bull."[21]

Thanks to *Taras Bul'ba*, the fictitious execution of the Cossack officers in Warsaw made a spectacular career in the historical imagination of Gogol's readers and admirers. The director of the Russian blockbuster *Taras Bul'ba* (2009), Vladimir Bortko, believed that the novel was based on historical fact. He also saw in the novel a call for Rus' or, rather, Russo-Ukrainian unity. As the basis for his screenplay Bortko used the second (1842) edition of Gogol's novel, where the writer, partly under the influence of a change in his own reading of Ukrainian history and partly yielding to ideological dogmas of the time, depicted Taras Bulba not only as a patriot of the Rus' land but also as an admirer of the Russian tsar. Bortko did not distinguish between Rus' and Russia, making the Ukrainian Cossacks into Russian patriots and loyalists of the Russian monarchy and the modern Russian nation. This reading of Gogol provoked a wave of protest in Ukraine, but the Kyiv-born Russian filmmaker defended himself by claiming that he had simply followed Gogol and used his language and terminology.[22]

If Bortko followed Gogol, Gogol followed the *History of the Rus'*. The terms that they all used to denote Cossack nationality were similar – Rus' or Russian (*russkii*) – but their meaning was quite different. For Bortko, the Cossacks were simply part of a larger Russian nation: in that sense, he followed in Pushkin's footsteps. For the author of the *History* and for Gogol, the Cossacks were a nation in their own right. In 1834, Gogol wrote announcing his plans for a history of Ukraine, which he called Little Russia: "We still do not have a full and satisfactory history of Little Russia, the nation [*narod*] that functioned for four centuries separately from Great Russia." He also referred to the Cossacks as a "warlike nation ... marked by complete originality of character and exploits." At the same time, Gogol considered Little Russia to be part of a larger entity called "Russia" and occasionally referred to "Russia" and "Great Russia" interchangeably. This left Gogol's works open to a variety of interpretations when it came to determining exactly what he meant by the term "Russian."[23]

---

[21] *Istoriia Rusov*, pp. 39, 56.

[22] "Rezhisser Vladimir Bortko v programme Viktora Rezunkova," Radio Liberty, April 15, 2009 www.svobodanews.ru/content/transcript/1610037.html.

[23] For divergent views of Gogol's Ukrainian identity, see Bojanowska, *Nikolai Gogol*, pp. 124–25, and Oleh S. Ilnytzkyj, "The Nationalism of Nikolai Gogol': Betwixt and Between?" *Canadian Slavonic Papers* 49, nos. 3–4 (September–December 2007): 349–68.

Taras Shevchenko, the Ukrainian poet whose views and plight we discussed at the beginning of this chapter, interpreted the heroism and self-sacrifice of Gogol's Cossack characters as a manifestation of their love not for the Russian Empire or nation but for their native Ukraine. In a poem of 1840 addressed to Gogol, Shevchenko treated Taras Bulba's killing of his pro-Polish son Andrii as a manifestation of Taras's Ukrainian patriotism, which was in direct conflict with the loyalty of Shevchenko's contemporaries to the Russian Empire. The poet wrote:

> No cannon roar now in Ukraine
> With voice of Liberty;
> Nor will the father slay his son,
> His own dear child, with pain,
> For honor, glory, brotherhood,
> The freedom of Ukraine.
> He'll rather rear him up to sell
> To Moscow's slaughterhouse.[24]

For Shevchenko, not only Gogol's *Taras Bul'ba* but also the *History of the Rus'* were records of the glorious Ukrainian past – the ideals expressed in those works were to be held dear and their heroes emulated. This Ukrainocentric reading of the *History* set Shevchenko apart not only from Ryleev and Pushkin but also from Gogol. Shevchenko was, of course, not the only Ukrainian intellectual who read the *History* in that way. The mysterious manuscript influenced his whole circle of friends, many of whom were arrested along with him in a police sweep in the spring of 1847.

According to police records, Shevchenko and his friends belonged to the clandestine Brotherhood of SS. Cyril and Methodius, whose declared goal was the national revival of their homeland and the creation of a Slavic federation led by Ukraine. The historical section of the brotherhood's program, entitled *The Books of the Genesis of the Ukrainian People*, was heavily influenced by the *History*. It claimed that Ukraine united first with Poland and then with Russia as equal with equal, treated the Cossack hetmans as Christian knights, and identified the Cossack tradition of free elections as the core of Ukrainian identity. It made the following affirmation: "Ukraine loved neither the tsar nor the Polish lord and established a Cossack Host amongst themselves, i.e., a brotherhood in which each

---

[24] *The Poetical Works of Taras Shevchenko*, p. 182; Shevchenko, *Zibrannia tvoriv*, I: 284, 710–12. On Gogol's and Shevchenko's interpretations of Ukrainian history and culture, see George Luckyj, *Between Gogol' and Ševčenko: Polarity in the Literary Ukraine, 1798–1847* (Munich, 1971).

upon entering was the brother of the others – whether he had before been a master or a slave, provided that he was a Christian."[25]

The Books of the Genesis were written by Mykola Kostomarov (1817–85), a professor of Russian history at Kyiv University and chief ideologist of the brotherhood. It was on the way to his wedding that Taras Shevchenko was arrested in April 1847. Kostomarov, who had been arrested a few days earlier, was the son of a Russian noble and a Ukrainian serf woman from the Ostrogozhsk region, the same area that had inspired Ryleev's interest in Ukraine and things Ukrainian. A graduate of Kharkiv University, he took up a professorship at Kyiv University in 1846 and became a founder of the Brotherhood of SS. Cyril and Methodius in the following year. By that time he was already familiar with the *History of the Rus'*, which had influenced his political views and historical writings since the late 1830s, among them a scholarly biography of Bohdan Khmelnytsky, which was first published in 1857. No less impressed by the *History* was another member of the brotherhood, Panteleimon Kulish (1819–97). Born into a petty gentry family with Cossack roots in the Chernihiv region of the former Hetmanate, Kulish became one of the most influential Ukrainian writers and folklorists of the nineteenth century. In the early 1840s there was no greater admirer of the *History* or more ardent promoter of the Cossack myth than Panteleimon Kulish. In 1843 he published two works heavily influenced by the *History*, the Russian-language novel *Mykhailo Charnyshenko, or Little Russia Eighty Years Ago* and a popular Ukrainian-language history entitled *Ukraine: From the Origin of Ukraine to Father Khmelnytsky*.[26]

The 1830s and 1840s marked the apogee of the *History*'s influence. Its heroes, real and imagined, were to be found not only in the literary and popular works of Ryleev, Pushkin, Gogol, Shevchenko, and Kulish, but also in multivolume histories of Ukraine. It served as one of the sources for the second edition of Dmitrii Bantysh-Kamensky's *History of Little*

---

[25] *Towards an Intellectual History of Ukraine: An Anthology of Ukrainian Thought from 1710 to 1995*, ed. Ralph Lindheim and George S. N. Luckyj (Toronto, 1996), p. 96. On the Brotherhood of SS. Cyril and Methodius, see Stefan Kozak, *Ukraińscy spiskowcy i mesjaniści: Bractwo Cyryla i Metodego* (Warsaw, 1990).

[26] "Avtobiografiia Nikolaia Ivanovicha Kostomarova," *Russkaia mysl'*, no. 5 (1885): 211; *Taras Shevchenko: Dokumenty i materialy do biohrafii, 1814–1861*, ed. Ie. P. Kyryliuk (Kyiv, 1982), pp. 88–159, here 116; Vozniak, *Psevdo-Konys'kyi*, pp. 31–32. On Kostomarov, his political views and historical writings, see Thomas M. Prymak, *Mykola Kostomarov: A Biography* (Toronto, 1996). On Kulish, see George S. N. Luckyj, *Panteleimon Kulish: A Sketch of His Life and Times* (Boulder, Col., 1983). The manuscript copy of the *History* that belonged to Kulish is preserved as "Istoriia Rusov ili Maloi Rossii," Manuscript Institute, Vernadsky Library, 1, no. 4094.

Russia (1830) and was the primary source for Mykola Markevych's five-volume *History of Little Russia*, which appeared in print in 1842–43. Among those fascinated with the mysterious document were not only historians, writers, and poets but also Ukrainian nobles, normally distant from intellectual pursuits. The German traveler J. G. Kohl, who visited Dnieper Ukraine in the late 1830s, wrote that the "Konysky history" (he spelled the archbishop's name "Kanevsky") was exceptionally popular among the local nobility, and in some regions one could find a copy on every estate.[27]

There was a demand for a printed edition of the *History*, but the plans of many admirers of the work, including its discoverer, Aleksandr von Brigen, to publish the manuscript remained unfulfilled. The first excerpts appeared in 1834 in the journal *Zaporozhskaia starina* (Zaporozhian Antiquity), published by the Kharkiv Romantics, a group of writers and poets whose central figure was Izmail Sreznevsky (1812–80), the author of numerous literary mystifications, some of them based on the *History of the Rus'*. As discussed above, in 1836 additional excerpts from the work were published by Alexander Pushkin. There were plans to publish the complete text, but nothing came of them. J. G. Kohl, who explained this as a consequence of the freethinking spirit in which the *History* was written, was right on the mark. When the *History of the Rus'* finally appeared in print in 1846, it was issued by the Imperial Society of Russian History and Antiquities at Moscow University, which was exempt from the regular censorship.[28]

The person responsible for the publication was the society's academic secretary, Osyp Bodiansky (1808–77). A native of Ukraine, Bodiansky graduated from Moscow University, where he became a professor of Slavic philology. A friend of Gogol and Shevchenko, he had a great interest in Ukrainian history and published numerous sources on the subject. In preparation for the publication of the *History*, Bodiansky collected a number of manuscript copies and, as he wrote in the introduction, "I selected the best of them, added readings from other copies, and then proposed that the Imperial Society of Russian History and Antiquities publish it, which is now accomplished." Regarding the censorship, Bodiansky wrote many years later: "Nor shall I conceal the hidden motive for beginning the publication of Ukrainian chronicles and other monuments with this particular work, bearing in mind the following: the publication of the *History of the Rus'*, for which Ustrialov, Pushkin, and Gogol strove in vain, might be undertaken successfully by the 'Society,' which was in charge of its own censorship at the time, especially at the start of its publishing activity."[29]

Bodiansky succeeded where others had failed. The censorship did not interfere, and the *History* hit the bookstores to the excitement of Ukrainian patriots. The year 1846 was probably the last in which a manuscript of that nature could have been published. In the following year, with the arrest of members of the SS. Cyril and Methodius Brotherhood, the authorities became vigilant toward anything that might smack of Little Russian separatism. Two years later, in the atmosphere of paranoia created by the revolution of 1848, the society's journal, in which the *History* had appeared, was shut down by the censors for publishing a Russian translation of Giles Fletcher's *Of the Russe Common Wealth*. In that account of a sixteenth-century English diplomat's mission to Muscovy, Emperor Nicholas I discerned "references insulting to Russia, to Russian monarchs, and the Russian church." Bodiansky was dismissed from his position in Moscow and transferred to the University of Kazan. The published *History* soon became a rarity, and many believed it to be officially banned. Mykhailo Maksymovych, the admirer and student of the *History* who first introduced it to Pushkin, wrote to Bodiansky in 1857: "And do you know that in Kyiv it is being sold for 10 or 12 silver rubles, and it is rumored throughout Ukraine that it is supposedly a forbidden book!"[30]

Few people could have benefited more from the publication of the *History* than Taras Shevchenko. A soldier in the Russian army, he wrote to Osyp Bodiansky from exile in the Caspian steppes, requesting a copy of the book. Bodiansky complied, and in the fall of 1854 Shevchenko was overwhelmed with joy. "Thank you again for the chronicles," he wrote to his benefactor. "I am now reciting them by heart. Reading them, my little soul revives! Thank you!" At that time Shevchenko, who, despite the tsar's orders, managed both to paint and to write, was working on a novel entitled *The Twins*. Its main character, a Ukrainian nobleman of Cossack

[29] *Istoriia Rusov*, p. v; Osip Bodianskii, "Ob"iasnenie," in *Chteniia v Imperatorskom obshchestve istorii i drevnostei rossiiskikh* 1 (Moscow, 1871): 221–22; For academic biographies of Bodiansky, see N. P. Vasilenko, *O. M. Bodianskii i ego zaslugi dlia izucheniia Malorossii* (Kyiv, 1904); N. A. Kondrashov, *Osip Maksimovich Bodianskii* (Moscow, 1956).
[30] Quoted in Vozniak, *Pseudo-Konys'kyi*, pp. 34–36.

origin named Nykyfor Fedorovych Sokyra, turned out to be a great admirer of the *History*. Shevchenko explained that his emotions were aroused most strongly by descriptions of wrongs done to Ukraine by its numerous enemies. "Nykyfor Fedorovych read it several times," wrote Shevchenko about the *History*, "but never to the very end. Everything – all the abominations, all the Polish inhumanities, the Swedish war, Biron's brother, who took infants at the breast from their mothers in Starodub and forced the mothers to breast-feed dogs for his kennel – that, too, he read, but whenever he got to the Holstein colonel Kryzhanovsky, he would spit, close the book, and spit again."[31]

As Shevchenko, faithful to the ideals of his youth, wrote *The Twins* in his Caspian exile, few of his Kyivan friends from the Brotherhood of SS. Cyril and Methodius shared his excitement about the *History*. Bodiansky's publication made its text available not only to admirers in Ukraine but also to scholars in the rest of the empire, many of whom raised doubts about its reliability as a historical source. Panteleimon Kulish, the former admirer of the *History*, was in the first ranks of the skeptics. Two years after Shevchenko completed *The Twins*, Kulish, well versed in the latest literature on the subject, celebrated the appearance of scholarly publications that undermined the credibility of the *History*. He wrote: "The sacred mantle of historian has been stripped from Konysky. He has been revealed, first, as a fanatic – a historian of Little Russia who, out of love for it, spared neither Poland nor the Muscovite state, contrary to the truth; second, as an unusually talented individual, a poet of chronicle narratives and an authentic painter of events only in those cases when he had no preconceived idea."[32]

There was more to Kulish's reassessment of Konysky than mere disappointment with the inaccuracy of the *History*'s data. Both he and Mykola Kostomarov had come to realize that the manuscript they once revered no less fervently than did Shevchenko's Nykyfor Sokyra was as far removed from their ideals of populism and egalitarianism as one could imagine. As political thinkers and writers, they continued to hold the popular masses in high regard and considered nobiliary conservatives their main enemies. That set them apart from the author of the *History of the Rus'*, for whom the masses were hopelessly in thrall to their uncivilized practices and superstitions. What they shared with the author of the *History* was their fascination with the Cossack past and their deep patriotism. For these former members of the Brotherhood of SS. Cyril and Methodius,

---

[31] Shevchenko, *Zibrannia tvoriv*, iv: 27; vi: 86.   [32] Quoted in Vozniak, *Pseudo-Konys'kyi*, p. 37.

the Cossacks were representatives not just of the Ukrainian nation but of the Ukrainian popular masses. When they realized that the *History* provided justification only for the national component of their beliefs, they ceased to be spellbound by it.

Taras Shevchenko remained the last Mohican of the old beliefs, but because of the enormous popularity of his writings, it was his interpretation of the *History of the Rus'* that prevailed in the long run. Shevchenko's poetry became the driving force that transformed the Cossack myth, inspired and promoted by the *History of the Rus'*, from a mainly Russian literary and cultural phenomenon into a mainly Ukrainian one. Shevchenko's works captured the moment when the first generation of Ukrainian national awakeners took over Ryleev's and Pushkin's fascination with the *History* but refused to accept their interpretation of it as a general appeal for political freedom or an expression of Russian imperial identity. For them, the *History* was a manifestation of Ukrainian national identity. In adopting this view, they reshaped the old Cossack myth in a way that corresponded not only to their national but also to their populist beliefs. When they finally became disillusioned with the *History* and decided to renounce it on grounds of historical and political unreliability, it was too late. The *History* could no longer be separated from the Cossack myth, which the awakeners so successfully established as the founding myth of the modern Ukrainian nation.

PART II

On a cold trail

CHAPTER 4

A noble heart

At first there were a few dozen of them, then a few hundred, and finally thousands of people, mostly students of Kyiv University and local secondary schools, who gathered in and around the Church of the Nativity in the Podil (Lower Town) of Kyiv on May 7, 1861. They were all in mourning, with a single purpose in mind: to say goodbye to Taras Shevchenko, who had died two months earlier in St. Petersburg. Kyiv was a major stop on the long road of the funeral cortège from the imperial capital to the town of Kaniv, in the vicinity of which the serf-born poet would be buried on a hill overlooking the Dnieper. The coffin with Shevchenko's earthly remains reached Moscow by train and then was brought to Kyiv on a horse-drawn carriage. There it would be transferred to a boat to continue its southward journey to Kaniv. In all the major towns through which the cortège passed, activists of local Ukrainian organizations held church services and led processions in which thousands took part.

The funeral procession presented the imperial authorities with a dilemma. They did not interfere with commemorations on Russian territory (in Orel, for example, the procession included not only clergy, local intelligentsia, and students of local schools, but also a military band), but in Ukraine the situation threatened to get out of hand. Anticipating that the funeral procession might turn into a mass manifestation, with subversive speeches delivered by Ukrainophiles, the governor general of Kyiv prohibited bringing the coffin into the city center. The Kyivans met the funeral procession on the left bank of the Dnieper, unharnessed the horses, and drew the carriage bearing the coffin onto a ferry and then into a church in Podil on the right bank. The governor general was still worried. Although he allowed no eulogies in the church, he could do nothing about young people who chose to address the procession of several thousand following Shevchenko's coffin from the church to the riverbank, where it was transferred to a boat.[1]

One of the most memorable eulogies was delivered that day by a young student of Kyiv University named Mykhailo Drahomanov. He was inspired by a scene that he witnessed in the Podil church: a young woman dressed in black had made her way through the crowd to place a crown of thorns on Shevchenko's coffin. Drahomanov got ahead of the procession and built a small brick podium from which he addressed the mourners. "Everyone who sets out to serve the people thereby dons a crown of thorns," he declared, calling on his compatriots "to show true respect for their great men and not to allow them to be tortured while they are still alive." The speech made a strong impression, and Drahomanov was among the handful of speakers who were later asked to prepare a text for publication. This was a token of recognition for a young man hitherto regarded by Shevchenko's Ukrainophile followers as a "cosmopolitan." When he unexpectedly showed up at the church, one of them had said to him: "Why have you come here? This is no place for you!" It was known that he did not share the Ukrainophiles' strong anti-Polish sentiments and their idealization of the peasantry.[2]

Mykhailo Drahomanov refused to leave the church. During the next decade he emerged as one of the leaders of the Ukrainian national movement in the Russian Empire and its foremost political thinker. Born in 1841 to a family of descendants of Cossack officeholders in the former Hetmanate, Drahomanov received his education at Kyiv University, where he became a professor of ancient history. In 1875 he was dismissed from his post for active involvement in the Ukrainian movement. Drahomanov emigrated to Western Europe and settled in Geneva, where he established the first modern Ukrainian political journal and laid the foundations for the rise of the Ukrainian socialist movement. Drahomanov also contributed to the formation of the Ukrainian movement in Austrian Galicia and shaped the thinking of generations of Ukrainian activists there and in Russian-ruled Ukraine. Drahomanov was a lifelong admirer of Taras Shevchenko. He also was a highly perceptive reader of his works and believed that Shevchenko's poetry could not have been written without the *History of the Rus'*. Given

---

[1] V. Anisov and Ie. Sereda, *Litopys zhyttia i tvorchosti T. H. Shevchenka*, 2nd rev. edn. (Kyiv, 1976), pp. 330–38, here 336–37.

[2] Mykhailo Drahomanov, "Avstro-Rus'ki spomyny (1867–1877)," in *Literaturno-publitsystychni pratsi*, 2 vols. (Kyiv, 1970), II: 151–288, here 157–58.

Drahomanov's importance in the Ukrainian political and cultural discourse of the era, this connection elevated the *History of the Rus'* to a special and highly privileged status in the history of Ukrainian political thought and the country's national awakening.[3]

Drahomanov's first foray into the study of the mysterious text took place at a time when the question of authorship began to dominate discussion of the work, its meaning and significance. Was Archbishop Konysky indeed the author of the *History*, as was believed by Ryleev, Pushkin, Gogol, Shevchenko, and scores of other readers and students? And if he was not, who was? The long and relentless hunt for the author began in the 1860s, and for the rest of the nineteenth century and all of the twentieth, numerous new candidates for authorship would rise to prominence, only to be questioned and eventually dismissed by scholars, who would put forward candidates of their own to replace the old and tarnished ones.

For Drahomanov, the authorship of the *History* was not an isolated issue or a matter of mere curiosity. It was closely linked to his understanding of the ideological origins of the mysterious text. Establishing the identity of its author had clear political ramifications, given the way in which Drahomanov linked the *History* with the writings of Taras Shevchenko. Although Drahomanov did not know who the author was, he was certain that he knew who could not have written it. He first commented on the question in his review of I. G. Pryzhov's "Little Russia (Southern Russia) in the History of Its Literature from the Eleventh to the Eighteenth Century," published in 1870 in the Russian liberal journal *Vestnik Evropy* (European Herald), Drahomanov claimed that Pryzhov "vainly ascribes primacy in South Russian historiography" to the *History of the Rus'* and "contests Maksymovych's view, now universally accepted, that the *History of the Rus'* was not written by Konysky." Drahomanov was not challenging Pryzhov without reason. His skepticism concerning Konysky's authorship of the text reflected a consensus that had emerged in the field in the 1850s and 1860s.[4]

---

[3] On Drahomanov's life and work, see Taras Andrusiak, *Shliakh do svobody: Mykhailo Drahomanov pro prava liudyny* (Lviv, 1998); Larysa Depenchuk, *Istoriosofiia ta sotsiial'na filosofiia Mykhaila Drahomanova* (Kyiv, 1999); Anatolii Kruhlashov, *Drama intelektuala: politychni ideï Mykhaila Drahomanova* (Chernivtsi, 2000).

[4] Mykhailo Drahomanov, "Malorossiia v ee slovesnosti," in *Vybrane* (Kyiv, 1991), pp. 5–45, here, 24; cf. I. G. Pryzhov, *Malorossiia (Iuzhnaia Rossiia) v istorii ee literatury s XI po XVIII vek* (Voronezh, 1869).

The first to indicate the deficiencies of the *History* as a historical source was the dean of Russian historiography, Sergei Soloviev, a professor at Moscow University and the author of a multivolume *History of Russia*. In 1848–49 he published in a number of installments a lengthy article entitled "An Outline History of Little Russia up to Its Subordination to Tsar Aleksei Mikhailovich." There he compared the entries in the *History of the Rus'* concerning the early history of the Cossacks with other sources, characterizing some of the anonymous author's accounts as "fables." Konysky's claim that the sixteenth-century Cossack hetman Dmytro Vyshnevetsky had helped the Muscovite army defend Astrakhan against the Ottomans in 1577 had no basis in the Russian sources, argued Soloviev, and his claim that the Council of Brest (1596) had been attended by an Orthodox bishop of Chernihiv was plainly unfounded, for Chernihiv then belonged to Muscovy, not to the Polish-Lithuanian Commonwealth.[5]

Soloviev's revelations shocked admirers of the *History* among its lay readers but did not come as a complete surprise to its more perceptive students. Dmitrii Bantysh-Kamensky was quite selective in his use of the *History*'s data when he first gained access to it while preparing for publication the second edition of his *History of Little Russia* (1830). In 1834 Izmail Sreznevsky, the first publisher of selected excerpts from the *History*, referred to its accounts as "tales." An author of literary mystifications himself, Sreznevsky knew what he was talking about. Panteleimon Kulish had been dubious about the *History*'s reliability at least since 1846, when he complained to the Moscow historian and philologist Mikhail Pogodin about Bodiansky's decision to publish it: "I do not understand … why the publication of Ukrainian historical sources has been initiated with Konysky's chronicle when we have sources in the stricter sense of the word, that is, historical works." The first potential problems with Konysky's authorship were already clear to Alexander Pushkin, who drew attention in 1836 to the numerous and detailed battle scenes in a manuscript supposedly written by an archbishop. He explained the contradiction away by citing Konysky's noble origins: "Evidently the heart of a noble still beats beneath his monastic robe." His remark would prove prophetic, but there was no interest at the time in a closer examination of the question of authorship.[6]

[5] S. M. Solov'ev, "Ocherk istorii Malorossii do podchineniia ee tsariu Alekseiu Mikhailovichu," *Otechestvennye zapiski*, no. 11 (1848): 1–34; no. 12 (1848): 147–66; no. 2 (1849): 215–70, here 270.

[6] Vozniak, *Psevdo-Konys'kyi i Psevdo-Poletyka* (Istoriia Rusov *u literaturi ta nautsi*) (Lviv and Kyiv, 1939), pp. 36–39; Aleksandr Pushkin, "Sobranie sochinenii Georgiia Konisskogo."

While the accuracy of the *History*'s data was questioned openly from 1849 on, it took another fifteen years to raise similar doubts regarding the authorship of the work. When Bodiansky published the *History* in 1846 under the name of Heorhii Konysky, he was following an established tradition, for Konysky figures as its author on the title pages of manuscripts dating from the early nineteenth century. But the title pages are at odds with the introduction to the *History*, according to which Konysky was at best the editor of the manuscript. Bodiansky, however, was not interested in undermining the notion of Konysky's authorship, since he had to guide the manuscript through the narrow gate of the tsarist censorship, and Konysky's name was one of the few assets available to him. The first to raise open concern about Konysky's role in the writing of the *History* was Mykhailo Maksymovych, one of the earlier admirers of the monument and the person who made it available to Alexander Pushkin. In his letters of 1865 to Mikhail Yuzefovich, the chairman of the Kyiv Archeographic Commission, who advocated restricting the use of the Ukrainian language in the Russian Empire, Maksymovych questioned whether Konysky was indeed the author of the *History*. He had serious doubts in that regard. Maksymovych argued that someone as well versed as Konysky in the history of the Orthodox Church and the legal norms of the Polish-Lithuanian Commonwealth could not have produced a text so full of major factual errors and misrepresentations.

"That unforgettable man," wrote Maksymovych about Konysky, "was well acquainted with the old documents pertaining to the history of the church in Western Russia and was very well read as regards Polish historical writers; this is attested to us by his book *Prawa i wolności* [Rights and Liberties], published in Warsaw in 1767, and his short work about the Union [of Brest], published in the [Moscow] *Chteniia*." And could Konysky have entered that arena, in which he worked with such renown, without a reserve of historical and factual knowledge? His historical knowledge would inevitably have resounded in the history he would have written, whatever its tendency and spirit. The *History of the Rus'* shows no sign of good knowledge of contemporary documents, nor of Polish historians, nor of the most important Little Russian chronicles: everything is taken from secondary sources, as if from hearsay, and refashioned according to the author's preference without preserving the veracity and accuracy of historical fact." Maksymovych argued that the *History* was a mystification: "It seems to me that the *History of the Rus'* was written by an author unknown to us who hid his name behind two Little Russian eminences [Heorhii Konysky and Hryhorii Poletyka] in order to state in the introduction that the history, having passed through these outstanding minds, should be reliable."[7]

While the unreliability of the *History* as a historical source led Maksymovych to question Konysky's authorship of the text, it did not shake his belief in its overall importance as a literary artifact. It was because the text was first and foremost a literary work, argued Maksymovych, that historical facts were often misrepresented in it. He wrote to Yuzefovich: "In that celebrated history, which is most remarkable from the artistic viewpoint, Little Russian Cossackdom of the sixteenth and seventeenth centuries is presented with the same poetical and willful reworking of historical reality with which Gogol in *Taras Bul'ba* and Shevchenko in his *Haidamaky* depicted their chosen epochs. All three showed no concern whatever for establishing and abiding by actual historical fact!" In his highly favorable assessment of the *History* as a literary work, Maksymovych followed in the footsteps of Alexander Pushkin, whom he quoted directly in posing a question to Yuzefovich: "Is it not pointless that his [the anonymous author's] name is contemned for its [the *History of the Rus'*] shortcomings on the factual side and praised for its merits on the artistic side, for which Pushkin himself called Konysky a great artist?"[8]

When in 1870 Mykhailo Drahomanov took upon himself the task of defending Maksymovych's position against the attack on him by Pryzhov, few people in the academic community still believed in Konysky's authorship. Pryzhov was rather an exception in that regard. But Drahomanov did not limit himself to defending Maksymovych or criticizing the *History* as an unreliable historical source. He actually introduced a new approach to the study of this now discredited monument of historical writing. If Maksymovych valued the *History* for its literary style, Drahomanov considered it a monument of political thought and was excited about its ideological message. He wrote: "That work should be regarded as a pamphlet in support of the rights and liberties of the Rus', that is, of the Little Russians; a pamphlet exceedingly caustic in places and even artistic (for instance, where it depicts the depredations committed by soldiers, according to whose words 'chickens, geese, girls, young women – they are all ours by right of warriors and by order of His Honor'), and not as an outwardly factual history: it will then constitute an irreplaceable monument of the condition of enlightenment and political ideas in Little Russia of the mid eighteenth century."[9]

---

[7] Mikhail Maksimovich, *Sobranie sochinenii* (Kyiv, 1876), 1: 305–6.
[8] *Ibid.*, 1: 301–2.   [9] Drahomanov, "Malorossiia v ee slovesnosti," p. 24.

Thus Drahomanov was attracted to the *History* by the same ideas of liberty and freedom that had inspired Kondratii Ryleev half a century earlier, but he considered those ideas as a historian, linking them to a very specific group in the Russian Empire. Drahomanov's dispassionate, academic, and generally positive reading of the *History* was a hard sell in the nationally and socially charged atmosphere of the 1870s. His interpretation was challenged by Russian and Ukrainian historians alike from opposing ideological perspectives. The Russian side was represented by Soloviev's student Gennadii Karpov, the Ukrainian one by none other than Mykola Kostomarov, the founder of the Brotherhood of SS. Cyril and Methodius. The two were rivals and ideological opponents, with Karpov defending the statist approach to Russian history and Kostomarov advocating a populist one. Their main battleground was the history of Ukraine, where Karpov attacked Kostomarov for allegedly ignoring Russian archival sources while being unduly influenced by such unreliable texts as the *History of the Rus'*. Kostomarov indeed relied heavily on the *History* in the first edition of his monograph on Bohdan Khmelnytsky but endeavored to purge it of such influence in the second and third editions. By 1870 he was no less critical of the *History* as a historical source than Karpov himself. But distrust of the *History* as a source was not the only thing shared by the two opponents in the 1870s: for their own disparate reasons, they did not like its ideological message.[10]

In his *Critical Survey of the Principal Russian Sources Pertaining to the History of Little Russia* (1870), published soon after the appearance of Drahomanov's review of Pryzhov in *Vestnik Evropy*, Karpov not only pointed out factual errors and misrepresentations, of which there was no shortage in the *History*, but also attacked the ideological underpinnings of the text. Where Drahomanov saw a defense of the rights and liberties of the Little Russians, Karpov detected subversive liberal ideas. He decried the *History* as a "false chronicle," elaborating as follows: "The basic characteristics of such chronicles are, first, outward liberalism, the profession of humanitarian ideas; the accusation of individuals and peoples uncongenial to the author of despotism, ignorance, barbarism, an inclination to deceit, cowardice, and stupidity, while all becoming qualities contrary to these are attributed to those whom the author takes under his patronage. The second distinguishing characteristic is an abundance of anecdotes: simple, everyday events are embellished with fantasies. The talent indispensable to all

---

[10] On the Karpov–Kostomarov debate, see John Basarab, *Pereiaslav 1654* (Edmonton, 1982), pp. 26–28.

this is not always to be found among the authors of false chronicles, so that the poetry of their narratives and their professions of liberalism strike a serious observer as vulgar, if only because they are too artificial, but they are more accessible to the uneducated masses than works of serious research. The *History of the Rus'* belongs to that class of chronicles; moreover, it was written by a man who lacked talent, by no means liberal, but extremely embittered ... It has enjoyed undeserved authority for so long, probably, both because of society's sympathy for a negative orientation and, on the other hand, because of the extreme ignorance of those among whom such a pamphlet was issued."[11]

Karpov not only tried to demolish the *History* as a historical source but also attacked its quality as a literary text and passionately denounced its ideological message. His outburst was fueled by his professional attachment to archival sources in preference to narrative ones and his indignation that a historical mystification could have been regarded as a legitimate source by so many for so long. Another of his motives was ideological. Karpov saw the *History* as an attack on the Russian nation as a whole and an attempt to spread dangerous liberal ideas. At that time, in the aftermath of the Polish uprising of 1861 and the prohibition of Ukrainian-language publications in 1863, Russian nationalists like Mikhail Katkov were campaigning in defense of the Russian Empire against real and imagined attacks by Polish and Ukrainian activists and representatives of the Russian radical and liberal intelligentsia. For Karpov, the *History* was a mouthpiece of ideas shared by those who, as he put it, favored the "negative orientation" in Russian political discourse.

If Karpov was negatively disposed to the *History* for its liberalism and glorification of Cossack leaders such as Pavlo Polubotok, whom he accused of having conspired with the foreign enemies of Russia, Mykola Kostomarov had his own reasons to dislike the work. For him, the *History* was nothing but a harmful product of nobiliary thinking. In his essay "From a Journey to Baturyn in 1878," published three years after the trip, Kostomarov indicated the immediate source of his distress: the popularity of the *History* among the most conservative strata of the Ukrainian landowning class. In Baturyn, the former capital of the Ukrainian hetmans, Kostomarov encountered a nobleman named Velykdan whose Ukrainian patriotism was based on the *History of the Rus'*. "According to the views of the landlords who were reared on Konysky," wrote Kostomarov,

---

[11] Karpov, *Kriticheskii obzor razrabotki glavnykh russkikh istochnikov, do istorii Malorossii otnosiashchikhsia* (Moscow, 1870), pp. 44–45, 118–20.

"the whole Cossack order was ideally good, and all evil came from Muscovite perfidy and the injustice and severity of Great Russian ills. The views suggested by Konysky's pseudohistory are still potent among the Little Russian gentry, and the superstition that it sowed has grown to such an extent that all the diligent research and publications of documents long unknown to anyone are as yet unable to dispel accepted errors: they do not read documents and research works but believe Konysky."

Kostomarov's passionate rejection of the *History of the Rus'*, not unlike Karpov's criticism of it, was informed by the political and social battles of the 1870s. In their writings one also feels the frustration of professional historians with the mythological nature of popular historical identity. Like Karpov, Kostomarov rejected the idealization of the Ukrainian past and the habit of blaming Russia for Ukraine's troubles. But that is where the similarities ended. If Karpov detested the *History* as a manifestation of liberalism, Kostomarov saw in it the roots of nobiliary conservatism – the political and ideological opposite of liberalism in the Russian Empire of the 1870s and 1880s. That led him to agree with Alexander Pushkin's much earlier observation about the "noble heart" of the author of the *History*. Kostomarov wrote in that regard: "Pushkin was mistaken in accepting, along with others of his day, that the *History of the Rus'* was 'written by the well-known Belarusian archbishop,' but he understood and accurately guessed that it was written by a nobleman."

Kostomarov actually stated something that Pushkin only implied. He also turned the poet's observation from one concerning the anonymous author's interest and expertise in military affairs into one with clear social overtones. "Indeed," wrote Kostomarov, "this history was written by one of the *arriviste* Little Russian nobles of Catherine II's day who made the views of the Great Russian lords their own and applied them in slapdash fashion to the past of their fatherland." While opposing the "nobiliary" ideology of the *History of the Rus'*, Kostomarov seems to have been unable to cast off the spell of the work entirely. Like the author of the *History*, he blamed things he did not like about his homeland on the "injustice and severity of Great Russian ills." Unlike Velykodan and other Ukrainian nobles, whom Kostomarov criticized, he blamed the problems not on Russians in general but on the Russian nobility and state apparatus. This was a distinction that Karpov was not prepared to make or appreciate.[12]

---

[12] Nikolai Kostomarov, "Iz poezdki v Baturin v 1878 godu," *Poriadok*, no. 97 (1881). Cf. Vozniak, *Psevdo-Konys'kyi*, p. 52.

Kostomarov's article inspired Mykhailo Drahomanov to return to his study of the *History of the Rus'*. Drahomanov, by then no longer a professor of Kyiv University but a political exile in Geneva, did not respond to Karpov's attacks on the author of the *History*. But Kostomarov's essay was a different matter. It was the work of a fellow Ukrainian attacking the historical legacy of a text that Drahomanov considered essential to the development of Ukrainian political thought. He responded in *Poriadok* (Order), the same St. Petersburg newspaper in which Kostomarov had published the account of his trip to Baturyn. Drahomanov's article, signed "V. K.," was entitled "In Defense of the Late Author of the *History of the Rus' or Little Russia*." The strange title of the essay reflected one of its main theses: a heated polemic with the long-deceased author of the *History* was a futile if not downright ridiculous undertaking. Drahomanov wrote that once scholars "noted a mass of errors" in the *History*, they "deemed it a falsification and began to speak of it with condescension and even with some exasperation." That was, of course, an understatement if one considers the heated tone of Karpov's polemic. "But it would seem," continued Drahomanov, "that the time has come to take a perfectly calm view of what is, in any case, a notable literary monument . . . and, most important, to value the spirit and social significance of the *History of the Rus'* not as a scholarly work but as a political treatise."

While Drahomanov's attitude to the *History* as a political pamphlet was the same in 1881 as it had been a decade earlier, this time he spelled it out in considerable detail. To rebut Kostomarov's claim that the author of the *History* shared and promoted the ideology of Russian landowners, Drahomanov quoted the anonymous author's invectives against the Muscovites as a nation of tyrants and slaves that had provoked such a vitriolic reaction from Karpov. Drahomanov also cited the *History*'s negative assessment of the role played in Ukraine by former Polish nobles who joined the Khmelnytsky Uprising in 1648. For Drahomanov, that assessment was proof of the anonymous author's support for the popular masses against the nobility. Drahomanov also rejected Panteleimon Kulish's earlier claim that the author of the *History* was a "sympathizer of nobiliary separatism." If the author of the *History* was not an admirer of the imperial order, a partisan of nobiliary rights, or a supporter of Ukrainian separatism, who was he?

Drahomanov believed that he was "a precursor of the very theory of which Mr. Kostomarov himself later became the scholarly exponent." In other words, the author was a forerunner of the Ukrainian national movement of the second half of the nineteenth century. Karpov would probably have agreed with that characterization of Kostomarov, but he would certainly have rejected Drahomanov's notion of what the author of the *History* and subsequent leaders of the Ukrainian movement had in common. For Drahomanov, the autonomous author was not a narrow Ukrainian nationalist but a defender of human rights and a promoter of European cultural values. He was also a fierce critic of the imperial order, including the bureaucracy that set itself above the law, the military that lashed out with arbitrary violence, and the pervasive intolerance of religious and ethnic diversity. Drahomanov saw the *History* as a precursor of Taras Shevchenko's *Kobzar* and attributed to its influence the lack of resistance among the nobility of the former Cossack lands to the emancipation of the serfs undertaken by the imperial government in 1861.[13]

A year later, in an article published in Geneva, beyond the reach of the imperial censors, Drahomanov gave a much more politically explicit account of what he considered the positive features of the *History*. He characterized it as an amalgam of "Cossack republicanism with the new liberalism and democratism – Ukrainian autonomism with all-Russian federalism." Drahomanov, a political refugee and proponent of Ukrainian autonomy and the federalization of the Russian Empire, saw in the author of the *History* not only a forerunner of Shevchenko and Kostomarov but also his own predecessor. For the first time since the exposure of the *History* as an unreliable source and a product of mystification, Drahomanov was bringing that monument back into Ukrainian political and academic discourse as a text that was not to be regarded with shame. Admittedly, the *History* was coming back not as a book of revelation, as it had been regarded in the first half of the nineteenth century, but as a historiographic monument of a different era.[14]

The question was: which era? Along with the related question of the authorship of the *History*, it constituted part of a great mystery that had surrounded the manuscript ever since Mykhailo Maksymovych rejected Konysky's authorship in 1865. Maksymovych did not have a candidate of his own. He believed, however, that the author of the *History* was active in the early nineteenth century. Maksymovych confided to Osyp Bodiansky that all traces of the *History* he had managed to find led him to the circle of intellectuals who gathered in the late 1810s in Poltava around Prince

[13] V. K. [Drahomanov], "V zashchitu neizvestnogo pokoinika avtora 'Istorii Rusov ili Maloi Rossii,'" *Poriadok*, 1881, no. 128. Cf. Vozniak, *Psevdo-Konys'kyi*, pp. 53–55.
[14] Mikhail Dragomanov, *Istoricheskaia Pol'sha i velikorusskaia demokratiia* (Geneva, 1882), p. 64; Vozniak, *Psevdo-Konys'kyi*, pp. 55, 59.

Nikolai Repnin, the governor general of Little Russia. The Masonic lodge established in Poltava in 1818 with the help of Repnin counted among its members such people as the founder of modern Ukrainian literature, Ivan Kotliarevsky; a leading literary figure of the empire and a passionate enemy of serfdom, the poet Vasilii (Vasyl) Kapnist; and the author of the first scholarly history of Ukraine, Dmitrii Bantysh-Kamensky. Drahomanov happened to be of the same opinion as Maksymovych. If the *History of the Rus'* was indeed first and foremost a monument of Ukrainian autonomism and liberalism, then there was no better place to seek its origins and author than the Poltava Masonic circle. In 1888 Drahomanov wrote to Ivan Franko, one of his followers and subsequently a prominent Ukrainian writer, publicist, and political activist: "The *History of the Rus'* was probably written around the 1820s in the circle of Prince Repnin."

Drahomanov's belief that he had identified the milieu that produced the *History* was short-lived. A few years later he moved its creation to a date preceding Repnin's arrival in Poltava and linked it with people who had no known association with Repnin or the Poltava Masonic lodge. The *History* "was written *c.* 1810 and is associated with the contemporary constitutional plans of Alexander I and his first minister, Speransky," claimed Drahomanov in 1894. Why such a drastic change of opinion, and where did the date of 1810 came from? Drahomanov's new hypothesis was based on the archival findings of two Ukrainian historians, Oleksandr Lazarevsky (1834–1902) and Vasyl Horlenko (1853–1907), published in the Kyiv Ukrainophile journal *Kievskaia starina* (Kyivan Antiquity).[15]

Lazarevsky's first article on the subject appeared in April 1891 under the title "Extracts from the Poletyka Family Archive" and included as a subsection a short essay entitled "A Surmise about the Author of the *History of the Rus'*." Lazarevsky was a recognized authority on the history of the Hetmanate and its territories. He belonged to the older generation of Ukrainophiles who shared the strongly populist beliefs of the members of the SS. Cyril and Methodius Brotherhood. In the last years of Taras Shevchenko's life, Lazarevsky, then a student in St. Petersburg, was in touch with him on a daily basis. They had regular lunches at the apartment of Lazarevsky's elder brother. After Shevchenko's death the young Lazarevsky accompanied his coffin to Moscow, the first leg of a grand tour

---

[15] Mykhailo Drahomanov, *Lysty na naddniprians'ku Ukraïnu*, in Mykhailo Drahomanov and Borys Hrinchenko, *Dialohy pro ukraïns'ku natsional'nu spravu* (Kyiv, 1994), pp. 154–55; Vozniak, *Psevdo-Konys'kyi*, p. 45.

that included Kyiv, where Drahomanov delivered his eulogy to the poet. Lazarevsky shared Shevchenko's attachment to Ukrainian history and his unshakable populism – features that characterized his first essay on the *History of the Rus'*, published in St. Petersburg a few months after Shevchenko's death.[16]

In that essay, entitled "Did Polubotok Deliver the Speech to Peter the Great Cited by Konysky?" Lazarevsky questioned the authenticity of the apocryphal speech of Acting Hetman Pavlo Polubotok in defense of Cossack rights and freedoms. On the basis of his populist convictions, Lazarevsky argued that such a speech could not have been given by a rich landowner known for his abuse of power. He believed that its text might have some basis in local tradition and in petitions submitted by Polubotok to St. Petersburg, but that it was essentially Archbishop Konysky's composition. When Lazarevsky returned to the study of the *History of the Rus'* in 1891, he no longer accepted Konysky's authorship. By that time he had a different candidate – Hryhorii Poletyka, a deputy to the Legislative Commission of 1767–68 and the second eighteenth-century Ukrainian celebrity mentioned in the introduction to the *History*.[17]

Lazarevsky was not the first to consider Poletyka as a possible author of the *History*. The first scholar to do so was V. S. Ikonnikov, a professor of Russian history at Kyiv University, who indicated such a possibility in a lecture course on Russian historiography given in 1874. Ikonnikov did not provide any support for his hypothesis. He also ignored the observations of Mykhailo Maksymovych, who doubted that Poletyka, "an intelligent man acquainted with the best historical chronicles, including that of Velychko," could have drawn on such an unreliable source as the *History* to write his well-researched memoranda for the Legislative Commission. One might also conclude, by the same token, that he could hardly have been the author of such an unreliable work. But Lazarevsky's case, as he presented it in 1891, was not based on a textual analysis of the *History* or on a close reading of Poletyka's historical works and memoranda. He offered new archival findings that, in his opinion, linked Hryhorii Poletyka to the *History*. Lazarevsky had

---

[16] On Lazarevsky, see Vitalii Sarbei, *Istorychni pohliady O. M. Lazarevs'koho* (Kyiv, 1961); *Oleksandr Matviiovych Lazarevs'kyi, 1834–1902: dopovidi ta materialy naukovo-praktychnoï konferentsiï "Ukraïns'ka arkheohrafiia: problemy i perspektyvy," prysviachenoï 160-richchiu vid dnia narodzhennia O. M. Lazarevs'koho*, ed. Pavlo Sokhan' (Kyiv and Chernihiv, 2002).

[17] Aleksandr Lazarevskii, "Govoril li Polubotok Petru Velikomu rech', privodimuiu Koniskim?" *Osnova*, 1861, no. 8: 9–10; *Istoriia Rusov ili Maloi Rosii. Sochinenie Georgiia Koniskago, Arkhiepiskopa Beloruskago* (Moscow: 1846), pp. i-ii.

accomplished what Maksymovych tried but failed to do: he had gained access to the Poletyka family papers.[18]

The papers were acquired from the heirs of Hryhorii Poletyka by a renowned Ukrainian collector, V. V. Tarnovsky, who allowed Lazarevsky to examine his collection. Lazarevsky immediately put the archive to use by reconstructing Hryhorii Poletyka's biography, which until then had been known only in general terms. Poletyka was born in 1725 into the family of the mayor of the town of Romny in the Lubny regiment of the Hetmanate. His maternal grandfather was the colonel of the Lubny regiment, and his father eventually left the mayor's office to join the Cossack service. The young Poletyka received his education at the Kyivan Academy at a time when its prefect was none other than the future archbishop of Mahiliou, the Reverend Heorhii Konysky. In 1746 Poletyka joined the St. Petersburg Academy of Sciences as a translator. His language skills were examined by one of the leading Russian poets of the day, Vasilii Trediakovsky, who found Poletyka's Latin excellent but assessed his Russian as mere "Little Russian dialect." Poletyka would soon master written and spoken Russian and make a respectable career in the imperial capital. He served as a translator not only at the Academy of Sciences but also in the Holy Synod, the ruling body of the Russian Orthodox Church, and eventually became general inspector of the navy school for nobles. Poletyka compiled and published a six-language dictionary, translated Greek philosophers, wrote an essay on the origins of Ruthenian education, and prepared instructions for converts to the Orthodox faith.

Poletyka's claim to fame derives from his service in the Legislative Commission convened by Catherine II in 1767. There the navy school inspector represented the interests of the nobility of his native Romny district. His fellow nobles could not have wished for a better deputy. Not only was Poletyka a skillful writer completely at ease in the St. Petersburg milieu, but he also was one of the richest landowners in the area. Thanks to his own inheritance, his marriage to the daughter of a retired general judge of the Hetmanate, and his successful land purchases, Poletyka amassed rich landholdings and owned close to three thousand serfs.

While serving his constituency in the Legislative Commission, Poletyka wrote two lengthy memoranda. In them he argued for the preservation of the Hetmanate's autonomy and defended the rights and privileges of the Little Russian nobility, which he represented as liberties granted by Lithuanian grand dukes and Polish kings and confirmed by the Russian

[18] Maksimovich, *Sobranie sochinenii,* 1: 305–6.

tsars and emperors. The preservation of regional and estate privileges was not what Empress Catherine II had in mind when she convened the commission. Inspired by the ideas of the French *philosophes*, the empress was a promoter of universal values interested in standardizing and rationalizing administrative practice. The demands of deputies such as Poletyka were ignored and the commission dissolved. Nevertheless, Poletyka became a hero to the Little Russian nobility. He retired from his position at the St. Petersburg navy school in 1773 and returned to his native Ukraine, where he continued to amass lands and serfs until his death in the middle of a property dispute with one of his relatives.[19]

In 1861 Lazarevsky would hardly have considered Poletyka, a defender of the rights and freedoms of the landowning elite, capable of writing the speech delivered by Polubotok to Peter I. Thirty years later, however, with Konysky eliminated as a possible author of the *History*, Lazarevsky was no longer so wedded to his view of the *History* as a manifesto of the rights and freedoms of the popular masses. The Poletyka correspondence in Tarnovsky's collection convinced him that Hryhorii Poletyka not only had the right qualifications to produce the *History* but could actually have done so. From Poletyka's correspondence with Archbishop Konysky and one of his relatives at the Russian embassy in Vienna, Lazarevsky learned that Poletyka had owned a large library and actively collected books dealing with Ukrainian history. A letter from Hryhorii's son, Vasyl, disclosed that while Hryhorii's first library was destroyed by fire in 1771, he continued to collect books and manuscripts on Ukrainian history until the very end of his life. He had also been writing a historical work of his own.

On November 25, 1812, Vasyl Poletyka wrote to Count Nikolai Rumiantsev, one of the first Russian manuscript collectors, that the books and manuscripts "collected with great effort and diligence by my father in the last days of his life and finally by me, and added to the previous ones, pertain mainly to Little Russian history, whose delineation was his and

---

[19] Aleksandr Lazarevskii, "Iz semeinogo arkhiva Poletik," in *Ocherki, zametki i dokumenty po istorii Malorossii* (Kyiv, 1892), 1: 32–51, here 32–37. On Hryhorii Poletyka, see Oleksander Ohloblyn, *Liudy staroï Ukraïny* (Munich, 1959), pp. 193–98; Zenon E. Kohut, "A Gentry Democracy within an Autocracy: The Politics of Hryhorii Poletyka (1723/25–1784)," *Harvard Ukrainian Studies* 3–4 (1979–80): 509–19; T. F. Lytvynova, "Prohresyvnyi konservatyzm – vypadkove slovospoluchennia, chy fakt ukraïns'koï suspil'noï dumky druhoï polovyny XVIII stolittia," in *Dnipropetrovs'kyi istoryko-arkheohrafichnyi zbirnyk*, vol. 1 (Dnipropetrovsk, 1997), pp. 372–86; "Maloross v rossiiskom istoricheskom prostranstve XVIII veka," in *Dnipropetrovs'kyi istoryko-arkheohrafichnyi zbirnyk*, ed. O. I. Zhurba, vol. 2 (Dnipropetrovsk, 2001), pp. 28–64.

finally became my object." On the basis of these words, Lazarevsky assumed that the *History* could have been written by Hryhorii Poletyka, while the introduction to the work was added later by his son, Vasyl, who knew about his father's relations with Archbishop Konysky and invented the story of the origins of the *History* in order to conceal the name of its true author – his own father. Lazarevsky found another argument in support of his hypothesis in the patriotism of Hryhorii Poletyka, which matched that of the author of the *History*: here he relied on the reconstruction of the anonymous author's patriotic credentials by Mykhailo Drahomanov in his polemic with Kostomarov. Another piece of circumstantial evidence came from the favorable treatment in the *History* of the seventeenth-century hetman Demian Mnohohrishny, a relative of the Poletykas.[20]

Lazarevsky's hypothesis did not remain unchallenged for long. The next year another student of Cossack history, Vasyl Horlenko, published a new series of letters that included some of Vasyl Poletyka's correspondence. The letters dated from 1809–10 and were found in the archive of a former governor general of Little Russia, Prince Nikolai Repnin. They comprised Poletyka's correspondence with another Poltava-area connoisseur of Ukrainian history and collector of historical documents, Andrian Chepa. Both were considered experts on Ukrainian history and were approached in 1809 by Vasyl Charnysh, the marshal of the Poltava gubernia nobility, with a request to help draft a memorandum on the rights and privileges of the Little Russian nobility. Both Poletyka and Chepa agreed. They also began to correspond with each other, and Horlenko believed that in one of his letters to Chepa, Vasyl Poletyka provided evidence that undermined Lazarevsky's hypothesis about Hryhorii Poletyka as the principal author of the *History*.

The letter that Horlenko found especially interesting was written on April 23, 1809. In it Vasyl Poletyka confided to his fellow antiquarian: "I am trying to obtain information everywhere pertaining to Little Russian history but finding little. We still have no full chronicles of our fatherland. According to my observations, their authentic and most important traces vanish almost as much in the unfortunate devastation of our lands and the destruction [of historical sources] as in the lacunae [occurring in those sources]. The writer of this history encounters these difficulties and lays his pen aside. Moreover, it is only posterity that will

---

[20] Lazarevskii, "Iz semeinogo arkhiva Poletik," pp. 41, 45–51.

read it dispassionately. My slight aptitude and poor knowledge already divert me from this task, no matter how much I think of taking it up."[21]

Vasyl Horlenko believed that his find, together with the letter from Vasyl Poletyka published by Lazarevsky, pointed to Vasyl, not Hryhorii, Poletyka as the likely author of the *History*. Horlenko also cited Maksymovych's opinion that Archbishop Konysky was too well versed in the history of his homeland to be the author of the factually unreliable *History of the Rus'*, and that Hryhorii Poletyka was too well educated to have used it as a source. Furthermore, Horlenko indicated a number of textual parallels between the *History of the Rus'* and Vasyl Poletyka's writings, which included a memorandum on the Little Russian nobility ("Zapiska o Malorossiiskom dvorianstve," 1809) prepared at the request of the marshal of the Poltava gubernia nobility. Horlenko argued that if the *History of the Rus'* had indeed been written by Hryhorii Poletyka, then Vasyl would have revealed the existence of such a history in his correspondence with Chepa in 1809–10. He did not do so, which Horlenko took as an indication that it was Vasyl, not Hryhorii, who had written the *History*. But why conceal the author's identity behind the name of Archbishop Konysky? Horlenko had an answer to that question as well: the work, written during the liberal rule of Alexander I, was completed only after the defeat of the Decembrist Uprising and could not have appeared under the author's name in the era of political reaction that followed the revolt.[22]

Vasyl Poletyka, the new candidate for the authorship of the *History*, was born in 1765. He spent the first years of his life in Ukraine. His father found a French teacher to educate Vasyl and his brothers at home but then sent his son to a Catholic-run school in Vitsebsk. Vasyl Poletyka mastered Latin, German, French, and Polish, apart from Russian and Ukrainian. He concluded his education at the University of Vilnius, which he entered on the recommendation of Archbishop Konysky. After a brief period of military service, Vasyl Poletyka returned to his father's homeland, where he served as leader of the local nobility and made a name for himself as a patriot, promoter of education, and supporter of the liberal reforms of Alexander I. Two speeches that he delivered on different occasions were published in the St. Petersburg journal *Vestnik Evropy*, making him known, if not renowned, throughout the empire and a local

[21] V. P. Gorlenko, "Iz istorii iuzhno-russkogo obshchestva nachala XIX veka," *Kievskaia starina*, no. 1 (1893): 41–76, here 51–52.
[22] *Ibid.*, pp. 68–72.

celebrity in the former Hetmanate. The correspondence published by Lazarevsky and then Horlenko showed that he was also interested in Ukrainian history and at least considered writing a comprehensive history of his homeland. He died in 1845 at the age of eighty, leaving no manuscript or publication on the subject.[23]

Now Horlenko was suggesting that Poletyka actually had left such a work. Titled the *History of the Rus'*, it was published by Osyp Bodiansky a year after its author's death. Horlenko saw further proof of his authorship in the fact that the author of the *History* showed particular interest in the fate of the citizens of Romny – Vasyl Poletyka's home ground – when he described the punishment inflicted on them by Russian troops after the defeat of the Mazepa Uprising in 1709. So convinced was Horlenko of his own hypothesis that he even visited the grave of Vasyl Poletyka in the village of Korventsi in the Romny district. He later described his visit in the following words:

> The thought that I was standing at the grave of the author of the *History of the Rus'* did not leave me. No matter that the idea of that book is false – the idea of identifying the old Cossack order with the notion of "liberty" and the view of representatives of "antiquity" as creators of "distinctiveness." Scholarship and the facts of history have exposed the falsity of that view, revealing the authentic character of Little Russian history and its democratic origins. But what remains is the ardent love of the homeland expressed in that book; the animation and brilliance of its narrative; the details taken from unrecorded sources and legends that served to substantiate a whole series of sources.[24]

If Horlenko tried to reconcile his appreciation of the *History* as a highly patriotic work with Kostomarov's rejection of it as a product of the conservative thought of the landowning classes, Mykhailo Drahomanov had no such problem when he read Horlenko's article. He was convinced by Horlenko's argument and eagerly embraced the hypothesis of Vasyl Poletyka's authorship of the *History*. Writing in 1894, a year after the publication of Horlenko's findings, Drahomanov declared: "The *History of the Rus'* of Pseudo-Konysky must be recognized as the first

---

[23] *Ibid.*, pp. 44–45. For a comparison of the historical and political views of the Poletykas, father and son, see T. F. Lytvynova, "Do pytannia pro istorychni pohliady ta sotsial'ni idealy Hryhoriia ta Vasylia Poletyk," in *Istoriia suspi'lnoï dumky Rosiï ta Ukraïny XVII–pochatku XX st.* (Dnipropetrovsk, 1992), pp. 53–64. On the Poletyka family papers and correspondence, see Lytvynova, "Papery rodyny Poletyk v arkhivoskhovyshchakh Ukraïny ta Rosiï," in *Istoriia i osobystist' istoryka: Zbirnyk naukovykh prats', prysviachenykh 60-richnomu iuvileiu Hanny Kyrylivny Shvyd'ko* (Dnipropetrovsk, 2004), pp. 202–17; also in *Arkhivy Ukraïny*, nos. 1–6 (2006): 47–70.

[24] *Ibid.*, p. 76.

manifestation of Ukrainian political liberalism. As may now be ascertained, it came from the Poletyka family ... It should be noted that even the father of the author of the *History of the Rus'*, Hryhorii Poletyka, a deputy in 1767, was one of the few Ukrainian liberals of Cossack and gentry origin who opposed serfdom. This time, fortunately, liberalism appeared together with democratism, corresponding to the discussions about the liberation of the serfs that went on in European Russian society and even in government circles as far back as the times of Alexander."

In Horlenko's hypothesis about Vasyl Poletyka's authorship Drahomanov found confirmation of what he already believed: the *History* was a product of the liberal era of Alexander I, and as such it could be regarded as prefiguring not only the Ukrainian movement in general but also its liberal and federalist trend. He saw the author as a precursor of the idea of constitutional rule in Russia and autonomy for its provinces, especially Ukraine. According to Drahomanov, the author of the *History* "was a great political patriot of his 'Little Russian Fatherland,' an autonomist after his own fashion, but no separatist in that regard, and least of all an ethnographic patriot. He idealized the political order of Cossack 'Little Russia' and thought that a constitutional Russia would be just like it."[25]

Mykhailo Drahomanov died in 1895 believing that the author of the *History of the Rus'* had finally been identified. This opinion was shared by many Russian and Ukrainian scholars at the time, but there were dissenters as well. Oleksandr Lazarevsky, for example, stuck to his guns, and until his death in 1902 maintained that the *History* had been written by Hryhorii Poletyka. Others argued that the *History* had been begun by the senior Poletyka and completed by his son. One way or another, the nineteenth century, which had seen the discovery and publication of the *History*, as well as its considerable impact on the Ukrainian historical imagination and national movement, was reaching its end with a new consensus among readers and students of the work. Most of them rejected the authorship of Archbishop Konysky and strongly believed in that of the Poletykas. The assumption prevailed that the author was a rich nobleman and that in some form the book reflected the opinions and interests of the Ukrainian nobility. Alexander Pushkin's remark about the heart of a noble beating under the cassock of a monk thus made an unexpected but spectacular career in the academic literature on the *History of the Rus'*. The next century would shake that consensus, producing significant discoveries and raising new doubts.

[25] Drahomanov, *Lysty na naddniprians'ku Ukraïnu*, p. 155.

CHAPTER 5

The Cossack prince

A few minutes before noon on the sunny morning of October 3, 1926, a car with government plates pulled over and stopped near the main entrance to the red-walled building of Kyiv University. A short, stocky man with a long silver-gray beard got out of the car and helped the woman accompanying him with the door. He then turned around and waved to the crowd that was eager to greet him. His gesture was met with applause: the onlookers, many of them young students, had been waiting for hours to see the silver-gray elder, and the atmosphere in the crowd was festive, the air full of excitement. "The old man is as energetic as he was in 1917. Neither time nor events nor circumstances affect him," observed a middle-aged man in the crowd to his student neighbor. "And you – did you know him once?" asked the student. "Well . . . it happened, young man, it all happened," the man managed to reply before the movement of the crowd rushing into the university building separated the two. The student was Hryhorii Kostiuk, a future writer and editor who emigrated to the United States after the Second World War and described the scene in his memoirs. His accidental interlocutor was Volodymyr Chekhivsky, the prime minister of the government of independent Ukraine in 1918–19 and a leader of the Ukrainian Orthodox Church independent of Moscow in the 1920s. The man being welcomed by the Kyiv students, and regarded with admiration by Kostiuk and Chekhivsky alike, was Mykhailo Hrushevsky, Ukraine's most prominent twentieth-century historian and the first head of the independent Ukrainian state during the Revolution of 1917.[1]

For Hrushevsky, the whole scene at the entrance to Kyiv University must have brought a sense of *déjà vu*. The last time he had been welcomed by Kyiv crowds was nine years earlier, in the revolutionary year of 1917. Back then, the 51-year-old Hrushevsky, recently released from exile in Russia, had led his young followers, like Volodymyr Chekhivsky, from

---

[1] Hryhorii Kostiuk, *Zustrichi i proshchannia. Spohady. Knyha persha* (Edmonton, 1987), pp. 186–89.

one victory for the Ukrainian cause to another. The Central Rada (Council), a small group of radical Ukrainians that Hrushevsky agreed to chair in March 1917, had become the parliament of autonomous Ukraine by the summer of that year; in the fall it proclaimed Ukrainian statehood, and in January 1918 it declared complete independence. Hrushevsky presided over the most inspiring and optimistic period of the Ukrainian Revolution, its parliamentary stage, which saw close cooperation between the Ukrainian government and Jewish, Russian, and Polish political parties and organizations. The year 1918 brought Bolshevik intervention, German occupation, civil war and, finally, massacres and pogroms. With the parliamentary period over, there was no longer a place on the Ukrainian political scene for people like Hrushevsky. He had no choice but to leave the country.

In emigration in Vienna, Hrushevsky returned to his academic pursuits, which had been interrupted by the outbreak of the First World War and the 1917 revolution. A graduate of Kyiv University, Hrushevsky had taught Ukrainian history for twenty years at Lviv University in Austria-Hungary. There he laid the foundations for Ukrainian nationhood by supplying the country, still divided by imperial borders, with a new narrative: eight volumes of Hrushevsky's monumental *History of Ukraine-Rus'* were published between 1898 and 1917. In Vienna, Hrushevsky wanted to continue work on his magnum opus, which he had managed to bring up to the mid seventeenth century, but he needed access to the archival sources. He was prepared to return to communist-controlled Ukraine, where he believed new opportunities had emerged for Ukrainian academic and cultural work. In order to buy the loyalty of the population, the victorious Bolshevik government had declared a policy of cultural Ukrainization. The authorities were inviting Hrushevsky back, but only on condition that he stay out of politics. The former leader of independent Ukraine agreed. He returned to Kyiv in the spring of 1924 with the rank of full member of the Ukrainian Academy of Sciences and the goal of organizing the academy's research in the discipline of history.[2]

The public event at Kyiv University in October 1926 that created such enthusiasm among the Kyiv intelligentsia and students was the officially sanctioned celebration of Hrushevsky's sixtieth birthday. For many in Ukraine it was an opportunity to pay homage to Hrushevsky the historian and politician, who had liberated Ukrainian history and attempted to free

---

[2] On Hrushevsky, see Thomas M. Prymak, *Mykhailo Hrushevsky: The Politics of National Culture* (Toronto, 1987); Serhii Plokhy, *Unmaking Imperial Russia: Mykhailo Hrushevsky and the Writing of Ukrainian History* (Toronto, 2005).

Ukrainian politics from Russian dominance. Hrushevsky's main scholarly accomplishment, his multivolume *History of Ukraine-Rus'*, was the culmination of a long phase of Ukrainian historiography that began with the *History of the Rus'*. The difference between the two works was not limited to the presence of the word "Ukraine" in Hrushevsky's title. His work was a *tour de force* of modern positivist scholarship. On the conceptual level, Hrushevsky refused to treat the Ukrainian past as part of a Russian or all-Russian historical narrative – a major departure from the practice brought into modern Ukrainian historiography by the *History of the Rus'*. At the public meeting that marked Hrushevsky's anniversary, his older colleague and former president of Kharkiv University, Dmytro Bahalii, welcomed Hrushevsky's accomplishment with the following words: "We, together with all those working in Ukrainian history … regard your *History of Ukraine-Rus'* as the first monumental synthetic work that … fulfills the requirements of European methodology, draws up the conclusions of Ukrainian historiography as presented in its sources and research works, and stands on the same level as analogous histories of other peoples."[3]

Dmytro Bahalii and other Ukrainian scholars paid tribute to Hrushevsky by issuing a festschrift in his honor – a two-volume collection of essays dedicated to the historian. The contributors wrote on topics that had either been researched by Hrushevsky himself or dealt with subjects in which he was interested. Two essays focused on the *History of the Rus'*, which Hrushevsky highly appreciated as a historiographic monument and encouraged others to study. In 1894, soon after the publication of essays by Oleksandr Lazarevsky and Vasyl Horlenko on the authorship of Hryhorii and Vasyl Poletyka, Hrushevsky expressed his own view on that contested issue. He did not side with Lazarevsky or Horlenko but endorsed the compromise hypothesis of Leonid Maikov, who argued that the *History* could have been started by Hryhorii Poletyka and completed by his son, Vasyl. "This notion also seems generally likely to us," wrote Hrushevsky, "although more detailed study of the *History of the Rus'* is required for a definitive elucidation of the matter." Mykhailo Hrushevsky's younger brother, Oleksandr, was among those who undertook the task. In 1906–8 he published two articles about the views of the anonymous author, claiming that the main theme of the work was the history of the people, or the nation. He had an eye for the markers of national histories:

---

[3] Kostiuk, *Zustrichi i proshchannia*, p. 190; cf. *Velykyi ukraïnets': Materialy z zhyttia ta diial'nosti M. S. Hrushevs'koho*, comp. A. P. Demydenko (Kyiv, 1992), pp. 308–425.

the history of the people/nation was also the leitmotif of his brother's *History of Ukraine-Rus'*.[4]

The two authors who contributed articles to Hrushevsky's festschrift of 1926 dealing with the *History of the Rus'* were Anatolii Yershov and Pavlo Klepatsky. Yershov, an associate of Hrushevsky's in his research expeditions to the Moscow archives, published an extremely interesting analysis of the time-sensitive terminology and references in the *History*, which led him to conclude that the work was most probably written after 1815. That year saw the conclusion of the Congress of Vienna, which made the notion of the balance of power – a concept repeatedly cited by the anonymous author – dominant in European political thought of the period. The latest possible date for the writing of the *History*, according to Yershov, was 1818, the year that appears on the title page of the first known manuscript of the work. Yershov's conclusions were highly significant for the debate on the authorship of the manuscript. Of all the possible candidates, only Vasyl Poletyka could fit his chronology. But the times when scholars limited their candidates to Konysky and the two Poletykas were quickly passing away.[5]

Pavlo Klepatsky did not share Yershov's views either on the time of writing of the *History* or on its potential author. Klepatsky felt it was time to break with the long-established tradition of seeking authors of the *History* among the individuals mentioned in its introduction. His candidate was not mentioned in the *History* at all but was well known to any student of eighteenth-century Ukrainian or Russian history. Klepatsky pointed his finger at none other than Prince Oleksandr (Alexander) Bezborodko (1747–99), the chancellor of Catherine II and the most powerful Ukrainian at the imperial court since Teofan Prokopovych, an ideologue of Peter's rule. Klepatsky found correspondence in the Poltava archives between Oleksandr Bezborodko and his father, Andrii, which convinced him that the younger Bezborodko had been working on a history of Ukraine. That history, in Klepatsky's opinion, was in fact the *History of the Rus'*. Klepatsky's hypothesis directly contradicted Yershov's

---

[4] Mykhailo Hrushevs'kyi, review of Leonid Maikov, "K voprosu ob Istorii Rusov," in *Zapysky Naukovoho tovarystva im. Shevchenka* 6 (1894): 190; Oleksandr Hrushevs'kyi, "K sud'be *Istorii Rusov*. Epizod iz ukrainskoi istoriografii XIX veka," in *Chteniia v istoricheskom obshchestve Nestora-Letopistsa* 19, no. 4 (1906): 51–70; Hrushev'skyi "K kharakteristike vzgliadov *Istorii Rusov*," in *Izvestiia Otdeleniia russkogo iazyka i slovesnosti* (1908): 396–427.

[5] Anatolii Iershov, "Do pytannia pro chas napysannia Istorii Rusov, a po chasty i pro avtora ïi," *Iuvileinyi zbirnyk na poshanu akademika M. S. Hrushevs'koho*, ed. P. A. Tutkivs'kyi, pt. 1 (Kyiv, 1928), pp. 286–91.

textual findings, but the editors of the Hrushevsky festschrift did not try to reconcile the two views and simply printed both essays. The disagreement was left for future scholars to untangle.[6]

Oleksandr Bezborodko, the new candidate for the authorship of the *History of the Rus'*, was a contemporary of both Konysky and the senior Poletyka. Born in 1747 to the family of one of the highest officials of the Hetmanate (his father twice held the post of general chancellor and de facto ruled the polity during the hetmancy of Kyrylo Rozumovsky), Bezborodko began his career in the Hetmanate after the abolition of the office of hetman in 1764. He first assumed the coveted post of military judge in the Hetmanate's Supreme Court and then took part in the Russo-Turkish War of 1768–74. He fought in the decisive battles of that war, including those of Larga and Kagul. The major leap in his career occurred when he became head of the chancellery of Count Petr Rumiantsev, the Russian military commander in the Russo-Turkish War and the new ruler of Ukraine. It was on Rumiantsev's recommendation that Bezborodko was promoted to the rank of colonel of the Kyiv regiment and then became petition secretary to Catherine II, moving from Ukraine to St. Petersburg in 1775.

Bezborodko was to spend the rest of his life in the imperial capital. He served Catherine II and then her son and successor Paul I for twenty-four years – one of the very few courtiers who managed to gain the trust of both rulers. Over many years Bezborodko served as a principal architect of Russian foreign policy. It was on his watch, and often with his direct participation, that the traditional enemies of the Hetmanate, the Ottomans, were defeated, Poland divided, and the Crimea annexed. Bezborodko's diplomatic skills helped the empire achieve these and other successes in the international arena. St. Petersburg gained unprecedented power and influence, but the elite of the former Hetmanate also benefited from these geopolitical changes in Eastern Europe. Many descendants of prominent Cossack families acquired positions and lands in the newly annexed territories of the empire. Bezborodko managed not only to preserve but also to improve his standing during Paul's reign. The new emperor bestowed the title of prince on this son of a Cossack officer and made him grand chancellor of the Russian Empire. At the time of his death at the age of fifty-two, in 1799, Prince Oleksandr Bezborodko was one of the most powerful men in the empire.[7]

---

[6] Pavlo Klepats'kyi, "Lystuvannia Oleksandra Andriiovycha Bezborod'ka z svoim bat'kom, iak istorychne dzherelo," *Iuvileinyi zbirnyk na poshanu akademika M. S. Hrushevs'koho*, pt. 1: 280–85.

[7] On Bezborodko's life and career, see N. I. Grigorovich, *Kantsler kniaz' Aleksandr Andreevich Bezborodko v sviazi s sobytiiami ego vremeni*, 2 vols. (St. Petersburg, 1879–81).

Klepatsky's theory about the authorship of Oleksandr Bezborodko, a Cossack prince in the employ of the Russian Empire, was a major departure from previous historiography on the subject. There were, however, two problems with the claim. First, Klepatsky was unaware that some of the materials he located in the Poltava archives had already been published in the mid nineteenth century. Second, Klepatsky's identification was not original: the same hypothesis had been advanced one year earlier by Mykhailo Slabchenko, a legal and economic historian from Odesa. Klepatsky knew Slabchenko's work on the subject but preferred not to mention it in his own essay. Later he found himself obliged to tell Slabchenko that he had "somehow forgotten" about the latter's earlier work. In subsequent historiography, the Bezborodko hypothesis was justly associated first and foremost with Slabchenko's name.[8]

Who was Slabchenko, and what was his main argument concerning the authorship of the *History of the Rus'*? Mykhailo Slabchenko was born in 1882 in the Odesa suburb of Moldavanka, known for its ethnic, religious, and cultural diversity. Moldavanka, whose plebeian inhabitants worked in the local factories and often engaged in criminal and semi-criminal activities, became a source of city lore and the subject of Isaac Babel's *Odesa Tales*. An alumnus of Odesa University and the St. Petersburg Academy of Military Law, Slabchenko began his political activity by joining the Revolutionary Ukrainian Party in 1903. He then became an active member of the Ukrainian Social Democratic Labor Party, which kept its distance from Lenin's Social Democrats and combined the goals of social liberation of the working masses and Ukrainian national liberation. After the 1917 revolution, Slabchenko quit politics and focused on academic work, becoming the leading Ukrainian-studies specialist in Odesa. His research was devoted to the social, economic, and legal history of the Hetmanate and the Zaporozhian Sich. In the fall of 1929 his scholarly accomplishments were recognized by his election to full membership in the Ukrainian Academy of Sciences.[9]

Slabchenko formulated his hypothesis about Oleksandr Bezborodko's authorship of the *History of the Rus'* in the first volume of his *Materials on the Economic and Social History of Nineteenth-Century Ukraine* (1925). In the chapter on "Nobiliary Historiography," Slabchenko presented the

[8] See Viktor Zaruba, ed., *Mykhailo Slabchenko v epistoliarnii ta memuarnii spadshchyni (1882–1952)* (Dnipropetrovsk, 2004), p. 140.
[9] On Slabchenko and his writings, see Viktor Zaruba, *Istoryk derzhavy i prava Ukraïny akademik Mykhailo Slabchenko (1882–1952)* (Dnipropetrovsk, 2004), pp. 47–232.

History of the Rus' as a historiographic tool of the Ukrainian nobility in its struggle for equality with its Russian counterparts. He discounted the notion that the *History* could have been the work of Hryhorii or Vasyl Poletyka, observing that there was nothing in the available sources to indicate that either the father or the son had actually written a history of Ukraine. True, they had collected historical materials, but that was not the same as producing a historical narrative, let alone the *History of the Rus'*. The fact that Yakiv Poletyka, a grandson of Hryhorii Poletyka, made a copy of the *History* for himself from the manuscript discovered in the late 1820s was a clear indication for Slabchenko that the Poletykas had had nothing to do with the origins of the *History*.[10]

If the Poletykas did not, who did? Slabchenko believed that the remaining traces led to Oleksandr Bezborodko. Slabchenko's hypothesis was based on textual parallels between the *History of the Rus'* and some of Bezborodko's own writings. The text that attracted Slabchenko's attention had appeared in print in St. Petersburg in 1777. Its title was *A Brief Chronicle of Little Russia from 1506 to 1776, with the Disclosure of a True Picture of the Local Administration and the Publication of a List of Earlier Hetmans, General Officers, Colonels, and Hierarchs*. The book was issued by Vasyl Ruban, an alumnus of the Kyivan Academy, one-time secretary to Prince Grigorii Potemkin, and publisher of some of the first Russian journals. The introduction to the book stated that the concluding section of the "chronicle," covering the period from 1734 to 1776, as well as the description of the form of government and the list of Hetmanate officials, had been compiled by the colonel of Kyiv and petition secretary to Empress Catherine II, Oleksandr Bezborodko.[11]

Ruban's own role in the project was that of compiler, editor, and publisher. He added a geographic description of Ukraine and a list of church hierarchs received from his Ukrainian friends. Ruban claimed that he had obtained the text of the *Brief Chronicle*, which ended with the events of 1734 and was continued by Bezborodko up to 1776, from his former professor at the Kyivan Academy, Archbishop Heorhii Konysky. That was just the beginning of the striking similarities between Ruban's publication and the *History of the Rus'*. Ruban further claimed that the text supplied to him by Konysky had been composed by chancellors who

---

[10] Mykhailo Slabchenko, *Materiialy do ekonomichno-sotsiial'noï istoriï Ukraïny XIX stolittia*, vol. 1 (Odesa, 1925), pp. 103–5.

[11] *Kratkaia letopis' Malyia Rosii s 1506 po 1776 god, s iz"iavleniem Nastoiashchego obraza tamoshnego pravleniia i s priobshcheniem spiska prezhde byvshikh getmanov, general'nykh starshin, polkovnikov i ierarkhov* (St. Petersburg, 1777).

served various Cossack hetmans, starting with Bohdan Khmelnytsky and ending with Danylo Apostol. That statement had clearly influenced the author of the *History*, who wrote not only that his own text originated with Konysky but also that its sources included "journals of memorable events and national deeds" kept at the time of Bohdan Khmelnytsky. "There is no need to write here of what the Little Russian people experienced before the fourteenth century," wrote Ruban in his introduction. "Its deeds are united with those of the Russian people, whose history has been and is being published by many writers." The author of the *History* was of the same opinion: "The history of Little Russia until the time of its invasion by the Tatars with their khan, Batu, is united with the history of All Russia, or indeed it is the only Russian history."[12]

There is no reason to question Ruban's assertion that he obtained the chronicle from Konysky. Ruban was indeed in touch with the archbishop of Mahilioŭ and even published two of his speeches in the journals that he was busily producing in the 1770s. One was the speech delivered before Catherine II during her coronation in Moscow in 1762; the other had been given before King Stanisław Poniatowski of Poland in 1765. Konysky was a well-respected figure in St. Petersburg, and mentioning him in the first printed work on Ukrainian history to be published in the Russian Empire since the Kyivan *Synopsis* of 1674 could by no means compromise the publisher. Still, the chronicle published by Ruban and apparently supplied by Konysky was far from original. It was a variant of a manuscript, otherwise known as the *Brief Description of Little Russia*, that began to circulate in Ukraine in the 1740s; by the time of Ruban's publication, it had become the most popular compendium of Ukrainian history in the Hetmanate.[13]

Studying the two publications in the 1920s, Mykhailo Slabchenko saw the references to Konysky both in Ruban's *Brief Chronicle* and in the *History of the Rus'* as more than coincidence or name-dropping for the sake of historical and political legitimacy. Slabchenko believed that the two histories were in fact related and written at least in part by the same author, Oleksandr Bezborodko. To strengthen his argument, he pointed out that one of the first known copies of the *History* had been found on

[12] *Kratkaia letopis'*, p. 31; *Istoriia Rusov ili Maloi Rosii. Sochinenie Georgiia Koniskago, Arkhiepiskopa Beloruskago* (Moscow, 1846) pp. i, ii, iv; Vozniak, *Psevdo-Konys'kyi i Psevdo-Poletyka* (Istoriia Rusov u literaturi ta nautsi (Lviv and Kyiv, 1939), pp. 148–49.

[13] See Andrii Bovhyria, *Kozats'ke istoriopysannia v rukopysnii tradytsiï XVIII st. Spysky ta redaktsiï tvoriv* (Kyiv, 2010), pp. 121–47. On Vasyl Ruban, see David Saunders, *The Ukrainian Impact on Russian Culture, 1750–1850* (Edmonton, 1985), pp. 119–26.

the Bezborodko family estate in 1828. Slabchenko further argued that ending the *History* with the events of 1768 made perfect sense if Bezborodko was indeed its author: that year the future imperial chancellor had absented himself from court to take part in the war against the Ottomans. But Slabchenko's main argument in favor of Bezborodko's authorship was of a different nature: he based it on textual parallels between the *History* and the *Brief Chronicle of Little Russia* published by Ruban. This was a turning point in the century-old debate on the question. For the first time, a textual analysis of the *History* and its possible sources was offered as a means of establishing its authorship.

Slabchenko was not the first scholar to point out textual parallels between the *Brief Chronicle* and the *History* – that honor belonged to a Kyiv historian, Vladimir Ikonnikov, who presented his argument in 1908. Slabchenko, however, was the first to suggest that the two texts were written by the same author. The textual parallels identified by Slabchenko were stunning indeed. "Hetman Count Razumovsky, having received a charter of privilege for his rank in the very same terms as those of the one given to Skoropadsky" went a passage in the Bezborodko portion of the *Brief Chronicle*. "In 1751 Hetman Count Razumovsky received a most lofty privilege for his rank in the very same terms as those of the one given to Skoropadsky," wrote the author of the *History of the Rus'*, mirroring Bezborodko's text. Slabchenko was able to point out many other examples of textual coincidence between the two works. His conclusion, based on the kind of evidence that proponents of Konysky or the Poletykas could not provide, was hard to dismiss. As Klepatsky supplemented Slabchenko's textual research with his own archival evidence, the case for Oleksandr Bezborodko, the Cossack colonel and imperial chancellor, as author of the mysterious *History of the Rus'* became stronger than that for any of his competitors.[14]

There were, of course, unanswered questions. One of them, most troublesome for Slabchenko, concerned Anatolii Yershov's findings about the time of writing of the *History*. Unfortunately, Slabchenko was never able to respond to Yershov or fully develop his ideas. In January 1930 he was arrested by Stalin's secret police at the Odesa railway station on his return from Kyiv, where he had lobbied on behalf of his son, Taras, who had been arrested a few weeks earlier. Both father and son, along with many other leading figures of the Ukrainian intelligentsia, were accused of

[14] *Kratkaia letopis'*, p. 212. Cf. *Istoriia Rusov*, p. 246; V. Ikonnikov, *Opyt russkoi istoriografii*, vol. ii, bk. 2 (Kyiv, 1908), p. 1648.

having participated in the illegal activities of the Union for the Liberation of Ukraine. The authorities charged that this organization was devoted to the violent overthrow of Soviet power in Ukraine and the establishment of an independent Ukrainian state, which the capitalist West would then use as a base for aggression against Soviet Russia. These were bogus charges, to say the least. There was no such organization in Soviet Ukraine in 1929, and all that united the accused was their active role in promoting Ukrainian culture and scholarship.

In the late 1920s the Stalin regime began to have second thoughts about the official policy of Ukrainization that had been pursued in Soviet Ukraine for most of the decade. That policy was now deemed dangerous to the stability of the Soviet regime: instead of forging an alliance between the Ukrainian-speaking peasantry and the Russian-speaking working class in order to strengthen the "dictatorship of the proletariat," it was giving the Ukrainian intelligentsia a platform to challenge the dominance of the Russian language and culture in Ukraine. Moscow regarded this as a manifestation of bourgeois nationalism. The arrest of alleged members of the Union for the Liberation of Ukraine in late 1929 and early 1930 was a signal to the Ukrainian intelligentsia in general that the party line had changed: in the Kremlin's view, the main threat was no longer Russian chauvinism, as proclaimed in the early 1920s, but local nationalism. The severe sentences meted out to the defendants indicated the seriousness of their political transgressions. Mykhailo Slabchenko was sentenced to six years of hard labor, which he served in a notorious Gulag camp on the Solovets Islands in northern Russia. His son, Taras, was initially sentenced to three years of hard labor; he was shot in 1937 at the height of the Great Terror in the USSR. Mykhailo Slabchenko survived imprisonment. After serving a six-year term in Stalin's Gulag, he was released but prohibited from returning to Odesa. He was lucky to find a job as a secondary-school teacher in a provincial town.[15]

The Soviet authorities could arrest a scholar and thus put a stop to his or her work. It was much more difficult to interfere with the development of scholarly ideas. In 1933, when Slabchenko was on the Solovets Islands serving his sentence for alleged membership in the Union for the Liberation of Ukraine, Andrii Yakovliv, a legal scholar and prominent Ukrainian political activist then living in Prague, wrote an article

---

[15] Zaruba, *Istoryk derzhavy i prava*, pp. 233–77; On the policy of Ukrainization, see Terry Martin, *The Affirmative Action Empire: Nations and Nationalism in the Soviet Union, 1923–1939* (Ithaca, N.Y., 2001), pp. 75–124.

supporting Slabchenko's hypothesis. The article, titled "On the Question of the Author of the *History of the Rus'*," was published in 1937, at the height of the Great Terror in the USSR. It appeared in the Lviv-based academic journal *Zapysky Naukovoho tovarystva im. Shevchenka* (Proceedings of the Shevchenko Scientific Society).[16]

A lawyer by training and a historian by vocation, Yakovliv had participated actively in the Ukrainian Revolution. In 1917 he was a member of the Central Rada, the first Ukrainian revolutionary parliament, which was headed by Mykhailo Hrushevsky. Yakovliv served on the Rada executive and later embarked on a diplomatic career, representing the Rada's interests in Austria-Hungary. With the overthrow of the Rada's government by the German military in the spring of 1918, Yakovliv joined the government of Hetman Pavlo Skoropadsky, serving as director of the foreign-relations department of the Ministry of Foreign Affairs. After the fall of Skoropadsky in December 1918, Yakovliv agreed to represent Ukraine's next government, the Directory, in the Netherlands and Belgium. Although Yakovliv worked for Ukrainian governments of different ideological stripes, he refused to serve the Bolsheviks and, unlike Mykhailo Hrushevsky, declined to return to Ukraine when its communist regime introduced the Ukrainization policy. After the revolution Yakovliv moved to Czechoslovakia, becoming a professor of law at the Ukrainian Free University in Prague and the Ukrainian Economic Academy in Poděbrady.[17]

Yakovliv's article, in which he not only enhanced Slabchenko's hypothesis but also criticized Yershov and other scholars who believed in the authorship of the Poletykas, inaugurated a period of strong interest in the mysterious Cossack text outside Soviet Ukraine. In the tumultuous year of 1939 Yakovliv, who also served as general secretary of the Ukrainian Mohyla-Mazepa Academy of Sciences, authorized the publication not of an article but an entire book dealing with the *History of the Rus'*. The book, titled *Pseudo-Konysky and Pseudo-Poletyka: The "History of the Rus'" in Literature and Scholarship*, was written by Mykhailo Vozniak, a Lviv scholar of Ukrainian literature. Vozniak, whose daily greeting was "Honor to Labor," was known to his friends as a bookworm who had no family and knew little in life other than daily work on his manuscripts. *Pseudo-Konysky and Pseudo-Poletyka* was one of many results of such

---

[16] Andrii Iakovliv, "Do pytannia pro avtora Istoriï Rusiv," *Zapysky NTSh*, vol. 154 (1937): 71–113.
[17] Arkadii Zhukovsky, "Andrii Yakovliv," in *Encyclopedia of Ukraine*, 5 vols. (Toronto, 1984–93), I: 373.

unremitting labor. The book turned out to be the most complete survey ever written of the debates on the origin and significance of the *History of the Rus'* up to 1939.[18]

Born in Habsburg-ruled Galicia in 1881, Mykhailo Vozniak graduated from Lviv University in 1908. He obtained a teaching position at a local secondary school, but even before graduation he had begun his career as a literary scholar, contributing to numerous publications of the Shevchenko Scientific Society. With the outbreak of the First World War, Vozniak entered politics as a supporter of the Union for the Liberation of Ukraine, a political organization of émigrés from Russian-ruled Ukraine that was based in Lviv and Vienna. The members of the Union aspired to create an independent Ukrainian state; under the auspices of the Central Powers they conducted political and cultural work among Ukrainian prisoners of war in Germany and the Habsburg Monarchy. This was the organization that prompted Stalin's secret police to invent the bogus Union for the Liberation of Ukraine in the late 1920s. Vozniak wrote a number of brochures for distribution by the original Union, including *Our Native Tongue*, which was first published in 1916. In 1918, the last year of the Union's activities, he published a brochure on *Ukrainian Statehood* in Vienna.

The young scholar fully established his credentials with the publication of a three-volume *History of Ukrainian Literature* (1920) in Lviv. With Poland taking full control of Galicia after the fall of Austria-Hungary, Vozniak, like many other Ukrainian scholars, remained unemployed but continued to publish his works with the Shevchenko Scientific Society, which survived the world war and the collapse of the dual monarchy in 1918. Mykhailo Hrushevsky, who took over the historical institutions at the Ukrainian Academy of Sciences in Kyiv in 1924, supported Vozniak with honoraria for his contributions to Soviet Ukrainian academic journals. In 1929 Vozniak accepted an offer to become a full member of the Academy of Sciences without leaving Lviv. This was a major boon to a prominent scholar without an academic position, but it was short-lived. In the early 1930s, when the purge of Ukrainian cadres began in Soviet Ukraine, Vozniak's membership in the academy was suspended. He was lucky to be out of reach of the Soviet authorities – many of his colleagues in the academy, including Mykhailo Slabchenko, ended up in Stalin's Gulag. In Lviv, Vozniak was free but penniless, as Ukrainian academics

---

[18] Mykhailo Vozniak, *Psevdo-Konys'kyi i Psevdo-Poletyka* (Istoriia Rusov *u literaturi ta nautsi*) (Lviv and Kyiv, 1939).

were barred from taking positions in Polish universities. He remained
unemployed throughout the interwar period.[19]

In the late 1930s inhabitants of Lviv often had occasion to observe the
"smallish, lean, somewhat slanted figure" of a gentleman in his late fifties
"walking quickly, almost running, down the street, waving his arm and
sometimes muttering something." Occasionally he would raise his voice,
and then passersby would hear the names of his enemies, whom he
occasionally cursed along with the Polish authorities – the objects of his
particular loathing. The man's name was Mykhailo Vozniak. His
grudges against the Polish authorities were closely related to the ethnic
antagonism that ravaged the eastern provinces of Poland during the
interwar period. Vozniak's academic activities ignored the political
borders that divided Ukraine in the first half of the twentieth century.
The content of his monograph *Pseudo-Konysky and Pseudo-Poletyka*,
which dealt with the history of "Russian Ukraine," was the best proof
of that.[20]

The title of Vozniak's book shows immediately that he rejected earlier
hypotheses about the authorship of either Heorhii Konysky or the
Poletykas, father and son. Vozniak was absolutely convinced, and did
his best to convince his readers, that the true author of the *History of the
Rus'* was none other than the eighteenth-century chancellor of the
Russian Empire, Oleksandr Bezborodko. Vozniak claimed that the
inspiration for his study came not from Slabchenko's book of 1925 or
Yakovliv's article of 1937 but from his reading of Vladimir Ikonnikov's
study of Russian historiography. He had read it in 1920, when he
was completing his *History of Ukrainian Literature*, and was struck by
Ikonnikov's observation concerning textual parallels between the *Brief
Chronicle of Little Russia*, issued by Vasyl Ruban in St. Petersburg
in 1777, and the *History of the Rus'*. Vozniak thought about a possible
connection between Bezborodko and the *History of the Rus'*, but at that
time he could not gain access to the text of the *Brief Chronicle*, which
was nowhere to be found in Polish libraries. He moved on to other
subjects, leaving his conjectures in abeyance. It was Slabchenko's book of
1925 that prompted Vozniak to resume his search for the *Brief Chronicle*.

[19] Mykhailo Vozniak, *Istoriia ukraïns'koi literatury*, 3 vols. (Lviv, 1920–24). On Vozniak's life and
work, see Mykhailo Nechytaliuk *et al.*, *"Chest' pratsi!" Akademik Mykhailo Vozniak u spohadakh ta
publikatsiiakh* (Lviv, 2000), pp. 9–178.
[20] Volodymyr Doroshenko, "Akademik Mykhailo Vozniak," in Nechytaliuk *et al.*, *"Chest' pratsi!"*,
pp. 365–83, here 365.

He finally managed to obtain it through the interlibrary loan service that was still functioning between Poland and the USSR in the later 1930s.[21]

A significant part of Vozniak's book was devoted to a critique of the Poletyka hypothesis. But it was Vozniak's comparison of the *History of the Rus'* with Ruban's *Brief Chronicle* that constituted the core of his argument. Vozniak indicated numerous structural parallels between the *History of the Rus'* and the part of the Ruban chronicle sent to him by Konysky. In the chronicle's statement that King Casimir IV of Poland had "made all the officials and courtiers of that Little Russian nation equal in honor and liberty with Polish servitors and nobles and confirmed this with an oath to their successors," Vozniak found the origins of what he characterized as the main idea of the *History of the Rus'* – the equality of the Ruthenian and Cossack elites with their Polish and Russian counterparts. But his attention was focused mainly on the parts of the chronicle written by Bezborodko, which covered slightly more than forty years of the history of the Cossack lands, from 1734 to 1776. There Vozniak found not only structural parallels but also textual borrowings, significantly increasing the number of similarities known to Slabchenko. For anyone reading Vozniak's book, there was no remaining doubt that the two texts were indeed related. It was also clear that the part of the chronicle written by Bezborodko was closer to the *History* than the portion supplied to Ruban by Konysky. But did this mean that it was Bezborodko who had written the *History*?[22]

Mykhailo Vozniak believed that it was. The scholar strengthened his case by bringing in as additional evidence Bezborodko's letters to his father. The first letter dated from August 1776. Writing from Tsarskoe Selo near St. Petersburg, the young Bezborodko asked his father to send him two chronicles, hetmans' articles, and the Magdeburg Statute. "For all these books are all the more necessary here because there are people who intend to publish a history of Little Russia and print a translation of the statute," wrote Oleksandr Bezborodko. The second letter, dated March 31, 1778, accompanied a copy of Ruban's *Brief Chronicle* that Bezborodko sent to his father. There the young Bezborodko referred to himself as the author of the final section of the chronicle, noting that its earlier part (presumably a reference to the *Brief Description of Little Russia*, which ended in 1734 and was supplied by Konysky) was full of inaccuracies. "This small composition," wrote Bezborodko about Ruban's publication, "now serves as a guide to our intended publication of a complete history of Little Russia, in which, of course, all the inaccuracies of the

---

[21] Vozniak, *Psevdo-Konys'kyi,* p. 137.   [22] *Ibid.,* p. 141–48.

chronicle will be corrected as soon as we manage to collect all the information we need." Bezborodko had begun working on that new compendium of Ukrainian history, "engaging in this work, which is pleasant to me, when I am free from other matters." He treated his history project as "a manifestation of my unalloyed zeal for my fellow citizens."[23]

Vozniak regarded these letters, first brought to the attention of scholars of the *History* by Pavlo Klepatsky, as an important piece of evidence that had remained unknown to Slabchenko. He believed that at the time Bezborodko wrote the second letter, he had been working on the *History of the Rus'* itself. Advancing his Bezborodko theory, Vozniak established a textual connection between the *History* and the political demands of the Chernihiv nobility in the second half of the eighteenth century. He found additional support for his hypothesis in certain elements of Bezborodko's life and career. The anonymous author of the *History of the Rus'* evinced a benevolent attitude toward Count Petr Rumiantsev, Bezborodko's own protégé, which was one biographical argument in favor of Vozniak's hypothesis. Another was the author's negative treatment of the imperial official Grigorii Teplov, whom Bezborodko had also disliked. Finally, the anonymous author's familiarity with the Chernihiv region, Bezborodko's homeland, was regarded by Vozniak as additional proof of Oleksandr Bezborodko's authorship and disqualification of the Poletykas, natives of the Poltava region. Vozniak also pointed out that Bezborodko had favored the restoration of Cossack military formations after the abolition of the Hetmanate and remained a patriot of his homeland until the end of his life.[24]

According to Vozniak, Oleksandr Bezborodko had written the *History of the Rus'*, possibly with assistance from Ruban, in 1778. Given the political restrictions imposed on Bezborodko by his spectacular career at court, the work could not be published at the time. It was allegedly preserved among Bezborodko's family papers and eventually discovered in the library of his brother, Ilia. The latter died in 1816, two years before the appearance of the first dated manuscript of the *History* known to scholars. It was on Ilia Bezborodko's former estate of Hryniv (Grinevo) near Starodub that one of the first known copies of the *History* was found. Discovered in Bezborodko's library, it was delivered to General Stepan Shyrai, a relative of Ilia Bezborodko's wife, who began to disseminate the manuscript after the Hryniv discovery of 1828. All these facts fitted

[23] *Ibid.*, pp. 137–38.   [24] *Ibid.*, pp. 146–52.

together neatly in Vozniak's scheme, leaving him convinced that it was indeed Bezborodko who had written the enigmatic manuscript. The Cossack prince had turned out to be a true Cossack after all.[25]

Vozniak's argument closely paralleled the dominant trend in Ukrainian historiography of the time. Vozniak's fellow historian and believer in Bezborodko's authorship, Andrii Yakovliv, and a score of Mykhailo Hrushevsky's students in Lviv all belonged to the "statist" trend in Ukrainian historical writing. The "statists" emerged on the ruins of the populist school immediately after the defeat of the Ukrainian Revolution. They dismissed the populism of the previous generation of Ukrainian intellectuals, blamed it for the defeat of the Ukrainian cause, and adopted as their goal the rehabilitation of the role of the state and elites in Ukrainian history. Vozniak's book returned to Ukraine one of its forgotten sons whom the populist historians had condemned as yet another aristocratic traitor to his homeland. It now turned out – or so it seemed at the time – that Bezborodko was not only a Ukrainian patriot but also a leading figure of the modern Ukrainian national revival. Elites were reclaiming a leading role in Ukrainian history.[26]

Mykhailo Vozniak published his monograph on the *History of the Rus'* before the outbreak of the Second World War and the fall of the Polish state in September 1939. The book listed as its place of publication not only Lviv, where it was in fact published, but also Kyiv, which was still on the other, Soviet, side of the Polish–Soviet border. This was a reflection of Ukrainian intellectuals' belief in the unity of Ukrainian lands. To be sure, they did not expect that unification would come so soon, or that it would be brought about by none other than Joseph Stalin. On September 17, 1939, two Red Army formations consisting of more than half a million soldiers crossed the eastern border of the Polish Republic and started their advance deep into its territory. The propaganda addressed to the "liberated" population of Western Ukraine claimed that the Soviets wanted to restore the unity of the long-suffering Ukrainian nation by consolidating all its lands in a single state. In proclaiming the unification of the Ukrainian lands as their primary goal, the Soviet propagandists took a page from the book of the Ukrainian national movement.[27]

[25] *Ibid.*, pp. 152–59.
[26] On the "statist school" in Ukrainian historiography, see Jaroslaw Pelenski, ed., *The Political and Social Ideas of Vjačeslav Lypyns'kyj* [=*Harvard Ukrainian Studies* 9, nos. 3/4 (1985)]; Plokhy, *Unmaking Imperial Russia*, pp. 330–32, 524–25.
[27] On the Soviet takeover of Western Ukraine, see Jan T. Gross, *Revolution from Abroad: The Soviet Conquest of Poland's Western Ukraine and Western Belorussia* (Princeton, N.J., 2002).

Like many other Ukrainian intellectuals, Mykhailo Vozniak had little
to lose from the end of Polish rule and, as it appeared for some time,
much to gain from the arrival of the Soviets. A somewhat eccentric man
who had been heard loudly complaining on the streets of Lviv about
Polish policies toward Ukrainians long before the Red Army crossed the
Soviet–Polish border, Vozniak was now appointed head of the department of Ukrainian literature at the University of Lviv. He was also
reinstated as a full member of the Ukrainian Academy of Sciences and
elected on the Communist Party list to the Supreme Soviet of the
Ukrainian Soviet Socialist Republic. His involvement in the Austrian-
sponsored Union for the Liberation of Ukraine during the First World
War was overlooked, if not entirely forgotten, by the new authorities. At
the same time, ironically enough, Mykhailo Slabchenko was still in exile,
having been found guilty of participation in a bogus political organization
whose name was "borrowed" by Stalin's secret police from the real Union
for the Liberation of Ukraine, to which Vozniak had belonged. While
Slabchenko was persecuted, Vozniak was elevated to the pinnacle of the
Soviet academic establishment. The fate of the two scholars, who shared
the same view of the *History of the Rus'* and its authorship, could hardly
have been more different.[28]

Mykhailo Vozniak's privileged status came to an abrupt end in June
1941, when Germany attacked the Soviet Union and took over Lviv.
Vozniak was now heard complaining about the policies of the Nazis.
He miraculously survived the years of German occupation. When the
Soviets came back in the summer of 1944, Vozniak, unlike many of his
Ukrainian colleagues, declined to emigrate to the West and stayed in Lviv.
He had been unemployed during the German occupation and believed
that he had no reason to fear the return of the Red Army. He was wrong.
With the war over and the Stalin regime anxious to establish full
ideological control over the recently incorporated western borderlands,
Vozniak found himself, along with other Ukrainian scholars, among the
targets of a state-sponsored campaign against "Ukrainian bourgeois
nationalism." He was accused of promoting nationalist ideas attributed
to Mykhailo Hrushevsky. In November 1946 Mykola Bazhan, one of the
foremost Soviet Ukrainian poets of the era, published an attack on Lviv
historians and literary scholars in the leading newspaper *Radians'ka
Ukraïna* (Soviet Ukraine). He accused them of continuing Hrushevsky's
traditions. According to Bazhan, Vozniak's three-volume history of

---

[28] Doroshenko, "Akademik Mykhailo Vozniak."

Ukrainian literature was "also constructed according to Hrushevsky's historical scheme."[29]

The twenty years that had passed between the fall of 1946, when the Soviet authorities launched a major attack on Hrushevsky's students and followers in Lviv, and the fall of 1926, when they had allowed a lavish celebration of his birthday at Kyiv University, saw a major change in the official attitude toward Ukrainian scholarship. The celebration, which resulted in the publication of the festschrift to which Vozniak contributed along with Mykhailo Slabchenko and Pavlo Klepatsky, took place at the height of the Ukrainization policy, intended to stabilize the regime in the rebellious Ukrainian borderlands and engage the local intelligentsia in socialist construction. That policy came to an end during the Ukrainian Famine of 1932–33, when the authorities blamed peasant resistance to the forced collectivization of agriculture on the nationalist activities of the Ukrainian intelligentsia. The man-made famine resulted in close to four million deaths. This about-face in party policy unleashed the persecution of Ukrainian cadres, causing some of the leading political figures and writers, including Ukraine's leading national Bolshevik, Mykola Skrypnyk, and the prominent writer and publicist Mykola Khvyliovy to commit suicide. Tens of thousands of others were arrested and sent to the Gulag.[30]

Many of those arrested were accused of sharing and disseminating Hrushevsky's views. When the party unleashed its secret police on the Ukrainian intelligentsia in the spring of 1933, Hrushevsky was no longer in Ukraine. He was arrested in the spring of 1931, then released and exiled to Moscow. He would be allowed to continue his academic work but not to return to Ukraine or publish his research there. Hrushevsky's last articles, written in Russian and published in Moscow, dealt with Cossack historiography. One of them, which appeared posthumously, dealt directly with the *History of the Rus'* and its links with West European historiography. Hrushevsky died under suspicious circumstances in southern Russia in the fall of 1934. The last volume of his unfinished *History of Ukraine-Rus'* was published by his daughter, Kateryna, in 1936. A few years later Kateryna would be arrested and sent to the Gulag. The same fate befell Hrushevsky's younger brother, Oleksandr, the author of prerevolutionary articles on the *History of the Rus'*,

---

[29] Nechytaliuk, "*Chest' pratsi!*" pp. 54–63.
[30] On the connection between the Great Famine and changes in the Ukrainization program, see Martin, *Affirmative Action Empire*, pp. 236–60.

and his nephew Serhii Shamrai. None of them returned from imprisonment and exile. The name "Hrushevsky" became a symbol of Ukrainian
nationalism, which the Soviet regime was now sworn to overcome. The
ranks of historians in Soviet Ukraine were purged in the 1930s. The turn
of Western Ukraine came in 1946.[31]

Mykhailo Vozniak survived the ideological attacks on him and his
scholarship almost unscarred. Although a target of numerous ideological
campaigns (in 1952 he was accused of contradicting the teachings of Stalin
himself), Vozniak managed to keep his job, membership in the Academy
of Sciences, and the right to train a new generation of scholars. When
Vozniak died in November 1954, the regime gave this former supporter of
the Austrian-sponsored Union for the Liberation of Ukraine a princely
funeral. Downtown traffic was halted, and hundreds of mourners, including students of the University of Lviv, solemnly moved through the
streets of the city, which in Vozniak's lifetime was known successively
as Austrian and German Lemberg, Polish Lwów, Ukrainian Lviv, and
Russian Lvov. Twenty years earlier, in the fall of 1934, the Soviet authorities had given a lavish funeral to their other leading intellectual opponent, Mykhailo Hrushevsky. He was buried at the prestigious Baikove
Cemetery in Kyiv in the presence of Communist Party officials and
academic brass.[32]

Little appeared to have changed in the Soviet Union since Stalin's
death in March 1953: scholars persecuted by the state were still getting
state funerals. But once each funeral was over, the published works of
the deceased scholar would be removed from bookstores and libraries.
That was the fate that befell all of Hrushevsky's writings and those of
Vozniak's works that were written before the Soviets took control of
Lviv: they were deemed nationalist and therefore consigned to restricted
sections of Soviet libraries, where they would be accessible only to a
limited number of scholars. Among the prohibited books was his work
on the *History of the Rus'*, whose listing of Lviv and Kyiv as places of
publication presaged the Soviet takeover of Western Ukraine in 1939–41.

---

[31] Mykhailo Hrushevs'kyi, "Z istorychnoï fabulistyky kintsia XVIII st.," repr. in *Ukraïns'kyi istoryk* (New York and Toronto) (1991–92): 125–29. On the fate of Hrushevsky and his family, see Plokhy, *Unmaking Imperial Russia*, pp. 264–80, 382–414. On the Soviet campaign against Hrushevsky's students in Galicia, see Iaroslav Dashkevych, "Borot'ba z Hrushevs'kym ta ioho shkoloiu u L'vivs'-komu universyteti za radians'kykh chasiv," in *Mykhailo Hrushevs'kyi i ukraïns'ka istorychna nauka*, ed. Iaroslav Hrytsak and Iaroslav Dashkevych (Lviv, 1999), pp. 226–68.

[32] Nechytaliuk, "*Chest' pratsi!*" pp. 9–90; Doroshenko, "Akademik Mykhailo Vozniak," *ibid.*, pp. 362–71; Plokhy, *Unmaking Imperial Russia*, pp. 275–80.

With the war over and the western Ukrainian lands reannexed to the Ukrainian SSR, any scholar making reference to Vozniak's publication of 1939 would be deemed unreliable by the authorities. The secrets of the *History of the Rus'*, previously revealed by Slabchenko, Klepatsky, Yakovliv, and Vozniak, would now be protected by the power of the Soviet state.

CHAPTER 6

The Kyiv manuscript

On November 7, 1943, the twenty-sixth anniversary of the Bolshevik Revolution of 1917, Soviet radio broadcast an address by Joseph Stalin to the people of the USSR. "The day is not far off when we will completely liberate Ukraine and White Russia, as well as the Leningrad and Kalinin regions, from the enemy," declared the Soviet leader. The audience was already prepared for the good news. "A few hours earlier Stalin had announced the year's richest victory: the recapture of Kiev," wrote *Time* magazine in its issue of November 15. "Moscow's walls echoed the jubilant salvos of 324 guns, the pealing of the Kremlin's bells, the happy tumult of the crowds." After the defeats of 1941–42, the Red Army had reversed the course of the war and was recapturing lost territory. The attack on Kyiv began on November 3, 1943, with the bombardment of German positions on the left bank of the Dnieper. On November 5 the tanks of General Pavlo Rybalko, a native of the Lebedyn district in the former Hetmanate, rolled into the city. The enemy was on the run, desperate to avoid being surrounded. The following day the liberation of Kyiv was complete.[1]

As the Red Army secured its control of the Ukrainian capital and the soldiers of the First Ukrainian Front advanced westward, troops of the People's Commissariat of the Interior, the dreaded NKVD, moved into the city to hunt down saboteurs, root out German spies, and punish those who had collaborated with the enemy. A small group of NKVD officers rushed to building no. 2 on one of Kyiv's most picturesque streets, Andriivskyi uzviz (St. Andrew's Descent). Their target was apartment 42, occupied until recently by the Nazi-era mayor of Kyiv, Oleksander Ohloblyn. The team consisted of archivists whose task was to secure

[1] "World Battlefronts: The Battle of Russia: The Ousting is at Hand," *Time*, November 15, 1943. On the battle for Kyiv, see Ernest Ledderey, *Germany's Defeat in the East: The Soviet Armies at War, 1941–1945* (London, 1955).

documents and archival materials abandoned by the Germans. Some of them had known Ohloblyn personally: before the outbreak of the war, he had been a professor of history at Kyiv University. In Ohloblyn's apartment the NKVD team found an abundance of papers, some lying on the floor and others in desk drawers. The archivists collected everything they could get their hands on. They felt themselves lucky: loose paper was a prized commodity in the cold city, and Ohloblyn's papers might easily have been snatched up by his former neighbors to heat their apartments.

Probably the most valuable portion of the NKVD loot came from a hiding place between the wall and a bookshelf, where the archivists found some of Ohloblyn's correspondence and the typescript of a long essay on Ukrainian historiography. Fedir Shevchenko, a young Soviet archivist and a member of the NKVD team, later remembered that the manuscript constituted the results of Ohloblyn's work on the *History of the Rus'*. Along with Ohloblyn's other papers, it was deposited in the NKVD archives. It also made a strong impact on Shevchenko, who already had in his library the Bodiansky edition of the *History of the Rus'*. In 1966, more than twenty years after his Kyiv find, he published an article on the *History of the Rus'* that helped bring the work back to the attention of Soviet historians. He was reluctant, however, to publicly recall his long-distance encounter with Ohloblyn and his manuscripts until the fall of communism.[2]

Who was Oleksander Ohloblyn, why he was interested in the *History of the Rus'*, and why was the NKVD interested in him? Born Oleksandr Petrovych Mizko in Kyiv in 1899, Ohloblyn was raised largely by his maternal grandmother, a descendant of a prominent Cossack family. In the revolutionary year of 1917, Ohloblyn enrolled at the University in Kyiv. His studies were cut short in 1919, and he began his teaching career in educational institutions created by the Bolshevik regime. He amazed his peers with his ambition and his knowledge of history as he sought to acquire through self-education and independent research what he had not had time to learn at the university. Ohloblyn's fascination with the history of economic and social relations was coupled with an interest in Ukraine and things Ukrainian. In academia, the young Ohloblyn found himself in

[2] Ihor Verba, "Zi spohadiv Fedora Pavlovycha Shevchenka pro Oleksandra Ohloblyna ta Nataliu Polons'ku-Vasylenko," in *Istynu vstanovliuie sud istoriï. Zbirnyk na poshanu Fedora Pavlovycha Shevchenka*, ed. Svitlana Baturina *et al.*, 2 vols. (Kyiv, 2001), I: 138–40; Fedir Shevchenko, "Istoriia Rusov ili Maloi Rossii: do 120-richchia z chasu vydannia tvoru," *Ukraïns'kyi istorychnyi zhurnal*, no. 7 (1966): 146–49; Svitlana Baturina, "Biblioteka F. P. Shevchenka iak dzherelo do rekonstruktsiï naukovoho svitohliadu vchenoho," in *Istynu vstanovliuie sud istoriï*, II: 55–63.

the same camp as Mykhailo Slabchenko, another believer in a communist Ukraine, and at odds with the older generation of Ukrainian historians led by Mykhailo Hrushevsky. Neither group was fully trusted by the authorities. In 1930 Ohloblyn was arrested and briefly imprisoned; subsequently he was forced to renounce his deceased mentor at Kyiv University, the prominent historian Mytrofan Dovnar-Zapolsky. The 1930s were anything but a happy time in Ohloblyn's life, but with the outbreak of the Second World War he found himself back in favor with the authorities. Along with other Soviet Ukrainian historians, Ohloblyn was entrusted with the Sovietization of historiography in Western Ukraine, which had just been annexed to the Ukrainian SSR. By this time, however, any illusions Ohloblyn may have had about Soviet rule were gone.

After the German invasion of the USSR on June 22, 1941, Ohloblyn's true attitude to the Soviet regime became apparent. In September 1941, when Kyiv was besieged by the Germans and many of his superiors, colleagues, and students at the Academy of Sciences' Institute of History fled, Ohloblyn decided to stay in the city. The capital of Ukraine fell to the Germans on September 19. Two days later, in a most unexpected turn of events, the forty-two-year-old Oleksander Ohloblyn was appointed mayor of the occupied city. He was persuaded to take the post by a faction of the Organization of Ukrainian Nationalists (OUN), a Western Ukraine-based radical political group that had closely associated itself with Nazi Germany in hopes of attaining Ukrainian independence. OUN members convinced Ohloblyn to take on the job by promising that he would be able to Ukrainize the city's public and cultural life. The nationalists needed a person who could command respect from both the Germans and the Kyivans. The occupation authorities appointed Ohloblyn to his new post on September 21. Fairly soon all parties realized that they had made a mistake. Although Ohloblyn did much to promote a Ukrainian cultural revival in the city, he had little influence on developments under the German occupation. The Germans, for their part, considered Ohloblyn a poor administrator who was interfering in matters that they considered their own prerogative. Ohloblyn submitted his resignation on October 25, barely a month after taking office.[3]

---

[3] On Ohloblyn's life and career, see Liubomyr Vynar (Lubomyr Wynar), *Oleksander Petrovych Ohloblyn 1899–1992: Biohrafichna studiia* (New York, 1994); Ihor Verba, *Oleksandr Ohloblyn. Zhyttia i pratsia v Ukraïni* (Kyiv, 1999); *Oleksander Miz'ko-Ohloblyn: doslidzhennia ta materialy. Do 100-richchia z dnia narodzhennia istoryka*, ed. Liubomyr Vynar (New York, Ostrih, Kyiv, and Toronto, 2000).

Ohloblyn's brief term as mayor witnessed the single most horrendous massacre of Jews during the Holocaust. On September 24, three days after he took office, powerful blasts shook central Kyiv: the building where the Germans had established their principal offices was blown up by bombs planted there by the NKVD before the Soviet surrender of the city. "The Germans had a clear ideological line to follow," writes Timothy Snyder about the events of September 1941 in Kyiv. "If the NKVD was guilty, the Jews must be blamed." On September 29 and 30, German SS, SD, and military police units, with the assistance of local police, massacred more than thirty-three thousand of the city's Jews in a ravine on the outskirts of Kyiv known as Babyn Yar. The decision to execute the Jews was made by the military governor of the city, Major General Friedrich Eberhardt. Ohloblyn later claimed that he had nothing to do with the massacre. Indeed, the decision was not his to make, and he could hardly have done anything to prevent it. But the massacre could not have occurred without cooperation on the part of the city authorities. We do not know what Ohloblyn knew or thought about the human tragedy unfolding before his eyes. It is known, however, that on one occasion at least the mayor tried to intervene with General Eberhardt on behalf of a Jewish woman whose family he had known before the war. The woman survived the Holocaust and later recalled: "Ohloblyn left the commandant's office looking very disturbed and pale. As it turned out, the commandant indicated to him that the Jewish question was subject to the exclusive authority of the Germans, and they would decide it as they pleased."[4]

It is safe to assume that, having spent a tumultuous and extremely tragic month of his native city's history at the top of its civil administration, Ohloblyn was glad to resign. He was lucky to leave the mayor's office when he did. His deputy and successor, Volodymyr Bahazii, was arrested by the Germans and executed along with other members of the OUN in February 1942 in the same Babyn Yar ravine where tens of thousands of Jews had been gunned down a few months earlier. In the course of the German occupation of the city, close to a hundred thousand people – Jews, Gypsies, Soviet prisoners of war, Ukrainian nationalists, hostages taken by the Nazis from the local population in retaliation for partisan attacks, and patients of a nearby psychiatric hospital – were executed on the slopes of Babyn Yar. The Germans decided to starve those who remained in the city, driving the survivors into the countryside,

---

[4] Victoria Khiterer, "Babi Yar: The Tragedy of Kiev's Jews," *Brandeis Graduate Journal*, no. 2 (2004): 1–16; Timothy Snyder, *Bloodlands: Europe between Hitler and Stalin* (New York, 2010), pp. 201–4.

where they would feed themselves and help feed the German Army. After a short stint as a city administrator, Ohloblyn found refuge from the realities of the terror-ridden and starving city in his academic work. He presided over a number of German-approved historical projects, often of questionable academic value, but it was the *History of the Rus'* that became his true passion. The mysterious manuscript remained at the top of Ohloblyn's agenda throughout the Nazi occupation of Kyiv.[5]

What drove Ohloblyn's interest in the *History*? He began his research on the *History of the Rus'* in the late 1930s, when, during the first years of the Second World War, the regime allowed a temporary resumption of Ukrainian historical studies to legitimize its annexation of territories acquired as a result of the Molotov–Ribbentrop Pact. By the outbreak of the German–Soviet war in June 1941, Ohloblyn had already done enough work on the *History* to present the results of his research to the academic community. No place was more appropriate for that purpose, and no audience more responsive, than that of the city of Lviv. Ohloblyn spent the first days of June 1941 there, delivering a paper whose title went to the core of the generations-old controversy, "On the Question of the Author of the *History of the Rus'*." Ohloblyn was prepared to pose a question that had not been asked before. He was interested not only in the ideology of the author and in the time period when the *History* might have been written but also in the place where it could have been composed. To the questions who, why, and when, he added a new one: where?[6]

Ohloblyn became the first scholar to consider the text from the perspective of historical geography. In his study of the *History*, completed in Kyiv in 1942 (this was probably the manuscript secured by the NKVD team a year later), he explained his method as follows: "Here one must take account of two factors, first, which locale prevails in the consciousness of the author; which one interests him personally, so to speak; second, how well does he know this locale; how precisely in detail, and not in his overall conception, does he make provision for various local features (events, geographic names, names of local activists and the like)."[7] Natalia Polonska-Vasylenko, Ohloblyn's close friend during the years of the

---

[5] "Iz svidetel'stva I. Minkinoi-Egorychevoi o ee spasenii sviashchennikom Alekseem Glagolevym v Kieve," *Kholokost* http://holocaust.ioso.ru/documents/10doc.htm.

[6] Verba, *Oleksandr Ohloblyn*, p. 319; V. A. Smolii, O. A. Putro, and I. V. Verba, "Slovo do chytacha. Pro zhyttia i naukovu diial'nist' profesora O. P. Ohloblyna," in O. P. Ohloblyn, *Do pytannia pro avtora "Istoriï Rusov"* (Kyiv, 1998), pp. 3–15, here 11.

[7] Ohloblyn, *Do pytannia pro avtora*, pp. 35–36.

German occupation of Kyiv, was astonished by the precision with which Ohloblyn scrutinized the text of the *History*. "Progressively, step by step, page by page he studied ... the toponyms with which the text is replete. Oleksandr Petrovych [Ohloblyn] knows the Siverian region well, and that gave him the opportunity, probably unavailable to any other scholar, to compare these toponyms with those of the present day – and this analysis has yielded brilliant results: villages, rivers, woods, all these correspond to current names."[8]

The "Siverian region," an area around Novhorod-Siverskyi, a small town in the northeastern corner of today's Ukraine, a mere 45 kilometers from the Russian border, had a special place in Ohloblyn's heart. His mother's family came from the Siverian region, and as a child Ohloblyn often stayed in the area, visiting his maternal grandmother, who came from the prominent local noble family of the Lashkevyches. When Ohloblyn began his systematic study of the *History*, he could hardly fail to notice that a preponderant number of geographic names mentioned in the text were intimately familiar to him from his childhood. The map of Ukrainian history, as presented in the *History of the Rus'*, did indeed tilt heavily toward the northwestern region of the Hetmanate, and the town of Novhorod-Siverskyi was at the center of that map. Ohloblyn was fascinated to observe how the seemingly unlimited imagination of the author of the *History*, amply demonstrated in his descriptions of events of the deep past, for which he had few if any historical sources, worked hand in hand with his knowledge of Siverian topography.

Especially interesting in that regard were the largely fantastic details of the siege of Novhorod-Siverskyi by the "Polish" army of the first False Dmitrii in 1604 – a remote period from the perspective of the anonymous author. The author of the *History* wrote that the Poles, "drawing nearer to Novhorod-Siverskyi, established their camp by Solene Ozero, at the head of deep and extensive ditches, overgrown with trees, that had once been filled with water and encircled Novhorod. The first of them was called the Ladeina landing ... and the left one was called the Yaroslav Stream, since it flowed into the Yaroslav Hills." "All these names were also in use in Novhorod-Siverskyi in the eighteenth and nineteenth centuries," concluded Ohloblyn after quoting this extract in his work. He was also able to indicate other passages of the *History* in which its author betrayed familiarity with the topography of Novhorod-Siverskyi and its environs.

---

[8] Nataliia Polons'ka-Vasylenko, "Oleksandr Petrovych Ohloblyn v ochakh suchasnytsi," in *Oleksander Miz'ko-Ohloblyn*, pp. 60–65; Verba, *Oleksandr Ohloblyn*, p. 263.

There was no doubt in Ohloblyn's mind that the author came either from Novhorod-Siverskyi itself or from the vicinity.[9]

True to his research method, Ohloblyn took notice of another of the author's proclivities that gave away his affinity with northwestern Ukraine. He apparently had no qualms about using local Novhorod-Siverskyi family names in describing episodes that he invented, or about placing people with local surnames at the center of actual historical events. Ohloblyn noted that one Novhorod-Siverskyi family, the Khudorbas, was especially close to the heart of the author of the *History*. Of all Novhorod-Siverskyi families, this was the one mentioned most frequently in the *History of the Rus'*. The reader first meets them in 1648, at the dawn of the Hetmanate. On the orders of Bohdan Khmelnytsky, the main protagonist of Cossack historical literature, Colonel Kindrat Khudorba (Khudorbai) leads his regiment into Siveria. Not only does he play an important part in the Khmelnytsky Uprising, but he also performs a most sacred task – the liberation of what appears to be the author's little homeland from the Polish yoke. A certain Colonel Khudorba saved part of the Cossack army from imminent defeat in 1655. Five years later he led the Uman regiment into Siveria, where, along with other colonels, he drove the Polish army out of Kyiv, Chernihiv, Novhorod-Siverskyi, and Starodub. The Khudorbas are last mentioned in the *History* under the year 1708, when the Novhorod-Siverskyi flag-bearer Pavlo Khudorba appears before Tsar Peter I in the village of Pohrebky to let him know that the local Cossacks are prepared to surrender that settlement, which had earlier been captured by the Swedes.

Ohloblyn believed that all four episodes involving the heroic Khudorbas were little more than inventions of the anonymous author, but he was excited to learn that there had actually been a Khudorba family in the Novhorod-Siverskyi region. He found information about numerous Khudorbas living in the area in the eighteenth and early nineteenth centuries. The most prominent of them, Arkhyp Khudorba, attained the rank of captain in the Starodub regiment in the late 1770s. Neither rich nor very prominent in the Cossack ranks, the Khudorbas claimed, and were granted, Russian nobility on the basis of a genealogy that began with a very real person, Mykhailo Kindratovych Khudorba. The *History* appears to have extended the Khudorba family tree back to the seventeenth century, providing Mykhailo Khudorba with a father – none other than a colonel who served under Khmelnytsky and liberated Siveria from the

---

[9] Ohloblyn, *Do pytannia pro avtora*, p. 41; cf. *Istoriia Rusov*, p. 43.

Poles, not once but twice in the course of his distinguished service in the Cossack Host. Ohloblyn discovered that the historical Khudorbas had lived in the village of Koman on the outskirts of Novhorod-Siverskyi and had owned lands next to the village of Pohrebky, which is mentioned in the *History*.

This was followed by a sensational development: Ohloblyn was able to make an all-important connection between the Khudorbas and the first known appearance of the text of the *History*. A member of the Khudorba family was mentioned in a letter from the first known "discoverer" of the manuscript, Colonel Aleksandr von Brigen. Reporting to Kondratii Ryleev in October 1825 that he had located the manuscript of the *History of the Rus'*, von Brigen added: "I shall make an effort to supply you with as much material about Little Russian history as possible; I intend to obtain such a history written by Khudorba, a contemporary of Konysky; it is unknown, for there is only one copy of it in the house where Khudorba lived. This history is valued here equally with Konysky's history; it is criticized only for being written very freely and against our government. Upon receiving it, I shall have two copies made, one for you and the other for myself." Von Brigen's letter was published prior to the First World War, but no one before Ohloblyn made the connection between von Brigen's Khudorba the historian and the Khudorba warrior clan of the *History of the Rus'*, to say nothing of the Khudorbas of Koman.[10]

But what exactly was the significance of that connection? At first, Ohloblyn was not entirely sure. He wondered whether the Konysky *History* that von Brigen obtained for Ryleev was indeed the *History of the Rus'*, published in 1846 by Osyp Bodiansky. In Ohloblyn's opinion, the question required further research, but he was provisionally prepared to treat the *History* and the unknown text by Khudorba as separate works. He did not exclude the possibility that the author of the *History* might have known Khudorba's manuscript (Ohloblyn would later espouse that view much more explicitly), but he was already convinced that the author was not Khudorba. Ohloblyn had a different candidate for the authorship. Who was he? Ohloblyn believed that the author, like Khudorba, was associated with the village of Koman. He was descended not from a simple Cossack officer family but from the Cossack elite, and his ancestors included the seventeenth-century hetman of Right-Bank Ukraine. The author's surname, claimed Ohloblyn, was Khanenko. "All the threads in

[10] V. I. Maslov, *Literaturnaia deiatel'nost' K. F. Ryleeva* (Kyiv, 1912), appendix, pp. 97–98; A. F. Brigen, *Pis'ma. Istoricheskie sochineniia* (Irkutsk, 1986), pp. 376–77.

the obscure matter of the authorship of the *History of the Rus'* lead to the Khanenkos," he declared. Not only did they own most of the village of Koman in the eighteenth and early nineteenth centuries, but, according to Ohloblyn, they were linked to the Khudorbas in the pages of the *History.* "The post of colonel of Uman, which, according to the *History of the Rus'*, was occupied by a Khudorba in the 1660s," argued Ohloblyn, had actually belonged in the second half of the seventeenth century to one of the Khanenkos, to wit, the future Right-Bank hetman Mykhailo Khanenko.[11]

The Khanenkos were the third most frequently mentioned Cossack family in the text after the Khmelnytskys and Khudorbas. One of the individuals mentioned is, as one might expect, Hetman Mykhailo Khanenko, whose rule under Polish tutelage is treated with great understanding, if not outright sympathy, by the generally very anti-Polish author of the *History.* There are also two mentions of another Khanenko, an alumnus of the Kyivan Academy and general flag-bearer of the Cossack Host, Mykola Khanenko (1693–1760), who left an interesting diary. He traveled to St. Petersburg twice in the course of his long career to demand the restoration of the hetman's office. In 1723, as a member of a Cossack delegation to the imperial capital, he was imprisoned by Peter I along with Acting Hetman Pavlo Polubotok. He was later released, fought in the Russo-Ottoman War, and rose to become a member of the Cossack general staff. In 1745 he took part in another Cossack delegation to St. Petersburg that lobbied for the restoration of the hetman's office, abolished by Anna Ioannovna. This time the mission was a success. Not only were its members not arrested, but Empress Elizaveta Petrovna appointed Kyrylo Rozumovsky, the president of the imperial Academy of Sciences and the younger brother of her lover, Oleksii Rozumovsky, as hetman of Ukraine. The *History* listed Khanenko as a member of both missions. In that regard, the author did not have to invent anything.

Ohloblyn believed that the *History* could have been coauthored by Mykola Khanenko's son Vasyl, who might have had access to his father's archive. Vasyl Khanenko (*c.* 1730–after 1790) was a prominent figure in the noble society of Novhorod-Siverskyi in the second half of the eighteenth century. In 1787, during Catherine II's triumphal progress to the Crimea, he met with the empress and apparently shared memories about her husband and predecessor on the Russian throne, Peter III. What a conversation it must have been: Peter was killed as the result of a coup engineered by Catherine. Vasyl Khanenko had every reason to be

[11] Ohloblyn, *Do pytannia pro avtora*, pp. 65–72.

inconsiderate of the empress's feelings, for the assassination of Peter had effectively ended his own career. Khanenko, who served as Peter's first adjutant, was relieved of his duties immediately after the emperor's death. An alumnus of Kiel University in Germany and a high-flying courtier in St. Petersburg, Khanenko was forced to spend the rest of his life on his estate in the Novhorod-Siverskyi area. There, Ohloblyn assumed, he maintained his father's archive and followed Catherine's policies with a critical eye. Ohloblyn regarded the *History's* favorable treatment of the rule of Peter III as evidence that Vasyl Khanenko might indeed have been the author of the manuscript. But there were still many questions outstanding. Ohloblyn never gave up his belief, based partly on the writings of Mykhailo Maksymovych and Mykhailo Drahomanov, that the *History*, at least in its final form, was a product of the liberal era of Emperor Alexander I.

Ohloblyn found a solution to his dilemma by bringing yet another Khanenko into the picture. Oleksandr Khanenko, a grandson of Mykola and a nephew of Vasyl, was born *c.* 1776 and still living in 1817. He served as secretary to the Russian ambassador in London in the early nineteenth century, the period of Alexander's liberal experiments; was personally acquainted with Russia's leading reformer of the time, Mikhail Speransky; and left government service in 1817, as Ohloblyn assumed, in connection with Speransky's fall from grace. Oleksandr Khanenko spent the rest of his days on his estates in the Surazh district (*uezd*), not too far from Novhorod-Siverskyi, where he became the custodian of the rich family archive. In Oleksandr Khanenko, Ohloblyn had found a perfect candidate for coauthorship or at least editorship of the *History*, which, according to him, summarized the life experiences, ideas, and aspirations of three generations of a leading Cossack family of the era. The Khanenko hypothesis mirrored the theory about the joint authorship of the *History* by Hryhorii and Vasyl Poletyka, and in that regard it reconciled the well-established claim that the work had been completed in or around 1768 with numerous indications that the *History* was in fact written later.[12]

As Ohloblyn completed his brief monograph on the *History of the Rus'* in German-occupied Kyiv in May 1942, he pleaded for further research. He did not know at the time that his own studies on the *History* would be cut short by developments at Stalingrad later that year. The tide of war turned against the Germans, and the prospect of an encounter with Stalin's secret police probably struck fear into Ohloblyn, who had already

[12] *Ibid.*, pp. 105–40.

experienced the hospitality of the NKVD. Caught between two opposing war machines in the fall of 1943, Kyiv and its inhabitants appeared to be doomed. Fire destroyed whole sections of the once flourishing city. "Darnytsia has been ruined and burned; Podil is burning," recalled one of the survivors. "At least half the Left Bank no longer exists. Day and night, the sky is red and smoky on that side of the Dnieper, and on this side there are clouds of dust, also resembling smoke, above the steppe roads from the constant movement of refugees. Whoever hides in order to remain here is killed by the Germans . . . As for those who manage to hide successfully, what fate awaits them under the Bolsheviks?"[13]

As a former mayor of the Nazi-occupied city, Ohloblyn had no illusions about his future under the communist regime. His path would therefore lead westward, ahead of the rapidly retreating German armies. On September 15, 1943, together with his wife and teenage son, Ohloblyn went to the Kyiv railway station to board a train for Lviv. The cultural elite of Kyiv was leaving *en masse*. It was hard to get a ticket for a westbound train and even harder to board one at the overcrowded station. Vasyl Krychevsky, Ukraine's greatest twentieth-century artist, who had designed the coat of arms of the young Ukrainian state in 1917, suffered a heart attack at the Kyiv station. When he regained consciousness on the train bringing him to the relative safety of Lviv, he was shocked to learn from family members that in the commotion following his heart attack two suitcases containing masterpieces of his, along with his wife's manuscript about early modern Ukrainian glass, had been stolen. None of these works were ever recovered.[14]

Ohloblyn was lucky. His luggage was not stolen, and his manuscripts were safe, but most of his archive, including his valuable genealogical tables of Cossack officer families, the Khanenkos and Khudorbas probably among them, had to be left in Kyiv. He moved his archive to the local Protection of the Mother of God (Pokrova) Church, which served as a depository of the Kyiv regional archives, but some of his papers remained in his apartment. The manuscript found by the NKVD archivists in November 1943 was probably the one that Ivan Krypiakevych, Ohloblyn's colleague, as well as his host and benefactor when the historian took refuge in Lviv, was eager to publish in the *Annals of the Shevchenko*

---

[13] Arkadii Liubchenko, *Shchodennyk*, ed. George Luckyj (Lviv and New York, 1999), p. 173. Cf. Valentyna Ruban-Kravchenko, *Krychevs'ki i ukraïns'ka khudozhnia kul'tura XX stolittia. Vasyl' Krychevs'kyi* (Kyiv, 2004), pp. 455–56.

[14] Ruban-Kravchenko, *Krychevs'ki i ukraïns'ka khudozhnia kul'tura*, pp. 455–58.

Scientific Society in 1942. It did not appear at the time because of the turmoil of war. Later Ohloblyn refused to publish it as written, since he changed his views on the authorship of the mysterious manuscript. When the historian left Kyiv for Lviv on September 15, 1943, he abandoned not only most of his manuscripts and book collection but also his belief that the *History* had been written by the Khanenkos.[15]

Soon after settling in Lviv, Ohloblyn gave a talk at the Shevchenko Scientific Society and published an article in the November issue of the Lviv journal *Nashi dni* (Our Days). In it he claimed that the *History* had been written not by the Khanenkos, as he believed earlier, but by another author whose name had never previously been mentioned in connection with the mysterious manuscript. The name of the new candidate was Opanas Lobysevych (1732–1805). Ohloblyn's article had an unexpected result: Mykhailo Vozniak, who had stayed in German-occupied Lviv and considered himself the foremost authority on the *History of the Rus'*, took personal offense that the Kyiv scholar had dared to attribute the *History of the Rus'* to someone other than Prince Oleksandr Bezborodko. In January 1944 Vozniak published an article in *Nashi dni* criticizing Ohloblyn's thesis. The Kyivan responded in February with an article of his own. This exchange led to a personal conflict between the two scholars. Ohloblyn's attack on Bezborodko's authorship upset Vozniak so much that soon his friends and visitors to Lviv libraries could overhear not only the old scholar's invectives against the Nazi regime but also his threats to beat up Ohloblyn. Vozniak was prepared to defend his theory with his fists. No confrontation ever took place, which was probably just as well for Vozniak, since he was eighteen years older than Ohloblyn.[16]

In 1944 Ohloblyn had successfully avoided encounters not only with Vozniak but also with the Red Army, which took the city in the summer of that year. From Lviv, Ohloblyn and other Ukrainian scholars unwilling to remain under Soviet rule went on to Prague. As the front approached, they moved farther west, and on May 8, 1945, at a railway station on the

[15] See "Lysty Ivana Kryp'iakevycha do Oleksandra Ohloblyna z 1941–1943 rr.," *Ukraïns'kyi istoryk*, nos. 1–4 (104–7) (1990): 175–77; Feodosii Steblii, "*Istoriia Rusiv* v kul'turnomu i naukovomu zhytti Halychyny," in *P'iatyi konhres Mizhnarodnoï Asotsiatsiï ukraïnistiv. Istoriia*, pt. 2 (Chernivtsi, 2004), pp. 134–44, here 142.

[16] Oleksander Ohloblyn, "Khto buv avtorom 'Istoriï Rusiv'?" *Nashi dni*, no. 11 (1943): 6–7; Mykhailo Vozniak, "I khto zh avtor Istoriï Rusiv?" *Nashi dni*, no. 1 (1944): 4–5; Ohloblyn, "Psevdo-Bezborod'ko proty Lobysevycha," *Nashi dni*, no. 2 (1944); Verba, *Oleksandr Ohloblyn*, p. 265; Smolii, Putro, and Verba, "Slovo do chytacha," p. 11; Volodymyr Doroshenko, "Akademik Mykhailo Vozniak," in Mykhailo Nechytaliuk *et al.*, "*Chest' pratsi!*" *Akademik Mykhailo Vozniak u spohadakh ta publikatsiiakh* (Lviv, 2000), p. 378.

Czech–German border, they learned that Nazi Germany had capitulated. By late May they reached Winterberg, where they turned the hall of the guesthouse into their makeshift home. Thirty-two people were housed in the hall. The youngest of them was less than a year old, while the most senior was aged seventy. The hall of the guesthouse was full of beds with straw mattresses, but in one corner there was a table built by the nineteen-year-old Dmytro Ohloblyn for his father, Oleksander. The elder Ohloblyn could hardly imagine a day without work on the subject that had become his obsession – the text of the *History of the Rus'*.[17]

Oleksandr Ohloblyn continued his research on the *History of the Rus'* while living in Displaced Persons' camps in Germany throughout the second half of the 1940s. The research he conducted at that time further strengthened his conviction that the author of the *History* was none other than Opanas Lobysevych. In 1949 he published an essay in the Paris-based journal *Ukraïna* in which he presented his arguments in favor of Lobysevych's authorship. Like Bezborodko, Lobysevych spent most of his career in St. Petersburg, and also like the grand chancellor of the empire, he was an author in his own right. But there the parallels between the two candidates end. Lobysevych never made it to the top of the imperial service. His highest post was head of the chancellery of Kyrylo Rozumovsky, the president of the Russian Academy of Sciences and the last hetman of Ukraine. In literary talent, however, he clearly surpassed the imperial chancellor. Lobysevych is widely considered a forerunner of the founder of modern Ukrainian literature, Ivan Kotliarevsky. The latter gave rise to the development of Ukrainian letters in 1798 by publishing the first volume of his *Eneïda*, a Ukrainian-language travesty of Virgil's *Aeneid*. It is believed that Lobysevych did the same, before Kotliarevsky, with Virgil's *Georgics*. The problem is that his poem, titled *Virgil's Shepherds ... Dressed in Little Russian Topcoats*, did not survive. What did survive were his translations from Latin and French.[18]

Why did Ohloblyn prefer Lobysevych as the author of the *History* not only to Bezborodko but also to the Khanenkos? A possible explanation is that Lobysevych's life and career fit the profile of the hypothetical author of the *History* better than those of any of the Khanenkos taken individually. Born in or around 1732 and deceased in 1805, Lobysevych not only lived through the last decades of the Hetmanate but was also exposed to

---

[17] Nataliia Polons'ka-Vasylenko, "Storinky spohadiv," *Ukraïns'kyi istoryk*, nos. 3–4 (7–8) (1965): 45.
[18] See Ohloblyn, "Do pytannia pro avtora Istoriï Rusiv," *Ukraïna*, no. 2 (1949): 71–75. Cf. Oleksander Ohloblyn, *Opanas Lobysevych (1732–1805)* (New York, 1966).

the enlightened ideas of St. Petersburg culture of the second half of the eighteenth century and even captured the dawn of the liberal reforms of Alexander I. Lobysevych as a candidate for the authorship of the *History* could do the job of two or even three Khanenkos. Like them, he came from the appropriate part of Ukraine. He was born to a distinguished Cossack family in the environs of Pohar (Pogar), which belonged to the Starodub regiment, not very far from Novhorod-Siverskyi. Even more important to Ohloblyn, Lobysevych began his education at the Kyivan Academy at the time when Archbishop Konysky served as its rector. In the 1790s, when Lobysevych retired from his service to Rozumovsky and lived in relative obscurity on his estates near Novhorod-Siverskyi, he wrote to Konysky, inquiring about the possibility of publishing one of archbishop's plays, the tragicomedy "The Resurrection of the Dead." Nothing came of the initiative, but the letter survived, turning Lobysevych in the eyes of future scholars into a true patriot of his Cossack fatherland, nation, and native tongue.

Lobysevych's retirement to the part of the Hetmanate where the *History* was eventually found, and interest in literature and writing made him a strong suspect and, according to Ohloblyn, a perfect candidate for the authorship of the *History*. After his retirement to Ukraine, Lobysevych became a marshal of the nobility, first of Novhorod-Siverskyi county (1783–85) and then of the Novhorod-Siverskyi vicegerency (1787–89). Those were the years when Novhorod-Siverskyi became the capital of a huge imperial province and a center of political, intellectual, and cultural life of the former Hetmanate elite. Ohloblyn was fascinated with the lives, career trajectories, and characters of the people who held office in Novhorod-Siverskyi at the time of its unexpected fame and prosperity. Most of those people belonged to old Cossack families whose members made brilliant careers in the imperial service. Ohloblyn was convinced that this milieu had produced the *History of the Rus'*, and that the *History* reflected the patriotic feelings of the town's new elite. He went so far as to declare the existence of a Novhorod-Siverskyi patriotic circle, a supposition that became Ohloblyn's mantra in his later writings but finds little support in the sources and is now almost unanimously rejected by historians who study the era.[19]

Ohloblyn's research was impressive, but few scholars were prepared to accept his hypothesis. One of the leading Ukrainian historians of the time, Dmytro Doroshenko, did not think that Ohloblyn had enough evidence

[19] Oleksander Ohloblyn, "Opanas Lobysevych," in *Liudy staroï Ukraïny* (Munich, 1959), pp. 137–49.

to prove the existence of a Novhorod-Siverskyi circle. In the same year another Ukrainian émigré historian, Illia (Elie) Borschak, published in Paris a monograph on the *History*, claiming among other things that the manuscript had been written by Vasyl Poletyka. Ohloblyn's argument also failed to persuade another scholar of the *History*, Andrii Yakovliv, who continued to defend his earlier thesis identifying Oleksandr Bezborodko as the author. Soon Ohloblyn began to have doubts of his own. The refusal of other authors to accept his hypotheses was one thing. Even more important, as Ohloblyn knew better than anyone else, too many particulars in the *History* did not match Lobysevych's biography and his particular experiences. To begin with, Lobysevych had never lived in Novhorod-Siverskyi and probably had no reason to feel any great attachment to it. He had no military experience, nor was he especially familiar with the topography of southern Ukraine – something that Ohloblyn considered essential for the author of the *History*, if one judges by his Khanenko hypothesis. In the late 1940s Ohloblyn had to bid farewell to another of his hypotheses. Lobysevych as the author of the *History* was gone.[20]

If the Khanenko hypothesis was buried in the ashes of Kyiv in 1943, the Lobysevych candidacy perished in the ruins of a Europe devastated by the Second World War. What Ohloblyn brought to the United States in 1951, aside from his manuscripts and a small library, was his continuing obsession with the text that had haunted him so long. In Ludlow, Massachusetts, Ohloblyn kept turning the pages of the *History*, shielded from the cares of everyday life by his son, who supported his father by becoming a manual laborer at one of the city's mills, and by his wife, who took on the burden of household duties. He drew a harsh lesson from his earlier "errors" and never again claimed any individual as the author of the *History*. Instead of advancing such hypotheses, he would focus his energies on studying the *History*'s sources and biographies of people who, in his opinion, had belonged to the Novhorod-Siverskyi patriotic circle and had inspired the author of the mysterious text.[21]

Ohloblyn summarized his views on the origins of the *History of the Rus'* in the introduction he wrote for the Ukrainian translation of the

---

[20] "Lysty Ivana Kryp'iakevycha do Oleksandra Ohloblyna z 1941–1943 rr.," *Ukraïns'kyi istoryk*, nos. 1–4 (104–7) (1990): 175–77; E. Borschak, *La Légende historique de l'Ukraine. Istoriia Rusov* (Paris, 1949).

[21] O. Ohloblyn, 'Where Was *Istoriya Rusov* Written?' *Annals of the Ukrainian Academy of Arts and Sciences in the U.S.* 3, no. 2 (1953): 670–95; A. Yakovliv, "*Istoriya Rusov* and Its Author," *Annals of the Ukrainian Academy of Arts and Sciences in the U.S.* 3, no. 2 (1953): 620–69; Ohloblyn, "Arkhyp Khudorba," in *Liudy staroï Ukraïny*, pp. 288–99; "Opanas Lobysevych," *ibid.*, pp. 137–49; Ohloblyn, *Opanas Lobysevych*.

book that appeared in New York in 1956. He did not advance any of his former hypotheses. Instead, he put forward three propositions concerning the origins of the text. The first had to do with the Novhorod-Siverskyi origins of the anonymous author and, possibly, the text itself. The second dealt with the period in which the text was written. Ohloblyn put it between 1802 and 1805, on the basis that the author allegedly knew some publications that had appeared in 1801 and 1802 but lacked knowledge of an important work issued in 1805. Ohloblyn argued that the *History* began to circulate in manuscript between 1822 and 1825. Finally, he claimed that the author came from the Novhorod-Siverskyi patriotic circle that allegedly existed in the 1780s and 1790s. No less intriguing was Ohloblyn's explication of the author's ideological and national assumptions, to which he referred as the "historiosophy" of the anonymous author. He believed that the work was inspired by the idea of Ukrainian statehood and built around the opposition of Ukraine and Muscovy. Ohloblyn concluded his introduction with a statement that predicted the continuing importance of the *History* in Ukrainian scholarship and political discourse: "The *History of the Rus'* as a declaration of the rights of the Ukrainian nation will remain an eternal book of Ukraine."[22]

Oleksander Ohloblyn on the one hand, and Andrii Yakovliv and Mykhailo Vozniak on the other, disagreed sharply about the authorship of the *History* but seemed to share the ideas promoted by the "statist" school of Ukrainian historiography, which searched the past for aspirations to Ukrainian statehood. That trend remained dominant in Ukrainian émigré historiography throughout the Cold War, and its adherents were prepared to regard the *History of the Rus'* as the forerunner of their own trend of thought, if not the earliest embodiment of "statism." Ohloblyn may not have solved the mystery of the authorship of the *History*, but he was determined to place that text at the service of the Ukrainian cause as it was understood in the West in the mid twentieth century. He achieved this in part by turning the descendants of the Cossack elite, whom Lazarevsky had called "the people of bygone Little Russia" and lambasted for their betrayal of the interests of the popular masses, into "the people of bygone Ukraine," and patriots to boot. Ohloblyn spent the late 1950s and early 1960s working hard on a monograph provisionally entitled "Studies on the *History of the Rus'*." He never abandoned hope of identifying the author of the mysterious text, but the goal kept eluding him. In 1964 he

---

[22] Ohloblyn, introduction to *Istoriia Rusiv*, trans. Viacheslav Davydenko (New York, 1956), pp. v–xxix.

declared: "My research on the *History of the Rus'* is not yet finished, and, what is considerably worse, it can no longer be finished. I emphasize my research, for all the sources required for a final resolution of this problem remain there in the Fatherland, where I shall never be again, as there is no time remaining for me." Ohloblyn would live another twenty-seven years. He died in February 1992, a few months after Ukraine declared independence and established a state of its own. He never published the long-promised "Studies."[23]

In 1966, two years after Ohloblyn all but gave up his research on the *History of the Rus'*, hope revived that the study of the mysterious manuscript might be resumed in Ukraine itself. That year Fedir Shevchenko, a member of the group of NKVD archivists who discovered Ohloblyn's manuscript on the *History* in his abandoned Kyiv apartment in November 1943, published an article devoted to that historiographic monument. Shevchenko's essay marked the 120th anniversary of Osyp Bodiansky's publication of the *History*. This questionable commemoration was used as a pretext to restore the *History*, marred in the eyes of the Soviet authorities by its close association with persecuted and émigré historians, as a legitimate object of study by Soviet historians and literary scholars. Shevchenko declared the author of the *History* to have been a true internationalist, a revolutionary noble, and a historian who appreciated the importance of the Pereiaslav council of 1654.[24]

Fedir Shevchenko had all the credentials required for the risky task of "rehabilitating" the author of the *History* in the eyes of the Soviet historiographic establishment. Born in 1914 to a peasant family in the Podilia region of Ukraine, he was a representative of the new Soviet intellectual elite. Shevchenko was educated at the prestigious Moscow Historical and Archival Institute, from which he graduated in the dreadful year 1937. The timing proved perfect for the launch of a successful career, as the regime was eager to replace the "old" cadres decimated by the Great Terror with a new crop of specialists with the right social background. Shevchenko clearly fitted the bill. In 1940, with the Soviet annexation of northern Bukovyna, he was sent to organize the archives in its capital, the city of Chernivtsi. After the outbreak of the Soviet–German war in June 1941, Shevchenko was evacuated along with his archival treasures to Central Asia. He was back in Ukraine in the fall of 1943, in time for the Soviet

[23] Smolii, Putro, and Verba, "Slovo do chytacha," pp. 12–13.
[24] Shevchenko, "Istoriia Rusov ili Maloi Rossii: do 120-richchia z chasu vydannia tvoru."

recapture of Kyiv. The rest of his life and academic career would be closely linked to the Ukrainian capital. After the end of the war, Shevchenko taught at Kyiv University and conducted research at the Ukrainian Academy of Sciences, where he headed the commission on the history of the "Great Patriotic War," the Soviet term for the Soviet–German conflict of 1941–45.

Shevchenko's career really took off in 1957 with his appointment as editor of *Ukraïns'kyi istorychnyi zhurnal* (Ukrainian Historical Journal), the first periodical of its kind since Hrushevsky's journal *Ukraïna* was closed down by the authorities in the early 1930s. In 1963 Shevchenko defended his second doctorate, writing on Russo-Ukrainian relations during the Khmelnytsky Uprising and establishing his credentials as both a distinguished student of Cossack history and a loyal adherent of the "friendship of peoples" paradigm that dominated the Soviet historiographic scene at the time. Shevchenko reached the pinnacle of his career in 1968, when he was appointed director of the Institute of Archaeology at the Ukrainian Academy of Sciences, becoming a corresponding member of the Academy soon afterwards. As editor of the historical journal and Academician, Shevchenko did a great deal to legitimize research on the Cossack past to the extent that it could be fitted into the Russocentric and class-based Soviet narrative of Ukrainian history. The publication of the article on the *History of the Rus'* in 1966 was only one of his many contributions.[25]

Shevchenko was not alone in trying to bring back the *History* as a legitimate subject of research in Soviet Ukraine. Since Ohloblyn's day, it had first resurfaced in Soviet historical publications at the beginning of Nikita Khrushchev's de-Stalinization campaign. In 1959 Mykhailo Marchenko published a survey of Ukrainian historiography in which he discussed the *History of the Rus'*. Two years later he published a short entry on the *History* in a Ukrainian encyclopedia. Marchenko's interest in the *History* was directly related to Ohloblyn's research on the subject during the first years of the Second World War. The two men had been friends. In 1939, when Ohloblyn was flying high in Soviet academic circles, Marchenko, a peasant-born and Soviet-educated historian with impeccable Bolshevik credentials, was appointed the first rector of Lviv

---

[25] On Shevchenko's life and career, see the account by another victim of the 1970s campaign, Olena Apanovych, *Fedir Pavlovych Shevchenko: istoryk, arkhivist, istoriohraf, dzhereloznavets', arkheohraf, orhanizator nauky, liudyna: spohady ta istoriohrafichnyi analiz* (Kyiv, 2000). See also the articles and documentary publications in *Istynu vstanovliuie sud istoriï. Zbirnyk na poshanu Fedora Pavlovycha Shevchenka*, 2 vols. (Kyiv, 2001).

University after the Soviet takeover of Western Ukraine and Belarus as a result of the Molotov–Ribbentrop Pact. He proved too effective in the Ukrainization of the former Polish university to be fully trusted by the authorities. Marchenko was soon removed from his position and sent back to Kyiv, where he was spotted by Soviet secret-police agents socializing with Ohloblyn. With the outbreak of the German–Soviet war in 1941, Marchenko was arrested and sent to the Gulag. It is not clear whether Marchenko was in a position after his release to follow the work that Ohloblyn did on the *History* in Europe and in the United States, but he certainly was not prepared to remove the monument from the record of Ukrainian historiography.[26]

The 1960s turned out to be a period of revival of academic interest in Cossack history and historiography. The next decade promised to be even more productive in that regard. It began on an upbeat for students of Cossack historiography in Ukraine. In 1971 a new academic edition of the *Eyewitness Chronicle*, one of the three major Cossack works of that genre, was published in Kyiv. Another chronicle attributed to the eighteenth-century Cossack colonel Hryhorii Hrabianka was being prepared for print. But then came the unexpected. In May 1972 the Moscow Politburo ousted Petro Shelest, the first secretary of the Central Committee of the Communist Party of Ukraine, who ruled the republic as a virtual viceroy. This maneuver was part of the power struggle in Moscow, but the center decided to use the occasion to strengthen its control over Ukraine, where the political and cultural elites had asserted their autonomy after Stalin's death in 1953. The political campaign against Ukrainian autonomy focused on the book *O Our Soviet Ukraine*, which appeared under Shelest's name but was ghostwritten for him. Shelest was accused of deviating from Leninist principles of nationality policy, downplaying the class factor in Ukrainian history and idealizing Cossackdom in the tradition of "Ukrainian bourgeois" historiography. The new Ukrainian leadership learned its lesson and, in effect, banned further research on the Ukrainian Cossacks and their culture, which they saw as a symbol of exclusive Ukrainian national identity and political independence.

---

[26] Mykhailo Marchenko, *Ukraïns'ka istoriohrafiia (z davnikh chasiv do seredyny XIX st.)* (Kyiv, 1959), pp. 102–7; Marchenko, "Istoriia Rusiv," *Ukraïns'ka Radians'ka Entsyklopediia*, vol. ii (Kyiv, 1961); O. S. Rubl'ov, "Malovidomi storinky biohrafiï ukraïns'koho istoryka," *Ukraïns'kyi istorychnyi zhurnal*, no. 1 (1996).

In the wake of Shelest's dismissal, the institutions of the Ukrainian Academy of Sciences were purged of "Cossackophiles." Among the victims of the purge was Fedir Shevchenko, whose promotion to full member of the academy was halted. He was removed as director of the Institute of Archaeology but allowed to continue as a researcher in the academy's Institute of History. Others were less lucky. Olena Apanovych, a specialist on the armed forces of the Cossack Hetmanate, was dismissed from the Institute of History, left unemployed for a time, and later allowed to return to the academy to catalogue manuscripts in the library. The editor of the Cossack *Eyewitness Chronicle*, Yaroslav Dzyra, was fired from the Institute of History and could not obtain work in his profession until the 1980s. Like many other specialists in Cossack history and Ukrainian political dissidents, he was blacklisted by the authorities, who allowed their victims to work only as manual laborers. Most scholars purged from the Academy of Sciences in the early 1970s were accused of harboring nationalist sympathies. Fedir Shevchenko was charged with Ukrainian nationalism and sympathy for Zionism – a deadly mix of accusations in the Soviet Union of the 1970s.[27]

After the crackdown of the early 1970s, any meaningful study of Cossack historiography became all but impossible. The manuscript found in Ohloblyn's apartment in November 1943 alerted Shevchenko to the importance of the *History* and helped reintroduce it into historiographic discourse, but it was not published and did not contribute to scholarship at the time. Whatever readers in Soviet Ukraine knew about the *History* was based largely on prerevolutionary research. Not only the works of Ohloblyn and Yakovliv but also those of Slabchenko and Vozniak were banned. The lack of independent research on the monument and the de facto ban on the study of the Cossack past helped turn the *History of the Rus'* back into what it had been in the early nineteenth century, before academic research on the text began – a mysterious and almost mystical account of the "true" Ukrainian past concealed from the Ukrainian public by evil forces in Moscow and Kyiv. It was only in 1997, six years after

---

[27] On the political and administrative campaign of the 1970s against Ukrainian nationalism and the fate of the Ukrainian intelligentsia targeted by the authorities, see Iurii Kurnosov, *Inakomyslennia v Ukraïni (60-ti–persha polovyna 80-kh rr. XX st.)* (Kyiv, 1994); Heorhii Kas'ianov, *Nezhodni: Ukraïns'ka intelihentsiia v Rusi oporu 1960–80-kh rokiv* (Kyiv, 1995); Anatolii Rusnachenko, *Rozumom i sertsem: Ukraïns'ka suspil'no-politychna dumka 1940–1980-kh rokiv* (Kyiv, 1999); Oleh Bazhan and Iurii Danyliuk, *Ukraïns'kyi natsional'nyi rukh: Osnovni tendentsiï i etapy rozvytku (kinets' 1950-kh–1980-ti rr.)* (Kyiv, 2000); Iurii Danyliuk, *Opozytsiia v Ukraïni: druha polovyna 50-kh–80-ti rr. XX st.* (Kyiv, 2000).

Ukrainian independence, that a version of Ohloblyn's manuscript on the authorship of the *History of the Rus'*, presented by him as a gift to acquaintances in May 1942, was found in the Kyiv archives and published as a brochure. Devoid of the "statist" overtones of Ohloblyn's émigré-era writings, the publication contributed immensely to rescuing the *History* from the embrace of latter-day Romantic mythology.[28]

[28] For the publication of Ohloblyn's manuscript of 1942, see Oleksii Tolochko, "O. P. Ohloblin ta ioho monohrafiia pro avtora 'Istoriï Rusiv,' *Kyïvs'ka starovyna,* no. 6 (1997): 67–68; Oleksandr Ohloblin, "Do pytannia pro avtora *Istoriï Rusiv,*" *ibid.,* pp. 69–94. Cf. Ohloblyn, *Do pytannia pro avtora.*

PART III

Pieces of a puzzle

CHAPTER 7

A matter of time

In the spring of 1979, the Ukrainian intelligentsia celebrated a major victory. Valentyn Malanchuk, the secretary of the Communist Party of Ukraine who had conducted a purge of "Cossackophiles" and "nationalists" in the Ukrainian Academy of Sciences and created lists of proscribed authors whose names and works were not to appear in print, was finally removed from his position. The changing of the guard on the ideological Olympus in Kyiv signaled the desire of the party leadership to improve its relations with the academic and "creative" intelligentsia, as writers, journalists, and artists were termed by the party apparatchiks. The same year witnessed the publication in Kyiv of an epic poem by Lina Kostenko, a leading Ukrainian poetess and one of the most severely proscribed writers of the 1960s and 1970s. The poem, titled *Marusia Churai*, had waited seven long years for publication – it was submitted to a publishing house in 1972, the year in which Petro Shelest was dismissed and exiled from Ukraine and the campaign against "nationalist deviations" began. The publication of the poem was a clear sign that the authorities were finally changing their attitude toward Ukrainian history and culture.[1]

Although Cossack studies were not yet "rehabilitated," the Cossack myth slowly but surely began to make its way back into the public realm. It was reemerging in the traditional garb of Romanticism, and its reappearance was again closely associated with the *History of the Rus'*. Lina Kostenko's poem was based on the story of the legendary folk poetess Marusia Churai, who allegedly lived in the Cossack town of Poltava in the mid seventeenth century, and to whom nineteenth-century writers and folklorists attributed a number of popular Ukrainian songs. Largely on

---

[1] Lina Kostenko, *Marusia Churai. Istorychnyi roman u virshakh* (Kyiv, 1990). On the difficulties with the publication of *Marusia Churai*, see Volodymyr Panchenko, "Samotnist' na verkhiv'iakh: Poeziia Liny Kostenko v chasy 'vidlyhy' i 'zamorozkiv,'" *Den'*, 30 July 2004; Panchenko, "Episodes from the history of Ukrainian literature of the early 1970s," *The Day Weekly Digest*, no. 7 (2004) www.day. kiev.ua/277/.

the basis of their own imaginations, they did their best to "reconstruct" Marusia's life story, which included her descent from Hordii Churai, a Cossack hero of the first half of the seventeenth century, her tragic love for a young Cossack named Hryts, and her death at the hands of an executioner for poisoning Hryts, whom she accused of betrayal. It was a compelling story, and Lina Kostenko presented it in a way that captured the imagination of readers, who discerned references in the poem to episodes of trust and betrayal that haunted Ukrainian society in the wake of the political purge of the early 1970s.

Lina Kostenko knew the story of Marusia Churai from the writings of the Ukrainian Romantics and believed it. She wanted to find documentary proof of the existence of a historical Marusia Churai but was unable to do so. Eventually she addressed the problem of missing historical sources in the same way as her Romantic predecessors, blaming it on the burning of the Poltava archives, which must have contained the "criminal case" of Marusia Churai, with details of her arrest and interrogation. "Perhaps that is why no evidence of her has come down to us – because the Poltava record books were burned by fire in the fighting during the pillage of the town," wrote the poetess. "But what if even one were to be found in some monastery or attic? What if it survived that conflagration, as indestructible as the burning bush?"[2]

The origins of the Marusia Churai legend can indeed be traced to one such miraculously preserved "monastic manuscript." It is hardly surprising that the title of that manuscript was the *History of the Rus'*. In the *History*'s gruesome description of the execution of the Cossack hetman Yakiv Ostrianytsia by the Polish authorities, which made such a strong impression on Pushkin and Gogol, there is mention of a regimental aide-de-camp named Churai, who, along with other Cossack officers, was "nailed to boards, covered with pitch and burned in a slow fire." This Churai, whose name does not appear in any historical source of the period, was singled out for special treatment, probably because of his Cossack-sounding surname, by the Romantic poet and philologist Izmail Sreznevsky. In 1831, in his almanac *Zaporozhskaia starina* (Zaporozhian Antiquity), Sreznevsky published excerpts from the *History of the Rus'*, including the scene of the execution of Ostrianytsia and his comrades-in-arms. Along with the excerpts, Sreznevsky published a number of literary mystifications based on the *History* and presented as Ukrainian folk songs. One of those allegedly authentic songs was called "Song to Churai at His

---

[2] Kostenko, *Marusia Churai*, p. 5.

Graveside." The literary legend of the aide-de-camp Churai had been launched. By the end of the decade the myth of his daughter, Marusia, the author of the Ukrainian folk songs, had been born.[3]

In 1839 the Russian playwright Aleksandr Shakhovskoy published a short novel titled *Marusia, the Little Russian Sappho* in which he presented a detailed biography of Marusia Churai, allegedly recounted to him by an old church servant. In reality, Shakhovskoy used the plot of a popular Ukrainian song about a betrayed girl who poisoned her lover in order to "reconstruct" the biography of Churai's daughter, including the year of her birth (1625), the names of her parents, and the details of her trial. None of these details could be confirmed by historians until the 1970s, when the literary scholar Yurii Kaufman published in Moscow a copy of a Poltava court record allegedly found by the Ukrainian poet Ivan Khomenko in the library of the Ukrainian Academy of Sciences in Kyiv. In 1973, the year of publication of the document, whose authenticity was questioned by specialists, Khomenko was safely dead – he passed away in 1968, and part of the library of the Ukrainian Academy of Sciences, in which the all-important document was supposedly preserved, was destroyed by fire in 1964. Ukrainian political dissidents believed that this was deliberate arson by the KGB intended to destroy an important part of the Ukrainian cultural heritage. This time the truth about Ukrainian history was not just hidden but completely annihilated. If history could not be recovered, it had to be reconstructed, and the *History of the Rus'* once again emerged as a basis for bringing the lost past to life.[4]

In the 1970s, however, it was almost impossible to get one's hands on the text of the *History*, which had not been reprinted since 1846. The taboo on its publication was finally broken in 1983, when the Institute of Literature of the Ukrainian Academy of Sciences published excerpts from the *History* in a volume devoted to eighteenth-century Ukrainian literature. How did the publication make its way past the Scylla and Charybdis of the Soviet censorship? The title of the *History* hinted at the presentation of the Ukrainian past as part of the Russian historical narrative, and the excerpts selected for publication dealt, among other things, with Cossack uprisings led by Severyn Nalyvaiko and Bohdan Khmelnytsky, as well as

---

[3] *Istoriia Rusov ili Maloi Rosii. Sochinenie Georgiia Koniskago, Arkhiepiskopa Beloruskago* (Moscow, 1846), p. 56; Izmail Sreznevskii, *Zaporozhskaia starina*, no. 1 (1831): 74–76; Mykhailo Vozniak, *Pseudo-Konys'kyi i Pseudo-Poletyka* (Istoriia Rusov u literaturi ta nautsi) (Lviv and Kyiv, 1939), pp. 17–24.

[4] Mykhailo Stepanenko, "Kolo Marusi Churai. Trahediia bezsmertnoï ukraïnky," *Den'*, January 27, 2007.

with Cossack resistance to the church union with Rome, all of which was in harmony with the dominant Soviet discourse. Oleksa Myshanych, the author of the introduction and commentary to the volume, went out of his way to stress that the *History* reflected the class interests of Cossack officeholders. On the positive side, he noted that the work portrayed Bohdan Khmelnytsky as a true defender of the "reunification of Ukraine with Russia." Such obligatory clichés helped the editors and compilers of the volume to maneuver excerpts of the otherwise suspicious text past the censors. It was a major coup.[5]

The *History of the Rus'* was finally back after decades of de facto prohibition. But the publication also demonstrated the troublesome state of research on the Cossack chronicles and general literature of the period in Soviet Ukraine. The editors of the *History* were not familiar with research undertaken outside the USSR or preferred not to betray their knowledge of works written by émigré scholars. This situation was very different from the one in neighboring Poland. There, a scholar of Ukrainian literature, Stefan Kozak, was able to devote two long chapters of his book on the origins of Ukrainian Romanticism to the *History of the Rus'*. He not only knew Ohloblyn's writings but made reference to the Ukrainian translation of the *History* that appeared in New York in 1956. If the *History of the Rus'* had finally been legitimized for research in Soviet Ukraine, scholars there still had to catch up with the considerable work done on the monument outside the Soviet Union. Nowhere was this more obvious than in the dating of the *History*. While the Kyiv editors included excerpts from the *History* in a volume on eighteenth-century literature, few scholars outside Ukraine believed that it had been written before 1800.[6]

If the *History of the Rus'* was not a product of the eighteenth century, when was it written? Up to this point we have sought to answer questions about the *History* by relying on research conducted by others. From now on, the only way to move forward is to conduct an independent inquiry, using evidence overlooked so far in the study of the mysterious text. The

---

[5] *Ukraïns'ka literatura XVIII st.: Poetychni tvory, dramatychni tvory, prozori tvory*, ed. V. I. Krekoten' (Kyiv, 1983), pp. 23–25, 584–640, 681–83.

[6] Stefan Kozak, *U źródeł romantyzmu i nowożytnej myśli społecznej na Ukrainie* (Wrocław, 1978), pp. 70–135. Ohloblyn claimed that the work must have been written between 1802 and 1805 but could have been edited later. He believed that the author was acquainted with some works published in 1801 and 1804 but missed an important publication that appeared in 1805. See Ohloblyn, introduction to *Istoriia Rusiv*, trans. Viacheslav Davydenko (New York, 1956), pp. v–xxix.

question of the time of production of the *History* seems a promising one with which to begin this new stage of research.

Let us first re-examine the data we already have, starting with a closer look at the claims of the author of the *History* regarding the time of creation of his work. As discussed earlier, the author of the *History* wanted his readers to believe that the work was written in or soon after 1769, the second year of the Russo-Turkish War of 1768–72. The *History* ends with an intriguing statement: "at the beginning of 1769 the troops set off on a general campaign, and a true war began with the Turks. How it will end, God knows!" Since the introduction to the *History* indicates that it was sent by Archbishop Heorhii Konysky to Hryhorii Poletyka, who needed it for his work in the Legislative Commission, one should assume that the manuscript was indeed completed in 1769, as the commission ended its work that year. This, at least, is what the author would have us believe. The year 1769 worked well for those identifying Konysky (d. 1795) or Poletyka (d. 1784) as the author of the *History*. It also suited those who believed that the *History* could have been written by Prince Bezborodko, who died in 1799.[7]

However, existing manuscripts of the *History* tell a very different story from the one suggested by its author or editor. The bulk of the manuscripts date from the 1830s and 1840s. They began to be produced in quantity following the alleged discovery of the *History* on the Hryniv estate of the Bezborodkos. There are earlier copies as well, but, with rare exceptions, the manuscripts of the *History* are not dated, which obliges scholars to rely on watermarks in order to determine their approximate dates. This method works well in establishing the *terminus post quem* a given manuscript was produced. Unfortunately for proponents of the eighteenth-century origins of the *History*, it does not favor their hypothesis. The earliest manuscript of the work (dated by watermarks) known to have been seen by anyone came from 1809. In the mid nineteenth century it was seen by Oleksandr Konysky, a Ukrainian cultural activist and namesake of Archbishop Hryhorii Konysky in the Zolotonosha region of Dnieper Ukraine.

The next-oldest manuscript of the *History* comes from 1817 (according to its watermarks) or 1818 (the year on the title page). Until 1944 the manuscript was preserved in the library of the Shevchenko Scientific Society in Lviv, but its location is unknown today. Another manuscript of the *History* comes from 1814, if one trusts Mykhailo Vozniak, or 1818, if

[7] *Istoriia Rusov*, pp. i–ii, 257.

one follows Oleksander Ohloblyn. The two scholars examined it in the library of the Ukrainian National Museum in Lviv but reached different conclusions about the watermarks. Our own examination of them points to 1818. We concur with Ohloblyn, who maintained that the figure 18 on the watermark pertains to the last two digits of the year 1818 and not to the first two digits of the year 1814, as Vozniak seems to have assumed. One more early manuscript of the *History* has been preserved in the collection of the Ukrainian Free Academy of Arts and Sciences in New York. It was written on paper watermarked 1819 and 1820.[8]

The surviving manuscripts of the *History* tell us that the work did not begin its "public life" before 1809 – or, more probably, before 1818. This proposition is supported by Anatolii Yershov's research, undertaken in the 1920s, on the time of production of the text. In his essay of 1926 in the festschrift for Mykhailo Hrushevsky, Yershov made a compelling case for dating the *History* to the second decade of the nineteenth century. He was the first to note that the anonymous author makes reference to the writings of Daniel Ernst Wagner, whose work *Geschichte von Polen* first appeared in print in 1775. This was two years before another source of the *History*, Vasyl Ruban and Oleksandr Bezborodko's *Brief Chronicle of Little Russia* (1777), was published in St. Petersburg. Yershov also drew attention to the author's discussion of ancient inscriptions on rocks located, among other places, on the Taman or Tmutorokan Peninsula. A stone with ancient inscriptions was indeed discovered on the Taman Peninsula in 1792. A reference to the rule of Catherine II in the past tense indicated to Yershov that the *History* must have been written after 1796, the year of her death. Numerous references to ministers and ministries in the *History* pointed to the period after Alexander I's reform of 1802, which created a ministerial system of administration in the Russian Empire. A wealth of references to nations and national rights in the *History*, claimed Yershov, might well indicate the era of Napoleon, whose wars provoked national awakening in many countries of Europe. Finally, references to the "system of the balance of power" could place the writing of the manuscript after

---

[8] Vozniak, *Psevdo-Konys'kyi*, pp. 5–6; Ohloblyn, introduction to *Istoriia Rusiv* (1956), pp. viii, xi–xii; Ohloblyn, "Spysky *Istorii Rusiv*," *Naukovyi zbirnyk Ukrains'koho vil'noho universytetu*, vol. VI (Munich, 1956): 167–80; Feodosii Steblii, "*Istoriia Rusiv* v kul'turnomu i naukovomu zhytti Halychyny," in *V Mizhnarodnyi konhres ukraïnistiv. Dopovidi. Istoriia*, no. 2 (Chernivtsi, 2004): 134–44, here 138–39. My dating of the manuscript titled "Istoriia Rusov ili Maloi Rossii," which is currently preserved in the Andrei Sheptytsky National Museum, Manuscript Division, no. 563 (old no. 520929), is based on the watermark reproduced in N. P. Likhachev, *Paleograficheskoe znachenie bumazhnykh vodianykh znakov* (St. Petersburg, 1899), II: 247; III: table DXXIV.

the Congress of Vienna (1814–15), which created such a system. Yershov believed that the *History* was probably written between 1815, the year of the Congress of Vienna, and 1818, the year on the title page of the first dated manuscript.[9]

This chronology effectively ruled out not only Konysky and Poletyka but also Bezborodko as possible authors and was dismissed by supporters of the Poletyka and Bezborodko hypotheses (the latter group being particularly influential in the field) on the grounds that the terms "minister" and "nation" and the idea of the balance of power were well known in Russia before the nineteenth century. The critics certainly had a point. But does this mean that Yershov's chronology was wrong? Not if we take into account the research done in the 1960s and 1970s by Yurii Shevelov, a professor of Slavic linguistics at Columbia University in New York. Like Ohloblyn, Shevelov was a native of Ukraine who immigrated to the United States in the aftermath of the Second World War. The two scholars knew each other and had some common interests. On August 25, 1969, Shevelov delivered a paper titled "The *History of the Rus'* through the Eyes of a Linguist" at the Ukrainian Free University in Munich. Eight years later he published a revised version of the paper in a collection of essays honoring Oleksander Ohloblyn on his seventy-fifth birthday. It constituted the first attempt by a professional linguist to address questions with which historians had been struggling for generations: where and when was the *History of the Rus'* written?[10]

Shevelov's essay offered insights into the history of the text that no historian was able to provide. First and foremost, Shevelov stated that the *History* was written not in Russian *per se* but in the language of the educated classes of Ukrainian society, which included numerous Ukrainisms. At the time, these were not considered errors but constituted an integral part of the written language of the Ukrainian elite. Shevelov also noted the author's mastery of Russian military vocabulary and his knowledge of French. Shevelov's analysis of (largely French) loan words in Russian-language works allowed him to make important observations about the

---

[9] Ohloblyn, introduction to *Istoriia Rusiv*, p. viii; Anatolii Iershov, "Do pytannia pro chas napysannia *Istoriï Rusov*, a po chasty i pro avtora ïï," *Iuvileinyi zbirnyk na poshanu akademika M. S. Hrushevs'koho*, pt. 1 (Kyiv, 1928), pp. 286–91.

[10] Natalia Polons'ka-Vasylenko, "Istoriia Rusiv ochyma movoznavtsia (lektsiia profesora Iuriia Shevel'ova v UVU, 25 serpnia 1969 r.)," *Vyzvol'nyi shliakh*, no. 7/8 (1970); Iurii Shevel'ov, "*Istoriia Rusov* ochyma movoznavtsia," in *Zbirnyk na poshanu prof. d-ra Oleksandra Ohloblyna*, ed. Vasyl' Omel'chenko (New York, 1977), pp. 465–82. For a brief biography of Shevelov, see Jacob Hurski, "Shevelov, George Yurii," *Encyclopedia of Ukraine*, vol. IV (Toronto, 1993), pp. 661–62.

time frame in which the *History* was created. Noting the first occurrences of individual foreign words in Russian dictionaries of the era, he concluded that the *History* could have been written in the 1790s and perhaps have undergone further editing in the first decade of the nineteenth century.

The most promising feature of Shevelov's analysis was his investigation of the first appearances in literary texts of legendary personages mentioned in the *History*. There we encounter a Cossack colonel called Gromval, whose name first appears in the title of a Russian romantic ballad, written in 1802 by Gavriil Kamenev. The ballad, prepared for publication by Vasilii Zhukovsky, was included in an anthology of Russian poetry and reprinted numerous times between 1804 and 1814. Another time-sensitive name spotted by Shevelov in the *History* is "Rogdai." It does not appear in that particular spelling in any work of literature or history until 1809, when Vasilii Zhukovsky published his short novel *Mary's Grove* in the popular Russian journal *Vestnik Evropy*. Last but not least, there is one more name that can link the text of the *History* with a particular point in time. This name, "Turnylo," is given to another mythical Cossack colonel of the *History*. Shevelov linked it with the name "Turn," which appears in Ivan Kotliarevsky's Ukrainian rendering of Virgil's *Aeneid*. That particular section of Kotliarevsky's poem appeared in print in 1809, just as the name "Rogdai" was entering Russian literature.[11]

Shevelov's analysis suggested that while the *History* could have been written in the last decade of the eighteenth century, it could not have been completed before 1804, or even 1809. But how certain are these dates? In the 1990s the Chernihiv historian Oleksandr Ilin indicated a literary parallel in the *History of the Rus'* that provides further support for Shevelov's chronology. Ilin wrote that the reference to the fable of the wolf and the lamb in the *History* (where the wolf accuses the lamb of interfering with his drinking when the lamb takes a drink twenty steps downstream from him) was inspired by Ivan Krylov's fable on this subject, first published in 1808. While Krylov's fable closely followed the version of Jean de La Fontaine, which in turn was based on Aesop's fable and could thus have been known to the anonymous author from other sources, the fable did in fact become especially popular in the Russian Empire after being rendered by Krylov. It was included in the first collection of Krylov's fables, published in 1809. Zhukovsky reviewed it in *Vestnik Evropy* in the same year. Putting together the evidence

11 Shevel'ov, "*Istoriia Rusov* ochyma movoznavtsia," pp. 477–80.

provided by the surviving manuscripts of the *History* and the results of the research conducted by Yershov, Ohloblyn, and Shevelov, recently supported by Ilin's observation, we can conclude that the *History* could not have been written, or at least completed, prior to 1809.[12]

Can we get any additional information about the time when the *History* was written from the text itself? Are there any indications that its author used historical sources or engaged in polemics with works that appeared in the first decades of the nineteenth century? Indeed there are. One of them comes directly from the introduction to the *History*, where the author attacks an unnamed writer of a textbook who, influenced by Polish and Lithuanian historians, used the name "Ukraine" to denote what the anonymous author calls Rus' and Little Russia. "Thus, for example," wrote the author of the *History* "in one paltry little history textbook, some new land by the Dnieper, here called Ukraine, is brought onto the stage from Ancient Rus' or present-day Little Russia, and in it Polish kings establish new settlements and organize Ukrainian Cossacks; and until then the land was allegedly empty and uninhabited, and there were no Cossacks in Rus'. But it is apparent that the gentleman writer of such a timid little history has never been anywhere except his school, and in the land that he calls Ukraine he has not seen Rus' towns, the oldest ones – or at least much older than his Polish kings. But for him all this is a desert, and he consigns to nothingness and oblivion the Rus' princes who sailed their great flotillas onto the Black Sea from the Dnieper River, that is, from those very lands, and made war on Greece, Sinope, Trabzon, and Constantinople itself with armies from those regions, just as [by his account] someone hands back Little Russia itself from Polish possession without resistance and voluntarily."[13]

The full title of the *History* (*History of the Rus', or Little Russia*) was not Bodiansky's invention. It appears in the absolute majority of surviving manuscripts of the text and leaves little doubt regarding the preference of its author or editor concerning the terms "Little Russia" and "Ukraine."[14] But why did the author attach such importance to that issue, and who

---

[12] Oleksandr Il'in, "Oleksandr Markovych – avtor 'Istoriï Rusiv'?" *Siverians'kyi litopys*, no. 1 (1996): 73–79; Vasilii Zhukovskii, "Kritika. Basni Ivana Krylova," *Vestnik Evropy*, no. 9 (1809).

[13] *Istoriia Rusov*, pp. iii–iv.

[14] See, e.g., the titles of manuscripts preserved in the Manuscript Institute of the Vernadsky Library in Kyiv: "Istoriia Rusov ili Maloi Rossii" (I, no. 4094); "Istoriia Maloi Rossii s rukopisi arkhiepiskopa Mogilevskogo i Belorusskogo Koniskogo" (I, nos. 707–9); "Malorossiiskaia istoriia G. Konisskogo" (I, no. 57); "Istoriia Maloi Rossii, sochinennaia Georgiem Koniskim, arkhiepiskopom Belorusskim" (I, no. 211). All these manuscripts can be dated with some precision to the 1830s and 1840s.

specifically of the Polish, Lithuanian, or "Rus'" historians was the object
of the anonymous author's attack? Identifying the writer whose work
provoked this polemical outburst can help us check our assumptions
about the time of writing of the *History*. We are not, of course, the
first readers of the *History* to attempt a solution to this puzzle. Andrei
Storozhenko suggested in 1918 that the reference was to two Polish
authors of the late eighteenth and early nineteenth centuries, Jan Potocki
and Tadeusz Czacki. While such a possibility cannot be ruled out, in
the above extract the author of the *History of the Rus'* does not argue
either against Potocki's theory linking Ukrainian origins with those of
the Polianians, Derevlianians, Tivertsians, and Siverianians or against
Czacki's theory that the Ukrainians were descended from a tribe called
"Ukr." Instead, he rejects the notion that credits Polish kings with the
establishment of Cossackdom and the settlement of the Dnieper region
even as it neglects the Rus' origins of the Cossacks, ignores their long and
determined struggle for union with Russia, and undermines the claim of
the Rus' nation to its glorious history. It should also be noted that the
anonymous author's protest was provoked not by Polish (and Lithuanian)
writings *per se* but by the adoption of the views set forth in those writings
by the authors of "Little Russian chronicles."[15]

Indeed, one should not look for authors promoting the term "Ukraine"
exclusively among Poles or Lithuanians: there were plenty of such writers
among the Ukrainians themselves. One of the last eighteenth-century
Cossack chroniclers was Petro Symonovsky, the author of a *Brief Description of the Cossack Little Russian Nation*. The major Cossack chronicles of
the early eighteenth century, including the one attributed to Hryhorii
Hrabianka – an important source for Cossack historiography of the later
period – were full of references to "Ukraine," used interchangeably with
"Little Russia." At the turn of the nineteenth century, most historians of
Ukraine were prepared to make a direct connection between Stefan
Batory, the Cossacks, and the name "Ukraine." Such views were expressed
by Symonovsky's contemporary Yakiv Markovych, who published his
Notes on Little Russia (1798), a historical, geographic, and ethnographic
description of his homeland.[16]

---

[15] A. V. Storozhenko, "Malaia Rossiia ili Ukraina?" (1918), repr. in *Ukrainskii separatizm v Rossii.
Ideologiia natsional'nogo raskola*, comp. M. B. Smolin (Moscow, 1998), pp. 280–90, here 287–88.
On Czacki, see Julian Dybiec, *Nie tylko szablą. Nauka i kultura polska w walce o utrzymanie
tożsamości narodowej, 1795–1918* (Cracow, 2004), pp. 75–80, 112–13.

[16] On Petro Symonovsky, see Oleksander Ohloblyn, *Liudy staroï Ukraïny* (Munich, 1959), pp. 219–36.
On the use of the term "Rus'" in the Cossack chronicles, see Frank E. Sysyn, "The Image of Russia

While there were quite a few Russian and Ukrainian authors who shared the kind of ideas that provoked outrage on the part of the author of the *History*, very few of them could be accused of writing "timid little history textbooks." In fact, there is only one such person known to us. His name was Maksym Berlynsky (1764–1848), and in the late eighteenth and early nineteenth centuries he taught a variety of subjects, including history, in a Kyiv school. Having been born in the vicinity of Putyvl into the family of an Orthodox priest, Berlynsky could certainly be considered a "native of Rus'," a term that the anonymous author of the *History of the Rus'* could have applied to Great Russians and Ukrainians alike. He was appointed a teacher at the recently opened secular school (later gymnasium) in Kyiv in 1788, after graduating from the Kyiv Mohyla Academy and training for two years at the teachers' college in St. Petersburg. Berlynsky taught at the Kyiv gymnasium until his retirement in 1834, thereby meeting another qualification – that of a lifelong teacher who had never been anywhere except his school, as specified by the author of the *History*.[17]

Probably the most important of Berlynsky's formal qualifications is that his many works on Ukrainian history included a textbook, *Short History of Russia for the Use of Young People* (1800), which, according to a member of the Berlynsky family, was written specifically for students of the Kyiv Theological Academy. Even more interesting in this connection is that the textbook included an essay on Ukrainian history entitled "Note on Little Russia." It was inserted into a basically Great Russian historical narrative, in the section dealing with the rule of Tsar Aleksei Mikhailovich, and covered the history of Ukraine from the Mongol invasion to the Truce of Andrusovo (1667). Subsequent Ukrainian history was treated within the context of imperial Russia. Thus Berlynsky perfectly matches

---

and Russian–Ukrainian Relations in Ukrainian Historiography of the Late Seventeenth and Early Eighteenth Centuries," in *Culture, Nation, and Identity: The Ukrainian–Russian Encounter, 1600–1945* (Edmonton and Toronto, 2003), pp. 108–43. On Markovych's interpretation of Ukrainian history, see Oleksii Tolochko, "Kyievo-Rus'ka spadshchyna v istorychnii dumtsi Ukraïny pochatku XIX st." in V. F. Verstiuk, V. M. Horobets', and O. P. Tolochko, *Ukraïna i Rosiia v istorychnii retrospektyvi*, vol. 1: *Ukraïns'ki proekty v Rosiis'kii imperiï* (Kyiv, 2004), pp. 250–350, here 303.

[17] Serhii Plokhy, "Ukraine or Little Russia? Revisiting an Early Nineteenth-Century Debate," *Canadian Slavonic Papers* 48, nos. 3–4 (September–December 2006): 260–78; Plokhy, *Ukraine and Russia: Representations of the Past* (Toronto, 2008), pp. 49–65; Oleksiy Tolochko, "Fellows and Travelers: Thinking about Ukrainian History in the Early Nineteenth Century," in *A Laboratory of Transnational History: Ukraine and Recent Ukrainian Historiography*, ed. Georgiy Kasianov and Philip Ther (Budapest and New York, 2009), pp. 161–62; M.-L. Chepa, "Khto napysav 'Istoriiu Rusiv'?" Instytut ukraïniky http://ukrainica.com.ua/rus/istoriya_rusov/istoriya_rusov_all/1886.

the image of the mysterious opponent invoked by the author of the
History of the Rus' in the introduction to that work.[18]

But does Berlynsky's textbook indeed use "Ukrainian" terminology
and include pro-Polish passages, as suggested by the anonymous author?
The very first sentence of Berlynsky's "Note on Little Russia" gives a
positive answer to this question, since it implies that the original name
of that land was indeed Ukraine. It reads: "Ukraine received its name of
Little Russia after its union with Russia." According to Berlynsky, King
Sigismund I of Poland, "seeing that the Ukrainians engaged in military
pursuits, who were known as Cossacks, were accomplishing very brave
and valiant exploits ... gave them permission to occupy places above
and below the town of Kiev and, in 1506, gave them their first leader
with the title of hetman, a certain Liaskoronsky [Lanckoroński], to
whom he granted the towns of Chigirin and Cherkassy as possessions."
King Stefan Batory, for his part, "confirmed the Ukrainians' previous
privileges in 1576 and gave them new ones; hence the empty lands
between the Dnieper, Bar, and Kiev were soon settled by them."[19] Thus
the author of the "Note on Little Russia" was indeed "guilty as charged"
by the author of the *History* when it comes to the origins of the name
Ukraine, the Polish kings' organization of the Cossack Host, and the
settlement of the steppe borderlands.

Berlynsky did not identify his sources, leaving us no direct evidence of
possible Polish influences on his work. A reading of Maksym Berlynsky's
textbook and his other writings on Ukrainian history leaves no doubt that
he was anything but a Polonophile. However, Berlynsky's general assessment of the Ukrainian past was damning of those who extolled the heroic
deeds of the Cossack nation. "In a word," he wrote in his article "On the
City of Kyiv," "this people groaned beneath the Polish yoke, made war
under Lithuanian banners, occupied itself with the Union under Polish
rule, and contended for privilege under Russian rule, producing nothing

---

[18] *Kratkaia rossiiskaia istoriia dlia upotrebleniia iunoshestvu, nachinaiushchemu obuchat'sia istorii,
prodolzhennaia do iskhoda XVIII stoletiia, sochinennaia v Kieve uchitelem Maksimom Berlinskim*
(Moscow, 1800), pp. 93–106. On the purpose behind the writing of the *Short History of Russia*, see a
letter to Maksym Berlynsky from his brother Matvii, dated March 2, 1817, in "Semeinaia perepiska
Berlinskikh," Manuscript Institute, Vernadsky Library, fond 175, no. 1057, fol. 7–7ᵛ. On Berlynsky,
see David Saunders, *The Ukrainian Impact on Russian Culture, 1750–1850* (Edmonton, 1985), pp.
209–12; Mykhailo Braichevs'kyi, "Maksym Berlyns'kyi ta ioho 'Istoriia mista Kyieva,'" in Maksym
Berlyns'kyi, *Istoriia mista Kyieva* (Kyiv, 1991), pp. 5–20; Volodymyr Kravchenko, *Narysy z ukraïns'
koï istoriohrafiï epokhy natsional'noho Vidrodzhennia (druha polovyna XVIII–seredyna XIX st.)*
(Kharkiv, 1996), pp. 80–84.
[19] Berlinskii, *Kratkaia rossiiskaia istoriia*, pp. 93, 96–97, 98–99.

for us except descendants."[20] Berlynsky was also quite negative in his assessment of the role of Cossackdom, especially the Cossack officer elite – an attitude that caused him difficulty when an excerpt from his "History of Little Russia" was considered for publication in 1844. On the recommendation of the prominent imperial Russian historian Nikolai Ustrialov, a negative characterization of the Cossacks was removed from the journal publication. It is entirely possible that the anti-Cossack attitudes of Berlynsky, whose writings clearly favored Ukrainian city dwellers, prevented the publication of his "History" year after year. Ironically, Berlynsky lived long enough to see the publication of the *History of the Rus'*, which contained an attack on his views and was potentially dangerous to the imperial regime, but not long enough to witness the appearance of his own works, such as the "History of Little Russia" and the "History of the City of Kyiv," which were perfectly loyal to the authorities.[21]

If our identification of Berlynsky as the object of the anonymous author's attack is correct, then the *History* could not have been written before 1800. But can we move the date further into the nineteenth century? It would appear so. The historiographic evidence we have is not conclusive, but it cannot be ignored and should be considered in our search for the *History*'s date of origin. Like our findings regarding Berlynsky's textbook, it is directly related to the anonymous author's rejection of the term "Ukraine." In 1816 the debate over the most fitting name for the former lands of the Hetmanate spilled onto the pages of the first Ukrainian journal, appropriately titled *Ukrainskii vestnik* (Ukrainian Herald). The journal was published by a circle of Kharkiv University professors and took its name from Sloboda Ukraine, a historical and administrative region whose capital was Kharkiv.

It all began with the publication in the February 1816 issue of *Ukrainskii vestnik* of an article by the Kharkiv-area antiquarian Illia Kvitka entitled "On Little Russia." There Kvitka presented a standard view concerning the origins of the Cossacks that was shared by many, including Maksym Berlynsky. With regard to events following the Union of Lublin (1569), Kvitka wrote: "Not long before this, inhabitants of Volhynia and other provinces in its vicinity, adopting the name of Cossacks, raided the Tatars of the Crimean Horde and even ventured to sail the Black Sea on

---

[20] Quoted in Kravchenko, *Narysy z ukraïns'koï istoriohrafiï*, p. 83. The article "O gorode Kieve," published in *Ulei* in 1811, was an excerpt from Berlynsky's larger study on the "History of the City of Kyiv."

[21] Kravchenko, *Narysy z ukraïns'koï istoriohrafiï*, pp. 8–84.

their light vessels near its northern and western shores, attacking Greek traders. The happy thought occurred to the Polish king Stefan Batory to make good use of these new Cossacks; he proposed that they constitute themselves as a decent army, gave them leave to elect a chief called a hetman, established the Ukrainian town of Trakhtemyriv as a residence for him, and reserved a certain territory on the borders of his kingdom so that they would serve as protectors against Tatar incursions into Polish domains." The unusual feature of Kvitka's presentation was his suggestion that Right-Bank Ukraine was called "Little Russia" by the Poles, while Left-Bank Ukraine became known as "Ukraine." "The Kingdom or Republic of Poland established its order in the newly annexed provinces and assigned that of Volhynia, as well as Lutsk with Podilia and Polisia, to Little Poland, while the city of Kyiv and its environs, as well as other towns located on the right side of the Dnieper, were called Little Russia, and those on its left side were called Ukraine," wrote Kvitka.[22]

The conventional wisdom at the time, which corresponded to eighteenth-century realities, was the exact opposite: the lands on the left bank of the Dnieper were known as "Little Russia," while those on the right bank were called "Ukraine." That was the main point of Mikhail Markov's "Comment on the Article about Little Russia," which appeared in the August 1816 issue of *Ukrainskii vestnik*. He not only dismissed Kvitka's suggestions but did so on the basis of numerous historical sources, including Polish ones – Kvitka's thesis rested, after all, on the claim that it was the Polish authorities who had introduced the terms "Ukraine" and "Little Russia." "While Little Russia appears in native Russian documents beginning in the mid seventeenth century, the Greeks gave that name as early as the mid fifteenth century to the provinces seized from Russia," wrote Markov. "But as far as Polish use of that name is concerned, however many charters of Polish kings I have seen from the very time of the union of Lithuania with Poland, and however many of their various constitutions I have read, I have never encountered it, just as I have not found it in their chronicles, nor in their geographies. That is why I conclude that the Poles referred to all our above-mentioned provinces simply as Rus' in general, and often by the names of palatinates." He later added: "As for Ukraine, the name supposedly used by the Poles for the towns on the left side of the Dnieper from 1570, while Little Russia was used for those on the right side, I have an old Polish atlas that tells against this."[23]

---

[22] Il'ia Kvitka, "O Maloi Rossii," *Ukrainskii vestnik*, no. 2 (1816): 146–47.
[23] Mikhail Markov, "Zamechanie na stat'iu o Malorossii," *Ukrainskii vestnik*, no. 8 (1816): 129–33.

The whole debate turned out to have been provoked by a simple misunderstanding. That was the explanation Kvitka gave in a letter printed in the October 1816 issue of *Vestnik*. He wrote: "What should have been said was 'Ukraine on the right side of the Dnieper and Little Russia on the left,'" and added: "such an error was made in copying or typesetting those words." The issue seemed to have been resolved, and there was no continuation of the "Ukraine vs. Little Russia" debate on the pages of *Ukrainskii vestnik*. But a comparison of the Kvitka–Markov exchange with the introduction to the *History of the Rus'* tells us that while the debate may have begun with a misunderstanding, it had a much broader historiographic and political significance. The origins of the Cossacks, the Polish role in the settlement of the Dnieper region, and the importance of Polish authors and sources for Ukrainian historiography are discussed in both publications. Was the author of the *History* reacting not to Berlynsky's textbook but to the exchange of 1816?[24]

To make such an assumption work, one would have to explain the anonymous author's reference to *uchebnaia istoriika*, which is no easy task. Mikhail Markov was the director of the Chernihiv gymnasium and the Chernihiv gubernia school system. He was an ardent student of the Ukrainian past and published a number of works on the history of Chernihiv and vicinity. In 1816–17, aside from his polemic with Kvitka, he contributed an essay to *Ukrainskii vestnik* discussing the origins of Rus' history. Thus Markov could indeed be accused of never going beyond the walls of his school, as the anonymous author wrote about his opponent. However, the problem with Markov's possible authorship of the textbook that so upset the author of the *History of the Rus'* is that although he contributed to publications dealing with education, he never wrote anything approaching a history textbook, and his eight-page essay ambitiously titled "An Introduction to Little Russian History" (*Ukrainskii vestnik*, 1817) advanced no further than the period of Kyivan Rus'.[25]

Even if one assumes that in referring to *uchebnaia istoriika* the anonymous author did not mean a textbook but a work written by a teacher, or that in the original the reference was not to an *uchebnaia istoriika* but to an *uchenaia istoriika* (a scholarly little history), Markov's response to Kvitka did not include any assertions undermining Cossack or Rus' claims to Dnieper Ukraine. Markov also avoided Ukrainian terminology in his

[24] Il'ia Kvitka, "Izdateliam," *Ukrainskii vestnik*, no. 10 (1816): 139.
[25] On Markov, see Oleh Zhurba, *Stanovlennia ukraïns'koï arkheohrafiï: liudy, ideï, instytutsiï* (Dnipropetrovsk, 2003), pp. 94–119.

writing and can hardly be suspected of Polonophilism. Kvitka would have been a much better target than Markov in that regard, but Kvitka had nothing to do with schools and should also be excluded from the list of possible suspects. Thus we return to Maksym Berlynsky as our main suspect, and to his textbook of 1800 as the main trigger for the anonymous author's attack on Polonophiles. Our discussion of the Kvitka–Markov polemic does indicate, however, that the attack directed primarily against Berlynsky may well have been provoked by the exchange on Ukraine and Little Russia published in *Ukrainskii vestnik* in 1816. Our venture into the historiographic debates of the period confirms the conclusions of those authors who refer to the *History* as a product of the nineteenth century, and it points to 1816 as a possible date before which the *History* could not have been completed. Hypothetically, we can limit the window of opportunity for the writing of the work to a period between 1809 and 1818. We can go on to suggest that the introduction to the *History*, which includes the attack on the use of the name "Ukraine" for the lands of the former Hetmanate, was written between 1816 and 1818.

Could it be that more than fifteen years after the publication of Berlynsky's textbook, someone was still taking issue with its author? There would be nothing unusual in such a development. In early nineteenth-century Ukraine it took a while for books to reach their readers. Andrian Chepa, a Poltava-based connoisseur of Cossack history and an expert on the rights of the Ukrainian nobility, received Berlynsky's book from its author only in 1810. Until then, he was unaware of the existence of a work that had been used for years as a textbook in the Kyivan Academy and provincial schools. If someone was unhappy with Berlynsky's treatment of Cossack history, he might have expressed his feelings long after its publication. There was no incentive to mention the author by name. Berlynsky lived a long time and was still alive not only when the *History of the Rus'* began its public career as a manuscript in the 1820s but even when it was first printed in 1846.[26]

Some debates can last a lifetime. Yurii Shevelov, the scholar on whose observations about the language of the *History* and its legendary characters we have based much of our analysis in this chapter, knew that as well as anyone. In 1953 he reviewed a novel by Oles Honchar (1918–1995), then a rising star in the Soviet Ukrainian literary establishment. A few years

[26] Oleksiy Tolochko, "Fellows and Travelers: Thinking about Ukrainian History in the Early Nineteenth Century," in *A Laboratory of Transnational History: Ukraine and Recent Ukrainian Historiography*, ed. Kasianov and Ther, pp. 161–62.

earlier Honchar had been awarded two Stalin Prizes for a trilogy, *Praporonostsi* (The Standard-Bearers), describing the liberating mission of the Red Army in Eastern Europe in 1944–45. In reviewing Honchar's new novel, *Tavriia*, dealing with the history of the Ukrainian Revolution (1918–20), Shevelov praised him as a talented writer but was very critical of the direction that Ukrainian literature was taking in Stalin's USSR. According to Shevelov, *Tavriia* was indicative of the "major loss of Ukrainian literature under the USSR – the *loss of culture*. These are bitter words, terrible words, but they must be spoken. Not only has Ukrainian literature in the Ukrainian SSR been driven back seventy years, but it does not possess even the level of culture it possessed then."[27]

It is unlikely that the review of 1953 was on Shevelov's mind when he first returned to Ukraine in 1990 after long years of emigration. But it was clearly on the mind of Oles Honchar, by that time the patriarch of Ukrainian literature and a symbol of Ukraine's national resilience. He had been accused of nationalist deviations in the early 1970s and left the Communist Party in the fall of 1990 in a public show of solidarity with his granddaughter, who, along with other Ukrainian students, participated in a hunger strike in downtown Kyiv to protest the hardliners' attempts to stop Ukraine's drive for independence. Honchar, as it turned out, had a long memory and was not only offended by Shevelov's review but also considered it a betrayal. Before the outbreak of the German–Soviet war in 1941, Honchar had taken classes with Shevelov, who was then a professor at Kharkiv University. During the war Honchar joined the Red Army. Taken captive by the Germans, he was held as a POW in a Kharkiv concentration camp. From there he tried to send a note to his former professor, who was then working for the local Ukrainian newspaper, begging that he take action to save him. There was no response, and it is unlikely that the message ever reached Shevelov. But Honchar believed that it had. He also believed that Shevelov's critique of his work was related to the note.

When in the early 1990s Honchar confronted Shevelov during one of his visits to Ukraine about his note of 1942 from the concentration camp, Shevelov denied ever having received it. The denial did not convince Honchar. In June 1995, a few weeks before his death, Honchar wrote his last literary work, entitled "An Uncontrived Story from Life." There he made the following statement: "I wonder where he [Shevelov] gets so

---

[27] Iurii Sherekh [Iurii Shevel'ov], "Zdobutky i vtraty ukraïns'koï literatury. Z pryvodu romana Olesia Honchara 'Tavriia,' 1953," *Krytyka* (May 2002): 24–27.

much pathological malice toward my work ... In the emigration the professor would sometimes mention my work as well, and each time extremely tendentiously, very negatively, with almost unexplained hatred toward me. And in blaming, for example, the blameless *Tavriia*, just when it was being eagerly read by steppe herdsmen and acclaimed by academics, my harsh trans-oceanic negativist would sometimes, having cast his aspersions, shed an insincere crocodile tear: 'bitter words, terrible words, but they must be spoken.' Just so! 'Bitter' and 'terrible,' professor, but I am obliged to turn them back to you, and I speak them in writing this uncontrived story from life, the story of a renegade."[28]

The dispute between these major figures in twentieth-century Ukrainian culture was never resolved. Shevelov, accused by Honchar of being a "renegade," died in New York in 2002, still maintaining that he had never received the note from Honchar in 1942. It would have been a miracle indeed if a note thrown over a barbed-wire fence had reached its addressee. It is no less difficult to imagine what Shevelov, who was of German background but never claimed *Volksdeutsche* status, could have done to save a Soviet prisoner of war in 1942. Today students in Ukraine write term papers on the relations between Shevelov and Honchar. The continuing debate focuses as much on the two personalities as on the role that the legacy of Second World War refugees like Ohloblyn and Shevelov should play in contemporary Ukrainian scholarship and culture. Framed in terms of a juxtaposition of Soviet, non-Soviet, and post-Soviet models of identity, the debate seems unlikely to reach any quick resolution. Another debate, the one concerning the terms "Ukraine" and "Little Russia," which involved the author of the *History of the Rus'*, also continues to this day. To be sure, its terms have changed: the name "Ukraine" is no longer associated with Polish intrigue but with the project of an independent Ukrainian culture and nation, while "Little Russia" symbolizes Ukraine's political and cultural dependency on Russia.[29]

---

[28] Oles' Honchar, *Katarsys* (Kyiv, 2000), pp. 133–35.

[29] For different interpretations of the Shevelov–Honchar controversy, see Bohumyla Berdykhovs'ka, "Praporonostsi nepohanoho mynuloho," *Krytyka* (May 2002): 22–25; Mykola Naienko, "Honchar i Shevel'ov, abo 'Vidriznyty zoloto vid imitatsiï,'" *Tainy khudozhn'oho tekstu (do problemy poetyky tekstu)*, vyp. 4 (Dnipropetrovsk, 2004): 49–56; [V. M. Halych], "Dyskursyvne pole 'Nevyhadanoï novely zhyttia' Olesia Honchara (referat)," www.ukrreferat.com/index.php?referat=66470. On the current discussion of the importance of the term "Rus'" for Ukrainian history and identity, see Oleksandr Palii, "Zapozychena istoriia," *Ukraïns'ka pravda* (August 13, 2010) www.pravda.com.ua/articles/2010/08/13/5296670/; idem, "Istoriia odniieï mistyfiktasiï," *Ukraïns'ka pravda* (September 2010), www.pravda.com.ua/columns/2010/09/14/5379524/.

CHAPTER 8

Uncovering the motive

In the summer of 1990 thousands of people in Lviv and other cities and villages of Western Ukraine put on their best embroidered shirts, packed their suitcases, got into their cars, boarded buses and trains, and set out for the city of Nikopol on the lower reaches of the Dnieper. The travelers, often led by men wearing colorful Cossack uniforms, would make stopovers in towns and villages along the way, meet with the locals, and tell them where and why they were going. The locals would listen with great interest. Some of them would even join the travelers, attracted by the stories they told and the songs they sang. Tens of thousands of people from all over Ukraine would take part in the Cossack festival that followed the march to Nikopol. There was something new, exciting, and liberating about that experience – the first popular event of that kind and on such a scale to take place in Ukraine since the Revolution of 1917. It was both striking and predictable that the manifestation took place under Cossack banners.

The march gave overwhelming proof of the resilience of Cossack mythology, which had miraculously survived decades of suppression and persecution. When it revived, it did so as an essential component of Ukrainian national ideology – a connection that had struck fear into the communist authorities since the 1970s. By the late 1980s the communist elite was losing its grip on the country and its monopoly on Ukrainian history. In the spring of 1990 the first free elections to local government offices took place throughout Ukraine. In three oblasts of Galicia in Western Ukraine that were known for their strong sense of national identity, the elections brought to power national democrats whose ultimate goal was political sovereignty. The major challenge for proponents of Ukrainian sovereignty was the attitude of the population of eastern Ukraine, which remained under the spell of communist ideology. This lent unexpected significance to the initiative of the amateur Nikopol historian Pavlo Bohush, who suggested the celebration of the quincenten-nial of Zaporozhian Cossackdom (the date was approximate at best).

The Cossack march to the east turned into an effort to awaken the politically dormant eastern population and convert it to the national ideology of the west. The Cossack myth, which originated in Orthodox eastern Ukraine and was subsequently adopted in the Greek Catholic west of the country because of its close association with Ukrainian national ideology, was now being redirected eastward in order to remind descend-ants of the Dnieper Cossacks of their glorious past and promote the cause of Ukrainian sovereignty. The march on Nikopol turned out successfully. The eastern population embraced the myth as its own. In the following year communist officials who had tried to stop the march bowed to the inevitable and sponsored Cossack festivals and celebrations of their own.[1]

The reemergence of the Cossack myth as a major factor in Ukraine's identity politics in the summer of 1990 was accompanied by the return to the public sphere of the *History of the Rus'*. Two years earlier Fedir Shevchenko, who survived the purge of the 1970s and maintained his membership in the Ukrainian Academy of Sciences, published an article about the *History* in which he basically repeated the information presented in his article of 1966, omitting declarations about the internationalism of its author. He also proposed a reprint of Bodiansky's edition of 1846, which he had in his possession. The imprimatur given the text by a renowned Ukrainian historian renewed interest in the monument among broad circles of the Ukrainian intelligentsia. In early 1991 a reprint of the *History* was published in Kyiv with a press run of 100,000 copies. The person directly responsible for the first reprint of the *History* since 1846 was not a writer or a dissident but a former historian of the Communist Party, Volodymyr Zamlynsky. With the beginning of glasnost, Zam-lynsky, a professor of history at Kyiv University, initiated a number of publication projects to make available to the mass reader many classic works of Ukrainian historiography, including the *History of the Rus'*. Zamlynsky's transformation was very much part of the political about-face undertaken by the Ukrainian "sovereign communists" of the 1980s. The chief representative of that group was Leonid Kravchuk, the long-serving ideological chief of the Communist Party of Ukraine, who

[1] Frank E. Sysyn, "The Reemergence of the Ukrainian Nation and Cossack Mythology," *Social Research* 58, no. 4 (Winter 1991): 845–64; Serhii Plokhy, *Ukraine and Russia: Representations of the Past* (Toronto, 2008), pp. 174–75. On Cossack themes in the music festival held in 1991 in the city of Zaporizhia, which is near Nikopol, see Catherine Wanner, *Burden of Dreams: History and Identity in Post-Soviet Ukraine* (University Park, Pa., 1998), pp. 130–32.

as chairman of the Ukrainian Supreme Soviet led the country to independence in December 1991.[2]

In May 1991, as the Soviet Union was about to enter the last summer of its existence, a new edition of the *History of the Rus'*, this time in Ukrainian translation, hit the shelves of Ukrainian bookstores. The press run of the book – 200,000 copies – was astonishing, especially given the dire economic circumstances of the time. The translation was undertaken by one of the most prominent political figures of the day, Ivan Drach. That distinguished Ukrainian poet and leader of a pro-independence coalition of political parties and civic organizations called Rukh (Movement) turned out to have been spending whatever nights were free from the frenzy of political activity translating the work attributed to the archbishop of Mahilioŭ. He believed it was the text that his nation desperately needed at that trying juncture in its history. "The *History of the Rus'* is the first stage of the rocket that launched you and me into the cosmic immensity of the history of nations and states," wrote Drach in his introduction to the book. He regarded the *History* as a true representation not only of Ukraine's past but also of its present, as well as a road map to the future. He went on: "This is a book to bring us to our senses. It always comes to Ukrainians at times of decision. Needless to say, this is just such a time."[3]

The author of the academic introduction to Ivan Drach's translation of the *History*, a fellow writer, Valerii Shevchuk, fully shared his view of the *History* as a book for the ages that kept reappearing in the history of Ukraine at its most decisive moments. He believed that the *History* had come into existence at another turning point, when Ukraine was undertaking its transition from the Cossack era to the age of national awakening. Like Drach, Shevchuk belonged to the group of Ukrainian writers and intellectuals known as the *shestydesiatnyky*, or the generation of the 1960s. They formed the backbone of the dissident movement in the 1960s and 1970s and were the first to become involved in perestroika in the late 1980s. Shevchuk's older brother, who had an enormous influence

---

[2] Fedir Shevchenko, "Istoriia Rusiv," *Pam'iatky Ukraïny*, no. 1 (1988): 36–39; Svitlana Baturina, "Spetsial'ni istorychni dystsypliny ta teoriia istorychnoï nauky v doslidzhenniakh F. P. Shevchenka," *Spetsial'ni istorychni dystsypliny: pytannia teoriï ta metodyky*, ed. Valerii Smolii, no. 15 (2007): 26–41; *Istoriia Rusov ili Maloi Rossii. Sochinenie Georgiia Koniskago, Arkhiepiskopa Beloruskago*, ed. V. A. Zamlynsky (Moscow, 1846; repr. Kyiv, 1991). For a collection of essays dedicated to Volodymyr Zamlynsky, see *Spetsial'ni istorychni dystsypliny: pytannia teoriï ta metodyky*, no. 6 (7) (Kyiv, 2001), 2 pts.

[3] *Istoriia Rusiv*, trans. Ivan Drach (Kyiv, 1991); Ivan Drach, "Kil'ka sliv perekladacha," in *Istoriia Rusiv* (1991), p. 29.

on Shevchuk, was sent to the Gulag in the 1960s for attempting to publish an article in the printshop where he worked about a fire that broke out in 1964 in the library of the Academy of Sciences. The *shestydesiatnyky* believed that it had been set deliberately in order to destroy priceless items of Ukraine's cultural and historical heritage.[4]

Shevchuk did an amazing job of catching up on the prerevolutionary, early Soviet, and émigré literature on the *History of the Rus'*, which was unknown to his predecessors in Soviet Ukraine. He also brought to his study of the *History of the Rus'* a full measure of Ukrainian patriotism, based on the desire to free Ukrainian culture from the dominance of its powerful Russian cousin. In the anonymous author of the *History*, Shevchuk saw first and foremost a Ukrainian patriot who had written his work to save his homeland from cultural Russification. "The individual who wrote it," asserted Shevchuk, "truly burned with great love for his unfortunate and enslaved land. Thus, at a time when everything Ukrainian was being barbarously destroyed, he managed the feat of casting this passionate pamphlet – a historical remembrance – before the eyes of his foolish and indifferent countrymen, who were scrambling, as Taras Shevchenko wrote, for 'tin buttons,' who 'knew all the ins and outs'; who were grasping for estates and jumping out of their skin to obtain Russian noble rank by any and all means; who had even forgotten their mother tongue."[5]

Was the author of the *History* indeed an antipode of those descendants of the Cossack officer families who were eager to integrate into the empire and a defender of "everything Ukrainian"? Quite a few students of the *History* would question this proposition. One of them, Andrei Storozhenko, writing in 1918, immediately after the fall of the Russian Empire, saw in the author of the *History* a promoter of all-Russian rather than Ukrainian identity. Storozhenko's interpretation of the author's agenda emanated not only from the title of the work itself (after all, it was the *History of the Rus'*, not the "History of the Ukrainians") but also from the discussion of Ukrainian and Rus' terminology in the introduction to the *History*, where the anonymous author claimed that the term "Ukraine" was nothing but a product of Polish intrigue, which had confused the Rus' historians of his age. Shevchuk believed that the "negative attitude of the author of the *History of the Rus'* to the notion

---

[4] Valerii Shevchuk, "Nerozhadani taiemnytsi 'Istoriï Rusiv,'" in *Istoriia Rusiv* (1991), p. 5. On Shevchuk's biography, see "Valerii Shevchuk," in "Biohrafiï pys'mennykiv," www.simya.com.ua/articles/71/18209/.

[5] Valerii Shevchuk, "Lipshe buty nikym nizh rabom," *Den'*, September 17, 2009; Shevchuk, "Nerozhadani taiemnytsi," pp. 27–28.

of 'Ukraine'" was merely a consequence of his poor knowledge of Ukrainian history. He wrote in that regard: "Considering, with perfectly good reason, that Rus' was the particular name of Ukraine, that the Rus' were the inhabitants of the Ukrainian land since time immemorial, and that this name had been usurped artificially in Muscovy because of political and dynastic pretensions, and clearly distinguishing the Rus' from the Russians and Belarusians, the author of the *History of the Rus'* anachronistically maintains that the name 'Ukraine' was foisted upon our land by the Poles; indeed, he does not delve more deeply into the history of this question, for he lacked sufficient historical knowledge."[6]

It is hard to agree with this supposition. The author's vocabulary was above all a reflection of the terminological choices available at the time. The Ukrainian Cossacks were treated as Rus' or even Russian (*Rossiiane*) by his immediate predecessors in the field of Cossack historiography, Petro Symonovsky and Aleksandr Rigelman. The anonymous author was following in the footsteps of Vasyl Ruban when he began his introduction to the *History* with the following statement: "The history of Little Russia until the times of its invasion by the Tatars, with their khan Batu, is one with the history of all Russia, or it is Russian history *per se*." The term *Rusy* (the Rus' people) in its ethnic application became popular in Russian historiography in the eighteenth century. It was popularized by the publication of Vasilii Tatishchev's *Russian History*, which began to appear in print in the 1760s, and was embraced by Empress Catherine II herself. There was, however, an important distinction between the use of this term by the author of the *History of the Rus'* and his illustrious predecessors.

If Tatishchev and Catherine II used the ethnonym *Rusy* to define an ethnic group distinct from the Slavs that came to the environs of the Dnieper River from the Baltic region, the author of the *History* used it to distinguish the ancestors of the Ukrainian Cossacks from the rest of the Slavic world, especially the Muscovites. According to the *History*, the *Rusy* settled the lands between the Danube in the west, the Dvina in the north, the Donets in the east, and the Black Sea in the south. The anonymous author divided these territories into Red and White Rus'. He believed that their political centers were located in what is now Ukraine. According to him, the land of Rus' historically belonged to the Kyiv, Halych, Pereiaslav, Chernihiv, Siverian, and Derevlianian principalities. With the formation of the Muscovite or Russian tsardom by Ivan the Terrible in the

---

[6] *Istoriia Rusov*, pp. i, iii–iv; Shevchuk, "Nerozhadani taiemnytsi," p. 27.

sixteenth century, Red and White Rus' adopted the name "Little Russia" to distinguish itself from the Great Russia of the tsars. [7]

On their first appearance in the *History*, the sixteenth-century Dnieper Cossacks are introduced to the reader as "Little Russian Cossacks." They were allegedly governed by descendants of the Rus' princes but also elected officers from their ranks who formed the backbone of the Little Russian nobility and the core of the Rus' nation. Thus the history of the Rus' nation, the Cossack estate, and the Little Russian noble stratum are linked together in a single narrative that covers some two hundred years. In geographic terms, the focus of that narrative switches from the history of the Rus' lands, defined as what are now Ukraine and Belarus, to the history of the Cossack Host and, later, the Hetmanate, first on both banks of the Dnieper and eventually on its left, Russian, bank. The author does not abandon the notion of Ukrainian-Belarusian Rus', but it recedes into the historical and cultural background as his narrative goes on. Occasionally he shows interest in the western Ukrainian territories, including Galicia, which was under Habsburg rule at the time of writing, and demonstrates readiness to treat the Ukrainian lands in general as a historical unit distinct from Muscovy and Belarus alike.[8]

The anonymous author does his best to follow the line set forth in the introduction to his work and stay away from the term "Ukraine." But once the author becomes involved in the discussion of seventeenth-century Cossack history, when the Cossacks themselves began to make frequent use of the term "Ukraine" and, indeed, made it the primary designation of their polity, even he fails to keep the accursed term out of his work. It penetrates the narrative despite the author's intentions proclaimed in the programmatic statement included in his introduction. He is overcome by his sources – apocryphal eighteenth-century letters, foreign histories, and Russian official documents of the late eighteenth and early nineteenth centuries, which were full of Ukrainian terminology. For example, in an apocryphal letter of May 1648 from Bohdan Khmelnytsky, the term "Little Russian Ukraine" appears four times in a variety of combinations, and there is a reference to "all Ukraine." The anonymous author also writes of Ukraine when referring to Voltaire's comment on Mazepa and the Ukrainian expedition of Charles XII of Sweden.[9]

---

[7] Vasilii Tatishchev, *Istoriia Rossiiskaia*, pt. 1, chap. 30; Plokhy, *Ukraine and Russia*, pp. 19–33; Ivan Dzyra, *Kozats'ke litopysannia 30-kh–80-kh rokiv XVIII stolittia: dzhereloznavchyi ta istoriohrafichnyi aspekty* (Kyiv, 2006), pp. 303–56.

[8] *Istoriia Rusov*, pp. i–ii, 1–16.

[9] See *Istoriia Rusov*, pp. 68–74, 161, 167, 172, 179, 208, 236, 242, 253.

Whatever his ideological postulates, the author of the *History of the Rus'* proves unable to divest himself entirely of the tradition established by earlier Ukrainian authors, for whom the term "Ukraine" had no negative connotations and entailed no suggestion of Polish intrigue. But why did he want to break with this tradition? The reason provided by the author himself is quite simple: it is rooted in his anti-Polish attitude. In Polish historiography the term "Ukraine" preserved its original meaning as first and foremost the land of the Cossacks, giving the author a good opportunity to strike at the Poles. His attack seems to have been well timed. The first decades of the nineteenth century were highly conducive to a renewed confrontation with the Poles. The activities of Adam Czartoryski, a personal friend and close adviser of Alexander I, who not only presided over the increasing cultural Polonization of the Vilnius educational district but also, as de facto foreign minister of Russia, was preparing to restore the Kingdom of Poland under the auspices of the Russian tsar, provoked a strong negative response from Russian society. Distrust of Poles grew in the second half of the decade, when Polish exiles in the West sided with Napoleon, and the French emperor, perceived by that time as Russia's worst enemy, carved a Polish polity known as the Duchy of Warsaw out of the Prussian part of the former Commonwealth. In 1806–7 the Poles were submitting proposals to Napoleon to make Podilia, Volhynia, and Right-Bank Ukraine part of a future Polish state. The elites of the former Hetmanate could by no means have endorsed the inclusion of the Right Bank (lands that the author of the *History of the Rus'* claimed as ancient Rus' territories) in a future Polish polity under Alexander I or Napoleon.[10]

The creation by the Congress of Vienna in 1815 of an autonomous Polish kingdom within the boundaries of the Russian Empire could not produce anything but resentment and jealousy in the hearts of the Ukrainian nobility. The persistent anti-Polish sentiment in the Russian Empire gave the Cossack elites of the former Hetmanate a good opportunity not only to settle historical scores with their traditional enemy but

---

[10] On the creation of the Kingdom of Poland, see Piotr S. Wandycz, *The Lands of Partitioned Poland, 1795–1918* (Seattle and London, 1974), pp. 33–42. On Napoleon's plans *vis-à-vis* Poland and Ukraine, see Il'ko Borshchak, *Napoleon i Ukraïna* (Lviv, 1937); cf. Vadym Adadurov, "Narodzhennia odnoho istorychnoho mitu: problema 'Napoleon i Ukraïna' u vysvitlenni Il'ka Borshchaka," *Ukraïna moderna* (Kyiv and Lviv) 9 (2005): 212–36, here 227, 233. On anti-Polish sentiments in the Russian Empire, see Andrei Zorin, *Kormia dvuglavogo orla … Literatura i gosudarstvennaia ideologiia v Rossii v poslednei treti XVIII–pervoi treti XIX veka* (Moscow, 2001), pp. 157–86; Zenon E. Kohut, *Russian Centralism and Ukrainian Autonomy: Imperial Absorption of the Hetmanate, 1760s–1830s* (Cambridge, Mass., 1988), pp. 248–84.

also to take credit for their age-old struggle with Poland. In the introduction to the *History*, the anonymous author does not hide his true feelings
toward the Poles and their interpretation of the history of his homeland.
He writes: "Polish and Lithuanian historians, rightly suspected of fabrica-
tion and self-advertisement, in describing the deeds of the Rus', who were
allegedly subject to the Poles, did their utmost to obscure the exploits of
the former, undertaken on behalf of their common fatherland with the
Poles." He was even more unforgiving with regard to those Rus' historians
who allegedly followed in the footsteps of their Polish and Lithuanian
predecessors: "[I]t must be said with regret that certain absurdities and
calumnies have unfortunately been introduced into Little Russian chronicles themselves by their creators, natives of Rus', who have carelessly
followed the shameless and malicious Polish and Lithuanian fabulists."[11]

The anonymous author concludes his introduction by posing the
rhetorical question of whether the "thirty-four bloody battles that it
required, with Rus' armies opposing the Poles and their kings and the
levy *en masse*, are of insufficient merit that this nation and its chieftains be
rendered due justice for their exploits and heroism." He regarded his book
as ultimate proof of his nation's heroic past and introduced it to the reader
with the words: "Come and see!" This was exactly the kind of narrative
that the Ukrainian elites wanted to read during the first decades of the
nineteenth century. History took center stage in public discussions of that
day, becoming an object of obsessive interest not only to antiquarians and
history buffs but also to leaders of noble society, governors general, and
high officials at the imperial court. The emperor himself became a
participant in historical debates and their ultimate judge.

In June 1809 Prince Yakov Lobanov-Rostovsky, the 49-year-old governor
general of Little Russia (1808–16), left his residence in Poltava and
embarked on a long and trying journey to St. Petersburg. He was going
to the imperial capital to see the young, reform-minded Emperor
Alexander I. In his bag he had an appeal to the tsar from the nobility of
Poltava gubernia, asking the sovereign to intervene on its behalf in its
conflict with the Heraldry Office, an imperial body in charge of the
recognition of noble status. The memorandum, entitled "On the Right
of Little Russian Civil Servants to Noble Dignity," argued that descendants of Cossack officeholders should enjoy the rights and privileges of the

---

[11] *Istoriia Rusov*, pp. iii–iv; Andrei Zorin, *Kormia dvuglavogo orla*, pp. 157–86; Kohut, *Russian Centralism and Ukrainian Autonomy*, pp. 248–84.

Russian nobility. The argument was as much legal as historical. The authors of the memorandum dug out official documents from the local archives and studied historical works and Cossack chronicles in an attempt to present the history of the Cossack officer stratum since the sixteenth century as that of a noble order. They protested against the rulings of the Heraldry Office, which questioned the claims to noble status advanced by many descendants of Cossack officeholders, and requested the governor general's intervention with the emperor.[12]

The conflict between the elite of the former Hetmanate and the Heraldry Office had its prehistory. Throughout a good part of the eighteenth century, the imperial authorities had sought the best way to incorporate the Cossack elite of the Hetmanate into the imperial noble estate, which was exempted from taxation, had the exclusive right to own serfs, and enjoyed extensive privileges with regard to education and career opportunities in the imperial army and civil service. The government was trying to incorporate the upper echelons of the Cossack officer stratum without opening the door too wide and allowing the ennoblement of tens of thousands of well-to-do Cossacks whose ancestors had held elective office in the army and the civil administration of the Hetmanate. The authorities were desperate to avoid a situation in which the number of recognized nobles in the former Hetmanate would be many times greater than in the Russian gubernias of the empire. They vacillated, recognizing the noble status of some officeholders but not others, granting it one day and taking it away the next. Policy remained in flux until the late eighteenth century, when Emperor Paul I decided to compile a new register of the imperial nobility. According to the imperial decree of 1797, families claiming noble status had to submit documents proving their noble origins, which turned out to be a problem for many of them.

In Ukraine, the Heraldry Office recognized the noble status and approved nobiliary coats of arms for those families that submitted documents proving that their ancestors had belonged to the Polish nobility. It also approved coats of arms for descendants of former Cossack officeholders whose ancestors had served in imperial institutions after the liquidation of the Hetmanate. Others were excluded. That was only the beginning of the "time of troubles" for those members of the Ukrainian gentry who claimed noble status exclusively on the basis of their ancestors' service in Cossack institutions. The conflict became more intense in the first years of the reign of Alexander I. In 1802 the Heraldry Office

[12] Volodymyr Sverbyhuz, *Starosvits'ke panstvo* (Warsaw, 1999), pp. 171, 177–78.

overturned the decision of a local nobiliary assembly and refused noble status to the Pidvysotsky family, one of whose members had been an acting colonel in the mid eighteenth century. Soon more than four hundred nobiliary coats of arms were returned to Chernihiv nobles, as their right to use them had been questioned by the Heraldry Office. In 1805 the office had ruled that service in the Hetmanate with officer rank at the company or regimental level did not constitute proof of noble origin. Hundreds of families hitherto treated as noble found their status revoked, their right to own serfs challenged, and their children turned away from educational institutions reserved for the nobility.[13]

The Little Russian nobility was up in arms. The best and, as it turned out, the only way to fight the Heraldry Office was to turn to history and prove that the noble status of Cossack officers had not only been recognized by Russian tsars and imperial agencies but actually predated Russian rule and was rooted in local tradition and grants of official privilege to its elite by Lithuanian dukes and Polish kings. Collecting historical documents to establish such grants suddenly became a matter of the utmost importance. Nobiliary assemblies charged their elected leaders, county and gubernia marshals, with the task of drafting historical memoranda to undermine the position taken by the Heraldry Office. The marshals of the nobility turned for assistance to people who had the reputation of history buffs. So did the imperial administrators of the region, who found themselves between the Scylla of the Heraldry Office and the Charybdis of the enraged nobiliary assemblies.

In 1804, relatively early in the crisis, the governor general of Little Russia, Prince Aleksei Kurakin (1802–8), met with an expert in Cossack history, a judge of the Chernihiv gubernia court named Roman Markovych, to discuss the historical evidence. Markovych was convinced that the Cossack officers were entitled to all noble rights traditionally pertaining to the "knightly estate or order." The governor promised to look into the issue. In November 1804 Markovych sent Kurakin a memorandum arguing that Cossack officers possessed not only personal but also hereditary rights and thus could pass on their noble status to their heirs. "The tsar ordered the hetman to confirm these officers, just

---

[13] *Ibid.*, pp. 165–66; D. Miller, "Ocherki iz iuridicheskogo byta staroi Malorossii. Prevrashchenie kazatskoi starshiny v dvorianstvo," *Kievskaia starina*, no. 4 (1897): 1–47; Kohut, *Russian Centralism and Ukrainian Autonomy*, pp. 247–58; Oleksiy Tolochko, "Fellows and Travelers: Thinking about Ukrainian History in the Early Nineteenth Century," in *A Laboratory of Transnational History: Ukraine and Recent Ukrainian Historiography*, ed. Georgiy Kasianov and Philip Ther (Budapest and New York, 2009), pp. 149–66.

like captains, on the basis of election," wrote Markovych, "with proclamations not for a certain period but for all time."[14]

Markovych's notion of the Cossack officers as members of a virtual
"knightly estate," which he equated with the corporate estate of the
hereditary nobility, was further developed by another Chernihiv history
connoisseur, Tymofii Kalynsky, the treasurer of the Chernihiv gubernia
nobiliary assembly. A migrant from the Polish-Lithuanian Commonwealth who had spent most of his life in the former Hetmanate, Kalynsky
claimed noble status as a descendant of Polish nobles. Nevertheless, one
could hardly imagine a more ardent defender of the noble rights of
Cossack officeholders than Kalynsky. In a memorandum written for the
nobiliary assembly in 1805, he went even further than Markovych and
argued that not only Cossack officers but Cossacks in general were
entitled to noble status. "In this land," wrote Kalynsky, "the Cossack
was endowed by Russian tsars, Polish kings, and Lithuanian princes with a
confirmed knightly rank and noble status according to which he was titled
and recognized; accordingly, on every occasion and at elections, even
those of hetmans themselves, he had a vote; hence at elections every
deserving candidate could be elected an officer holding some post, which
entitled him to a noble landed estate."[15]

The question of the noble status of Cossack officeholders and their
descendants was discussed at length at an assembly of the Chernihiv
nobility in January 1806. The nobles listened to the reports of their leaders
and historical arguments presented by experts, including Kalynsky. Those
in attendance commissioned Mykhailo Storozhenko, the marshal of the
Chernihiv nobility, to prepare a petition to be submitted on their behalf
to Governor General Aleksei Kurakin. Storozhenko lost no time in doing
so, relying largely on the memorandum written by Roman Markovych.
The petition was submitted to Kurakin in March 1806. As one could
expect of an official appeal, it was heavily freighted with references to the
proclamations of Cossack hetmans and decrees of the Russian imperial
authorities, and light on statements of a general nature. There was
nothing to indicate that the author was concerned with anything other
than particular rulings of the Heraldry Office or had any purpose other
than to redress the injustices inflicted by those rulings on a specific group
of Hetmanate officeholders. However, behind the bureaucratic language

[14] Sverbyhuz, *Starosvits'ke panstvo*, pp. 177–78.
[15] *Ibid.*, pp. 178–83; Miller, "Ocherki," p. 20; Oleksander Ohloblyn, *Liudy staroï Ukraïny* (Munich,
1959), pp. 33–48.

of the petition there was the growing conviction that the rulings of the Heraldry Office were not only an attack on the noble status of individual community members but also an assault on the historical identity and honor of the community as a whole.

Struggle with the Heraldry Office became a patriotic duty for members of the elite, and Storozhenko, while careful to keep such sentiments out of his official document, was quite prepared to appeal to the patriotic feelings of his compatriots in his private correspondence. "I am convinced, Honorable Sir, that you will take part in this matter as a patriot and will not decline to lend your support for the benefit of the land as a whole," he wrote in March 1806 on sending a copy of the petition to a fellow Ukrainian, Dmytro Troshchynsky. A former associate of Prince Oleksandr Bezborodko, Troshchynsky was the imperial minister in charge of land reform. He was indeed a local patriot, and in the previous year he had mediated a conflict between Kurakin and some Little Russian nobles. He could not, however, help much on this occasion. In 1806, Troshchynsky was already on his way out of office. He soon resigned his cabinet post and returned to his estate in the Poltava gubernia. The Chernihiv petition gathered dust in the governor general's office until Kurakin resigned in 1808 and was replaced by Prince Yakov Lobanov-Rostovsky.[16]

The appointment of the new governor general encouraged the Little Russian nobility to resume its efforts in what was increasingly considered an affair of honor. This time it was the Poltava nobles who took the lead. The "patriots," as the opponents of the Heraldry Office and promoters of the rights and privileges of the local nobility became known in Ukraine, found their new leader in Vasyl Charnysh, who was elected marshal of the nobility of the Poltava gubernia in January 1809. Charnysh's own noble status was never in doubt, as he was a descendant of a prominent Cossack family: one of his ancestors was a general judge of the Hetmanate. Vasyl Charnysh was also a rich landowner and master of almost two thousand serfs in Hadiach county of the Poltava gubernia. He was elected to the office of Poltava marshal three times between 1801 and 1820, and each time he did his utmost to defend the rights of his fellow nobles. Even before Charnysh's election, the Poltava nobles requested a copy of the

---

[16] "Predstavlenie Chernigovskogo gubernskogo marshala Storozhenko Malorossiiskomu general-gubernatoru s iz"iasneniem tochnogo znacheniia malorossiiskikh chinov i s prilozheniem iskhodataistvovaniia peremeny zakliucheniia ob onykh gerol'dii" (dated February 28, 1806), Manuscript Institute, Vernadsky Library, VIII, no. 1602, fols. 1–4; Sverbyhuz, *Starosvits'ke panstvo*, pp. 183–85; Miller, "Ocherki," pp. 27–30; David Saunders, *The Ukrainian Impact on Russian Culture, 1750–1850* (Edmonton, 1985), pp. 90–100.

Chernihiv petition of 1806 for study. They found it unsatisfactory on a number of legal and historical points and decided to produce a petition of their own that would make the case of the Little Russian nobility in the strongest possible terms.

Some preliminary work on a petition from Poltava had been done by Charnysh's predecessors in the marshal's office, Semen Kochubei and Mykhailo Myloradovych. The latter, who had served in that capacity from 1806 to 1808, had already been in touch with Roman Markovych and Tymofii Kalynsky in Chernihiv. Kalynsky sent Myloradovych two note-books filled with excerpts from historical sources on Cossack offices, accompanied by his own comments, which apparently were not entirely loyal to the imperial regime. In his letter of April 1808 to Myloradovych, Kalynsky appealed to the patriotism of his addressee. "I graciously request of you," he wrote, referring to his comments, "since I perhaps write too frankly in them, nourishing particular hope with regard to your patriotism toward our land, do not allow just anyone to read or, even more, to copy these notebooks." Kalynsky also declared his own patriotic credentials: "Roman Ivanovych [Markovych] calls their [the Cossack officers'] organ-ization an order of fellows of the Host. I would gladly give my life in defense of the order and our common privileges and liberty. I have lived in this land for almost sixty years, and I can say that that is where my fatherland is, where I live well and find the smoke of my fatherland pleasant."[17]

Vasyl Charnysh apparently inherited the Kalynsky notes from Myloradovych. But he did not want to rely exclusively on the work of the Chernihiv experts. Charnysh also turned for advice to local "patriots" known for their interest and expertise in history. Among them were Andrian Chepa, Vasyl Poletyka, and Vasyl Lomykovsky – all Poltava-area nobles. Like Storozhenko a few years earlier, Charnysh was not reticent about appealing to the local patriotism of his helpers. He appealed to their national feelings, introducing elements of national discourse into legal and historical debates on the rights and privileges of the Ukrainian nobility. "Again, I know how much you love your nation; consequently, it only remains for me to ask you most humbly to take upon yourself the trouble of augmenting and correcting the attached note in every respect according to your own views," wrote Charnysh in February 1809 to Andrian Chepa, a local collector of historical texts, on sending him the first draft of his memorandum. Chepa was happy to oblige. "I have augmented that note as much as I could, kind Sir, no less out of zeal

[17] Sverbyhuz, *Starosvits'ke panstvo*, p. 185; Miller, "Ocherki," pp. 30–31.

and love for my nation than out of my desire to be of service to you," he wrote to Charnysh in March 1809.[18]

Chepa also produced his own memorandum on the issue. He collected as much material as possible and even got in touch with Maksym Berlynsky, who sent him his textbook of 1800. Another memorandum was written at Charnysh's request by an amateur historian from the Poltava region, Vasyl Poletyka, whose candidacy for the authorship of the *History* was promoted by Vasyl Horlenko and Mykhailo Drahomanov. Both Chepa and Poletyka argued in favor of recognizing the noble status of descendants of the Cossack officers of the Hetmanate. Chepa quoted from the Lithuanian Statute of the sixteenth century, which referred to the rights and privileges of knights and nobles, presenting these two groups as belonging to one category (the statute did not distinguish between personal and hereditary nobility). Poletyka followed in the footsteps of Markovych and Kalynsky, arguing that the Cossack officers "constituted, so to speak, a particular knightly order." He regarded the actions of the Heraldry Office *vis-à-vis* individual members of that group as an insult to the historical memory of the whole "Little Russian nation." "The little Russian nation serves the Russian tsars faithfully and diligently. Not only does it not succumb to any enticements on the part of enemies of the Russian state, but, not sparing its possessions or its life, it has always valiantly and bravely taken up arms against such people ... But now the Little Russian officeholders, who commanded the Little Russian soldiers and deserve glory and gratitude, are being reduced to the lowest degree by the Heraldry Office."[19]

When Charnysh finally sat down to write the final draft of the petition, he combined historical and legal arguments pertaining to the noble status of Cossack officeholders with statements about the honor and dignity of the entire nation. The Poltava marshal represented the policies of the Heraldry Office not simply as an assault on the rights of the less prominent

---

[18] V. Gorlenko, "Iz istorii iuzhno-russkogo obshchestva nachala XIX veka (Pis'ma V. I. Charnysha, A. I. Chepy, V. G. Poletiki i zametki k nim)," *Kievskaia starina*, no. 1 (1893): 41–76, here 46. On Chepa, see Hanna Shvyd'ko, "Chepa, Andrian Ivanovych," in *Dovidnyk z istoriï Ukraïny*, vol. III (Kyiv, 1999), pp. 562–63; Oleh Zhurba, "Predstav'te Vy sebe kakoi zver' byl getman! Èto byli prenechestivye despoty! (Z lysta svidomoho ukraïns'koho patriota, avtonomista ta tradytsionalista XIX stolittia)," in *Dnipropetrovs'kyi istoryko-arkheohrafichnyi zbirnyk*, ed. Oleh Zhurba, no. 3 (Dnipropetrovsk, 2009), pp. 161–220.

[19] "Zapiska o nachale, proiskhozhdenii i dostoinstve Malorossiiskogo dvorianstva," Manuscript Institute, Vernadsky Library, VIII, no. 1604, fols. 1–10. Cf. "Zapiska o Malorossiiskom dvorianstve marshala romenskogo poveta Vasiliia Poletiki," *Kievskaia starina*, no. 1 (1893): appendix, pp. 1–8; "Zapiska o malorossiiskikh chinakh Andriana Ivanovicha Chepy (1809)," *Kievskaia starina*, no. 4 (1897): appendix, pp. 23–32; no. 5: appendix, pp. 33–39; Sverbyhuz, *Starosvits'ke panstvo*, pp. 186–87.

Cossack officer families but as an encroachment on the rights, privileges, and honor of Little Russia. "Such denial of nobility to Little Russian officials," read Charnysh's memo, "demeans them and their achievements, insults their dignity and that of their descendants, and undermines the rights and privileges of the whole nation granted by Polish kings and later by all-Russian autocrats." Charnysh traced the roots of his nation all the way back to Kyivan Rus'. "It is well known," wrote the Poltava marshal, "that the Little Russian nation, which comprised the grand principalities of Kyiv, Chernihiv, and Pereiaslav, was torn away from the Rus' scepter in 1321 and spent more than three centuries under the Tatar yoke or in Lithuanian and Polish bondage, until at last, by force of arms, after many signal victories over the Poles, it threw off its subjection and adhered to the rule of Russia."[20]

The leitmotif of Charnysh's memo was clear: in questioning the rights of individual nobles, the Heraldry Office was actually raising its hand against the nation. It was no longer a question of estate rights but of national rights. And Little Russia was a nation proud of its ancient origins, boasting a glorious past and a long record of loyalty to the monarchy. Charnysh's use of national discourse was not entirely unprecedented in early nineteenth-century Ukraine, where the Little Russian nation was regarded as a living organism with deep historical roots. In 1801 the nobility of Zolotonosha county south of Kyiv requested that Alexander I "establish a school in the town of Lubny for the whole nation." Thinking of the former Hetmanate as a separate nation was a sign of distinct group identity on the part of the Ukrainian elites, but not necessarily an indication of anti-Russian or anti-imperial tendencies. The same memorandum of the Zolotonosha nobility argued in favor of billeting imperial troops in the region, admittedly on economic grounds. "It would be not without utility and even necessary," reads the petition, "that in this nation, political and governmental circumstances permitting, cavalry regiments be introduced for billeting, whereby a sum of money would be contributed to the nation in return for its produce." The Zolotonosha nobles clearly wanted to reap full advantage for their nation from the empire to which it belonged.[21]

---

[20] Sverbyhuz, *Starosvits'ke panstvo*, p. 188; I. F. Pavlovskii, *Poltavtsy: ierarkhi, gosudarstvennye i obshchestvennye deiateli i blagotvoriteli* (Poltava, 1914), pp. 90–92; *Poltavshchyna: entsyklopedychnyi dovidnyk*, ed. A. V. Kudryts'kyi (Kyiv, 1992), pp. 489–99.

[21] T. F. Litvinova, "'Soslovnye nuzhdy i zhelaniia' dvorianstva Livoberezhnoï Ukraïny na pochatku XIX stolittia," *Ukraïns'kyi istorychnyi zhurnal*, no. 2 (2005): 67–78.

Vasyl Charnysh's emphasis on the rights of the nation were informed by, or closely resonated with, Roman Markovych's stress on service to one's countrymen, Tymofii Kalynsky's readiness to die defending the rights and freedoms of the Cossack order, and Vasyl Chepa's and Vasyl Poletyka's concern for the fatherland. Whether all these students of history used the terms *narod* and *natsiia* or not, their references to the fatherland, patriotic duty, and the interests of the nation contributed to the formation of a new type of discourse in early nineteenth-century Ukraine. Thinking about the former Hetmanate as a separate nation with a history, territory, and economic interests of its own, distinct from the rest of the empire, signaled an early stage in the development of a national identity among the descendants of the former Cossack elite. Like any other nation-building project, the Ukrainian one was moving forward with its face turned back to the past. In the opinion of the Ukrainian elite, there was no better argument for the distinctiveness of its homeland than its historical evolution, which was very different in political, economic, legal, and cultural terms from that of the rest of the empire.

In 1809 the new governor general, Yakov Lobanov-Rostovsky, faced with growing discontent among the local nobility, was eager to put the whole issue of noble status to rest and negotiate the best possible deal with the imperial authorities. He did what his predecessor, Prince Kurakin, had failed to do, submitting the petition of the nobility to the cabinet along with his own appeal. In November 1809, having heard the report of the minister of justice, the cabinet decided to loosen the rules applied by the Heraldry Office in the Hetmanate and return to the policy of entrusting the local nobiliary assemblies with the task of verifying their members' credentials. News reached Ukraine that Alexander I himself had issued oral instructions to the Heraldry Office to recognize the noble status of most Cossack officeholders. The Little Russian nobility was ecstatic. Poletyka wrote to Chepa, expressing his patriotic exaltation: "Recently I was delighted to hear the pleasant news that upon the report of our governor general the sovereign Emperor instructed the Heraldry Office to recognize the Little Russian nobility in its ancient noble dignity according to our ranks and other proofs. This news is sweet to my heart. Believe that I love my fatherland: I love my countrymen more than myself."[22]

The Ukrainian patriots and their historical advisers could celebrate a victory of sorts. The cabinet decision was soon suspended, but the outbreak of the Napoleonic Wars made it politically dangerous for the

---

[22] Gorlenko, "Iz istorii iuzhno-russkogo obshchestva," p. 56; Miller, "Ocherki," pp. 38–39.

imperial authorities to continue questioning the noble status of the families of former Cossack officeholders. Lobanov-Rostovsky issued an appeal to the Cossacks to join the new military formations. He also called on the nobles to enroll serfs in the auxiliary units. They complied. But when the conquerors of Paris returned to their homeland, the imperial institutions resumed their attacks. In 1816 the Cossack regiments were disbanded and the system of recruiting serfs into the Russian army resumed. Two years later, in December 1818, it was ruled that descendants of Cossack officers who had held the ranks of aide-de-camp, flag-bearer, captain, or fellow of the Host should not be considered nobles. Their forefathers, it was argued, had been entitled to personal but not hereditary nobility. The erstwhile peace in relations between the Ukrainian nobility and the imperial authorities turned out to have been a mere armistice.

Given the resumption of hostilities, some of the old commanders returned to the front lines to prepare a new attack on the capital. Among them was Vasyl Charnysh, reelected in January 1818 (for the third and last time) as marshal of the Poltava gubernia. In October 1819 the Poltava nobiliary assembly adopted a resolution that repeated verbatim entire paragraphs from the petition prepared by Charnysh in the summer of 1809. It claimed once again that "denial of noble status to Little Russian officials . . . undermines the rights and privileges of the whole nation." The national cause seemed as important in 1819 as it had been a decade earlier. Once again, the whole Little Russian noble nation was up in arms. The war would go on for another fifteen years until it was ended in March 1834 by an imperial decree recognizing the noble status of descendants of most Cossack officeholders, including company captains and fellows of the Host. Residual discontent among the Ukrainian elite in the wake of the Polish uprising of 1830–31 made the government more conducive to an agreement than it had been in the wake of the victorious Napoleonic Wars.[23]

The Little Russian nobility and its Cossack heritage were under attack in the opening decades of the nineteenth century, which in the atmosphere of the struggle for the noble status of the descendants of Cossack officeholders best explains the motivation, arguments, and tone of the *History of the Rus'*. This applies particularly to the author's emphasis on the history of the Rus' nation, to which he refers as *narod* but also, occasionally, as *natsiia* (including the use of the adjective *natsional'nyi*).

[23] Sverbyhuz, *Starosvits'ke panstvo*, pp. 172–77, 191–94; Miller, "Ocherki," pp. 40–47; Kohut, *Russian Centralism and Ukrainian Autonomy*, pp. 255–58.

The discourse of nation resonated well with the Ukrainian nobility of the early nineteenth century, whose members employed national terminology in the defense of their rights and privileges. Placing the nation at the center of a narrative was a historiographic innovation that contributed to the popularity of the *History* at a time when modern nationalism was slowly but surely making its way into Eastern Europe. But it was not all about the likes and dislikes of the nineteenth century.

The anonymous author's interest in the nation was also deeply rooted in the Ukrainian intellectual tradition, since the "nation of Rus'" had emerged as the main object of loyalty of religious polemicists as early as the first half of the seventeenth century. That nation, which included both Ukrainians and Belarusians at the time, was transformed in the works of the eighteenth-century Cossack chroniclers into the Little Russian or Cossack Little Russian nation of the Hetmanate. On the pages of the *History*, "nation" became the primary object of loyalty, replacing "fatherland," which had occupied a central place in eighteenth-century Cossack historiography and maintained its appeal to Ukrainian patriots of the early nineteenth century, including Vasyl Poletyka and Andrian Chepa. The anonymous author's emphasis on nationhood helped transform the Cossack historiography of the premodern era into the Ukrainian national narrative of the nineteenth and twentieth centuries.[24]

But why did the anonymous author call his nation Rus'? Why not call it the "Little Russian nation," as did Charnysh, or the "Cossack Little Russian nation," as did the last great Cossack chronicler of the eighteenth century, Petro Symonovsky, in the title of his chronicle? In fact, the anonymous author called his nation "Little Russia" much more often than he called it "Rus'." The term "Rus'" was probably included in the

---

[24] On the importance of the concept of "fatherland" in Cossack historical writing, see Frank E. Sysyn, "Fatherland in Early Eighteenth-Century Ukrainian Political Culture," in Giovanna Siedina, ed., *Mazepa and His Time: History, Culture, Society* (Alessandria, 2004), pp. 39–53; Siedina, "The Persistence of the Little Rossian Fatherland in the Russian Empire: The Evidence from the *History of the Rus' or of Little Rossia* (*Istoriia Rusov ili Maloi Rossii*)," in *Beispiele und Ansätze aus osteuropäischer Perspektive: Festschrift für Andreas Kappeler*, ed. Guido Hausmann and Angela Rustemeyer (Wiesbaden, 2009): 39–49. On the notion of "fatherland" in eighteenth-century Russian politics and culture, see essays by Ingrid Schierle, "'For the Benefit and Glory of the Fatherland': The Concept of Otechestvo," in *Eighteenth-Century Russia: Society, Culture, Economy. Papers from the VII International Conference of the Study Group on Eighteenth-Century Russia, Wittenberg 2004*, ed. Roger Bartlett and Gabriela Lehmann-Carli (Berlin, 2007), pp. 283–95; Schierle, "'Otečestvo' – Der russische Vaterlandsbegriff im 18. Jahrhundert," in *Kultur in der Geschichte Russlands. Räume, Medien, Identitäten, Lebenswelten*, ed. Bianka Pietrow-Ennker (Göttingen, 2007), pp. 143–62; Schierle, "Patriotism and Emotions: Love of the Fatherland in Catherinian Russia," *Ab Imperio*, no. 3 (2009): 65–93.

title of his work because the author or his editor wanted to make a point in contention with Russian imperial historiography. Well aware of the close ethnic and religious affinity between Great and Little Russians, the anonymous author sought to exploit it to the benefit of the latter. In that regard, he was following in the footsteps of the authors of nobiliary memoranda of the period. "Could the Little Russian nobility," wrote Vasyl Poletyka in his memorandum, "having freely united with the Russians as its brothers by common birth and faith, and having served the throne and the fatherland together with them so faithfully and so long, have expected such offensive abasement in return for the military valor and merits it had demonstrated and sealed with its blood?"[25]

While noting the ethnic and religious affinity of the Great and Little Russians, the anonymous author argued that primacy in that family relationship belonged to his compatriots, who happened to be direct descendants not only of the heroic Cossacks but also of the glorious princes of Kyiv. As such, they were not merely equal to the Great Russians but superior to them. This was an argument made by many Ukrainian patriots of the early nineteenth century. Tymofii Kalynsky, for example, claimed that not only the Cossack officers but also rank-and-file Cossacks were superior to the Russian nobility, which had originally been recruited to the tsar's court from the "rabble." Andrian Chepa made a similar argument in 1809 in a letter to Vasyl Poletyka. Referring to the writings of Vasyl's father, Hryhorii Poletyka, he noted the superior privileges of the Little Russian nobility prior to 1762 and recalled that "when the Little Russian nobility was told about the drafting of those laws [concerning the rights of the Russian nobility], the nobles of Starodub and Nizhyn, fearing, evidently not without reason, that they would be subjected to the status of Russian courtiers, thought it better to be in chains than to agree to those laws."[26]

The claim that one's own people were the only true Rus' natives, not junior partners of the Great Russians, was a good rhetorical device for propelling one's countrymen to the summit of the imperial hierarchy. This was a strategy of overcompensation – stressing the glorious past of the Cossack ancestors and claiming the superiority of the rights and freedoms of the Little Russian nobility as a way of asserting equal status with the Great Russians and negotiating the best possible conditions for integration into the imperial elite. That would appear to have been the main goal of the author of the *History*, who stressed not only Cossack

[25] Miller, "Ocherki," p. 11.   [26] Gorlenko, "Iz istorii iuzhno-russkogo obshchestva," p. 54.

heroism and the rights granted to the Little Russian nobles by the Polish kings but also the exclusive claim of his compatriots to the name and heritage of Rus', which was the core of the Russian imperial identity.

There are many similarities between the *History of the Rus'* and the legal and historical memoranda of 1804–19. But there are also profound differences between them. Comparing the *History* and the noble petitions of the period leaves little doubt that not only Vasyl Poletyka but also Roman Markovych, Tymofii Kalynsky, and Andrian Chepa do not qualify as possible authors of the mysterious text. To put it simply, their knowledge of the Cossack past and the details of Cossack legal history was far superior to that of the anonymous author. His strength was of a different kind. Adopting many arguments adduced by Ukrainian patriots of the early nineteenth century, the anonymous author went further than they ever could, given the genre of their writings, in developing those arguments. Tymofii Kalynsky could only dream of including stories of "national heroes ... who defended faith and freedom, gaining rights for this country through struggle" in his memorandum. The author of the *History* was actually in a position to do so.[27]

Rus' terminology helped the author assert the Cossack claim to the heritage of Kyivan Rus', but that was not its only function. Helping Cossack officers prove their equality to those in the imperial service was a prime task of research and historical writing at the time, and the *History*'s assertion of Cossack primacy over their Russian counterparts was an important contribution to a debate based largely on references to old royal and imperial charters and resolutions. But there was also a drawback to this strategy: by promoting the idea of a Rus' nation distinct from Russia, the author of the *History* left a confusing legacy. His insistence on the name "Rus'" and rejection of "Ukraine," while facilitating the admiration of his work by such Russian literary luminaries as Kondratii Ryleev and Alexander Pushkin, allowed Ukrainians of the Little Russian persuasion like Andrei Storozhenko to consider him a proponent of all-Russian identity. The project of turning the Little Russians of the early nineteenth century into modern Ukrainians, for which the anonymous author provided considerable historical ammunition, was both strengthened and weakened by the *History*. In the final analysis, that project was saved by the decision of Ukrainian intellectuals of the 1830s and 1840s to abandon the confusing Rus' terminology of their predecessors and embrace the Ukrainian one.

---

[27] Quoted in Sverbyhuz, *Starosvits'ke panstvo*, p. 185.

Although there is good reason to consider the author of the *History* a precursor of modern Ukrainian identity, as did Valerii Shevchuk and many scholars before and after him, it would be an error to see him as an opponent of those of his countrymen who did their utmost to gain Russian noble status and speed up their integration into the empire. While the author was clearly a patriot of his native land, he was far from being an exemplar of modern Ukrainian national identity, which draws a clear distinction between Ukrainians and Poles on the one hand and Ukrainians and Russians on the other. His rejection of "Ukrainian" terminology shows that his identity was exclusivist with regard to the Poles but still very porous when it came to Ukraine's Russian neighbors. He clearly set out on the path to modern Ukrainian identity but remained very far from the destination. The identity and motivation of the author of the *History of the Rus'* were much more complex than their representation by the Ukrainian writers and political activists who rediscovered the "eternal book of Ukraine" on the eve of Ukrainian independence. Like many of their predecessors of the nineteenth and twentieth centuries, they found answers in the *History* to the questions that most preoccupied them at the time. Long after historians had discarded the *History* as unreliable invention, poets and national awakeners would not allow the text to recede into the past, finding in it an inspiration that no other piece of historical writing could provide.[28]

---

[28] *Istoriia Rusov*, p. 43.

CHAPTER 9

How did he do it?

On Christmas Day 1991, viewers of CNN throughout the world witnessed a ceremony that few of them had ever expected to see. The red banner of the Union of Soviet Socialist Republics, inherited from the Russian Revolution of 1917, was lowered for the last time on the flagstaff of the Kremlin, the seat of tsars and commissars who for centuries had governed one of the largest empires in the world. Now the empire was gone. The Soviet Union fell apart, becoming the victim not so much of the Cold War, which by then had receded into the past, as of a peaceful revolt of its constituent nations. No nation contributed more to this major geopolitical coup than Ukraine. On December 1, 1991, more than 90 percent of Ukrainians voted for independence, sealing the fate of the Soviet Union and opening a new era in their own and world history. With more than fifty million Ukrainians gone, the leaders of Russia saw little point in continuing the imperial experiment. On Christmas Day, Gorbachev gave his farewell address as the first and last president of the Soviet Union.

For Western observers, one of the immediate outcomes of the disintegration of the USSR was not only the disappearance from newspapers of that familiar acronym but also the deletion of the definite article in media references to Ukraine. For decades, the leaders of the Ukrainian diaspora in North America had argued for dropping the article, since in their eyes it showed disrespect for their homeland: the article denoted a region, not a nation. The first to adopt the new norm was the former speechwriter for President Richard Nixon and *New York Times* columnist William Safire. Reporting from Kyiv in November 1991, on the eve of the fateful referendum, Safire wrote in his column, entitled "Ukraine Marches Out": "Ukraine (the article 'the' is dropped when referring to a country, not a province) is the great, hobnailed boot that will drop on Dec. 1 on top of Moscow center's pretensions to empire." Safire's article changed the way in which Western writers would refer to Ukraine for years to come.[1]

The person who convinced Safire to introduce the change was Ivan Drach, the leader of the pro-independence organization Rukh, whom Safire interviewed in Kyiv. During the first decade of Ukrainian independence, Drach emerged as one of the most influential figures on the Ukrainian cultural scene. No one who knew him was surprised that he used his new role in society to promote the text that had made such a great impression on him in the months leading up to independence. That text was the *History of the Rus'*. The 1991 Ukrainian edition of the *History* was published in an astonishingly high print run, but, given prevailing shortages, the paper was of poor quality, and the edition was devoid not only of illustrations and maps but also of commentary. Drach addressed these deficiencies of the first edition when in 2001, under much better economic circumstances, he decided to reissue the book. The publication was funded by the Ukrainian State Committee on Information Policy, Television, and Radio as part of a national program for the dissemination of "socially necessary publications." Drach was the head of the committee at the time.[2]

The 2001 edition of the *History* in Ukrainian translation encountered a different kind of reader and a new awareness of the text and its significance. Marko Pavlyshyn, one of the most perceptive observers of the Ukrainian cultural scene, noted in the early 1990s that the *Istoriia Rusov* had returned to the literary and cultural scene of Ukraine in the aftermath of independence as part of an anticolonial discourse. That discourse had turned the old Russian and Soviet colonial myths upside down without rejecting mythological thinking as such. Pavlyshyn also noted the appearance in Ukrainian humanities scholarship of post-colonial and postmodern discourses whose creators were trying to free themselves from ideological control and orient their scholarship toward more pragmatic and less ideological values. Indeed, in the first half of the 1990s, the loudest voices belonged to those who saw in the *History* nothing but the prophecy of an independent Ukraine, which was finally realized in 1991. Changes emerged in the second half of the decade, when attempts were made to treat the *History* like any other work of Ukrainian historiography.[3]

[1] Robert McConnell, "William Safire and Ukraine," *Aha! Network*, posted October 2, 2009 http://ahanetwork.org/?p=2251.
[2] *Istoriia Rusiv*, trans. Ivan Drach (Kyiv, 2001; repr. 2003), pp. 316–44.
[3] Marko Pavlyshyn, "Kozaky v Iamaitsi: postkolonial'ni rysy v suchasnii ukraïns'kii kul'turi," *Slovo i chas*, nos. 4–5 (Kyiv, 1994): 65–71. On the study of the *History* in independent Ukraine, see

The new edition of the *History* appeared in a print run of only five thousand copies, but what was lost in quantity was gained in quality. The volume was richly illustrated with color portraits of Rus' princes and Cossack hetmans painted by the renowned artist Oleksii Shtanko, who had won the prestigious Narbut Prize a year earlier for the best-designed Ukrainian postage stamp. Shevchuk expanded his earlier introduction, adding a lengthy analysis of the *History* as a literary text. Indexes were also provided, but perhaps the most important addition was that of scholarly commentary by two historians, father and son – Yaroslav and Ivan Dzyra. The commentators gave background information on major personalities and events discussed in the *History* and explained discrepancies between its text and historical reality first noted by scholars in the mid nineteenth century. The choice of the two Dzyras as commentators was anything but random.

Like Valerii Shevchuk, Yaroslav Dzyra (1931–2009) belonged to the generation of the sixties. He first became interested in the *History of the Rus'* when in the late 1950s he began work on his graduate thesis, which concerned the impact of Cossack history-writing on Taras Shevchenko's historical imagination. In 1971 Dzyra published the *Eyewitness Chronicle*, one of the major works of Cossack historiography. In the following year he began work on the *Chronicle* of Hryhorii Hrabianka, another monument of Cossack historical writing. It was a promising beginning, but Dzyra's career, like those of many of his colleagues, was disrupted in 1972 by a sudden turn of nationality policy in Soviet Ukraine. He was one of a number of historians fired from the Ukrainian Academy of Sciences. For years he was not allowed to publish his research. When in 1989, in the middle of Gorbachev's reforms, Dzyra submitted to the organizers of an international conference devoted to the life and works of Taras Shevchenko a paper proposal entitled "Taras Shevchenko and the *History of the Rus'*," it was rejected.[4]

In 1995, four years after Ukraine became independent, Dzyra was finally reinstated in his old position at the Institute of History of the Ukrainian Academy of Sciences. In the following year he published a number of essays in which he returned to the *History of the Rus'* and its author. Dzyra's argument was not entirely new. He maintained that the author of the *History* was none other than Hryhorii Poletyka. Why? Dzyra believed that

Volodymyr Kravchenko, "*Istoriia Rusiv* u suchasnykh interpretatsiiakh," in *Synopsis: Essays in Honour of Zenon E. Kohut*, ed. Serhii Plokhy and Frank E. Sysyn (Edmonton, 2005), pp. 275–94.

[4] On Dzyra's life and work, see "Dzyra, Iaroslav Ivanovych," *Ukraïns'kyi istorychnyi zhurnal*, no. 5 (2009): 235–37; Serhii Bilokin' and Mariia Dmytriienko, "Iaroslav Ivanovych Dzyra (12.05.1931–21.08.2009)," *Ukraïns'kyi arkheohrafichnyi shchorichnyk* (Kyiv) 13–14 (2009): 824–32.

Poletyka's surname was derived from the Greek Hippolytos, which means "unleasher of horses." Thus, argued Dzyra, Konysky (a name possibly derived from *kin'*, the Ukrainian word for "horse") was evidently Poletyka's pseudonym. Many readers who had heard about Dzyra's multi-year research on the *History* reacted with disappointment. Dzyra originally stuck to his guns, but with the passage of time he was obliged to reconsider his argument. The comments that he wrote for Drach's 2001 edition of the *History* did not mention Poletyka as a possible author of the *History*. With Dzyra's retraction of his "unleasher of horses" hypothesis, it appeared that the Poletyka era in the interpretation of the *History*, which began in the late nineteenth century, had finally come to an end. The retraction also marked the victory of the pragmatic approach to the study of the *History* over its romantic interpretations, which had dominated the field in the first years of Ukrainian independence.[5]

The new approach was represented by the work done by such historians as Volodymyr Kravchenko, who placed the *History of the Rus'* in the broad context of the development of Ukrainian historiography, and Nataliia Shlikhta, who researched the elements of nobiliary ideology in the mysterious text. Yaroslav Myshanych, the son of Oleksa Myshanych, who had published excerpts from the *History* in 1983, wrote a monograph examining the literary style of the monument. Finally, very promising work was done by Ivan Dzyra, the son of Yaroslav. The study of the *History* was becoming something of a family business. In 1998 Ivan Dzyra published his first article on the *History of the Rus'*. Five years later, in his most important study of the *History*, the young scholar analyzed the impact on the *History of the Rus'* of the *Annales de la Petite-Russie*, a two-volume history of the Ukrainian Cossacks published in Paris in 1788 by the French diplomat Jean-Benoît Scherer. Ivan Dzyra was not the first author to consider these works in relation to each other, but he was the first to conduct a thorough textual comparison between them. The result was fresh insight into the creation of the *History* and the impact of eighteenth-century French historiography on its author.[6]

---

[5] Iaroslav Dzyra, "Pidsumky dvokhsotlitnikh doslidnyts'kykh poshukiv avtorstva *Istoriï Rusiv*," in *Istoriohrafichna spadshchyna nauky istoriï Ukraïny (pohliad z kintsia XX stolittia)* (Kyiv and Hlukhiv, 1996), pp. 17–19; Dzyra, "*Istoriia Rusiv* – vydatna pam'iatka ukraïns'koi istoriohrafiï: novi dani pro ïï avtora," in Dzyra, *Avtoportret natsiï* (Kyiv, 1997), pp. 123–32; Dzyra, "Shliakhets'ko-kozats'kyi rid Polytyk (Poletyka, Pol'tyka, Polityka, Polytkovs'kyi)," in *Spetsial'ni istorychni dystsypliny: pytannia teoriï ta metodyky*, no. 12 (Kyiv, 2005): 237–48.

[6] Volodymyr Kravchenko, *"Poema vil'noho narodu" ("Istoriia Rusiv" ta ïï mistse v ukraïns'kii istoriohrafiï)* (Kharkiv, 1996); Nataliia Shlikhta, "Elementy richpospolyts'koï ideolohiï ta politychnoï rytoryky v *Istoriï Rusiv*," *Moloda natsiia: al'manakh*, no. 1 (2000); Iaroslav Myshanych, *Istoriia Rusiv: istoriohrafiia,*

Probably the first scholar to note the impact of French Enlightenment historical writing on Ukrainian historiography of the period was Mykhailo Hrushevsky. In a short essay published in Moscow in 1935, a year after his death, Hrushevsky stressed the importance of works by French authors such as Jean-Benoît Scherer on the formation of Ukrainian political and historical thought in the late eighteenth and early nineteenth centuries. He also indicated parallels between the *History* and the *Annales*, treating them as examples of the anonymous author's borrowings from the work of Scherer. Jean-Benoît Scherer was not the only French author who influenced the way in which the *History of the Rus'* was written. Another influence came from Voltaire himself. The anonymous author cited Voltaire's *History of Charles XII* (1739) in his account of the Battle of Poltava (1709), its preconditions and aftermath.[7]

Voltaire had enormous influence on the development of French and European historiography. He helped develop social history, including accounts of customs, law, and the arts. He also was a skeptical writer who regarded fables as intentional misrepresentations, considered it important to examine historical sources critically, and tried to replace unsystematic methods of research with scientific ones. But the *History of Charles XII*, which was known to the anonymous author of the *History of the Rus'* either in its French original or in one of its Russian translations, was one of Voltaire's early historical works in which he had not yet completely divested himself of the influence of seventeenth-century humanist historiography. He considered history a form of belles lettres that should be cast in dramatic terms and presented in an impressive style, and in the *History of Charles XII* he used such features of humanist historiography as invented speeches and anecdotes. The anonymous author of the *History of the Rus'* not only knew that work but was also influenced by its method and style.[8]

problematyka, poetyka (Kyiv, 1999); Ivan Dzyra, "*Istoriia Rusiv* ta istoryko-literaturnyi protses pershoï polovyny XIX st.," in *Spetsial'ni istorychni dystsypliny: pytannia teoriï ta metodyky*, no. 2 (1998): 156ff.; Dzyra, "Vplyv *Litopysu Malorosiï* Zhana Benua Sherera na *Istoriu Rusiv*," in *Problemy istoriï Ukraïny XIX–pochatku XX st.*, no. 6 (2003): 412–25. Cf. Dzyra, *Kozats'ke litopysannia 30-kh–80-kh rokiv XVIII stolittia: dzhereloznavchyi ta istoriohrafichnyi aspekty* (Kyiv, 2006), pp. 388–410.

7 Mykhailo Hrushevs'kyi, "Z istorychnoï fabulistyky kintsia XVIII st.," in *Akademiku N. Ia Maru. Iubileinyi sbornik* (Leningrad, 1935), pp. 607–11; repr. in *Ukraïns'kyi istoryk* (New York and Toronto) (1991–92): 125–29. See references to Voltaire in *Istoriia Rusov ili Maloi Rossii. Sochinenie Georgiia Koniskago, Arkhiepiskopa Beloruskago* (Moscow, 1846), pp. 184, 200, 208.

8 See Voltaire, *Histoire de Charles XII, Roi de Suède* (multiple editions). For one of the early Russian translations of the book, see Voltaire, *Istoriia i opisanie zhizni Karla XII, korolia Shvedskogo. Perevedena s nemetskogo iazyka [Petrom Pomerantsevym]* (St. Petersburg, 1777). On Voltaire's historical views, see J. H. Brumfitt, *Voltaire, Historian* (Westport, Conn., 1958), pp. 26–30, 129–64.

In his description of Ivan Mazepa's revolt against Peter I, the anonymous author declared himself in agreement with Voltaire's interpretation of the hetman's actions as guided by wounded honor. "The Czar, who began to be over-heated with wine, and had not, when sober, always the command of his passions, called him a traitor, and threatened to have him impaled," wrote Voltaire, describing a legendary episode about Peter's clash with Mazepa during one of the tsar's drinking parties. "Mazeppa, on his return to the Ukraine, formed the design of a revolt." The anonymous author found support for Voltaire's version of events in a local legend that placed the same episode at a dinner hosted by Peter's close associate Aleksandr Menshikov, whom the author considered a sworn enemy of Ukraine. According to this version, Peter slapped Mazepa in the face as a result of the conflict. "Both these stories, taken together, show the same thing – that Mazepa had a most harmful intent, inspired by his own malice and vengefulness, and not at all by national interests, which, naturally, ought in that case to have moved the troops and the people to support him, but instead the people fought the Swedes with all their might as enemies who had invaded their land in hostile fashion."[9]

Like Voltaire, the anonymous author of the *History of the Rus'* had a taste for drama and loved anecdotes. He also mixed traditional methods of humanist historiography with an Enlightenment belief in science and laws directing human history. Moreover, he attacked fables and fabulists of the past. Not all of this was necessarily derived from Voltaire, as similar ideas and approaches are to be found in the works of other writers of the day. The historical works of Jean-Benoît Scherer have many features in common with those of Voltaire, and, as Ivan Dzyra has shown, Scherer's *Annales* had a most profound impact on the author of the *History of the Rus'*.

Jean-Benoît Scherer (1741–1824) was born in Strasbourg, received his degree in law from the University of Jena and taught at the University of Tübingen from 1808 to 1824. He spent a significant part of his life in the French diplomatic service, beginning his career at the embassy in Russia; he was later stationed in Stockholm, Copenhagen, and Berlin. He retired from the diplomatic service in 1780, having spent the previous five years in France. Most of his published works dealt with or were inspired by his experiences in the Russian Empire. In 1774 he published a study of the Primary Chronicle, and a work discussing Russian international trade

---

[9] Voltaire, *History of Charles the Twelfth, King of Sweden* (New York, 1858), pp. 127–28; *Istoriia Rusov*, p. 200.

appeared in 1778. Ten years later, Scherer published the *Annales de la Petite-Russie, ou Histoire des Cosaques-Saporogues et des Cosaques de l'Ukraine*. A German version appeared in Leipzig in 1789. In 1792 Scherer returned to "Russian" subjects and published a multivolume collection of vignettes about Russian history and politics entitled *Anecdotes intéressantes et secrètes de la cour de Russie*.[10]

The *Annales de la Petite-Russie* consisted of two parts. The first was a geographic and historical description of Little Russia produced by Scherer himself. The second was a French translation of the *Brief Description of Little Russia*, the most popular compendium of Ukrainian history at the time. A version of the *Brief Description* was used by Vasyl Ruban and Oleksandr Bezborodko for their edition of the *Brief Chronicle of Little Russia* in 1777. But Scherer's second volume was not a translation of the Ruban-Bezborodko edition, or at least not only a translation of that edition. Scherer claimed to have obtained his manuscript from Kyiv. Indeed, there were parts of the text that found no parallel in any known version of the *Brief Description*. Either they were derived from other sources or they were inventions of the "publisher" himself, although he denied any "improvement" of the chronicle on his part.

What exactly did Ivan Dzyra find in the *Annales* and the *History* that scholars had not seen before? In 1948, Oleksander Ohloblyn devoted an article to the relationship between the two texts, noting a number of parallels between them. He came up with three possible reasons for their existence: Scherer's use of the *History* as one of his sources; the use of the *Annales* by the anonymous author of the *History*; or, finally, both authors' use of a source not known to posterity. Ohloblyn found the third hypothesis most promising. He suggested that the impulse for the writing of both the *History* and the *Annales* and their common source base came from the same place: the circle of Ukrainian autonomists in Novhorod-Siverskyi. Dzyra knew Ohloblyn's article but took his cue from Mykhailo Hrushevsky. Following Hrushevsky, Dzyra argued that the anonymous author took more than mere data from Scherer.[11]

Indeed, there can be little doubt that many of the ideas expressed in Scherer's *Annales* made their way into the pages of the *History*. A good example of such an intertextual connection is the use of the term "nation"

[10] Jean-Benoît Scherer, *Annales de la Petite-Russie, ou Histoire des Cosaques-Saporogues et des Cosaques de l'Ukraine*, 2 vols. (Paris, 1788). On Scherer, see Ludwig Stieda, "Scherer, Johann Benedict," *Allgemeine Deutsche Biographie*, vol. XXXI (Leipzig, 1890), p. 103ff.

[11] Oleksander Ohloblyn, *"Annales de la Petite-Russie* Sherera i *Istoriia Rusov*," *Naukovyi zbirnyk Ukraïns'koho Vil'noho Universytetu* (Munich, 1948), pp. 87–94.

in Scherer's *Annales* (*peuple*) and in the *History* (*narod*). That term is central to Scherer's narrative. In the dedication of his work and in the introduction to it, he writes about the Cossacks as forming not one but two nations (*peuples*). He treats the Cossacks of the Hetmanate (whom he calls the Cossacks of Ukraine) and the Cossacks of the Zaporozhian Host beyond the Dnieper rapids not only as distinct groups but as separate nations. However, in volume II, which was Scherer's retelling of the *Brief Description of Little Russia*, there is only one nation, and the whole story concerns its struggle for freedom. Scherer even adds a sentence to the *Brief Description*'s account of the Treaty of Zboriv (1649), asserting that the Polish king agreed to recognize the Cossacks as a *peuple libre*. Scherer's *peuple* and the anonymous author's *narod* worked very well together in transforming the history of the Cossacks as a social estate into that of a nation. Of course, as we now know, the anonymous author did not borrow the national idea from Scherer alone. The eighteenth-century Cossack chronicles as well as the nobiliary petitions of the early nineteenth century were full of references to *narod* and *natsiia*, but it was probably heartening to see them echoed in one of the anonymous author's French sources.[12]

Probably no less important than the borrowing of historical data and ideas was the stylistic influence of Scherer's narrative on the anonymous author. In the *Annales* one sees the emergence of some important elements of Romantic historiography. The French author is eager to call forth strong emotions and use the power of imagination to exert the strongest influence on the reader's feelings. Scherer's reworking of the dry factual narrative of the *Brief Description of Little Russia* may well have been an inspiration to the anonymous author of the *History*. Writing in an era when Romantic emphasis on emotion as the source of aesthetic experience was becoming a norm, the anonymous author unleashed his own historical imagination to produce an even more emotionally charged narrative than that of his model. One of the best examples of such a refashioning of a dry narrative taken from a Cossack chronicle is an episode that Alexander Pushkin included in his publication of excerpts from the *History* in 1836. This was the description of the Polish authorities' execution of the Cossack leader Ostrianytsia, which provided Nikolai Gogol with the historical data and emotional impulse for the description of the torture and execution of Ostap Bulba in his novel *Taras Bulba*.

[12] Scherer, *Annales*, II: 38.

The original text, which both Scherer and the author of the *History* knew from the *Brief Description of Little Russia*, reads as follows: "[The Poles] ... killed Ostrianytsia and Hunia in Warsaw, and they impaled Kyzym, the captain of Kyiv, along with his son, and quartered many eminent ones, hanging others on hooks by the ribs; and from that time they deprived the Cossacks of great liberty and imposed onerous and fantastic taxes in unusual fashion, sold off churches and ecclesiastical images to Jews, and boiled Cossack children in vats, crushed women's breasts with pieces of wood, and the like." Scherer used this text, adding a description of torture that is not to be found in the original. He also compared tortures invented by savages and those employed by "civilized nations" – a comparison not flattering to the latter:

[The Poles] ... were so perfidious as to kidnap Ostrianytsia and Hunia and so barbaric as to take their lives after the most horrific tortures. Captain Kasym of Kyiv died in the same way along with his son. Many other Cossacks fell victim to the cruelty of the Poles: some were broken on the wheel, while others were subjected to such tortures as would never enter the head of the most terrible savage but match the refined cruelty of enlightened nations. They were hung on long spikes with which their bodies were pierced between the ribs; others were quartered; and nothing could mollify the Poles or incline them to mercy. They even roasted children on gridirons and impaled others, lighting bonfires beneath them, and those whom they did not kill they turned into slaves. Even churches did not escape destruction: they were plundered, and chalices for the blessed sacrament were sold to Jews.[13]

The author of the *History* further developed the theme of Ostrianytsia's execution, first by inventing a detailed account of his victory over the Poles and then by using his imagination to describe the horrors of the Polish retaliation:

Hetman Ostrianytsia, General Quartermaster Surmylo, and Colonels Nedryhailo, Boiun, and Ryndych were broken on the wheel, and, as their arms and legs were incessantly broken, their veins were stretched across the wheel until they expired. Colonels Haidarevsky, Butrym, Zapalii, and Quartermasters Kyzym and Suchevsky were pierced with iron spears and raised up alive on stakes; the regimental quartermasters Postylych, Harun, Sutyha, Podobai, Kharkevych, Chudak, and Churai and Captains Chupryna, Okolovych, Sokalsky, Myrovych, and Vorozhbyt were nailed to boards, covered with pitch, and slowly burned. Standard-Bearers Mohyliansky, Zahreba, Skrebylo, Okhtyrka, Poturai, Burlii, and Zahnybida were torn to pieces with iron nails resembling bears' paws.

---

[13] "Kratkoe opisanie Malorossii," in *Letopis' Samovidtsa po novootkrytym spiskam*, ed. Orest Levitskii (Kyiv, 1878), pp. 211–319, here 238. Cf. Scherer, *Annales* (1788), ii: 20–21.

Officers Mentiai, Dunaievsky, Skubrii, Hliansky, Zavezun, Kosyr, Hurtovy, Tumar, and Tuhai were quartered. The wives and children of those martyrs, on seeing the initial execution, filled the air with their shrieks and weeping, but they soon fell silent. Those women, according to the unbelievable brutality of that time, had their breasts cut off and were slaughtered to the last, and their breasts were used to beat the faces of the men who were still alive; the children who remained after their mothers, clinging to them and crawling on their corpses, were all roasted before the eyes of their fathers on gridirons beneath which coals were strewn and blown into flame with hats and brooms.

The principal body parts hacked off the Little Russian officials who had been tortured to death, such as heads, arms, and legs, were distributed throughout Little Russia and hung up on stakes in the towns. The Polish troops who occupied all of Little Russia in connection with this did to Little Russians whatever they wanted and could think up: all kinds of abuse, violence, plunder, and tyranny, surpassing all description and understanding. Among other things, they subjected the unfortunate Little Russians several times to the cruelties perpetrated in Warsaw; several times they boiled children in vats and burned them on coals before the eyes of their parents, subjecting the parents themselves to the cruelest tortures. Finally, having plundered all the godly Ruthenian churches, they leased them to the Jews, and church utensils, such as chalices, patens, vestments, and surplices were sold off and drunk away to those same Jews, who made themselves tableware and clothing of church silver, turning vestments and surplices into skirts for Jewesses, who boasted before Christians, showing off bodices and skirts on which traces of crosses that they had torn off were still to be seen.[14]

The anti-Polish and anti-Jewish animus of the *Brief Description*; the civilizational discourse of Scherer's *Annales* – all these elements of earlier texts found their way into the *History* and were further elaborated by the rich imagination of its author, who not only inflated the descriptions of torture and execution but also came up with dozens of names for the victims of those horrendous acts of violence, making the story feel real. The images he presented filled generations of readers with hatred of Polish Catholics and Jews. Pushkin and Gogol were the best-known but by no means the only admirers of that episode of the *History*. The account taken from an old Cossack chronicle, retold by a French intellectual and embellished by a Ukrainian historian, appealed to their Russian patriotism, Orthodox upbringing, cultural sensitivities, and Romantic imagination in a way that the original story could not.

Although imagination was an important instrument in the employ of the author of the *History*, he used it not only to appeal to the emotions and

---

[14] *Istoriia Rusov*, pp. 55–56.

sensibilities of the Age of Romanticism but also in the service of reason – the mainstay of the fading Age of Enlightenment. Faced with a lack of historical sources, gaps in coverage of what he considered the most important periods of Cossack history, and contradictions in the sources at his disposal, the anonymous author used both reason and imagination to reconstruct the history of his land and nation. Like Voltaire, Scherer and others who took their cues from humanist historiography, he was happy to make his characters deliver long speeches that allowed him to interpret their motives, addressing both the "how" and the "why" of their actions. Yet, like his French models, he also insisted that he was not inventing anything or adding to what he had found in old and trust-worthy chronicles. His readers' tastes were just as contradictory: they wanted an enthralling, emotionally charged account that was nevertheless based on authentic historical sources.

The demand for mystification was in the air, and the author of the *History* had only to satisfy it – taking care, of course, to cover his tracks. How did he do it? How did he fashion his cover story and establish the credentials of his manuscript to meet the conflicting demands of his French models and the expectations of his readers? So far we have examined the surface elements of that story – the parts related to Archbishop Konysky and Heorhii Poletyka. Let us now take a close look at its deeper layer, which concerns the creation of the manuscript. According to the anonymous author, it was written "from times of old at the cathedral monastery of Mahiliou by sagacious people who obtained requisite information by communicating with learned men at the Kyivan Academy and at various prominent Little Russian monasteries, especially those where Yurii Khmelnytsky, the former Little Russian hetman, had lived as a monk. There he left many notes and papers of his father, Hetman Zinovii Khmelnytsky, and the actual journals of national records and events, which he reviewed and corrected anew."[15]

The anonymous author sought to establish the authenticity of the *History* by bringing in as part of the cover story not only Konysky and Poletyka but also Hetman Bohdan Khmelnytsky and his son Yurii (1641–85). His emphasis on Khmelnytsky was nothing new, since the hetman figured as the main character in all the Cossack chronicles. The "Articles of Bohdan Khmelnytsky," which enumerated the rights and privileges granted to the Cossack officers by Moscow in the winter and spring of 1654, were the cornerstone of Cossack legal and historical identity in the Russian Empire.

---

[15] *Ibid.*, p. ii.

Bringing in Yurii Khmelnytsky was a different matter. The meek successor of a strong-willed father, he assumed and resigned the hetman's office at various times, often serving as an instrument of the Cossack elite and neighboring rulers. Despite his checkered political career, however, Yurii Khmelnytsky remained an important part of the Cossack officers' usable past. In manuscript collections of historical documents that were widely distributed in the Hetmanate in the second half of the eighteenth century, the "Articles of Yurii Khmelnytsky" as confirmed by the tsar's officials and the Cossack officers in 1659 often followed the "articles" of his father. They served to confirm the rights and privileges of the Hetmanate and its ruling estate in the Russian Empire.[16]

Seen from the Russian imperial viewpoint, the two Khmelnytskys were strikingly different: the father was treated as a benefactor of Russia, and his son as a traitor. But for the Cossack officers the two Khmelnytskys were linked by the evolution of the rights and privileges of their corporate estate, making both of them highly positive figures. The assertion in the foreword to the *History* that its alleged authors had access to the papers of the two Khmelnytskys bolstered its actual author's claim that the manuscript was authentic. Not surprisingly, there is a direct link between the author's introductory mention of Orthodox monasteries in which the papers of the Khmelnytskys were preserved and his subsequent discussion of the fate of Yurii Khmelnytsky in the main body of the work. Describing the events of 1663, he claims that Yurii "was ordained a monk in the monastery of Lubny, which was his last refuge. In order to remove himself from anything that might disturb him in such an illustrious monastery as that of Lubny, he concealed himself most secretly in the wilderness of Moshny, which is below the Kaniv monastery, in the forests and ravines, but even here ill luck did not cease to pursue him."[17]

Apparently, the two monasteries that the author of the *History* had in mind when writing about the Khmelnytsky papers were those of Lubny and Kaniv. Why those two? The answer lies in the anonymous author's narrative strategy and his methods of reconstructing events with the aid of the limited source base at his disposal. He probably found information about Yurii Khmelnytsky's tonsure in the *Brief Description of Little Russia*, which is silent about where the younger Khmelnytsky took his monastic

---

[16] See descriptions of Cossack documentary codices that included the "Articles of Yurii Khmelnytsky" in Andrii Bovhyria, *Kozats'ke istoriopysannia v rukopysnii tradytsii XVIII stolittia. Spysky ta redaktsii tvoriv* (Kyiv, 2010), pp. 44–45, 252, 256, 258, 260, 273, 274, 275, 282, 288, 290 291, 294, 297; Oleksander Ohloblyn, *Liudy staroï Ukraïny* (Munich, 1959), pp. 128–36.

[17] *Istoriia Rusov*, p. 156.

vows. However, this information follows an entry about the Muscovite army proceeding to the town of Lubny immediately after defeating Khmelnytsky's forces. Scherer, who was the first to use his powers of reason and imagination in making sense of the *Brief Description*'s cryptic account of Khmelnytsky's tonsure, decided that after his defeat Yurii retreated to Lubny. He stated as much, while dropping the sentence about the Muscovite army's march there. Then came the anonymous author, who linked the story of Yurii's tonsure with Scherer's claim that he had retreated to Lubny by reaching the "logical" conclusion that the younger Khmelnytsky became a monk in the Lubny monastery.[18]

That was not the end of the story. Since this was the only mention of the Lubny monastery in the entire *History* – a tenuous link to the Khmelnytsky papers – the anonymous author decided to conflate the Lubny story with that of the Kaniv monastery, which he had represented earlier in the work as the monastery of the Cossack land. The Kaniv monastery first appears in the *History* in connection with the alleged funeral there of the Cossack leader Ivan Pidkova after his execution by the Polish authorities in Lviv in 1577. That information corresponds to the account of the *Brief Description*, from which it was taken by Scherer. But there the similarities end. After 1577 the Kaniv monastery disappears from the pages of the *Brief Description*, as it does from Scherer's *Annales*, but not from the *History*, whose author associates the monastery with the fate of Pidkova's successor, Hetman Shakh. According to the *History*, on the orders of the Polish king, Shakh "was dismissed from the hetmancy and sentenced to confinement in the Kaniv monastery for life; there he was voluntarily ordained a monk and ended his life peacefully in the monastic order." The anonymous author also turned the Kaniv monastery into the venue where the Polish authorities arrested Hetman Ostrianytsia, whose execution is one of the emotional focal points of the work. It was probably difficult for him to imagine Yurii Khmelnytsky becoming a monk in any other monastery than that of Kaniv. Needless to say, there is no surviving indication that Yurii Khmelnytsky was a monk in any of the Orthodox monasteries in the vicinity of Kaniv or Lubny. It was a complete invention or, rather, a result of the anonymous author's historical "reconstruction," whose ultimate goal was to establish the authenticity and reliability of the *History* as a historical source.[19]

---

[18] "Kratkoe opisanie Malorossii," p. 216; Scherer, *Annales*, II: 10.
[19] *Istoriia Rusov*, pp. 30–31, 55, 156.

Few historical events discussed by the author of the *History* better demonstrate the methods he used to "reconstruct" Cossack history than his discussion of the Union of Hadiach, a treaty concluded in September 1658 between Bohdan Khmelnytsky's successor, Hetman Ivan Vyhovsky, and representatives of the Polish-Lithuanian Commonwealth. The Union of Hadiach envisioned the creation of a tripartite Commonwealth – the Kingdom of Poland and the Grand Duchy of Lithuania, as well as a Principality of Rus' with the Cossack hetman as its official head. The Union was the culmination of the activities of moderate forces among the Polish and Ukrainian elites and the embodiment of the hopes and dreams of the Ruthenian (Ukrainian and Belarusian) nobility of the first half of the seventeenth century. Nevertheless, the compromise embodied in the Union was rejected by mainstream forces on both sides. The Commonwealth Diet ratified the text of the treaty with a number of important omissions, but even in that form it was viewed with suspicion and rejected by the Polish nobiliary establishment, which could not reconcile itself to the prospect of Orthodox Cossacks enjoying equal rights with Catholic nobles. On the Ukrainian side, the Cossack rank and file rejected a treaty that proposed to give all rights in the new Principality of Rus' to a limited number of representatives of the Ukrainian noble and Cossack elite at the expense of the Cossack masses and the rebel peasantry, which would have to submit once again to the noble landlords' jurisdiction and control.[20]

Needless to say, the Union had its fair share of critics among Ukrainian historians. But the author of the *History of the Rus'*, surprisingly, was not one of them. In fact, the *History* stands out as the work that contributed most to the popularization of a positive image of the Union, laying the foundations of the "Hadiach myth." One of the challenges that the anonymous author encountered in creating that myth was his own anti-Polish attitude. Judging by the introduction to the *History*, one of its major tasks was to debunk the "tales" of Polish and Lithuanian authors and their followers in Ukraine. The anonymous author set out to prove that Ukraine had been settled by the Rus' princes, not by the Polish kings; that Little Russia had fought numerous battles with Poland for its liberation, joined the Russian state of its own free will, and deserved recognition for its martial deeds. Could the Union of

---

[20] Wacław Lipiński (Viacheslav Lypyns'kyi), *Z dziejów Ukrainy* (Kyiv and Cracow, 1912), pp. 588–617; Tetiana Iakovleva, *Het'manshchyna v druhii polovyni 50-kh rokiv XVII stolittia. Prychyny ta pochatok Ruïny* (Kyiv, 1998), pp. 305–23.

Hadiach really fit this historiographic paradigm? Apparently it could, though not without certain modifications.[21]

The Hadiach Union emerges from the pages of the *History* in a version most unexpected to anyone familiar with its actual history and the texts of the agreement. Indeed, the anonymous author offers the most counterfactual account of the Union ever written. First of all, we learn from the *History* that although the treaty was based on the Hadiach Articles, it was not negotiated at Hadiach at all but in the town of Zaslav (Zaslavl) at an international congress attended by the representatives of European great powers. Second, its principal Ukrainian initiator was not Ivan Vyhovsky but Yurii Khmelnytsky, who allegedly lost his hetmancy for agreeing to the conditions of the Union. The text of the agreement presented in the *History* finds little corroboration either in contemporary versions of the treaty or in the variant summarized in Polish and Cossack chronicles.

According to the *History*, the treaty was mainly concerned with the rights and prerogatives of the Rus' nation, not with the hetman or the Cossack state – the two subjects that took center stage in the account of the treaty given in the Cossack chronicles. The Rus' nation of the *History* came from the same Sarmatian stock as did the Polish nation and was equal to it under the king's rule. Its leader was the Cossack hetman, who assumed supreme command in wartime and held the title of Prince of Rus' or Sarmatia. The right to elect the hetman and the palatines belonged exclusively to the local Cossack elite ("knights"); foreigners were excluded. The treaty guaranteed the equality of all representatives of the Rus' knightly estate and nation with their Polish counterparts and the equality of the "Rus' Catholic, or Greek, religion" with the "Polish or Roman Catholic" one.[22]

The anonymous author was clearly an admirer of the Hadiach Articles. He returned to them again and again in the text of his *History*, writing about Yurii Khmelnytsky's second election to the hetmancy, his appointment as prince of Sarmatia by the Ottomans, and the election of Mykhailo Khanenko as hetman. Each time he referred to the Hadiach or Zaslav Articles, he mentioned that they had been approved and guaranteed by representatives of the great powers. It was easy for the author of the *History* to endorse the agreement, given that not only the Zaslav Congress but also most of the Hadiach text was of his own creation. Most of the text of the Hadiach Agreement as it appears in the *History* came from a source that had nothing to do with the Union of 1658. This was the text of the Zboriv

---

[21] *Istoriia Rusov*, p. 4.   [22] *Ibid.*, pp. 143–45, 150, 157, 170.

Agreement of 1649, which appears about a hundred pages before the account of the Union of Hadiach. That text, in turn, bore little resemblance to the actual text of the Zboriv Agreement.[23]

Why would someone create a forgery by recycling a document cited earlier in the same work? It would appear that the anonymous author thought of himself as a careful researcher of historical fact, not a literary plagiarist. His sources claimed that the Hadiach Articles had originally been proposed by Khmelnytsky. In fact, Hrabianka, who may have been known to the anonymous author through other versions of his abridged chronicle, stated that these were the "well-known" articles of Khmelnytsky. The only well-known articles of the old hetman to which the anonymous author seems to have had access were the ones negotiated at Zboriv. He presented a long and elaborate history of the negotiation of the Pereiaslav Agreement but summarized its text in a few relatively short sentences. Thus he used an apocryphal text of the Zboriv Agreement in his possession to reconstruct the text of the Hadiach Articles. In his view, the latter could not be less advantageous to the Cossacks than their precursor, the Treaty of Zboriv. Zaslav, the center of a short-lived Iziaslav vicegerency (1793–95), looked like a city important enough to host a seventeenth-century international congress.

A nineteenth-century reader of the *History of the Rus'* might have concluded that the Rus' nation emerged from the Hadiach Agreement with a larger territory than the one provided by the Treaty of Zboriv, with a much more powerful hetman who could act as an independent prince in wartime, and a much stronger elite that deprived the rank and file of the Cossack Host of the right to elect its hetman and its local governors. The numerical strength of the Host remained the same, as did the status of the Rus' nation in the Commonwealth. The only negative feature of the Union in this account, it would seem, was its association with Ivan Vyhovsky. The anonymous author continued the well-established tradition of Cossack historical writing that distanced the good agreement from the evil Vyhovsky. He added another negative feature, referring to Vyhovsky as an ethnic Pole (*prirodnyi poliak*) – in a world of rising nationalism, this served to explain Vyhovsky's treasonous actions better than earlier references to his Polish schooling and sympathies.[24]

---

[23] *Ibid.*, pp. 94–95.

[24] *Ibid.*, p. 143. For a detailed discussion of the treatment of the Union of Hadiach by the anonymous author, see Serhii Plokhy, "Hadiach 1658: Tvorennia mifu," in *Hadiats'ka uniia 1658 roku*, ed. Pavlo Sokhan' *et al.* (Kyiv, 2008), pp. 281–305.

The image of the Hetmanate that emerges from the text of the Hadiach Articles as presented by the author of the *History* may be distant from mid-seventeenth-century realities, but it was fairly close to what prevailed – or, at least, to what the Cossack officers wanted – in the mid eighteenth century. Strong rule by the hetman; the political dominance of the Cossack elite; the establishment of a local Diet – all these were features of the reform program for the Hetmanate advanced by its last hetman, Kyrylo Rozumovsky. This was the image remembered and cherished by the Ukrainian nobility at the turn of the nineteenth century. The anonymous author ascribed special importance to the Rus' nation, depicted as equal to other nations, its rights not only recognized by the Kingdom of Poland but also guaranteed by the major European powers. This was a nation that tolerated other major religions, in the spirit of the Enlightenment, and whose own religion was tolerated in return. It was a nation of which the reader could be proud, and the author of the *History* could also be well satisfied, knowing that the purpose declared in the introduction to the work – to pay homage to the glorious deeds of the Rus' nation and its leaders – was well served by his account of the Hadiach Agreement.[25]

The introduction to the *History* proposed that such homage could best be rendered by narrating the numerous battles of the Rus' nation against the Poles, but the anonymous author's treatment of the Union of Hadiach proved that agreements concluded with the Poles, presented in an appropriate light, could do just as well. Indeed, the author of the *History of the Rus'* – the most anti-Polish work in Ukrainian historiography – managed to appropriate even the myth of Hadiach for his purpose. While the author clearly located his Rus' nation within Russian imperial historical space, he needed the Polish "other" to fully define his people within that space. His account of the Cossack wars with Poland was meant to emphasize the importance of the Rus' nation to the empire, while the Cossack treaties with the Polish kings – evidence of the seriousness with which the Cossacks were treated in the Commonwealth – gave the Rus' nation a claim to special status in the imperial setting. Both elements promoted national pride among the Ukrainian elites. Myths like that of Hadiach were indispensable to the success of the national project.

Our discussion of the ways in which the *History* was created provides an insight into the question of why it was so much admired not only by

---

[25] *Istoriia Rusov*, pp. iii–iv. On Rozumovsky's attempted reforms in the Hetmanate, see Zenon E. Kohut, *Russian Centralism and Ukrainian Autonomy: Imperial Absorption of the Hetmanate, 1760s–1830s* (Cambridge, Mass., 1988), pp. 86–94.

nineteenth-century poets and writers like Ryleev, Pushkin, Gogol, and Shevchenko but also by the generation of the 1960s, whose members helped bring about the Ukrainian independence of 1991. They did not have far to go in search of anticolonial mythology, which they were eager to introduce into public discourse: some of it was already there, in the pages of the *History of the Rus'*. What had to be done was to translate the text into Ukrainian, as Ivan Drach eventually did.

The literary and historiographic ethos of the Enlightenment and Romanticism helps one understand why and how the anonymous author populated his work with heroes and villains, devoting page after page to feats of valor and descriptions of horrendous crimes. While the author's material was taken from the Cossack chronicles, his literary inspiration came from Voltaire and Scherer. If the sources did not provide enough material for the kind of history his French models inspired him to write, the anonymous author used his imagination to a degree unmatched either by his predecessors or by his followers. He created history as much as he recorded it. Drawing both on the Enlightenment and on early Romanticism, the author produced a narrative that not only promoted the ideas of freedom, patriotism, struggle against tyranny, and human and divine justice but also inspired the imagination of the reader, who wanted to hear the voice of the past and see history evolve before his and, increasingly, her eyes. One reason for the *History*'s popularity was that it did not follow established trends but anticipated readers' changing tastes.

CHAPTER 10

The Cossack treasure

When Ukraine declared independence in December 1991, few of its citizens doubted that a bright economic future awaited their country. In the months leading up to the referendum on independence, Ukrainian newspapers wrote about the country's disproportionally large contribution to the Soviet Union's coffers and its enormous economic potential. Experts of the Deutsche Bank, claimed the media, were impressed by the country's industrial infrastructure, its fertile soil, and its highly educated and skilled population. They predicted that Ukraine would do better economically than any other post-Soviet republic, including Russia. And even if something should go wrong with the Ukrainian economic miracle, thought some of the country's most prominent writers, there was a trump card that economists did not know about but historians did – the treasure deposited in Britain by one of the leaders of Cossack Ukraine, Acting Hetman Pavlo Polubotok (*c.* 1660–1724). If converted into gold, claimed one of Ukraine's newspapers, the Polubotok deposit would provide every citizen of an independent nation of 52 million with 38 kg of gold.

Belief in the existence of Polubotok's gold was so strong and pervasive among some leaders of the Ukrainian intelligentsia that in June 1990, when Prime Minister Margaret Thatcher visited Kyiv, two deputies of the Ukrainian parliament, the prominent writers Volodymyr Yavorivsky and Roman Ivanychuk, submitted an official request to the Ukrainian government to investigate the fate of the treasure. The gold had allegedly been deposited with the Bank of the East India Company in the 1720s. Pavlo Polubotok had sent it there in anticipation of the hard times that were to befall him and Ukraine in the very near future. Indeed, he was soon arrested in the course of a mission to St. Petersburg, where he argued for the restoration of the hetman's office abolished by Peter I. The Russian officials sent to Ukraine to investigate Polubotok's "treason" were unable to locate a barrel of gold coins supposedly in his possession. It was assumed that the coins – as many as 200,000, according to some suggestions – had been smuggled to Britain.

If that were the case, the original deposit and the accrued compound interest would indeed amount to an astronomical sum – sufficient to bankrupt the Bank of England, which took over the assets of the East India Company in 1858, impoverish Britain, and destroy the world financial system. It could turn Ukraine into the Kuwait of Eastern Europe. But there was a catch stipulated by Polubotok's will: Ukraine must be independent in order to claim the deposit. So went the story that circulated in the Ukrainian media in the summer of 1990. With independence around the corner, the Ukrainian government had no time to lose. A special commission headed by the country's vice-premier was dispatched to England in search of Polubotok's gold. The fate of the country, if not the financial stability of the whole world, might depend on the outcome.

Ironically, the Ukrainian government was not the first political actor to lay claim to what became known as Polubotok's gold. The first to do so, back in the early twentieth century, were the Russian imperial authorities. In 1908, on orders from St. Petersburg, the Russian consul in London reviewed all unclaimed deposits in the Bank of England. Although he found nothing of the appropriate order of magnitude, that was not the end of the story. In the 1920s Soviet Ukrainian officials in Vienna were approached by a certain Ostap Polubotok, who claimed to be an heir to the Polubotok fortune, with documents to prove his bona fides. The sensational news was reported to Kharkiv, then the capital of Ukraine, and aroused interest among the Bolshevik rulers, but the subsequent purges of the Soviet leadership in Ukraine precluded any further investigation. The matter was forgotten for decades.

The ghost of Hetman Polubotok returned to haunt the Soviets in the early 1960s. The KGB allegedly informed the Soviet leadership that the British government was using money from the Polubotok deposit to fund anti-Soviet activities in the United States in connection with the "Ukraine Day" proclaimed by President Dwight Eisenhower. The Soviet leaders commissioned a secret report. Among the investigators was one of Ukraine's leading historians of the Cossack era, Olena Apanovych, who got on the trail of two carts of salt and salted fish dispatched to Arkhangelsk by Polubotok on the eve of his visit to the tsar and then placed on a British vessel to be shipped to London. The assumption was that the cargo actually consisted of gold. Apanovych was sworn to secrecy, and no one was supposed to know the results of her investigation. Then came the campaign of 1972 against Ukrainian bourgeois nationalism. Apanovych was fired from her position at the Institute of History of the Ukrainian Academy of Sciences. She never returned to her search for Polubotok's gold.

When the memory of Polubotok's treasure reemerged on the eve of Ukrainian independence as part of the revived Cossack myth, it ignited the imagination of the public but once again proved evanescent. The members of the Ukrainian delegation that went to London in 1990 were in for a major disappointment. Like many other Polubotok treasure hunters who had visited the Bank of England, they left that institution empty-handed. There were no Polubotok deposits in the bank, they were told. What they probably were not told was that even if such deposits should be discovered, the government of Ukraine would have to deal not only with the Bank of England but also with numerous heirs of Hetman Polubotok. The historical record pertaining to the Polubotok affair is sketchy at best, and, given the lack of any clear distinction between the hetman's personal funds and those of the Hetmanate treasury, it would be all but impossible to establish whose gold was deposited in the Bank of the East India Company – that of Ukraine or of Pavlo Polubotok and his family. Indeed, it was not a government of any kind – tsarist, Soviet, or Ukrainian – but the heirs of Polubotok who were the first to lay claim to the mysterious treasure.[1]

The world was first alerted to the possible existence of such a treasure in the 1880s. Count Hryhorii Myloradovych, one of the many heirs of Pavlo Polubotok who took it upon himself to represent the extended Polubotok family in the search for the hetman's gold, made the first inquiries in London banking circles. Those inquiries convinced him that the gold of Polubotok was nothing but a myth. He made a statement to that effect in one of the leading Russian newspapers, *Novoe vremia* (New Times), but few of the heirs and potential beneficiaries were convinced. Eventually, anywhere between 150 and 350 claimants gathered for a strategy session in the town of Starodub, the center of the Polubotok family's ancestral possessions. "Starodub, 15 January," read the dateline of a Russian newspaper report in early 1908. "An imposing convention of the heirs of Hetman Polubotok took place here. From every corner of the Russian State – from St. Petersburg, Moscow, Kyiv, Kharkiv, Poltava, Khabarovsk, Chita, Ufa, Odesa, Kherson, the Don oblast, Saratov, Kronstadt, and even from Galicia. Starodub, a peaceful, impoverished little regional town, has no recollection of such a gathering of nonresidents in its annals."

---

[1] Serhy Yekelchyk, "Cossack Gold: History, Myth, and the Dream of Prosperity in the Age of Post-Soviet Transition," *Canadian Slavonic Papers* 40 (September–December 1998): 311–25; Ihor Malyshevs'kyi, "Detektyv z het'mans'kym zolotom," *Dzerkalo tyzhnia*, December 22–28, 2001; Sofiia Sodol', "Istoriia odniiei spadshchyny. Iak SRSR i Velykobrytaniia borolysia za klad Polubotka," *Postup*, July 21, 2001; Serhii Plachynda, *Kozak – dusha pravdyvaia: povisti, ese, fresky z istorii Ukraïny* (Kyiv, 2006), p. 177ff.

For the rest of the year, Russian newspapers covered the development of the Polubotok saga. A leading expert on the history of the Ukrainian Cossacks, Dmytro Yavornytsky, and his friend, the popular Moscow journalist and socialite Vladimir Giliarovsky, considered the whole thing to be a hoax. The latter believed that Polubotok, a victim of the tsar and a champion of the Hetmanate's rights and liberties, was not the kind of the person who would amass possessions and smuggle his money to Britain. He wrote in *Russkoe slovo* (Russian Word):

Pavlo Polubotok became a legendary fighter for the freedom of Little Russia. It is said that Peter I went time and again to the arrested man's cell but did not manage to obtain any concessions from the hetman. Historians cite the statement that Polubotok, ringing his chains, made to Peter in response to his wish: "Standing up for my fatherland, I fear neither chains nor prisons, and it would be better for me to die the worst possible death than to see the complete destruction of my countrymen." This incident of Peter I's visit to the imprisoned Polubotok is depicted on a large canvas by one of the southern painters. I saw that painting long ago and do not remember whose work it was. But I recall the setting of the cell, the chains, and the two mighty, heroic figures in semidarkness. Such was Hetman Pavlo Polubotok. Obviously, he was not one of those capable of placing rubles in a London bank! And in that day and age! All those millions are an absolute lie. There are no Polubotok millions in any London bank. There are only speculators in Russia, active for a long, long time, who are seeking what does not exist and counting on human trust or on millions. Meanwhile, from Moscow alone, dozens of people are getting ready to go out in search of Polubotok's mythical legacy.[2]

Giliarovsky was right: Polubotok's millions were indeed a hoax. They were never found either by the hetman's heirs or by the governments of the Russian Empire, the Soviet Union, or independent Ukraine. However, in rejecting one historical myth associated with the hetman, Giliarovsky swallowed another one that pitted the hetman against an all-powerful tsar in the last days of his life and presented the hetman as a victor in that confrontation of values and characters. It was the persistence of this tradition that helped revive the myth of Polubotok's gold in the 1990s in the version claiming that only an independent Ukraine had the right to the hetman's treasures. That tradition was largely created by the *History of the Rus'*, whose author also quoted Polubotok's reply to Peter I. It was also the *History* that inspired the Russian artist Vasilii Volkov to produce the dramatic painting that made such a lasting impression on Giliarovsky.

---

[2] Vladimir Giliarovskii, "Lzhe-milliony getmana Polubotka," *Russkoe slovo*, January 8 (21), 1908.

Why did the anonymous author choose Pavlo Polubotok to embody the traditions and aspirations of eighteenth-century Cossackdom? In his early life, the historical Pavlo Polubotok was an unlikely rebel and thus a poor candidate for historical lionization. He was one of the few Cossack colonels who never fully supported Ivan Mazepa; hence he was not named a colonel until relatively late in his life. During the Mazepa Revolt, he remained loyal to the tsar but was too sagacious and independent for Peter's taste (the tsar believed that he might become the next Mazepa) to be promoted to the hetmancy. Thus a weaker candidate, the Starodub colonel Ivan Skoropadsky, was elected with Peter's blessing to take Mazepa's place, while Polubotok was compensated with a grant of new lands. These included the town of Liubech and two thousand peasant households – the basis of Polubotok's spectacular wealth and the foundation on which the legend of the hetman's gold was constructed by later generations of the Cossack elite. When Skoropadsky died in 1722, Polubotok was again passed over for the hetmancy. This time there were no new grants, and the tsar abolished the post of hetman altogether, replacing it with the Little Russian College.

Polubotok was appalled. So was the Cossack officer elite, which resented the new college, detested the additional taxes introduced by it, and sought the restoration of the hetman's office, as well as the rights and privileges guaranteed to the Cossacks in the days of Bohdan Khmelnytsky and confirmed by Peter himself. In 1723, when the tsar summoned Polubotok to St. Petersburg, the Cossack officers in the Hetmanate sent a petition of their own to the tsar with the same demand. The tsar smelled a revolt and ordered the arrest of Polubotok and his entourage. Investigators were sent to the Hetmanate to assess the situation. Meanwhile, Polubotok died in prison in December 1724, slightly more than a year after his arrest and a few weeks before the death of Peter himself. After the hetmancy was restored in 1727, Polubotok emerged in Ukrainian tradition not only as a martyr for a just cause but also as a symbol of Cossack moral victory over the imperial authorities. The text of Polubotok's petition to the tsar was included, along with the "articles" of other hetmans, in a number of documentary collections that were copied and recopied in the Hetmanate in the second half of the eighteenth century.[3]

It is hardly surprising that the anonymous author showed great sympathy for Polubotok and his plight. But the tragic story of Polubotok's

---

[3] V. Modzalevskii, *Pavel Polubotok* (St. Petersburg, 1905); Oleksander Ohloblyn, "Polubotok, Pavlo," in *Encyclopedia of Ukraine*, 5 vols. (Toronto, 1984–93), IV: 137; Andrii Bovhyria, *Kozats'ke istoriopysannia v rukopysnii tradytsiï XVIII st. Spysky ta redaktsiï tvoriv* (Kyiv, 2010), pp. 282, 295.

journey to St. Petersburg and his death in prison does not fully explain why he emerges in the pages of the *History* as the most positive Cossack leader since Bohdan Khmelnytsky. The full meaning of the Polubotok image in the *History of the Rus'* and the significance of the Polubotok legend in general can hardly be understood without considering the historical context in which Polubotok acted, especially Hetman Ivan Mazepa's revolt against the tsar and the impact of the Battle of Poltava (1709) on the Cossack state and its elites.

As discussed earlier, the Mazepa Revolt was by far the most important event in Cossack history since the Khmelnytsky Uprising of the mid seventeenth century. Initially a loyal servant of the tsar, Ivan Mazepa sided with Charles XII of Sweden in the fall of 1708, amid the turmoil of the Northern War. Tsar Peter I ordered Mazepa anathematized. This anathema, repeated every year in the churches of the vast empire, turned Mazepa into the most hated figure of the imperial political and historical imagination. The tsar even had a mock Order of Judas produced so that he could bestow it on the elderly hetman once he was captured. Peter won the Battle of Poltava in June 1709 but never caught up with Mazepa. Instead, for generations to come his name was turned into a symbol of treason to the ruler and the state; an object of government-sponsored hatred, association with whom was tantamount to sacrilege – a betrayal not only of secular authority but also of the Christian faith.[4]

The situation began to change in the first decades of the nineteenth century. It was then that Mazepa emerged as a hero of the new Romantic age, glorified by Lord Byron, who in 1819 published *Mazeppa*, a poem inspired by Voltaire's *History of Charles XII*. There Voltaire recounted an apocryphal story according to which the young Mazepa, then a page at the Polish royal court, fell in love with the young wife of a Polish aristocrat. When the affair was discovered, the aristocrat ordered Mazepa to be stripped naked and tied to the back of a horse that was unleashed to run wild in the steppe. Mazepa was allegedly saved by the Cossacks, who caught the horse days after it was let loose and untied the half-dead young lover. Thus began Mazepa's career among the Cossacks, which led eventually to his hetmancy. Voltaire's story concerned love and honor. He claimed that Mazepa had joined the advancing army of Charles XII because he never forgot another insult to his dignity allegedly suffered

---

[4] On the anathematization of Mazepa, see Nadieszda Kizenko, "The Battle of Poltava in Imperial Liturgy," in *Poltava 1709: The Battle and the Myth*, ed. Serhii Plokhy (Cambridge, Mass., 2012).

at the hands of Peter I. The French author's themes appealed to the sensibilities of nineteenth-century readers.

In Ukraine, admiration for the fallen hetman had different sources and took different forms. In 1810, just over a century after the Battle of Poltava, a young officer in the Russian military and a descendant of an old Cossack family, Oleksii Martos, visited Mazepa's grave in the Moldavian town of Galaţi. A few years after that event, most probably around 1819, the year that Byron's *Mazeppa* was published, Oleksii Martos left the following record in his memoirs:

Mazepa died far from his fatherland whose independence he defended; he was a friend of liberty, and for this he deserves the respect of generations to come ... He is gone, and the name of Little Russia and its brave Cossacks has been erased from the list of nations, not great in numbers but known for their existence and their constitutions. Besides other virtues, Mazepa was a friend of learning: he enlarged the Academy of the Brotherhood Monastery in Kyiv, which he renovated and embellished; he supplied it with a library and rare manuscripts. Yet the founder of the academy and of many churches and philanthropic institutions is anathematized every year on the Sunday of the first week of Great Lent along with Stenka Razin and other thieves and robbers. But what a difference! The latter was a robber and a blasphemer. Mazepa was a most enlightened and philanthropic individual, a skillful military leader, and the ruler of a free nation.[5]

The author of the *History* was caught between two conflicting interpretations of Mazepa's actions. The one advanced by Voltaire stressed the motive of personal revenge, while the one put forward by Martos portrayed the hetman as a champion of his country's independence. The anonymous author of the *History* declared himself in support of Voltaire's interpretation of Mazepa's actions as driven by personal insult and a desire for revenge. But the author's attitude to Mazepa was by no means simple. His characterization of Mazepa as an irresponsible leader driven to avenge a personal insult seems full of contradictions. On the one hand, he denounces Mazepa's actions in light of their reception by the Cossack elite (the Cossack Host) and ordinary people. On the other hand, he considers this reaction, especially on the part of the Cossacks, to be ill-informed, if not completely ridiculous.

---

[5] A. I. Martos, "Zapiski inzhenernogo ofitsera Martosa o Turetskoi voine v tsarstvovanie Aleksandra Pavlovicha," *Russkii arkhiv*, no. 7 (1893): 345. On Oleksii Martos, see Volodymyr Kravchenko, *Narysy z istoriï ukraïns'koï istoriohrafiï epokhy natsional'noho Vidrodzhennia (druha polovyna XVIII– seredyna XIX st.)* (Kharkiv, 1996), pp. 91–98. On Ivan Martos, see I. M. Gofman, *Ivan Petrovich Martos* (Leningrad, 1970).

Writing after the French Revolution, the author was prepared to judge his protagonist's actions by the level of public support that they generated. Did he, however, approve not only the actions of the Cossack elites but also those of the popular masses? Throughout the *History of the Rus'*, its author shows very little regard for the masses as such, and his assessment of their behavior toward the Swedish army in the months leading up to the Battle of Poltava is no exception. "The local people," he declares, making little effort to hide his contempt for the unenlightened and savage plebs, "then resembled savage Americans or wayward Asians. Coming out of their abatis and shelters, they were surprised by the mild behavior of the Swedes, but, because the latter did not speak Rusian among themselves or make the sign of the cross, they considered them non-Christians and infidels, and, on seeing them consuming milk and meat on Fridays, concluded that they were godless infidels and killed them wherever they could be found in small parties or individually." The masses emerge from this description as xenophobic, superstitious, and uncivilized, while the account itself exhibits all the characteristics of enlightened Orientalism.[6]

Depending on the nature and circumstances of the episodes described in the book, its author can be either critical or supportive of Mazepa, judgmental or forgiving. He appears to be seeking a balance between a frankly negative assessment of the hetman and an apology for him. In the process, he creates quite a contradictory figure. Speaking in his own voice, the author is more critical than supportive of the old hetman. His attitude changes when he allows his characters to speak on their own behalf, shielding the author from direct responsibility for what he has written: after all, he is only quoting existing sources without endorsing their views. More often than not, however, those sources were of the author's own invention, or at least a product of his heavy editing. This is particularly true of the speech allegedly delivered by Mazepa to his troops at the beginning of the revolt and cited at length in the *History*. It was in this speech that the author of the *History* gave Mazepa an opportunity to state his case. The long speech was allegedly delivered at the moment, decisive for Mazepa and his homeland, when the hetman decided to switch sides and join Charles XII. In order to maintain the loyalty of his men, Mazepa had to convince the Cossack Host of the justice of his cause. Mazepa (or, rather, the anonymous author) makes the fullest use of this opportunity to explain his view not only of the revolt but of Ukrainian history in general.

[6] *Istoriia Rusov ili Maloi Rossii. Sochinenie Georgiia Koniskago, Arkhiepiskopa Beloruskago* (Moscow, 1846), p. 209.

In his speech to the Cossack Host Mazepa emerges as a protector of Ukrainian independence. He also raises his voice in defense of the ancient rights and freedoms violated by the Muscovites, who allegedly deprived the Cossacks of their prior claim to the Rus' land, of their government, and of the very name of Rus'.

Mazepa's call to arms was based on the dire circumstances in which his fatherland and the Cossack nation found themselves. "We stand now, Brethren, between two abysses prepared to consume us if we do not choose a reliable path for ourselves to avoid them," begins Mazepa's apocryphal speech, referring to the fact that two imperial armies were approaching the borders of Ukraine and that a clash between them was all but inevitable. The hetman tars Peter I and Charles XII with the same brush, depicting them as tyrants who rule arbitrarily over conquered peoples: "Both of them, given their willfulness and appropriation of unlimited power, resemble the most terrible despots, such as all Asia and Africa have hardly ever produced." The hetman claims that the victory of either despot would bring nothing but destruction to Ukraine. The Swedish king would reestablish Polish rule over Ukraine, while the Russian tsar, who refused to confirm the rights and privileges guaranteed to Ukraine in the times of Bohdan Khmelnytsky, has treated the Cossack nation and its representatives in autocratic fashion. "If the Russian tsar is allowed to become the victor," argues the apocryphal Mazepa, "then threatening calamities have been prepared for us by that tsar himself, for you see that, although he comes from a line elected by the people from among its nobility, yet, having appropriated unlimited power for himself, he punishes that people according to his arbitrary will, and not only the people's will and property but their very lives have been subjugated to the will and whim of the tsar alone."

Mazepa's solution to the seemingly insoluble problem of choosing between the two despots was most unusual. He proposed to remain neutral in the conflict between them, but that neutrality was of a particular kind. Ukraine would accept the protectorate of the Swedish king and fight only against those forces that attacked its territory, which under these circumstances could only be Russian forces. The Swedish king, along with other European powers, would guarantee the restoration of Ukrainian independence. Mazepa's speech, at once passionate and highly rational, left no doubt that he was acting in defense of his nation (*natsiia*), which he wanted to save from destruction and lead to freedom, restoring its independence and placing it on a par with other European nations. Parts of his speech specifically countered the arguments of his critics, including the anonymous author's own claim that Mazepa had betrayed the tsar for personal advantage. "And so it remains to us, Brethren," says the apocryphal Mazepa to his troops, "to choose the lesser of the visible evils that have beset us, so that our descendants, condemned to slavery by our incompetence, do not burden us with their complaints and imprecations. I do not have them [descendants] and, of course, cannot have them; consequently, I am not involved in the interests of our descendants and seek nothing but the welfare of the nation that has honored me with my current post and, with it, has entrusted me with its fate."[7]

If the author of the *History of the Rus'* preferred to express his support for Mazepa's cause through a speech attributed to the hetman, he used his own voice to express his (and, by extension, his readers') loyalty to the Russian ruler and to declare his support for Peter. Where the author speaks on his own behalf, he takes a position that, unlike Mazepa's speech, does not tar both rulers with the same brush by depicting them as tyrants but differentiates them, favoring Peter at the expense of Charles. Sympathizing with Mazepa on the strength of his argument while remaining loyal to the ruler was no easy task, partly because the anonymous author disapproved of many of the tsar's actions and those of his Great Russian troops. He assuaged this dilemma by shifting responsibility to the tsar's advisers for those of Peter's actions of which he did not approve.

To judge by the text of the *History*, Aleksandr Menshikov was the main culprit. He is depicted as the embodiment of absolute evil, especially in the vivid description of the Russian massacre of the defenders and peaceful inhabitants of Mazepa's capital, Baturyn. The author goes out of his way to describe the atrocities carried out by Menshikov's troops and to stress their commander's low social origins, apparently seeking not only to explain his cruelty but also to distance him as much as possible from the tsar. "Menshikov assaulted the unarmed burghers, who were in their homes and had no part whatsoever in Mazepa's designs; he slaughtered them to a man, sparing neither sex nor age, nor even suckling infants. This was followed by the troops' plundering of the town, while their commanders and torturers executed the bound Serdiuk officers and civil authorities."[8]

In one case, referring to the massacres of Mazepa's Little Russian supporters by Great Russian troops, the anonymous author even puts Russian persecution of the Little Russian (Rus') nation on a par with its past persecution by the Poles. His attribution of the cruelty of those

[7] *Ibid.*, pp. 203–5.   [8] *Ibid.*, pp. 206–7.

massacres to Aleksandr Menshikov does little to hide the fact that, in his mind, the Great Russian regime has proved as oppressive to his nation as was the Polish one, which created the first Rus' martyr, Severyn Nalyvaiko. Describing the massacre of Mazepa's supporters in Lebedyn, the anonymous author writes:

That punitive action was Menshikov's usual employment: breaking on the wheel, quartering, and impaling; the lightest, considered mere play, was hanging and decapitation ... It now remains to consider and judge – if, according to the words of the Savior himself, written in the Gospel, which are immutable and not to be ignored, 'all blood spilled on earth will be required of this generation' – what requirement awaits for the blood of the Rus' nation shed from the blood of Hetman Nalyvaiko to the present day, and shed in great streams for the sole reason that it sought liberty or a better life in its own land and had intentions in that regard common to all humanity.[9]

The author of the *History of the Rus'* was caught not only between two conflicting interpretations of the Mazepa Revolt but also between two contradictory imperatives: his loyalty to the ruler and the Romanov dynasty conflicted with his clear admiration for Mazepa as an embodiment of the Enlightenment ideals of struggle against tyranny, defense of human dignity, and protection of national rights. The solution to this conundrum was found in the concept of the nation, deeply rooted in Ukrainian historical writing of the previous era. While the anonymous author of the *History* remained loyal to the tsar in his description of the Poltava episode and shifted responsibility for Peter's ruthlessness and cruelty to his advisers, he found no difficulty in denouncing the tsar's Great Russian nation. If revolt against the tsar remained illegitimate for the author, the struggle of one nation against another in defense of its freedom and liberties certainly did not. Hetman Pavlo Polubotok emerges in the pages of the *History* as an embodiment of this solution. He personifies the role of an ideal hetman prepared to die defending the interests of his nation without betraying the principle of loyalty to the ruler.

Polubotok spells out this vision of appropriate relations between the tsar and his subjects in a speech that the anonymous author makes him deliver upon his arrest by the Privy Chancellery, the most hated of all the imperial institutions described in the work. "The guilt imputed to us," Polubotok allegedly told the tsar,

---

[9] *Ibid.*, pp. 212–13.

"is nothing but our duty, and a sacred duty at that, so considered in every nation, and by no means contrary to law or deserving censure. We have pleaded and plead now on behalf of our people for mercy to our fatherland, which is being unjustly persecuted and pitilessly destroyed; we plead for the restitution of our rights and privileges affirmed by solemn agreements that you, Sovereign, have also confirmed several times." He claimed that his people had been "subjected to the basest slavery, obliged to pay a disgraceful and unbearable tribute, and forced to dig trenches and canals and drain impassable marshes, fertilizing all this with the corpses of our dead, who have fallen by the thousands from oppressive burdens, hunger, and climate. All those misfortunes and miseries of ours have finally been worsened to the utmost by our government. The Muscovite officials lording it over us, who do not know our laws and customs and are almost illiterate, know only that they are empowered to do anything at all to us, leaving only our souls untouched."

Thus Polubotok was first and foremost the representative of his nation and the defender of its legitimate rights. The interests of the people and the fatherland were central to his claim, as they had been central to the pronouncements made by Hetman Mazepa on the eve of his rebellion against the tsar. Unlike Mazepa, Polubotok did not raise a revolt against the tsar but petitioned him in an attempt to reconcile conflicting loyalties – to the nation and to the sovereign. Believing that compromise was possible, he wanted the tsar to abolish the new taxes and labor obligations imposed on the Cossacks and to do away with the Little Russian College, which was run by Great Russian officers. Judging by the known demands of the Cossack elites, this was supposed to lead to the restoration of the hetmancy.

Pavlo Polubotok's argument was rooted in his belief in the political and historical legitimacy of both the nation and the monarch. Part of Polubotok's argument, enunciated at both the beginning and the end of his speech, concerned his understanding of the rights and obligations of the sovereign. "I see, Sovereign, and understand," he began, "from what source you have drawn the wrath that is not native to your heart and unbecoming to the character of one anointed of God. Righteousness and humility, justice and mercy are the sole possession of all the Monarchs of this world, and the laws governing all humanity and preserving it from evil are a precise mirror to Tsars and Rulers of their duty and conduct, and they should be their foremost keepers and guardians. Whence comes it that you, O Sovereign, placing yourself above the laws, torment us with your exclusive power and cast us into eternal imprisonment, taking possession of our property for your own treasury?" The acting hetman's answer to his question about the source of the tsar's bad behavior was simple. It was the fault of the sovereign's advisers, especially Aleksandr

Menshikov: "And so, beset on all sides by persecution and attack, to whom should we turn with our cries if not to you, Most August Monarch? You are our protector and guarantor of our well-being. But the malice of your favorite, our implacable enemy and persecutor, has driven you from the true path and corrupted your rule."[10]

Polubotok's speech was not an invention of the author of the *History of the Rus'*. Whether or not Polubotok actually made any speech to Peter, texts of a Polubotok speech similar to the one we find in the *History* had been circulating in Ukraine long before the appearance of this historical pamphlet. The speech was so popular that an extract from it was used as an inscription on portraits of Polubotok that hung in the homes of the Hetmanate elite as late as the first decades of the nineteenth century. According to Dmitrii Bantysh-Kamensky, who encountered such inscriptions while working on his *History of Little Russia* toward the end of the second decade of the century, they read as follows: "Standing up for my fatherland, I fear neither chains nor prison, and it would be better for me to suffer the worst death than to see the total destruction of my countrymen."[11]

Thanks to Bantysh-Kamensky, this inscription became widely known in the nineteenth century and was quoted by Giliarovsky, among others. It derived from a fuller variant of the speech that must have been very close to the one found in Jean-Benoît Scherer's *Annales*. Translated into French from Ukrainian, possibly via Russian, that particular extract of the speech read as follows: "'I know that chains await me, and that, locked up in the horrors of a dark prison cell, I will be left to die of hunger according to Rus' custom, but what of it: I speak for my fatherland, and I readily prefer the cruelest death to the terrible spectacle of the total ruin of my nation." The "countrymen" of the portrait inscription are turned into a "nation" in Scherer's French version, but otherwise the two extracts are as similar as might be expected under the circumstances.

Since the portrait inscription reflects some peculiarities of written eighteenth-century Ukrainian, it could not have come from Scherer's French text. Because Scherer's text is fuller and more elaborate than that of the portrait inscription, it would be logical to assume that both the portrait inscription and Scherer's variant of Polubotok's speech have a common source – a text circulating in Ukraine before the publication of

[10]   *Ibid.*, pp. 228–30.
[11]   Dmitrii Bantysh-Kamenskii, *Istoriia Maloi Rossii* (Moscow, 1822), vol. IV, pp. 64–65.

Scherer's work. We can speak with even more certainty about the relation between Scherer's *Annales* and the *History of the Rus'*. The latter's version of Polubotok's speech is based on Scherer's text, as attested by the close lexical and structural correspondence between the two extracts. "I know that chains and dark dungeons await us," said Polubotok, according to the author of the *History*, "where we shall be worn down by hunger and oppression according to Muscovite custom." The anonymous author replaced the increasingly confusing "Rus'" with "Muscovite," but otherwise he stayed close to his source, which he loyally followed in other parts of the speech as well.[12]

What, if anything, did the anonymous author add to Polubotok's speech as rendered by Scherer? One of several things that we encounter in the *History* but not in Scherer is Polubotok's historical argument. Scherer's version of the speech contains nothing about the ethnic affinity between the Rus' nation and that of the tsar, nor about the loyal service of the Rus' nation from the time of its voluntary submission to the tsar up to the Northern War and the defeat of Charles XII.

"Our people, being of the same stock and faith as yours, strengthened it and exalted your tsardom by voluntary unification at a time when all that was in it was as yet immature, emerging from the chaos of troubled times and from almost complete poverty," claimed Polubotok. "And this alone would not allow our people to forfeit its recompense from you; but even more than that, we, along with our people, did not cease to render distinguished service to you in all your military levies and conquests; and, to say nothing of the Smolensk region and Poland, the Swedish War alone proves our unexampled zeal for you and for Russia. For it is known to all that we completely destroyed half the Swedish army on our soil and in our habitations, without yielding to any flattery or temptation, thereby putting you into a position to overcome the amazing bravery and desperate courage of the Swedes; but for this we brought down on ourselves nothing but contempt and animosity, and, instead of gratitude and reward, we were subjected to the basest slavery."

These additions to the Polubotok speech derive from the national and political views of the author of the *History*. The idea of the affinity between the Rus' and the Muscovites, along with the author's insistence on the important services rendered by the Cossacks to the Russian Empire, is one of the leitmotifs of the *History*, and he is only too happy to incorporate it into the text of Polubotok's speech as well. Another point

[12] Jean-Benoît Scherer, *Annales de la Petite-Russie, ou Histoire des Cosaques-Saporogues et des Cosaques de l'Ukraine*, 2 vols. (Paris, 1788), II: 207–11; cf. *Istoriia Rusov*, p. 230.

not to be found in Scherer is Polubotok's distinction between the good
Christian monarch and the bad Asian tyrant. Scherer's Polubotok already
thinks in national terms, speaking of national rights and the threat
of destruction hanging over his nation, but the Polubotok of the *History*
goes further and introduces elements of Orientalism into his discourse.
While absolving the tsar of direct responsibility for unjust acts, Polubotok
did not exculpate him entirely. Whether caused by bad advisers or not,
his behavior was not in keeping with that of an enlightened monarch:
"To subject peoples to slavery and lord it over slaves and bondsmen is
the task of an Asiatic tyrant, not of a Christian Monarch, who should
be exalted as and indeed act as the supreme father of [his] peoples,"
claimed Polubotok.

While Polubotok ended his speech with an explicit threat to the tsar, it
was not one of rebellion but of punishment that would befall the ruler
after his death. He concluded with the following words: "I know that
chains and dark dungeons await us, where we shall be worn down by
hunger and oppression according to Muscovite custom, but, while I still
live, I speak the truth to you, O Sovereign! You will certainly render an
accounting to the King of Kings, God Almighty, for our destruction and
that of our whole nation." Having heard out Polubotok without managing to refute his claims or the logic of his exposition, Peter resorted
to repression and sent him to prison. Although Polubotok was punished
for his "presumption," the justice of his claim remained unchallenged in
the *History*.[13]

Pavlo Polubotok and, by extension, the author of the *History of the Rus'*
were nothing if not followers of Jean Bodin's theory of the sovereignty of
rulers. Bodin had argued at length in his *Six livres de la république* (1576)
in favor of the absolute power of the monarch. His decisions were not
subject to appeal. Subjects might have just grievances against the monarch
and his rule, but God alone could judge him. Subjects could refuse to
obey the ruler's orders if they violated the laws of God or nature, but they
could not rebel against him. Like Aristotle before him, Bodin believed
that despotic monarchies were associated with Asia, not Europe. The
author of the *History* apparently held the same belief. The part of
Polubotok's speech in which he appeals to the tsar to remain a Christian
monarch and not become an Asiatic tyrant ruling over slaves is not to be
found in Scherer and was probably the author's own creation. Although

---

[13] *Istoriia Rusov*, pp. 230–31.

Bodin did not consider Muscovy a tyranny, the anonymous author evidently saw the possibility of its becoming one.[14]

An element of the Polubotok story that might be attributed to the author's special access to the Polubotok family is the visit of Peter I to the imprisoned hetman on the eve of his death. This was the episode that made the strongest impression on readers throughout the nineteenth and early twentieth centuries and inspired Vasilii Volkov to paint his picture of Peter's last encounter with his nemesis. The source of that story, according to the author of the *History*, was oral tradition. "Concerning the death of Polubotok," wrote the anonymous author,

tradition has left the following record: that when he was ill, felt his end approaching, and asked the prison guards to summon a priest for him, and the guards told the sovereign of it, the sovereign came to him to apologize, and he said to him, "I never had any enmity toward you, nor do I now, and with that I die as a Christian. I firmly believe that for my innocent suffering and that of my kinsmen we shall be judged by our common and undissembling Judge, God Almighty, and soon we shall both stand before him, and justice will be rendered to Peter and Paul." Soon afterwards – on January 28, 1725, to be precise – the sovereign indeed met his end.

Pavlo Polubotok, the hero of post-Mazepa Ukraine, preferred imprisonment and death to rebellion, but, for the readers of the *History*, his death strengthened the moral force of his argument. Ironically, during the 1917 revolution in Ukraine the Pavlo Polubotok military regiment, named after the hetman who had served so long as a symbol of nonviolent resistance, was the first to rise in the name of independent Ukraine. In the long run, it was the ideas embodied in Polubotok's apocryphal speech, not his mythical gold, that became his most valuable legacy to his nation.[15]

---

[14] Johann Sommerville, "Absolutism and Royalism," in *The Cambridge History of Political Thought, 1450–1700*, ed. J. H. Burns (Cambridge, 1991), pp. 347–73; Marshall Poe, *"A People Born to Slavery": Russia in Early Modern European Ethnography, 1576–1748* (Ithaca, N. Y., and London, 2000), pp. 151–56, 169–70.

[15] *Istoriia Rusov*, pp. 229–31; "Polubotok Regiment," *Encyclopedia of Ukraine*, vol. IV (Toronto, 1993), p. 137.

PART IV

Unusual suspects

CHAPTER II

People and places

There are few small towns in Ukraine more deserving of tourist attention than Novhorod-Siverskyi, located in the northeastern corner of the country. It has the highest per capita concentration of architectural monuments in Ukraine. Its current population is only about fourteen thousand, but Novhorod-Siverskyi is the proud custodian of numerous architectural jewels, some of which date back to the times of Kyivan Rus'. It also has a modern hotel complete with a swimming pool featuring artificial waves, according to the tourist guides. The online English-language description of the town highlights its location on hills surrounded by deep ravines and the broad valley of the Desna River, as well as the exceptional beauty of the Dormition Cathedral (seventeenth century) and the ensemble of the Transfiguration Monastery (eleventh to eighteenth centuries), one the oldest monasteries in Ukraine.[1]

Novhorod-Siverskyi is an ancient town indeed. It is first mentioned in the eleventh-century Rus' chronicle, and in the next two centuries it served as the capital of a Rus' principality. Aside from the Transfiguration Monastery and the Dormition Cathedral, notable monuments include the wooden Church of St. Nicholas, built in the Cossack baroque style in 1760; a triumphal arch erected in 1786–87 to welcome Catherine II in the course of her trip to the Crimea; and the "commercial rows" of the early nineteenth century. There are also numerous recent monuments celebrating characters from the most mysterious narrative in East Slavic literature, *The Tale of Igor's Campaign*. The statues of an ancient minstrel called Boian and of Princess Yaroslavna were created to immortalize these characters of the *Tale*. More than any of the town's architectural monuments, its literary connection with the *Tale* put it on the cultural and historical map of Eastern Europe. The entire

---

[1] *Sivershchyna Travel Guide*, Tourist Information Portal http://siver.org.ua/?p=181&lang=en.

Novhorod-Siverskyi architectural ensemble is part of a historical preserve named after the *Tale of Igor's Campaign*.[2]

What is the *Tale of Igor's Campaign?* Historians still argue about the
origins and meaning of the text. The narrative, which first became known
to scholars in the late eighteenth century, describes a campaign undertaken in 1185 against the nomadic Polovtsians by Prince Igor (Ihor) of
Novhorod-Siverskyi. The *Tale* was lauded by generations of Russian
and Ukrainian scholars as the most outstanding monument of old Rus'
literature. The pride of Russian and Ukrainian literature and culture, it is
thought to put Rus' civilization on a par with, if not significantly ahead of,
West European culture of the same period. The *Tale* became the source of
Alexander Borodin's opera *Prince Igor*, first performed in 1890. The prince
himself is immortalized in the monument erected in the city center. It
stands proudly in the middle of a square that, to the surprise and
confusion of foreign visitors, is named not after Igor or the *Tale* itself
but after Vladimir Lenin, the main character of a very different tale. If
anything, this is one more proof that the town does not take its history
lightly. But the paradoxes involving the *Tale* and the town of Novhorod-
Siverskyi do not end here.[3]

At a time when the civil authorities and cultural leaders in Kyiv
continue to pour money from Ukraine's strained budgetary resources into
the construction and maintenance of monuments to the characters of the
Tale, more and more scholars are raising questions about the authenticity
of the text. The skeptics, who include the founder of the "skeptical
school" in Russian historiography, M. T. Kachenovsky, came to the fore
soon after the publication of the mysterious text in 1800. They were quick
to point out that the publishers never produced their original. It allegedly
perished in the fire of Moscow during Napoleon's occupation of the city
in 1812. Bad luck, claimed believers in the authenticity of the text. Too
suspicious, argued the skeptics. Debate continues to the present day.
Academic research on the text has long featured heated exchanges between
self-proclaimed patriots and those who, their opponents claim, are not
patriots at all. Naturally, most non-Russian and non-Ukrainian scholars
in this field fall into the "non-patriotic" category. Recently the authenticity of the *Tale* was questioned once again in a monograph by a renowned

---

[2] "Novhorod-Sivers'kyi," *Entsyklopediia ukraïnoznavstva*, 14 vols. (Paris and New York, 1949–95), III:
623–25.

[3] On the *Tale*, see *Éntsiklopediia "Slova o polku Igoreve,"* 5 vols., ed. L. A. Dmitriev, D. Likhachev
et al. (St. Petersburg, 1995).

specialist in early modern Russian history, Edward L. Keenan. His book met with strong criticism in the academic press of the region. In the Novhorod-Siverskyi preserve, few scholars are prepared to take seriously Keenan's contention that the *Tale* is a mystification dating from the late eighteenth century. After all, if Keenan should prove right, the government of Ukraine could hardly continue funding an institution devoted to the study and promotion of a literary hoax![4]

While Novhorod-Siverskyi's claim to fame may start with the *Tale*, it does not end there. Ever since Ukrainian independence and the publication in Ukraine of the works of Oleksander Ohloblyn, the town has also become known as the home of a Ukrainian patriotic circle that allegedly existed there in the last decades of the eighteenth century. Among the believers in the existence of the "Novhorod-Siverskyi patriotic circle" are such heavyweights of Ukrainian scholarship and politics as Volodymyr Lytvyn, the long-serving chairman of the Ukrainian parliament and vice-president of the National Academy of Sciences of Ukraine. Not surprisingly, the "circle" has made its way into school textbooks. A historical dictionary for school teachers includes an entry on the grouping, which it defines as a "secret circle of Ukrainian autonomists." The entry suggests that the circle "existed in the Novhorod-Siverskyi vicegerency in the 1780s and 1790s. The circle included A. Hudovych, H. Dolynsky, M. Znachko-Yavorsky, V. Shyshatsky, T. Kalynsky, M. Myklashevsky, A. Khudorba, and others. The goal of the circle was to develop national culture and win the independence of Ukraine. Members of the circle helped disseminate patriotic and publicistic writings, as well as works on the history and ethnography of Ukraine (Yakiv Markevych's *Notes on Little Russia*, the *History of the Rus'*, Opanas Lobysevych's *Virgil's Shepherds*, etc.)."[5]

Ohloblyn's ideas made their way even into a book ghostwritten for Lytvyn's one-time boss, Ukraine's second president, Leonid Kuchma. A native of the Novhorod-Siverskyi region, Kuchma published *Ukraine Is Not Russia* in 2004, the last year of his presidency. In it he made a brief excursus not only into Ukrainian history generally but also into the past of his smaller homeland. Ohloblyn's name was not mentioned in the

---

[4] Edward L. Keenan, *Josef Dobrovský and the Origins of the Igor' Tale* (Cambridge, Mass., 2003). For reaction to Keenan's hypothesis in the West, see Simon Franklin, "The Igor Tale: A Bohemian Rhapsody?" *Kritika* 6 (4) (2005): 833–44; Ireneusz Szarycz, review of *Josef Dobrovský and the Origins of the Igor' Tale* by Edward L. Keenan, *Slavic Review* 61, no. 1 (spring 2005): 218–19.
[5] Volodymyr Lytvyn, *Istoriia Ukraïny. Pidruchnyk* (Kyiv, 2006), p. 295; *Dovidnyk z istoriï Ukraïny (A–Ia). Posibnyk dlia seredn'oho zahal'noosvitn'oho navchal'noho zakladu* (Kyiv, 2001), p. 520.

book, but, following the line taken by Ohloblyn's close friend and fellow émigré Natalia Polonska-Vasylenko, Kuchma embraced the notion that a Novhorod-Siverskyi patriotic circle had existed. He praised the work done by the Poletykas and Opanas Lobysevych and claimed that the *History* might have been written collectively by members of the Novhorod-Siverskyi circle. Like Polonska-Vasylenko and another émigré historian, Dmytro Doroshenko, as well as Mykhailo Drahomanov, whose name he forgot to mention, Kuchma considered the *History* a work of extraordinary importance, comparing its impact on the formation of Ukrainian identity to that of Taras Shevchenko's collection of poetry, the *Kobzar*. He also saw himself as a continuator of the work begun by the anonymous author. "The *History of the Rus'* was meant to remind readers that Ukraine is not Russia (two hundred years later, one finds oneself having to do this again)," claimed Kuchma. He endorsed the idea of establishing a museum devoted specifically to that work. "I ask myself," wrote Kuchma or one of his ghostwriters, "whether the 'eternal book of Ukraine' does not deserve its own museum. A museum devoted to a single work is a great rarity in the world. I would note that there is already a museum of the *Tale of Igor's Campaign* in Novhorod-Siverskyi. If a museum devoted to the *History of the Rus'* is built, then Novhorod-Siverskyi will probably become the world's only city with two such museums."[6]

Ohloblyn could celebrate a victory of sorts. The ideas that he had first advanced in his wartime writings on the *History of the Rus'* and developed in the course of long discussions with Natalia Polonska-Vasylenko in cold and hunger-stricken Kyiv became accessible to a new generation of readers. His Second World War-era manuscript on the author of the *History* was now available in print. His essay collection about *People of Bygone Ukraine* that postulated the existence of a Novhorod-Siverskyi patriotic circle and linked the *History* with it was reprinted. Most of this newly received wisdom was accepted uncritically. In schools, the *History* was studied as a product of Ukrainian autonomist thought. Yet Ohloblyn was never able to provide sufficient evidence that the links between those whom he considered members of the Novhorod-Siverskyi circle went beyond the mere coincidence of their working and living in the same town. Ukrainian scholars who examined Ohloblyn's argument came away utterly disappointed. There was no evidence whatever that the Novhorod-Siverskyi circle had existed, despite the claims of people as

[6] Leonid Kuchma, *Ukraina – ne Rossiia* (Moscow, 2004), pp. 112–14.

highly placed in the Ukrainian political and academic hierarchy as Leonid Kuchma and Volodymyr Lytvyn.[7]

Whatever the fate of Ohloblyn's hypothesis about the Novhorod-Siverskyi patriotic circle, his designation of Novhorod-Siverskyi as the birthplace of the *History of the Rus'*, gained considerable support not only among authors of general histories and historical dictionaries but also among more serious students of the *History*. Not only were those findings generally accepted, but they became the basis for a new hypothesis. In his introduction to a translation of the *History* first published in 1991 and issued in a revised and expanded version in 2001, Valerii Shevchuk took Ohloblyn's ideas about the connections between the Khudorba History mentioned in Aleksandr von Brigen's letter to Kondratii Ryleev, the Khudorbas of the *History*, and the Khudorbas of the village of Koman in the environs of Novhorod-Siverskyi one step further.

"Was not Khudorba's manuscript, which supposedly existed in a single copy, the holograph of the *History of the Rus*?" asked Shevchuk. "We cannot solve this problem in our day, though we might offer the following completely hypothetical picture," he continued. "Let us assume that Khudorba's History and the *History of the Rus'* are one and the same work. In the eighteenth century, until the author's death (and Khudorba wrote it when he went into retirement in the 1790s), it did not circulate, that is, it existed in one copy – the author, having written it, had every reason to be cautious. After his death, which occurred before 1810, several copies or a single copy were made, and this copy or these copies circulated; it was in fact the copyists who wrote Konysky's name on the work (there are copies that do not bear this name). These copies circulated locally, for it was a question of preserving an illegal book. The author did not sign his name, also for reasons of conspiracy. And so, from that time on, the *History of the Rus'* began to exist separately, with no link to Khudorba's name."[8]

Although Shevchuk's hypothesis was grounded in Ohloblyn's findings, which we discussed at length in Chapter 6, it also contradicted many of them, including his claim that the *History* had been written in the first decade of the nineteenth century. Where the professional historian Ohloblyn enjoined caution, the writer-turned-historian Shevchuk invoked

[7] Oleksander Ohloblyn, "Istoriia Rusiv," *Dnipro*, no. 9 (1991): 35–49; Ohloblyn, *Do pytannia pro avtora "Istorii Rusov"* (Kyiv, 1998); Ohloblyn, *Liudy staroï Ukrainy ta inshi pratsi* (Ostrih, 2000); O. Il'in, "Chy isnuvav Novhorod-Sivers'kyi patriotychnyi hurtok?" *Siverians'kyi litopys*, no. 6 (1997): 125.
[8] Valerii Shevchuk, "Nerozhadani taiemnytsi 'Istorii Rusiv,'" (2001), pp. 14–16. Cf. Ohloblyn, *Do pytannia pro avtora "Istorii Rusov"* (Kyiv, 1998), pp. 69–71.

his powers of literary imagination. He admitted that he had no proof to support his hypothesis. Under the circumstances, however, it was as good as anyone else's. He had every right to put the book aside and focus on other projects. Arkhyp Khudorba is a much stronger candidate for the authorship of the *History* than Archbishop Konysky, either of the Poletykas, or Prince Bezborodko. But there are also problems with this identification.

First of all, it must be admitted that the very notion of Arkhyp Khudorba as the author of the text known to von Brigen is little more than a hypothesis. Von Brigen never mentioned the first name of the author of the Khudorba History. Writing in 1941–42 in occupied Kyiv, Ohloblyn, the "discoverer" of the Khudorbas, never claimed that it was Arkhyp rather than any other member of the clan who had written the mysterious history. He simply indicated Arkhyp as the most prominent of the Khudorbas. It was only in emigration that Ohloblyn took a different position on the issue. In the essay of 1959 on Arkhyp Khudorba that appeared in his collection on *People of Bygone Ukraine*, Ohloblyn identified Arkhyp as the probable author of the history mentioned by von Brigen. "Speaking in favor of this are the rich life experience of Arkhyp Khudorba and his personal abilities, as well as the fact that of all the Khudorbas who were contemporaries of Hryhorii Konysky, he had no competitor in such an enterprise." Ohloblyn was certainly right in asserting that if Khudorba the author was indeed a contemporary of Konysky, as claimed by von Brigen, then Arkhyp Khudorba had all the appropriate qualifications to be the writer of a historical tract. Deprived of his Kyiv collections, however, Ohloblyn was unable to furnish any additional evidence supporting this claim.

Who was Arkhyp Khudorba? He was born in the mid eighteenth century to a rank-and-file Cossack family in the village of Koman and began his career as a secretary of the Novhorod-Siverskyi Cossack company in the early 1760s. Arkhyp clearly had the abilities required to advance through the Cossack ranks in both war and peace. He soon joined the Cossack officer stratum, obtaining promotions during the Russo-Turkish War (1768–74), which brought him to the walls of the Ottoman fortresses of Dubăsari (Dubosary) and Bender in Moldavia and to Perekop and Kaffa in the Crimea. By 1777 Arkhyp Khudorba was already a captain of the Sheptaky company to the north of his native Novhorod-Siverskyi region. But the abolition of the Hetmanate put an end to Khudorba's administrative career. He retired in 1783 with the Cossack rank of "companion of the banner," which guaranteed him

Russian noble status. By that time he had also become an owner of serfs – in 1785 he had twelve peasants to his name. These were too few to provide him with a sufficient income, and in that year Khudorba returned to the service, joining the Starodub carabineer regiment of the regular imperial Army as a second major. As far as Ohloblyn knew, Arkhyp Khudorba was last mentioned in 1790 as a premier major in the lists of the Novhorod-Siverskyi nobility.

The entire Khudorba family was granted noble status in 1799. That cumbersome process, with its uncertain outcome for many descendants of Cossack families in the region, was probably advanced by Arkhyp's spectacular career and accomplishments. There were other Khudorbas around, but none of them was as prominent as Arkhyp – a consideration that influenced, if it did not predetermine, Ohloblyn's choice of him as the possible author of the history mentioned by von Brigen. Ohloblyn saw additional proof of his hypothesis in the fact that after joining the Starodub regiment, Arkhyp served under the command of none other than von Brigen's father-in-law, Mykhailo Myklashevsky, who might well have known about Khudorba's historiographic efforts and informed his son-in-law about the existence of the text. Thus, according to Ohloblyn and, later, Shevchuk, it was Arkhyp Khudorba who wrote the "freedom-loving" tract. But where do these hypotheses leave seekers for the author of the *History of the Rus'*?[9]

Unlike Shevchuk, Ohloblyn never believed that the Khudorba History and the *History of the Rus'* could be one and the same text. He treated them as separate works on the basis of the only source that mentions Khudorba's History – von Brigen's letter to Kondratii Ryleev. "This History is valued here equally with Konysky's History," wrote von Brigen with reference to the historical work attributed to Khudorba. How, then, is one to explain the extraordinary interest shown by the author of the *History of the Rus'* in the family history of the Khudorbas? Ohloblyn offered the most logical suggestion that could be made under the circumstances: Khudorba's work may have served as one of the sources of the *History of the Rus'*. He was prepared to attribute to that particular source and, by extension, to Arkhyp Khudorba many characteristics that he had earlier ascribed to the author of the *History of the Rus'*. Not only did Khudorba have some practice in the art of writing (as his stint as company secretary could well attest), but he was also an officer who knew military

---

[9] Ohloblyn, *Do pytannia pro avtora*, pp. 65–72; Ohloblyn, *Liudy staroï Ukraïny* (Munich, 1959), pp. 288–99.

terminology and was intimately familiar with southern Ukraine – the theater of the Russo-Turkish War. Ohloblyn even believed that the year 1769 as the terminus of the *History of the Rus'* could be explained with reference to Khudorba's career, since he had left Novhorod-Siverskyi that year to take part in military campaigns in the South.[10]

Considered on the scale of probability and grounding in the historical sources, Ohloblyn's supposition that the Khudorba History served as a source for the *History of the Rus'* is much more persuasive than Shevchuk's hypothesis, which does not take full account of – or even explain – von Brigen's reference to the Khudorba History as a text separate from the one attributed to Konysky. Nor did Shevchuk explain the presence in the *History of the Rus'* of terms, ideas, and attitudes clearly suggesting an early nineteenth-century date for the work. But if Ohloblyn was right, Shevchuk wrong, and Khudorba (either Arkhyp or some other member of his family) indeed the author of a text used by the author of the *History*, what did that text look like? Answering this question would help determine the anonymous author's original contribution to the text of the *History* and perhaps lead to the author himself.

What period did the Khudorba History cover? Ohloblyn assumed that the year 1769 as the terminus of *History of the Rus'* made sense in terms of Khudorba's career, suggesting that Khudorba's historical account ended with that year. Thus, in Ohloblyn's imagination the two histories covered the same time period – up to 1769. But did they? There is an important feature of the *History* that undermines this otherwise solid hypothesis. The Khudorbas, who, according to Ohloblyn, were central to Arkhyp's narrative, disappear from the text of the *History of the Rus'* not in 1769 but more than sixty years earlier: they are last mentioned in 1708! According to the *History*, it was then that the flag-bearer Pavlo Khudorba of Novhorod-Siverskyi met with Tsar Peter I in the village of Pohrebky near Koman to let him know that the citizens were prepared to surrender the town to the Russian army. This episode had some basis in fact: as Ohloblyn showed, there was indeed a Pavlo Khudorba in the environs of Novhorod-Siverskyi in 1723. Moreover, some of the Pohrebky land belonged to the Khudorba family as late as the turn of the twentieth century. Unlike previous mentions of the Khudorbas, which appeared to be pure invention on the part of the unknown author or authors, the episode of 1708 mixed fact and fiction.

One may speculate that the Khudorbas do not subsequently figure in the *History*, and perhaps not in Arkhyp Khudorba's work either, because

---

[10] Ohloblyn, *Liudy staroï Ukraïny*, pp. 293–98.

there was no eighteenth-century heroism in the family history to write about, and the era was too close to the author's own times to allow for any invention. That is possible, but the Khudorbas do not disappear from the pages of the *History* alone. They take along a whole group of characters associated with Novhorod-Siverskyi, as well as individuals whose surnames correspond closely to known surnames of people in the vicinity of the town and among the inhabitants of Khudorba's native Koman well into the nineteenth century. Some of these people play a positive role in the *History*, others a negative one, but it does not stand to reason that they should all disappear from the narrative after 1708.

Who were these people? Let us begin with a list of the *History's* villains possessing Novhorod-Siverskyi connections. The name of Mykhailo Kunynsky in the *History* – the alleged proponent of the church union of 1596 – corresponds to that of a real person, Jan Kunicki, the Polish captain of the Novhorod-Siverskyi castle in 1648. Another Polish commander of the period discussed in the *History* is Wroński. Not surprisingly, a Polish nobleman named Jan Wroński was remembered by peasants of the village of Yukhnov, adjacent to Koman, as late as the nineteenth century. Iraklii Shvernytsky, the alleged bishop of Volhynia who supported the union of 1596, bore the same last name as a Novhorod-Siverskyi noble family whose heirs lived in the village of Pohrebky (next to Koman) as late as the end of the nineteenth century. No less surprising than the presence of these Novhorod-Siverskyi names in the text of the *History* is their disappearance from its narrative after 1708.

Positive characters with Novhorod-Siverskyi connections disappear as well. The Skabychevskys, another family of local provenance, make their only appearance in the *History* in 1648, when one of its members cuts off the moustache of Khmelnytsky's arch-enemy Czapliński. The Tomylovskys, another prominent local family, appear in the 1650s, represented by the apocryphal acting hetman Yakiv Tomylo. The Pashynskys, who lived in the village of Chulativ near Koman, figure in the person of Symeon Pashynsky, a devoted defender of Orthodoxy against the church union. References to the Malchyches, Lysovskys, and Zhoravkas – representatives of Novhorod-Siverskyi Cossack and Cossack officer families – also appear in the narrative before 1708. The same applies to individuals whose names are based on those of archimandrites of the Novhorod-Siverskyi Transfiguration Monastery: Berezovsky, Lezhaisky, and Tuptalsky (Tuptalo). The abundance of names from Novhorod-Siverskyi and its environs in the *History* was first noted by Ohloblyn in 1941–42 and remains one of his major contributions to the study of the mysterious text. But neither then nor later did he pay any attention to 1708 as a cut-off date for the author's reference to Novhorod-Siverskyi family names.[11]

The explanation may lie, as suggested above, in the circumstance that eighteenth-century events were too close to the time of writing of the *History* for its author to engage in telling fantastic stories without being caught. That would seem quite plausible. But there is another feature of the *History* that rules out this explanation. It is not only the glorious Khudorba clan and its next-door neighbors who disappear from the text after 1708, but something even more central to Ohloblyn's understanding of the *History* – the town of Novhorod-Siverskyi itself. There is no mention of Novhorod-Siverskyi or its immediate environs after 1708. None! The author might well have chosen to omit apocryphal stories about his own family and those of his friends and enemies, but, having paid so much attention to Novhorod-Siverskyi, he could hardly have dropped it from his account (as well as the village of Koman, which was long under the jurisdiction of the Novhorod-Siverskyi magistracy) at the very point when his narrative begins to rely more and more heavily on oral tradition and local lore.

The most obvious way out of this conundrum is to suggest that it is in 1708, or soon thereafter, that one of the major sources of the *History* – a narrative paying special attention to the Khudorbas, their neighbors, and their beloved Novhorod-Siverskyi – comes to an end. It is quite possible that this particular source was the Khudorba History mentioned by von Brigen. If that is the case, then its narrative ended in 1708, not 1769, as suggested by Ohloblyn, and it certainly was not the same text as the one published under the title *History of the Rus'* by Bodiansky, as Shevchuk suggests. Ironically, Shevchuk himself indicated the stylistically distinct section of the *History* that begins with 1708, the year of Mazepa's revolt and the election of Ivan Skoropadsky to the hetmancy. Knowingly or not, in this regard he followed Oleksandr Lazarevsky, who wrote in 1894: "The events of the eighteenth century in this history, especially beginning with Mazepa's treason, were written largely on the basis of living tradition, and probably in part on the basis of the author's personal knowledge. Hence the anecdotal character of the exposition of those events."[12]

[11] Ohloblyn, *Do pytannia pro avtora*, pp. 35–64. Cf. Ohloblyn, "Where Was *Istoriya Rusov* Written?" *Annals of the Ukrainian Academy of Arts and Sciences in the US* 3, no. 2 (1953): 670–95.
[12] Shevchuk, "Nerozhadani taiemnytsi 'Istoriï Rusiv,'" (2001), p. 51. Cf. Aleksandr Lazarevskii, "Prezhnie izyskateli malorusskoi stariny," *Kievskaia starina*, no. 12 (1894): 349–87, here 350–51. On the linguistic differences between different parts of the *History*, see S. N. Plokhii and

The post-1708 section of the *History* appears to have been written by someone with different religious concerns than the author of the preceding text. Although the prevailing authorial attitude throughout the work is one of staunch support for Orthodoxy, the principal religious opponents change. If before 1708 those opponents are the Uniates, after that year they are displaced by the Old Believers, whom the author hates with a passion probably surpassing his loathing of the Catholics. The anti-Uniate discourse can easily be traced back to the Khudorba History. Much of the land in the vicinity of Koman belonged to the Novhorod-Siverskyi Transfiguration Monastery, whose archimandrites and monks cherished memories of their predecessors' struggle against the church union in the first half of the seventeenth century. Whoever took it upon himself to continue the Khudorba History did not live in Koman nor, for that matter, in the environs of Novhorod-Siverskyi, and his negative attitude toward the Union was anything but personal. His concern about the Old Belief, by contrast, was real and ongoing. There was however a half-hearted attempt in the final editing of the *History* to connect the two sections. In the pre-1708 part of the *History*, the author of its last part plants a reference to the "Armenian monk Martin," whom he considers a forerunner of the Old Belief, in the protest allegedly issued by the Orthodox bishops after the Council of Brest (1596). But his last-minute addition does not affect the profound difference in the religious discourses of the two parts of the *History*: anti-Uniate prior to 1708 and anti-Old Belief after that date.[13]

If we try to reconstruct the scope and content of the Khudorba History on the basis of the episodes of the *History of the Rus'* directly linked to Novhorod-Siverskyi, the following picture emerges. The narrative may have begun with the earliest times: Novhorod-Siverskyi is first mentioned in the *History* in relation to the legend of St. Andrew's visit to the Dnieper region. Important episodes of the Khudorba History include the Union of Brest (1596), the False Dmitrii's siege of Novhorod-Siverskyi (1604), the Khmelnytsky Uprising and the history of the Cossack polity in the second half of the seventeenth century and, finally, the Northern War and the Mazepa Revolt. It most certainly ended there. The author would not have been the first to conclude his narrative at that turning point in Ukrainian

L. S. Shvarts, "Iz opyta primeneniia lingvisticheskikh metodov dlia atributsii tekstov ('Istoriia Rusov')," in *Problemy primeneniia kolichestvennykh metodov analiza i klassifikatsii istochnikov po otechestvennoi istorii*, ed. M. Koval's'kyi (Dnipropetrovsk, 1989), pp. 52–57.

[13] *Istoriia Rusov ili Maloi Rosii. Sochinenie Georgiia Koniskago, Arkhiepiskopa Beloruskago* (Moscow, 1846), pp. 32–35.

history. He would simply have followed in the footsteps of the Chronicle of Hryhorii Hrabianka, the most popular "long" Cossack chronicle of the era. It is possible but not likely that the Khudorba History went even further, let us say to the year 1734, as did the *Brief Description of Little Russia*, first published by Vasyl Ruban and Oleksandr Bezborodko in 1777, but there is no evidence associated with Novhorod-Siverskyi to support even this "extension," to say nothing of one that goes all the way to 1769.

The Khudorba History must have been based on local legends and family stories. It also had to rely heavily on the author's imagination, which was especially active when it came to the history of his family. The Khudorbas of Koman were of low social origin and needed as much proof of noble roots as one could get. Rank-and-file Cossacks and recent newcomers to the Cossack officer stratum had a hard time getting into the Russian nobility in the late eighteenth and early nineteenth centuries. The Khudorbas' official genealogy began with a certain Mykhailo Kindratovych Khudorba, whose noble origins were anything but certain. They become ironclad in the *History of the Rus'*, whose account of the matter is apparently based on the Khudorba History. There Kindrat Khudorba, the apparent father of Mykhailo, figures as nothing less than a colonel, a close collaborator of Khmelnytsky, and the liberator of the entire Siverian region from the Polish yoke. Few families in the Hetmanate could attribute so much to the alleged founder of a not very prominent Cossack family.

One of the very few things we know for sure about the Khudorba History is that, in the eyes of von Brigen's informants, it was written "very freely and against our government." It is hard to establish what exactly made the Khudorba History so anti-governmental, but the governments that one must consider under the circumstances are those of the Muscovite tsars between the second half of the seventeenth century and the beginning of the eighteenth – from Aleksei Mikhailovich to Peter I. It was probably the History's harsh treatment of Peter's actions in Ukraine on the eve of the Battle of Poltava and subsequent to it that alerted the attention of von Brigen's acquaintances. Whatever the content of the Khudorba History, it certainly appears to have lacked something that the *History of the Rus'* had in abundance – speeches and letters that served as vehicles for the expression of the author's own thoughts, beliefs, and attitudes. None of the Novhorod-Siverskyi characters ever delivers a speech or is even mentioned in any of the speeches in the *History*. On the other hand, when the anonymous author introduces his own characters into what by all accounts was Khudorba's story, he does so through the medium of speeches and letters, as is the case with the "Armenian monk Martin," who is "parachuted" into the text of a letter allegedly issued by Orthdox bishops protesting against the Union of Brest.

What are the possible implications of these new discoveries and observations for the authorship of the *History*? As for Ohloblyn's work, they cast doubt on his main contribution to the field – his belief in the Novhorod-Siverskyi origins of the text, which was shared by all subsequent students. At the same time, they confirm Ohloblyn's supposition that the Khudorba History may have been one of the sources of the *History of the Rus'*. With regard to Shevchuk's hypothesis, they completely exclude Arkhyp Khudorba as a possible author. But if the author was not a Khudorba and did not live in Novhorod-Siverskyi and its environs, who was he, and where did he live?

One way to answer these questions is to distinguish the author of the *History* from its numerous sources. Separating the text written by the anonymous author from what seems to be one of its most influential sources, the Khudorba History, is certainly a step in the right direction. It is difficult to accomplish a further separation with regard to the pre-1708 narrative, as we can only guess what was and what was not in the Khudorba History. But the task seems feasible with regard to the post-1708 part of the work. Previous scholars, especially Mykhailo Slabchenko, Andrii Yakovliv, and Mykhailo Vozniak, have supplied enough evidence to show that Ruban's publication of the *Brief Description of Little Russia* and Oleksandr Bezborodko's addition to it were among the important sources for the post-1708 or, in our reading, post-Khudorba part of the *History*. Examining that part and identifying what came from Bezborodko can help us not only double-check the validity of the Bezborodko hypothesis but also get closer to the true author of the *History*.

For anyone who compares Oleksandr Bezborodko's essay with the *History of the Rus'*, there can be no doubt that the Bezborodko addition to the *Brief Description of Little Russia* was indeed the main source of the author of the *History of the Rus'* for the post-1734 history of the Hetmanate. It defined not only the chronological terminus of the narrative (1769) but also its structure. The impression one gets is that the anonymous author simply followed Bezborodko's narration, adding to his source a discussion of specific episodes known to him largely from the oral tradition. Occasionally the author would engage in covert polemics with Bezborodko (and, by extension, with the imperial version of Ukrainian history) without identifying his principal source. That polemic becomes especially obvious in the *History*'s coverage of the rule of Catherine II, which Bezborodko praised in the most strenuous terms. "The favors showered by Her Imperial Majesty upon her subjects," Bezborodko wrote, "also extended to the Little Russian people." Among those "favors" he listed the abolition of taxes and tariffs that had restrained the Hetmanate's trade with the Polish-Lithuanian Commonwealth, restoration of the local court system, the empress's positive attitude toward the recognition of Cossack ranks, the enserfment of the peasantry, and the completion of the census, "the first in Little Russia." One could hardly imagine a more favorable account of the effects of Catherine's rule in the Hetmanate, nor would one expect anything less from Bezborodko, whose career benefited immensely from her rule.[14]

The anonymous author had no such reasons for gratitude to the empress. Although he maintains a façade of loyalty, there is an ironic undertone to his account of Catherine's reforms. He begins with an excessively positive assessment of the empress's rule, even in comparison to that of Bezborodko. Through her efforts, writes the anonymous author, "Russia has been raised to the summit of greatness and glory, to the amazement and envy of all nations." He then undercuts that statement by describing the impact of Catherine's reforms on "Little Russia." The outcome was the Pikemen's Revolt of 1769–70, which the author regards with obvious sympathy.

The section of the *History* that begins with exaggerated praise of Catherine's rule ends with the following description of the punishment meted out to the Cossacks who took part in the revolt:

this punishment was beyond measure and appears to have exceeded even the tyranny of Nero. The condemned were taken to all the small company towns designated for the Pikemen's Regiment and beaten mercilessly with knouts in every one of them. Those beaten to death were tied to the tails of horses and drawn through the streets of the towns; finally the bodies thus torn to pieces were thrown into manure pits and buried in them like dead livestock, without any Christian or even human interment. This execution was carried out by the Pikemen's colonel, some baptized Turk named Adobash, with Don Cossacks, and those executioners were picked men deserving of a judicial sentence and of having it applied to them. In every small town, having driven the people out of their houses onto the square to witness the execution, they robbed the houses in thoroughly Tatar fashion and divided the booty with their Turk – behavior in

[14] *Kratkaia letopis' Malyia Rossii s 1506 po 1776 god, s iz''iavleniem Nastoiashchego obraza tamoshnego pravleniia i s priobshcheniem spiska prezhde byvshikh getmanov, general'nykh starshin, polkovnikov i ierarkhov* (St. Petersburg, 1777), pp. 222–24.

which their kind has distinguished itself since time immemorial – and that is what constitutes their true worth, glorified as military honor.[15]

This description evinces the anonymous author's fierce resentment of Catherine's policies intended to abolish the special rights and privileges of the Cossack stratum and its polity. He tried to be a good subject and never challenged the ruler openly but pulled no punches when characterizing imperial policies. The objects of his attacks were individual officials who almost always possessed clearly defined national characteristics that distinguished them from the "Little Russians." Muscovites, Turks, Poles, and Jews certainly belonged to that category. As in the case of the Pikemen's Revolt, the author gives horrifying descriptions of their crimes against the Cossacks. We have such descriptions of events before and after 1708, which suggests that their author was not Khudorba but whoever wrote the post-Khudorba part of the text. Another conclusion that can be drawn from the description of the Pikemen's Revolt is that Bezborodko and the author of the *History* were indeed different individuals. It is well-nigh impossible to imagine Bezborodko mocking not only Catherine but also the inner logic of his own narrative in such a way. A further parallel reading of Bezborodko's narrative and the post-1734 part of the *History* can give us even more information about the author. Probably the best way to continue our inquiry is to return to a question that Ohloblyn answered to the satisfaction of many students of the *History*: where was it written?

Thus, the author of the *History* was neither Khudorba nor Bezborodko. He also did not live in Novhorod-Siverskyi. But where did he live? A close reading of the post-1708 part of the text points to lands north of Novhorod-Siverskyi. This applies particularly to the town of Starodub and its vicinity – a major center of Cossack life in the Siverian region. For a short period of time in the 1780s and 1790s, when Novhorod-Siverskyi became the seat of a vicegerency, Starodub took orders from Novhorod-Siverskyi, but for most of the region's history it was the other way around. During the Hetmanate, Starodub served as headquarters of the Cossack regiment that included the Novhorod-Siverskyi company. Jean-Benoît Scherer presented a very positive image of Starodub in his *Annales*. "Among the inhabitants of the town there are people of higher rank," wrote the French author, "including the colonel and his officers, civil servants of the same rank, and a good number of nobles ... The inhabitants of Starodub

[15] *Istoriia Rusov*, pp. 252–54.

surpass all others in their zeal for work; they work as much and even more than the peasants of Great Russia. The Starodub nobles and peasants are the wealthiest of all. The Starodub regiment and part of the Chernihiv regiment have more forests than their inhabitants require." From the Cossack perspective, Starodub was certainly a much more important center than Novhorod-Siverskyi, but one does not get that feeling from reading the eighteenth-century segment of the *History*. There Novhorod-Siverskyi overshadows Starodub in various ways. The balance shifts, however, after 1708, when Novhorod-Siverskyi disappears from the narrative altogether, while Starodub and its immediate area enjoys a historiographic revival.[16]

That revival is manifested not only in the number of mentions of the town but also in the quality of information about its history. The author first demonstrates his intimate knowledge of the region around Starodub when discussing Aleksandr Menshikov's seizure of territory in the northern Hetmanate in the 1710s. The episode is related in Ruban's *Brief Chronicle of Little Russia*, but Ruban fails to mention the inclusion of part of the Pohar company in Menshikov's possessions around Pochep (northeast of Starodub), which is duly noted by the anonymous author. He also provides another piece of information that almost certainly derives from local sources: Menshikov drew the borders of his realm with the aid of "the omnipotent astrolabe, which had never existed anywhere in Rus' and before which everyone fell silent, considering the direction and effect of its magnet a divine or magic manifestation." The anonymous author further betrayed his connection to the region when he wrote:

The landowners, officials, and Cossacks included in those boundaries were assigned to Pochep and burdened with all the obligations of the local commoners, as the whole Pochep region of that time was considered Menshikov's appanage principality, and the princely coats of arms bearing his title that were posted in many places, the title usually ending with the following words: "and so on, and so on, and so on," forced everyone to think that the disastrous old division of Rus' into principalities had erupted again. Meanwhile, the landowners and officials who found themselves in this chemical Principality were assigned to serve as town burgomasters and village heads throughout the settled area, and they long bore that yoke as if stunned or insensible.[17]

---

[16] Jean-Benoît Scherer, *Annales de la Petite-Russie, ou Histoire des Cosaques-Saporoagues et des Cosaques de l'Ukraine*, 2 vols. (Paris, 1788), 1: 52–53.

[17] *Ibid.*, p. 221.

The author of the *History* was also very specific about another "crime" commited by Menshikov against the Starodub notables – the transfer of their lands to the Old Believers, whose villages were first established on Cossack lands in the late seventeenth and early eighteenth centuries. Cossack officers initially welcomed the arrival of the new settlers, expecting to increase their revenues. But the imperial government had different plans. It was interested in collecting taxes from the Old Believers that it could not impose on the gentry landowners. It therefore turned the Old Believer settlers into state peasants, taking over land that had previously belonged to Cossack officers. Enraged by this development, the former landowners developed a hostility to the Old Believers that lasted into the early nineteenth century. The author of the *History* held Menshikov responsible for this upheaval. "These Old Believers have multiplied in Russia as they have been persecuted, and they have fled it in all directions in the same measure. They have filled all of Poland, Prussia, Moldavia, and Bessarabia with their migrants, but it is only the Little Russian landowners – and laymen at that – who have suffered for them. But the monasteries, having made up to Menshikov, maintained them constantly among their peasants and got rid of them only when they fell into total ruin." The author probably came from the same region, but he was clearly no monk![18]

The *History*'s account of the abuses of the brother of Ernst Johann von Biron, the favorite of Empress Anna Ioannovna (1730–40), also has clear Starodub origins, along with the author's trademark ability to describe the horrors of the imperial regime in the Hetmanate. "The inhabitants of Starodub and environs shudder at the very memory of the rages of his brother, the very lame and almost legless Biron," wrote the author of the *History*.

Being a complete invalid, he nevertheless held the rank of full Russian general, and, maintaining quarters near Starodub with his army and a large staff, resembled the proudest of Asian sultans in display and haughtiness, while his conduct was even more replete with barbarian caprice. And, to say nothing of his expansive seraglio, established and replenished by force, they seized women, especially those who were nursing, and took away the infants from their breasts; instead they forced them to breast-feed puppies from among the hunting dogs of that monster; his other niggardly actions beggar the human imagination itself.[19]

There is enough evidence to suggest that if the Khudorba History indeed originated in Novhorod-Siverskyi and its environs, then the *History of*

---

[18] *Istoriia Rusov*, p. 223.   [19] *Ibid.*, p. 243.

the Rus' was the product of an area around Starodub. The focus on the Starodub region changes little in our interpretation of the author's outlook, motives, and intentions, but it does make the search for him somewhat easier. As we seek to track him down, we shall have to move somewhat north of the area originally suggested by Ohloblyn and, in fact, cross the border between Ukraine and Russia. Starodub, the ancient capital of one of the Hetmanate's strongest Cossack regiments, is now part of the Russian Federation. Could it be that the "eternal book of Ukraine" was indeed produced on territory that is now part of Russia?

CHAPTER 12

The Cossack aristocrats

Few members of the Russian delegation that accompanied President Boris Yeltsin to a meeting with his Ukrainian and Belarusian counterparts in the Belavezha hunting lodge in western Belarus in December 1991 believed that the dissolution of the Soviet Union they helped orchestrate would lead to the creation of truly independent states. After all, they established a Commonwealth of Independent States (CIS) to replace the old Soviet empire and thought that close political links between Russia, Ukraine, and Belarus would soon be restored. That was certainly the impression of Yeltsin's chief bodyguard and confidant, Aleksandr Korzhakov, who later claimed that members of the Russian delegation believed they were establishing a new state with enhanced rights for the constituent republics. The true implications of the Belavezha Act became clear to the Russian political and intellectual elites only later, in 1992–93, when the Ukrainian leadership insisted that the CIS was not a state in its own right but an association intended to help the former Soviet republics divide the assets of the USSR and establish their sovereignty. All of a sudden the Russian elites were confronted with a newly independent country on their south-western border – a country they had considered indissolubly bound to their own by historical experience and tradition going back to the times of Kyivan princes and Cossack hetmans – and how to deal with it was anything but clear.[1]

As in Ukraine, intellectuals in Russia turned to the works of prerevolutionary and émigré authors in search of their new identity. Bereft of their old myths, they began to search desperately for new ones. In 1996 the Indrik publishing house in Moscow issued a reprint of a book by the

[1] Interview with Aleksandr Korzhakov, *Bul'var Gordona* (December 4, 2007); "Soviet Leaders Recall 'Inevitable' Breakup of Soviet Union," Radio Free Europe, December 8, 2006 www.rferl.org/content/article/1073305.html. On the Belovezha agreements, see Timothy Colton, *Yeltsin: A Life* (New York, 2009), pp. 205–6.

exiled Russian historian Nikolai Ulianov. Its title, *The Origins of Ukrainian Separatism*, aroused immediate interest in post-Soviet Russia. The book had originally appeared in New York in 1966 and was now reprinted at the initiative of Professor Vladimir Volkov, director of the Institute for the Study of the South and West Slavs at the Russian Academy of Sciences. A specialist on the diplomatic history of Eastern Europe in the twentieth century, Volkov had to undertake a major "retooling" after the fall of the Soviet Union. His institute was unexpectedly handed a new area on which to provide expertise – Ukraine and Belarus, the East Slavic "brethren" of Russia, previously covered by academic institutions dealing with the history and culture of constituent parts of the USSR. Now Ukraine and Belarus were in the "near abroad" beyond Russia's borders, and Volkov and his colleagues had to master a new field in record time – the funding authorities needed expertise and propaganda writings, and they needed them now.[2]

Volkov had heard about Ulianov's book on the origins of Ukrainian nationalism long before he got hold of it. Having searched for it in the academic libraries of North America (it was unavailable in post-Soviet Russia), he finally acquired a copy after visiting the widow of Nikolai Ulianov in the United States. Volkov obtained permission from Mrs. Ulianov to reprint her husband's book in Moscow. In the work of a post-Second World War émigré, the director of the Russian academic institution found a source of knowledge and inspiration that he had previously lacked. In his introduction to the reprint, Volkov wrote, "Nikolai Ivanovich Ulianov's book, *The Origins of Ukrainian Separatism*, here offered to the reader's attention, is the only scholarly work in all of world historiography specially devoted to this problem." From the publisher's viewpoint, the book was a major success. It was reprinted once again in 2007 and is now available on numerous Russian websites. To a public shocked by the rapid disintegration of the Soviet empire, Ulianov's work explained that the Ukrainian movement was to blame for that cataclysm. The movement lacked a distinct ethnic base (Russians and Ukrainians, claimed the author, were one and the same people) and was an invention of evil-spirited intellectuals.[3]

The root of this evil, according to Ulianov, was none other than the *History of the Rus'*, to which he devoted a whole chapter of his book.

---

[2] Nikolai Ul'ianov, *Proiskhozhdenie ukrainskogo separatizma* (Moscow, 1996).

[3] [Vladimir Volkov], "Ot redaktsii," in Ul'ianov, *Proiskhozhdenie* (1996). On Volkov's life and career, see I. V. Volkova, "Vladimir Konstantinovich Volkov: chelovek i uchenyi," fpp.hse.ru/data/974/434/1241/BKB.doc.

Ulianov treated the *History* not as a historical monument to be studied but as an ideological text to be discredited and refuted. In that regard he followed in the footsteps of Gennadii Karpov, a nineteenth-century critic of the *History*. Unlike Karpov, however, Ulianov never pretended to be interested in academic study of the work. His goal was different – to lay bare the author's "true" intentions. He titled his chapter "The Catechism" and characterized the *History* as the "Koran of the separatist movement." Ulianov accused the anonymous author of knowingly misrepresenting facts. "His distortions are not the result of ignorance but of deliberate falsification," he wrote. Ulianov rightly believed that the discontent expressed in the *History* actually derived from conflict with the imperial authorities over the recognition of Cossack officer ranks but protested against treating Cossack social grievances as national ones. That, he claimed, was the perverse attitude adopted by the author of the *History of the Rus'*.

"All that Cossackdom used to justify its treason and 'deceptions,' its hatred of Moscow, was collected here as a legacy to posterity," wrote Ulianov. "And we know that 'posterity' built up that Zaporozhian polit-ical wisdom into a credo. One need only start a conversation with any independentist for it to become immediately apparent that the baggage of his 'national' ideology consists of fables from the *History of the Rus'*, of the wrath of the 'accursed' Catherine II, who 'suspended our Ukrainian Cossacks on hooks by their ribs and hanged them on scaffolds.' Cossack ideology was turned into Ukrainian national ideology." Ulianov's attitude appeared to mirror that of his opponents, Ukrainian nationalist writers who also saw the author of the *History* as a conscious promoter of Ukrainian ideology. The anonymous author emerged as a hero to one camp and a villain to the other. The reprinting and translation of the *History* in Ukraine after 1991 and the reissue of Ulianov's book in Russia set these opposing evaluations in stone. The *History*, which had finally returned from forced emigration in 1991, became a welcome guest on one side of the Russo-Ukrainian border and an unwelcome intruder on the other.[4]

Among the many Russian websites that posted Ulianov's book online for their readers was one located in Starodub, now a regional center of the Russian Federation. In the first decade of the new millennium, the site began to host the publication of numerous materials dealing with the history and culture of that important region of the former Hetmanate.

---

[4] Ul'ianov, *Proiskhozhdenie* (New York, 1966), pp. 102–39.

Russian Old Believers, invited to the area as settlers by Cossack officers in the eighteenth century, eventually grew in numbers, and by the time the political fate of the region was decided in 1919, they constituted a majority in those former Cossack lands. Starodub and its environs, which were claimed by the short-lived Ukrainian People's Republic (1917–18), were allocated to Russia. Ulianov's book was posted on the website devoted to the history of Starodub with the following injunction from the webmaster Mikhail Roshchin: "Although the book mentions Starodub only about ten times, I still recommend that it be read by all who consider themselves Little Russians and Russians. I recommend that it be read by all who are not indifferent to the efforts of certain politicians to divide our fraternal peoples, to sow enmity and hatred."[5]

The question of historical identity and Russo-Ukrainian relations remains sensitive for Starodub, the only region in Russia that lists monuments of the Ukrainian Cossack baroque among its architectural treasures. After the disintegration of the Soviet Union, the search for historical roots created difficulties for Starodub historians, who found themselves in a bind as they sought to reconcile the Russian identity of the region with its Ukrainian history. One solution to the problem was found in embracing the Ukrainian national paradigm and stressing the Ukrainian roots of the region – the vision promoted by a series of publications posted on Ukrainian websites by an author using the Internet nickname "Faithful from the Starodub region." Another solution was adopted by the webmaster of the Starodub historical website, who chose to apply pre-1917 terminology: the former Cossack masters of the Starodub area were referred to as Little Russians. The same strategy is used by V. M. Pus, the author of numerous essays dealing with the history of Starodub regional centers that have been posted on the city's official website.

Neither solution resolves the contradiction created by placing Ulianov's book, which treats the *History of the Rus'* as a source of Ukrainian nationalism and "enmity and hatred" of Russia, on the Starodub historical website next to biographies of Starodub notables who held that work in high regard. Among these is the biography of Mykhailo Myklashevsky, the imperial governor and senator from whose estate we first hear of the existence of the *History*. The contradiction grows deeper if one assumes that the *History* was not only read and disseminated but also produced by natives of Starodub. How could the imperial careers and loyalties of people such as Myklashevsky coexist peacefully with texts like the *History*

---

[5] N. I. Ul'ianov, *Proiskhozhdenie ukrainskogo separatizma*, Starodub www.debryansk.ru/~mir17/.

of the Rus? A closer look at the Starodub notables of the early nineteenth century who were involved in the distribution of the *History* can help answer the larger question about the nature of imperial and national identities in the Russian Empire.[6]

Was it mere coincidence that the first news of the *History*'s existence reached the outside world from the Myklashevsky family estate in Ponurivka? On one level, it certainly was: after all, the *History* existed before it was "discovered" by Aleksandr von Brigen in the fall of 1825. On another level, "coincidence" seems the wrong word to describe the relationship between the Myklashevskys and the *History* on the one hand and the *History* and the Decembrist conspiracy on the other. In the early nineteenth century Ukrainian noble estates like Ponurivka became hotbeds of opposition to the imperial regime. It was there, in the homes of descendants of Cossack officers, that the old autonomist tradition of the Hetmanate came together with new trends of political and social thought associated with the Decembrist movement to create an unexpected alliance against the authoritarian policies of St. Petersburg. The "fathers," removed from the imperial center of power and threatened by official efforts to deprive them of the last vestiges of their regional privileges, embraced the rebellious "sons," who wanted a constitution and liberal reforms. History, especially the redefined Cossack myth, emerged as an intellectual and emotional ground on which "fathers" and "sons" could see eye to eye.

Mykhailo Myklashevsky, the owner of Ponurivka, was an important figure on the Starodub scene in the first half of the nineteenth century. Born in 1757 to a family that traced its lineage to the Starodub colonel Mykhailo Andriiovych Myklashevsky, the young Mykhailo Myklashevsky began his military career at seventeen, joining the Izmailovskoe guards regiment in the imperial capital. Between 1780 and 1782, as an imperial diplomatic courier, he traveled to European capitals, including London and Paris. In 1782 he switched military units, becoming an officer in the Semenovskoe guards regiment. He took part in the First Russo-Turkish War, distinguishing himself during the capture of Ochakiv (1788). In the following year, with the rank of colonel, he took command of the Starodub carabineers, who were part of Suvorov's army. He gained further

[6] Virnyi iz Starodubshchyny, "Starodub. Narys ukraïns'koho zhyttia." www.haidamaka.org.ua/page_starodubvirnyj.html; "Vidrodzhennia Starodubshchyny," *Surma. Kozats'kyi zhurnal* http://surma.moy.su/publ/1–1–0–1021; "Kolonka avtora," Starodub www.debryansk.ru/~mir17/; V. M. Pus', "Starodubskie kazaki: ot istokov do sovremennosti," http://starburg.ru/starodubskie_kazaki/index.html.

distinction in the battles of Rymnik (1789) and Machin (1791). Myklashevsky commanded the Starodub carabineer regiment until 1792. During the third partition of Poland in 1795, he was put in charge of three imperial regiments that occupied Volhynia. In 1797 he became governor of Volhynia and then of Little Russia.

As was the case with many other Starodub notables, Myklashevsky's imperial career depended on the fortunes of Prince Oleksandr Bezborodko. The young Myklashevsky was introduced to the powerful courtier by the first commander of the Starodub carabineer regiment, Ivan Maksymovych. Bezborodko encouraged his young compatriot to remain in the service and gain combat experience. In December 1786, he wrote to his protégé: "Sharpen your saber, get your musket in order for spring, and go to war: in your place I would weep if I were not allowed to go; I would not give a damn about anything if only I got the mere chance to watch the fighting." In the following year he was glad to hear that Myklashevsky had taken his advice. "I am glad that you are finally getting used to warfare," wrote Bezborodko. "There can be no better or more pleasant exercise for a young man." Bezborodko was happy to introduce the young officer to Catherine II during her trip to the Crimea in 1787. The empress even spent a night at Myklashevsky's home in the village of Nyzhnie, not far from Ponurivka. In October 1797, on the eve of Myklashevsky's marriage, Bezborodko wrote to his protégé, then already governor of Volhynia: "If I advised you to adhere to the rule of marriage given to Jacob in Holy Scripture – do not take a wife born of foreign sons – then I have a double reason to approve your intended marriage to my niece." Myklashevsky was marrying not just a Ukrainian woman but also a niece of the powerful chancellor, Nastasia Bakurynska. He became a member of the Bezborodko family, and just a month later he was appointed governor of Little Russia, which encompassed the entire territory of the former Hetmanate.

It is hardly surprising that Oleksandr Bezborodko's death in April 1799 had a major impact on Myklashevsky's life and career. Along with other Ukrainian officers with Starodub roots, he lost his powerful protector and promoter. Other groups and aristocratic parties were making their way to the throne and pushing the Starodub crowd aside. In May 1800, slightly more than a year after Bezborodko's death, Emperor Paul dismissed Myklashevsky "for poor attention to duty." Those "wrongly dismissed" by Paul, like Myklashevsky, were returned to the imperial service by Alexander but never recovered the influence they had enjoyed in Bezborodko's heyday. In 1802 Alexander appointed Myklashevsky civil governor of the New Russia gubernia, an enormous but sparsely populated administrative unit created in southern Ukraine out of former Zaporozhian lands and newly acquired territories of the Crimean Khanate. When the New Russia gubernia was divided into three parts, Myklashevsky had to accept the governorship of the part centered around Katerynoslav (Ekaterinoslav, present-day Dnipropetrovsk). He resigned in 1804, citing poor health. After spending two years in Ponurivka, Myklashevsky made his way back into the imperial service, commanding the Katerynoslav militia in the Russo-Turkish War of 1806–12. He soon became a senator, but his influence in St. Petersburg was never as strong as it had been in the closing years of the century.

The imperial senator was no stranger to the interests and concerns of the local nobility. The most important of these was the preservation of Cossack military units, which freed local landowners from the need to enlist their serfs in the imperial army and allowed the nobles themselves to claim active service in the military without leaving their homes and estates. In 1812 Myklashevsky prepared a memorandum arguing for the restoration of Cossack military units. It was based on a similar proposal written by Vasyl Kapnist, who had gone to Prussia in 1791 to look for allies in the event of a future revolt against Russia – a revolt to be fueled by the Russian imperial government's abolition of Cossack formations. In 1812, in the face of Napoleon's invasion, the Russian government allowed the recruitment of Cossack formations that turned out to play an important role in the war. Cossacks who joined their formations were promised that they would retain their privileges after the end of the conflict. Those who survived the fighting (more than one-quarter of the sixteen thousand Cossack recruits perished in battle) were in for a major disappointment after their return in 1815. Their rights and privileges were revoked in the following year, causing great dissatisfaction not only among the Cossacks themselves but also among the local nobility.

There can be little doubt that the old Myklashevsky shared the general dissatisfaction. Having made an enemy of a member of the tsar's family, he retired from the imperial service in 1818 to his Ponurivka estate. His forced retirement could not have made him sympathetic to the government. Toward the end of the 1810s and throughout the 1820s, Myklashevsky was the most prominent figure in the Starodub region. In August 1825, a few months before von Brigen wrote from Ponurivka to Ryleev about the *History of the Rus'*, Myklashevsky was visited at his estate by Emperor Alexander I himself. At this stop on his way to Taganrog, where he would die a few months later, the emperor was impressed by the paintings on the ceiling of Myklashevsky's house. They were the work of one of the best artists of imperial Russia, Giacomo Quarenghi. The failure of the Decembrist Revolt half a year later spelled disaster for the Myklashevsky family. Not only Aleksandr von Brigen but also Myklashevsky's own son, Oleksandr, were members of the Decembrist conspiracy. Von Brigen was fortunate enough to survive arrest and exile. Oleksandr, who was dispatched to fight in the Caucasus, never came home – he was killed in 1831. The old Myklashevsky could do very little to improve the lot of either his son or his son-in-law. He died in September 1847 and was buried, as he had wished, "among his people" in Ponurivka.[7]

Given what we know about Mykhailo Myklashevsky today, it does not seem strange that a work such as the *History of the Rus'* would have been known and read on his estate. The same applies even more strongly to the Khudorba History – Mykhailo Myklashevsky was Arkhyp Khudorba's commander in the Starodub carabineer regiment in the 1780s. Myklashevsky was part of a circle in which these texts circulated, were read, discussed, and probably created as well. Our discussion of Myklashevsky's links to the *History* would not be complete, however, without a consideration of the way in which his family is depicted in the pages of that work. One of its prominent representatives, Mykhailo Myklashevsky's great-grandfather, the Starodub colonel Mykhailo Andriiovych Myklashevsky (?–1706), receives a good deal of attention. He is mentioned twice. The description of Myklashevsky's service in the *History* is not only highly positive but also includes details absent in other historical sources.

Mykhailo Andriiovych Myklashevsky is portrayed by the anonymous author as a brave and skillful military commander. During the campaign of 1702, Myklashevsky, according to the *History*, "joining up with the Polish army of King August's party, led by their commander, Chalecki, routed the enemy forces and drove their leader, Beltsynevich, into the town of Bykhaŭ; then, making an assault on that town, he took it by storm and, taking Beltsynevich into captivity along with other officials who were with him, sent him to the hetman in Baturyn." The Starodub colonel not only lived but died a hero. "Myklashevsky," wrote the anonymous author concerning the events of March 1706, "fighting the enemy at Niasvizh and unable to overcome his large numbers, made his

---

[7] N. I. Grigorovich, *Kantsler kniaz' Aleksandr Andreevich Bezborod'ko v sviazi s sobytiiami ego vremeni*, 2 vols. (St. Petersburg, 1879–81); D. Poklonskii, "Miklashevskii Mikhail Pavlovich," in *Starodubskaia starina, XI–XIX vv. Istoricheskie ocherki*, vol. II (Klintsy, 2002), p. 243ff.; Oleksander Ohloblyn, *Liudy staroï Ukraïny* (Munich, 1959), pp. 150–67; Boris Petrov, "Poèt pushkinskoi pory," in Ivan Petrovich Borozdna, *Pisano v sele Medvedovo ...* (Klintsy, 2004), pp. 7–86, here 16–17.

way through the enemy ranks into the Niasvizh castle and fought them off for five days; finally, overcome by the enemy's efforts, he was slaughtered with all his regiment." The author of the *History* blamed Myklashevsky's death on Ivan Mazepa, who, "temporarily clearing the path along which his excessive courage and extreme bitterness were leading him to an immeasurable abyss, distanced from himself all suspect individuals incapable of imitating him in his endeavors and sought death itself for some of them." A brave commander and a victim of Mazepa's intrigues, Colonel Myklashevsky emerges from the pages of the *History* as an ideal Cossack hero who would have made his ancestors proud.[8]

The Myklashevskys were not the only Starodub family who could endorse the *History of the Rus'* for its favorable portrayal of their ancestors. This applied particularly to the Hudovyches, a well-established Starodub Cossack family whose prominence at the imperial court preceded Bezborodko's rise to power. The general treasurer of the Hetmanate, Vasyl Hudovych (d. 1764), who received especially generous treatment in the pages of the *History*, had numerous sons, quite a few of whom made impressive careers in the Russian imperial service. At least three of the Hudovych brothers – Andrii, Vasyl, and Petro – resided in the Starodub area.

The first to enter imperial service was Andrii Vasyliovych Hudovych (1731–1808). Andrii was educated in Germany (he attended the University of Königsberg) and became a close associate of the future Emperor Peter III. When Peter gained the throne in 1762, Andrii Hudovych became his adjutant and was promoted to the rank of major general at the age of thirty-one. The assassination of Peter III and the accession to the throne of Catherine II put an end to Hudovych's rise. After his brief arrest, Andrii first went abroad and then retired to his estate in the Starodub region, where his possessions were dramatically increased at the expense of Old Believer settlements granted to him by Emperor Peter. It was a long and lonely exile for Andrii Hudovych, one that lasted throughout the reign of Catherine II. But the death of the empress in 1796 revived his hopes for a triumphal return to the center of political life. Paul I awarded Hudovych the rank of general, and there were rumors that he would be appointed regent of Little Russia, an old/new province reuniting the territories of the former Hetmanate. Although Hudovych proceeded to St. Petersburg, something went wrong: no regent was appointed, and the region was entrusted to Bezborodko's relatives, including Mykhailo Myklashevsky. Nor did Hudovych's fortunes improve with the enthronement of Alexander I. He died at his Starodub estate in 1808, the promise of his life and career never fully realized. Hudovych evidently had good reason to be dissatisfied with the status quo, but we know nothing about his views or attitudes toward the authorities during his long decades of exile in Starodub.[9]

No less dramatic but much more spectacular was the fate of Andrii Hudovych's younger brother Ivan (1741–1820). Ivan's early career was helped by his brother's close association with Peter III. Like Andrii Hudovych, Ivan became one of the emperor's adjutants. Then came the coup of 1762 and the assassination of Peter. Upon the accession of Catherine II, Ivan was briefly arrested along with his elder brother. Upon his release, Ivan returned to the service and made a name for himself during the two Russo-Turkish wars that Catherine fought during her long reign. Ivan Hudovych took Hadzhibei (the future Odesa) and Anapa, a major Ottoman fortress on the Kuban Peninsula, for the Russian Empire. Paul I awarded Hudovych the title of count and appointed him military governor of Kyiv. In 1800, after the death of Bezborodko, Paul dismissed Ivan Hudovych from his post, but Alexander I brought him back in 1806, placing the old commander in charge of Russian troops in the Caucasus. In the next few years Hudovych brought Derbent and Baku under imperial control. He lost an eye but was promoted to field marshal. After a few years as commander of the Moscow garrison, member of the State Council, and senator, Hudovych retired in 1812, this time definitively, to his estates in Right-Bank Ukraine.[10]

But how might the Hudovyches – Andrii, Ivan, or any other member of their extended family – have been involved with the *History of the Rus*? The best way to begin answering this question is to note that the Hudovych family was related to Mykhailo Myklashevsky. General Treasurer Vasyl Hudovych, the founder of the dynasty, married into the Myklashevsky family. His wife was Mariia Stepanivna Myklashevska, a granddaughter of the Mazepa-era colonel of Starodub, Mykhailo Andriiovych Myklashevsky. In the family duet of the Hudovyches and the Myklashevskys, the Hudovyches took pride of place. While Ivan was

[9] Ohloblyn, *Liudy staroï Ukraïny*, pp. 7–13.
[10] *Istoriia Rusov*, pp. 197, 200; Ohloblyn, *Liudy staroï Ukraïny*, pp. 155–56; D. N. Bantysh-Kamenskii, *Biografii rossiiskikh generalissimusov i general-fel'dmarshalov*, 4 vols. (Moscow, 1990), vols. III–IV, pp. 10–25.

busy with his career in the imperial service, the rest of his brothers either lived permanently in the Starodub region or were frequent visitors there. They were all prominent figures on the Starodub political and social scene for more than forty years, and Andrii Hudovych's stories about the good old days under Peter III must have circulated in Starodub circles. The author of the *History of the Rus'*, for example, was favorably disposed to Peter III, whose assassination ended the career of Andrii Hudovych and condemned him to a lonely retirement on his family estate in the Starodub region. An even more promising connection between the Hudovyches and the mysterious text has to do with the exceptionally positive portrayal of Vasyl Hudovych, the patriarch of the family and general treasurer of the Hetmanate, in the pages of the *History*.

The anonymous author attributes to Hudovych a patriotic speech allegedly delivered in St. Petersburg in 1745. The speech features some of the leading motifs of the *History*, including the rejection of allegations that the Ukrainians were disloyal to the tsars:

"As far as zeal for Russia is concerned," replied Deputy Hudovych, "none of the free nations has shown such devotion and zeal for it as the Little Russians. And this is shown by the very fact that they, being free, having beaten off Poland, preferred Russia to all other nations extending protection to them, and they chose it alone because of their unity of origin and faith, to which they were constantly loyal and never wavered, rejecting and scorning the flattery and intimidation of powerful neighboring states, even the recent Swedish overtures, which were best suited to temptation. As for certain hetmans, with regard to them one may aptly cite the well-known saying: 'As you created them, so you have them.' For it is indisputable that only those hetmans lacked zeal for the Russian government who were chosen by it or chosen at the insistence of that government."[11]

The anonymous author put into Hudovych's mouth what he wanted to say himself and said more than once in the pages of his work. He insisted on the voluntary nature of Ukraine's subordination to the tsars, professed his nation's loyalty to the monarchy, and stressed the ethnic and religious affinity between the Little and Great Russians. There is good reason to suggest that views similar to those attributed by the author to Vasyl Hudovych were shared by many Starodub landowners of the early nineteenth century and appealed to members of the Hudovych clan – Vasyl Hudovych's numerous sons and daughters and their children. Even though the spectacular career of Ivan Hudovych had won the title

[11] *Istoriia Rusov*, p. 245.

of count for all of them, they must have shared the oppositional mood prevailing in the high society of Starodub.

A unique insight into the life of the Hudovych clan and the Cossack aristocracy in general is provided by the memoirs of a French medical doctor, Dominique de la Flise, who was taken prisoner by the Russians during Napoleon's campaign of 1812 and spent most of 1813 officially in captivity but actually as a guest of honor of Mykhailo Skorupa and other landowners in the area. While the Starodub Cossacks marched across half of Europe to bring the Russian imperial banner to Paris, this French officer spent his time visiting the homes of the Starodub elite and enjoying good food, wine, and conversation. Given his profession, he was needed and welcomed by the local notables, and, as a perceptive observer, he left us vignettes of local nobiliary life that we would otherwise lack.[12]

De la Flise attended a reception hosted by Count Vasyl Hudovych, a lieutenant general and a brother of Andrii and Ivan Hudovych. Among the guests were Iskrytskys and Markevyches, representatives of old Cossack families who were related to Vasyl Hudovych. There were others as well. "Many neighbors arrived around noon," recalled de la Flise, "some of whom were very wealthy. I remember some of the surnames: two Pokorsky brothers, Lashkevych, Savytsky, Sokolovsky, Hubchyts, Roslavets (three families), and the Messrs. Skorupa. In all, there were about sixty people. That whole society, regardless of some diversity, was distinguished by bon ton." It would appear that Starodub society also cherished good memories of times long past. In the home of one of Hudovych's guests, a certain Pokorsky, the French doctor saw portraits of Emperor Paul I and Generalissimo Aleksandr Suvorov. At Zavadovsky's palace, de la Flise saw a portrait of Catherine II. He did not notice a portrait of the ruling monarch, Alexander I, in either place.[13]

Apart from obvious nostalgia for the good old days, there was one more feature of Starodub aristocratic society that attracted De la Flise's attention – its strong anti-Polish sentiment. Descendants of traditional enemies and rivals – Ukrainian Cossacks and Polish nobles – the two groups found themselves in close proximity where the former Hetmanate bordered on the former Polish-Lithuanian Commonwealth. The lands of the former Starodub regiment were just such an area. Polish Catholic

[12] See Dominik de lia Fliz, "Pokhod velikoi armii v Rossiiu v 1812 g.," *Russkaia starina* (1892), LXXIII: 51–68, 339–63, 575–604, here 587–94.

[13] *Ibid.*, pp. 591, 595.

nobles generally had an easier time proving their noble status in the Orthodox empire than their Orthodox Cossack foes. Moreover, Alexander I toyed with the idea of Polish autonomy and granted the Polish nobility enough rights and privileges in the borderlands to upset former Cossack officers, who could only dream of the restitution of their own autonomy. As the Poles had sided with Napoleon in 1812, the Starodub landowners took the opportunity to get back at their more successful enemies. De la Flise described one such episode involving Petro Hudovych, one of the Hudovych brothers.

In 1812, at the head of the local militia, Petro Hudovych had availed himself of wartime disorder to pillage the estates of one Halecki, a rich Polish landowner in the neighboring Mahilioŭ gubernia. "But hardly had the younger Hudovych entered Lithuania with his forces," wrote de la Flise about Petro Hudovych (his elder brother Vasyl was in charge of the entire Chernihiv militia), "than he began to rob Polish landowners, making a clean sweep and sending the booty back to his estate, which lay beyond Mhlyn [Mglin]. There was everything here: arms, silver, furniture, carriages, supplies of food, vodka, herds, stud horses, factory-made linens and textiles, and so on. Among other things, an expensive saber worth 60,000 rubles, a gift from Peter the Great to Halecki's grandfather, was stolen . . . The excuse for that robbery was the intention to leave nothing as booty for the French and to prevent the Poles from offering assistance to the enemy, but, after all, Halecki was devoted to Emperor Alexander, and four of his sons were serving in the guards; indeed, the whole conduct of the Poles, who found themselves in a difficult situation, threatened by both the French and the Russians, revealed not even a shadow of treason on their part."[14]

The end of the war did little to improve relations between the two groups, if one judges by de la Flise's description of a ball that he attended in the village of Hordiivka, the estate of the Shyrai family. The guests included Ukrainians (whom de la Flise called Russians) and Poles, and tensions in the ballroom ran high. Both sides danced the polonaise and the krakowiak, but there the understanding ended. "The Poles were in despair at having come under the yoke of their despised enemies, but they did not dare to show their malice, all the more because no swift liberation was in view," wrote de la Flise:

On the contrary, they manifested a surface desire to come together. Something resembling a comedy was going on in that society, in which everyone was playing

---

[14] *Ibid.*, pp. 578–79.

a role, for there was not a hint of sincerity in their mutual politeness. The Russians frowned on the Poles for their superiority in worldly manner and education, nor did they like their Polish costume, which made a glaring display of their nationality . . . There was similar discord between the ladies of the two nations. The Russian mothers were most offended with their sons and their young comrades for lavishing attention on the Polish girls and flirting with them . . . The Polish mothers, in turn, looked askance at their young men if they delighted in the Russian beauties and deliberately spoke Russian with them. They took umbrage at every word in that hateful language that reached their ears.

The French doctor's observations readily call to mind the anti-Polish animus of the *History of the Rus'*. Whatever the origins of the *History*, it is no wonder that it was popular in the places visited by de la Flise.[15]

The Starodub notables lived in a very peculiar world that was informed as much by the past as by the present. They often had the same enemies as their fathers and grandfathers. Old religious and cultural disputes remained unresolved despite numerous changes of political fortune. The French Revolution provided new legitimacy and a new language for the expression of old hatreds and suspicions. The hopes, sympathies, and fears of the Starodub nobility were not limited to their corner of the world. They also resonated in many high offices of the imperial capital, where in the last decades of the eighteenth century some of the Starodub notables drafted international treaties and shaped policy toward Ukraine's traditional neighbors, the Polish-Lithuanian Commonwealth and the Russian Empire. Starodub and St. Petersburg were connected in ways unimaginable today.

The rise and fall of the Hudovych brothers and Myklashevsky reflected the ups and downs of the "Ukrainian party" at the imperial court. Their careers were made possible by the rise to power in St. Petersburg of Oleksandr Bezborodko and Petro Zavadovsky, the two protégés of the chief "liquidator" of the Hetmanate and governor general of Little Russia, Petr Rumiantsev-Zadunaisky. Zavadovsky was the first to gain prominence in St. Petersburg, briefly becoming a lover of Catherine II, but Bezborodko soon overshadowed his countryman. Except for a brief period, the two remained close friends and allies. Bezborodko helped advance the career of Dmytro Troshchynsky, another powerful St. Petersburg Ukrainian who rose to the post of state secretary by 1793. All three Ukrainian notables in St. Petersburg supported their compatriots and lobbied on behalf of their homeland, which they wanted to improve with imperial reforms and

---

[15] *Ibid.*, p. 561.

educate in the spirit of the Enlightenment without forsaking the rights and privileges inherited from Cossack times. Oleksandr Bezborodko's brother Illia was only half joking when he remarked that he would have to put up a sign identifying his St. Petersburg house as the "Little Russia Inn," as so many of his countrymen were turning to him for help in the capital.

The first year of Emperor Paul's rule marked the apogee of Ukrainian power at court. It was then that Oleksandr Bezborodko, having distanced himself from Catherine II in the last years of her rule, became even more influential under her successor. Ukrainians were now the strongest group at court, and they used their power not only to advance their careers and those of their protégés but also to bring back the administrative unity and some of the traditional institutions of their homeland. Mykhailo Myklashevsky, who became the civil governor of a "reunited" Little Russia, was an important participant in the "restore the homeland" project. It all ended abruptly with Bezborodko's death at the height of his power in April 1799. Zavadovsky was placed under surveillance at his Starodub estate of Lialychi. Myklashevsky was dismissed, as was Ivan Hudovych.

Belittlement by Paul during the last year of his rule turned into an advantage when the mercurial emperor was assassinated and replaced by his liberal-minded son, Alexander I. The Ukrainians made their way back into the imperial service. Zavadovsky became the first minister of education in the Russian Empire, Troshchynsky was appointed minister of justice, and Myklashevsky became a senator. Hudovych rose to the rank of field marshal. But the Ukrainian party never regained the status and influence it had enjoyed at court in the days of Catherine and Paul. Little Russia was again divided into a number of provinces whose governors general, Aleksei Kurakin, Yakov Lobanov-Rostovsky and, later, Nikolai Repnin, were all Great Russians primarily devoted to the imperial center. They all married into local noble families, but that gave them only a limited attachment to the region. The locals complained to the remaining highly placed Ukrainians in St. Petersburg, who included Bezborodko's protégé, Count Viktor Kochubei, minister of the interior under Alexander I and chairman of the State Council and the Committee of Ministers under Nicholas I. The complaints did not help very much. The Starodub notables were left to bemoan their fate and recall the good old days, whether those were the times of Cossack autonomy or of the emperors and empresses who had helped destroy it.[16]

---

[16] David Saunders, *The Ukrainian Impact on Russian Culture, 1750–1850* (Edmonton, 1985), pp. 65–112.

In the case of Myklashevsky and the Hudovyches we are dealing with high-flying imperial officials whose careers were cut short or seriously curtailed by a reversal of fortune at court. Like all former high officials forced into retirement by a competing group at the center of power, they harbored resentment against the new crop of governors and were eager to recall the good times of their service. A popular Russian poet of the era, Aleksandr Griboedov, complained about the backwardness of imperial old-timers in his celebrated play *Woe from Wit* (1823), which dealt with the generation that had fought the Russo-Ottoman wars and was out of touch with the liberal aspirations of the nineteenth century:

> Who are these judges? Old men whose hostility
> To freedom knows no bounds. Their judgment's formed by queer
> Forgotten papers, where the latest news will be
> Ochakov – or the annexation of Crimea.
> Always prepared to criticize,
> Keep droning out the same old chorus;
> Don't see the beam in their own eyes –
> These old men who deplore us.[17]

Griboedov's portrait of the older generation of imperial officials was certainly accurate with regard to the Russian political scene, but the situation in Ukraine was altogether different. Rejected by the Russian imperial establishment of the early nineteenth century, the Ukrainian old-timers found common ground with Griboedov's generation. That unexpected alliance of old and new was a mixture, extremely dangerous from the imperial viewpoint, of dreams of the autonomous Cossack past and plans for a liberal and constitutional future. What was going on in the mansions of the Starodub aristocrats in the early nineteenth century was probably not very different from developments in the circle of Dmytro Troshchynsky, an associate of Bezborodko and Zavadovsky and a promoter of the integration of the borderlands into the imperial core who later changed his integrationist stand. After his retirement from the imperial service in 1817, Troshchynsky lived on his estate of Kybyntsi in Lubny county of Poltava gubernia, where he collected a library of more than 4,500 volumes. His home became a haunt of local antiquarians like Andrian Chepa and Vasyl Lomykovsky, who first met there in the summer of 1811. It also served as a meeting place for local freethinkers.[18]

---

[17] Mary Hobson, *Aleksandr Griboedov's* Woe from Wit: *A Commentary and Translation* (Lewiston, N.Y., 2005), p. 51.

[18] See Saunders, *The Ukrainian Impact*, pp. 90–100; Ohloblyn, *Liudy staroï Ukraïny*, pp. 159–60; Oleh Zhurba, "Predstav'te Vy sebe kakoi zver' byl getman! Ėto byli prenechestivye despoty! (Z lysta

The Russian general Aleksandr Mikhailovsky-Danilevsky, whose unit was stationed in the area in 1824, wrote about the Troshchynsky circle in his memoirs:

I also noted that at every available opportunity the Little Russians condemned Alexander's rule and praised that of Catherine. The dissemination of this view was promoted mainly by the former minister of justice, Troshchynsky, who lived not far from Lubny – an old man of about eighty who was respected as an oracle in Little Russia. It is characteristic of the elderly to recall with satisfaction their youth and the time in which they acted as the equals of ministers; finding themselves at a remove from court, they are wont to extol the days when they were in their prime. That was also the case with Troshchynsky, who praised Catherine's rule without measure at the expense of Alexander's; the Little Russians, among whom he was considered the most distinguished landowner, served him as an echo, forgetting that they might well grumble against Catherine for the abolition of their ancient privileges.[19]

Another observation in Mikhailovsky-Danilevsky's memoirs corroborates what we know from other sources about Starodub attitudes toward Russians. According to the general, the Lubny nobles, who were critical of Alexander's rule, were even more critical of Russians or, in their language, "Muscovites" in general. "I did not find a single individual in Little Russia with whom I had occasion to speak," wrote Mikhailovsky-Danilevsky, "who was well disposed to Russia. An overt spirit of opposition prevailed among them all. They have a saying: 'He is fine in every way, but he is a Muscovite,' that is, a Russian, and thus an evil or dangerous person. Such hatred originated in the violation of the rights of Little Russia; in the decline of credit in industry; in the increase of taxes, which have caused general poverty in Little Russia; and in the foolish disposition of court appointments, where conscience was for sale." Mikhailovsky-Danilevsky had no problem in linking Troshchynsky's dreams about the past and ramblings about the present with the hopes and dreams of the Decembrists: "in Little Russia Troshchynsky's home served as a gathering place for liberals; for example, it was a constant haunt of one of the Muraviev-Apostols, who was later condemned to penal servitude, and of Bestuzhev-Riumin, who ended his life on the scaffold."[20]

---

svidomoho ukraïns'koho patriota, avtonomista ta tradytsionalista XIX stolittia)," in *Dnipropetrovs'kyi istoryko-arkheohrafichnyi zbirnyk*, ed. Oleh Zhurba, no. 3 (Dnipropetrovsk, 2009), pp. 176, 193.
[19] "Iz vospominanii Mikhailovskogo-Danilevskogo," *Russkaia starina* 104, no. 10 (1900): 201–18, here 213–14.
[20] *Ibid.*, pp. 212, 214.

Mikhailovsky-Danilevsky's reference to the Decembrists reminds us once again of those conspirators who had a hand in the "discovery" of the *History of the Rus'* – Aleksandr von Brigen, Kondratii Ryleev, and, possibly, Mykhailo Myklashevsky's son, Oleksandr. Troshchynsky's Kobryntsi and Myklashevsky's Ponurivka had much in common in the early nineteenth century. The owners of the two estates knew and respected each other. In 1812, Troshchynsky was one of the supporters of Mykhailo Myklashevsky's project to restore the Cossack regiments; he also corresponded regularly with Myklashevsky to discuss local and imperial politics. The two clearly saw eye to eye on quite a few matters of past and present. Their links with the Decembrists were one of the many things that drew them together. But was there ever a "Starodub patriotic circle" like the one that Oleksander Ohloblyn posited in Novhorod-Siverskyi? That is hard to say, but there is plenty of evidence pointing to a circle of rich Starodub landowners linked by family ties and the common experience of imperial service. They had good reason to be involved in reading and producing the *History of the Rus'*, which not only reflected many of their own views but was also exceptionally kind to their relatives and ancestors.

CHAPTER 13

The liberated gentry

"The 'stately homes of England' have long lorded it over the country estates of imperial Russia's elite," wrote John Randolph, the author of a number of insightful studies on the history of private life in imperial Russia. His comparison of the *longue durée* history of the Russian country estate with its British prototype was by no means flattering to the former. "The Russian country estate is now the Russian ruin, its owners executed by revolution, its treasures rudely confiscated, and its sanctuaries defiled. Meanwhile, English country houses prosper as never before. Their owners are still rich, and have many friends in times of need. Two million members swell the ranks of the English country house's defending army, the mighty National Trust for Places of Historic Interest or Natural Beauty."[1]

One of the changes in Russia since the fall of the Soviet Union is a steady revival of interest in the country's architectural heritage that was either deliberately destroyed or neglected during the Soviet era. That interest led to the restoration of imperial-era buildings in Moscow and St. Petersburg. It also reached the provinces, where enthusiasts and local businessmen, with the support and encouragement of the authorities, turned their attention to the country estates of the noble elite. Thousands of lovers of architecture and history enthusiasts have traveled to the most remote parts of Russia to document what is still there. They have posted on the web not only reports about their trips and numerous pictures of beautifully restored palaces and churches but also photos showing the deterioration of most of the remaining noble mansions in the Russian provinces. The Starodub region became one of the beneficiaries of that search for a lost heritage and a new historical identity. The "Wonders of Russia" website, sponsored by a number of Russian media powerhouses in

[1] John Randolph, "The Old Mansion: Revisiting the History of the Russian Country Estate," *Kritika: Explorations in Russian and Eurasian History*, no. 4 (2000): 729–49, here 729–30.

order to promote the Russian national heritage, features photos and descriptions of quite a few historical monuments and noble mansions in that part of the former Hetmanate. They include the former estate of Petr Rumiantsev in the village of Velyka Topal (present-day Velikaia Topal), constructed in the 1780s; the estate of Petro Zavadovsky in Lialychi (Lialichi); the mansion of Illia Bezborodko in Hryniv; and the estate of Mykhailo Myklashevsky in the village of Ponurivka (Ponurovka). The architectural monuments in all these places, most of which are churches, are now in various states of decline and disrepair.[2]

There is much to be done in order to preserve and restore the Starodub architectural heritage that has miraculously survived the Soviet era. It is even more important to reconstruct the historical and cultural landscape that defined and linked the Starodub-area noble estates and their inhabitants. In the early nineteenth century, not only did the estates of Cossack aristocrats like Myklashevsky, Hudovych, and Troshchynsky become centers of cultural activity in the provinces, but the smaller and more modest estates of much less prominent nobles became centers for the production and dissemination of new political and cultural knowledge. This was partly in line with the role envisioned for the provincial nobility by the imperial government. When in 1762 the Russian imperial nobility was granted liberty from the obligatory state service first introduced by Peter I, the practice emerged whereby nobles devoted only a small part of their lives to imperial service and spent most of their active years on their country estates. Catherine II completed the process of emancipation from state service when she issued the Charter to the Nobility in 1785. While granting new rights and privileges to the nobility, the empress and her advisers expected something in return. The charter ordered the creation of noble assemblies on the county and gubernia levels, effectively transferring to the local nobility many of the administrative functions and responsibilities earlier reserved for the state. The nobles were to decide who would hold noble status, elect their leaders and representatives to higher levels of self-government and, most importantly, run local affairs. Their "retirement" years would be spent not in idle pursuits but in volunteer service to the imperial Enlightenment project.[3]

That was the vision, and it would be unfair to say that it did not bring its fruits. The nobility became involved in local affairs, and the government got

---

[2] "O proekte. Istoriia," Chudesa Rossii www.ruschudo.ru/about.html.
[3] See Robert E. Jones, *The Emancipation of the Russian Nobility* (Princeton, 1973); I. V. Faizova, *Manifest o vol'nosti i sluzhba dvorianstva v XVIII stoletii* (Moscow, 1999).

the power base and administrative resources in the provinces that it had lacked before. St. Petersburg also began to exercise significant cultural influence in the provinces. In the non-Russian borderlands of the empire, that also meant the embrace by local elites of the Russian literary language and imperial Russian culture, which linked the privileged few with the capital and alienated them from the population at large. The centers of this new imperial presence in the provinces were the mansions and country estates of the local notables. As noted above, however, these same mansions and estates often turned into nests of opposition to it. In the late eighteenth and early nineteenth centuries the noble assemblies of the Hetmanate became fortresses of a noble Fronde, perpetually in conflict with the imperial administrators of the region. In 1791 a group of nobles in the Hetmanate sent Vasyl Kapnist, a Poltava-area nobleman and a prominent poet renowned throughout the empire, to King Frederick William II of Prussia to offer their services and request support in the event of a war with Russia. In 1812 they eagerly submitted proposals to the authorities for the restoration of Cossack formations. After the Napoleonic Wars, upset by harsh economic conditions in the region and the disbandment of temporary Cossack formations, they were glad to provide a home away from home for future Decembrists – imperial Russian officers stationed in Ukraine.[4]

Opposition-minded descendants of the Cossack elite gathered at their country estates to exchange news and ideas and to plot ways of preserving, if not restoring, their old privileges. It was also on the noble estates that new knowledge and new historical mythology were produced. Most of the Hetmanate's "antiquarians," including Vasyl Poletyka, Andrian Chepa, and Vasyl Lomykovsky, labored on their estates. They turned to their intellectual pursuits and the collection of historical documents after retirement from the imperial service. If Hryhorii Poletyka, who began his service before the Charter to the Nobility was issued, spent most of his active life in St. Petersburg, his son Vasyl spent his on the family estate in Ukraine. The production of historical texts, which began in the Cossack chancelleries of the Hetmanate in the early eighteenth century, shifted in the last decades of the century to the St. Petersburg apartments of publishers and intellectuals like Hryhori Poletyka, Vasyl Ruban, and

---

[4] John Randolph, *The House in the Garden: The Bakunin Family and the Romance of Russian Idealism* (Ithaca, N.Y., and London, 2007), pp. 23–24, 30–40; Priscilla Roosevelt, *Life on the Russian Country Estate: A Social and Cultural History* (New Haven, Conn., 1995), pp. 2–32; Iaroslav Dashkevych, "Berlin, kviten' 1791 r. Misiia V. V. Kapnista. Ï peredistoriia ta istoriia," in *Postati: Narysy pro diiachiv istoriï, polityky, kul'tury* (Lviv, 2006), pp. 200–41.

Vasyl Tumansky, and then, in the early nineteenth century, to the noble estates of descendants of the Hetmanate's elite.

Some of those estates were located in the environs of Starodub, and many of the local nobles had historical and intellectual interests ranging far beyond the confines of their home region. As a rule, these nobles were descendants of the local Cossack officer stratum and, unlike the Hudovyches and Myklashevskys, did not hold high imperial office. Instead, they spent most of their lives on their country estates, amassing their holdings, running the local affairs of the "liberated gentry" and occasionally indulging in recollections of family history. Like the main characters of the previous chapter, they all "made it" into the *History of the Rus'* through the intermediacy of relatives and ancestors mentioned in its text.

In Starodub noble society of the early nineteenth century, few people could claim a better educational background or higher intellectual credentials than Ivan Lashkevych. He was related by marriage to Pavlo Polubotok, the *History*'s most prominent eighteenth-century hero, and inherited part of Polubotok's immense fortune. Lashkevych was a remarkable figure on the Starodub social and cultural scene of the early nineteenth century. He was a published translator from English and probably the first Starodub notable to receive his education at the University of Moscow. He was born in 1765 to the family of the judge of Pohar county and a scion of an established Starodub family, Stepan Lashkevych. The Lashkevyches traced their origins to Starodub burghers who had joined the Cossack service in the early eighteenth century. Ivan's father, Stepan, began his career as a secretary in the Hetmanate's General Chancellery. He was a well-educated and intellectually curious individual who had a good library, for which he bought books in the imperial capital, and kept a diary. He also took care of his son's education and set him on a path toward a promising career. In 1775, at the age of ten, Ivan was enrolled with the rank of corporal in the Izmailovskoe guards regiment – one of three guards regiments in the empire. Three years later, still listed in the guards regiment, Ivan Lashkevych became a student at the University of Moscow. Thus Stepan Lashkevych ensured that his son got the best possible education in the empire.[5]

Gone were the days when the sons of Cossack officers went to the Kyiv Mohyla Academy and then continued their education at Central European, especially German, universities. In the late eighteenth century the Starodub elite found its way to the first and best secular institution of

---

[5] Vadim Modzalevskii, *Malorossiiskii rodoslovnik*, 4 vols. (Kyiv, 1908–14), III: 29, 32–33.

higher learning in the empire, the University of Moscow. It was founded in 1755 as an alternative to similar institutions in Central Europe. Ukrainian students sent there by their parents brought home friends, books, and ideas. Ivan Lashkevych studied in Moscow under the direction of such prominent figures as Khariton Chebotarev (1745–1815), who became the first rector of the university (1803–5) and one of the first university professors to study Russian history. Chebotarev served as a translator into Russian of Hieronymus Freyer's *Erste Vorbereitung zur Universal-Historie* (1724), published Mikhail Lomonosov's *Short Russian Chronicle*, and helped Empress Catherine II with her work on *Notes on the Earliest Russian History*. In his early years at Moscow University, Chebotarev was friends with Nikolai Novikov (1744–1818), the leading figure of the Russian Enlightenment. Both Chebotarev and Novikov were members of a Masonic lodge at a time when Masons were in the forefront of Russian political and cultural life. Ivan Lashkevych maintained good relations with his teacher after graduation, and in 1801 he brought his own son, Petrusha, to Chebotarev when he was ready to enrol at the university.[6]

Whether or not Ivan Lashkevych followed his teacher into the Masonic movement, there is little doubt that during his student days he was close to both Chebotarev and Novikov. It was with Novikov's press at the University of Moscow that Ivan Lashkevych published (in 1781) his student work, a Russian translation of Elizabeth Bonhote's novel *The Rambles of Mr. Frankly*. It was a promising beginning, but Lashkevych did not pursue either an academic or a literary career. Instead he returned to military service, attaining the rank of guard sergeant in 1783 and then leaving the guards to become a captain in a regular unit of the Russian army. But his military career soon came to an end as well. Like many of his Starodub neighbors, upon transferring to a regular army unit Lashkevych was dispatched to the Starodub carabineer regiment. This was usually just a step toward retirement, and in 1785, two years after his father's death, Ivan Lashkevych retired with the rank of second major. Only twenty years old at the time, he probably considered it his duty to go home in order to take care of his widowed mother and the family possessions. He would spend the rest of his life at his estate of Brakhliv (Brakhlovo) in the Starodub area,

[6] On Chebotarev's historical views, see Cynthia Hyla Whittaker, "The Idea of Autocracy among Eighteenth-Century Russian Historians," in *Imperial Russia: New Histories for the Empire*, ed. Jane Burbank and David L. Ransel (Bloomington, Ind., 1998), p. 45. On the history of Russian and Ukrainian Masonry, see Douglas Smith, *Working the Rough Stone: Freemasonary and Society in Eighteenth-Century Russia* (DeKalb, Ill., 1999); Andrei Serkov, *Rossiiskoe masonstvo: Slovar'-spravochnik* (Moscow, 2001); Oksana Kryzhanovs'ka, *Taiemni orhanizatsii: masons'kyi rukh v Ukraïni* (Kyiv, 2009), pp. 84–107.

serving in 1798 as a deputy of the local nobility. In 1809 Lashkevych was promoted to the rank of lieutenant colonel and served in that capacity for the next two years. He continued to live on his family estate of Brakhliv and died in 1822, at the age of 57.[7]

Lashkevych spent most of his "retirement years" running his estate and amassing new possessions. They increased significantly in May 1789, when the twenty-four-year-old Lashkevych married one of the richest brides in the Hetmanate, an heiress to part of Pavlo Polubotok's fortune, the twenty-year-old Nastasia Petrivna Myloradovych (1769–1833). The marriage also brought Lashkevych into the extended family of the heirs of the former acting hetman. Neither the marriage nor Lashkevych's entrance into the family was easy to achieve. The retired second major had to overcome a host of obstacles and diversions raised by the bride's family, and his pursuit of happiness entailed both a lengthy court case and extensive private correspondence that give us an inside view of Hetmanate society of the late eighteenth century. These documents also provide more information about one of Starodub's first published authors, who may well have been involved in the creation of the *History*.

At the center of the Lashkevych marriage saga stood Nastasia Stepanivna Polubotok (1732–1802), known locally as Grandmother Polubotok. She was married to Hetman Pavlo Polubotok's grandson, Semen Yakovych Polubotok. Together they had two daughters, one of whom, Sofiia (1747–73), was married to Colonel Petro Myloradovych of Chernihiv (1723–99). Sofiia Polubotok-Myloradovych died young, at the age of twenty-six, leaving behind her husband and three children – a son and two daughters. One of the daughters, Nastasia Petrivna Myloradovych, eventually became the wife of Ivan Lashkevych, but not before their romance and marriage divided the Polubotok-Myloradovych family. On one side of the family feud were Grandmother Polubotok and her grand-daughter, Nastasia; on the other side were Colonel Petro Myloradovych and his son, Hryhorii. The conflict was as much about good looks and love as about money and land.

According to the Lithuanian Statute, which, along with imperial legisla-tion, regulated family and property relations in the Hetmanate, a daughter could claim half the dowry of her deceased mother. Given the amount of Sofiia Polubotok's dowry, her daughter, Nastasia Myloradovych, emerged in the 1780s as one of the richest and thus most attractive brides in the

---

[7] Modzalevskii, *Malorossiiskii rodoslovnik*, III: 29, 32–33; *Liubetskii arkhiv grafa Miloradovicha*, vyp. 1, ed. Aleksandr Lazarevskii (Kyiv, 1898), p. 157.

Hetmanate. There was no shortage of young and not so young men eager for her hand, but Nastasia and her father could not agree on a suitor: those suggested by Colonel Myloradovych were rejected by his daughter, and vice versa. In this contest of wills, Nastasia Myloradovych was backed by Grandmother Polubotok, on whose estate she had lived since the age of fourteen. When Nastasia turned nineteen, and her father gave up looking for suitors for his rebellious daughter, Grandmother Polubotok took the matter into her own hands: timing was crucial, for, by the standards of that day, in a year or two Nastasia would be too old to attract a good match.

Fairly soon the grandmother found a suitable candidate, whom Nastasia also favored – the 25-year-old retired second major Ivan Lashkevych. Without the blessing of the bride's father, however, the legality of the marriage could easily be challenged in court. And Colonel Myloradovych refused to give his blessing, or even to allow Nastasia's favored suitor to visit her. Grandmother Polubotok suspected that her son-in-law was playing for time, hoping to postpone the marriage indefinitely and take over the entire estate of his deceased wife, Sofiia Polubotok, for himself. To her pleas about Nastasia's "advanced" age, Colonel Myloradovych responded that that problem could be solved if the grandmother were to will Nastasia her own estate in the village of Borovychi.[8]

The case, which was a contest not only between family members but also between the Lithuanian Statute and imperial legislation, went all the way to the imperial Senate in St. Petersburg. Both parties managed to find patrons among the powerful Ukrainian officials residing in the capital. The Myloradovyches enlisted the help of Oleksandr Bezborodko, to whom they were related. Grandmother Polubotok mobilized her own contacts, and Ivan Lashkevych gained the ear of another Ukrainian potentate, Count Petro Zavadovsky. He kept his relatives in Ukraine informed about the latest developments in the court intrigue by means of letters from the capital – more general ones were dispatched by regular mail, more candid ones delivered by friends heading from the capital to the Starodub region. The breakthrough in the case came about through Zavadovsky's personal intervention. "On the 15th of this month I went to Petro Vasyliovych [Zavadovsky's] dacha," wrote Ivan Lashkevych to Nastasia Myloradovych (now Lashkevych) from St. Petersburg in June 1790. "He talked with me a great deal about extraneous matters; when I began to entreat him about the case, he said to me that one should begin

---

[8] *Liubetskii arkhiv grafa Miloradovicha*, pp. 49–98; Modzalevskii, *Malorossiiskii rodoslovnik*, III: 29.

in peaceable fashion ... Then [Osyp Stepanovych] Sudiienko, whom I had given up visiting, came for the noon meal; what a surprise it was to me that he began to treat me politely and asked about our case."

Zavadovsky's patronage meant a great deal. It was undoubtedly because of him that Osyp Sudiienko, Bezborodko's all-powerful assistant, who had long refused to see Lashkevych, finally changed his mind and showed some signs of favor. The two parties eventually reached a compromise: Nastasia got her part of her mother's dowry, while Grandmother Polubotok divided her properties among all her grandchildren: one of them was Nastasia's brother, Hryhorii Myloradovych, who had backed his father in the original quarrel and could have been disinherited by his grandmother. The deal was reached in Zavadovsky's presence and then confirmed in front of Osyp Sudiienko, who represented Oleksandr Bezborodko. Thus the two most powerful Ukrainians in St. Petersburg brokered and guaranteed the agreement that made Lashkevych not only a lawful possessor of part of the Polubotok inheritance but also a respected member of the Myloradovych family. Lashkevych returned home from St. Petersburg in the company of Hryhorii Myloradovych, writing to Nastasia that they were coming back "as friends." Hryhorii would later serve as godfather to two of Ivan and Nastasia's sons. Ivan Lashkevych was accepted into the aristocratic (by Hetmanate standards) Myloradovych family. By that time he was acquainted or on good terms with quite a few members of the Hetmanate elite. His letters from St. Petersburg indicate that he knew not only Petro Zavadovsky and Osyp Sudiienko but also Bezborodko's secretary, Dmytro Troshchynsky, and was introduced to Oleksandr Bezborodko himself – he once bumped into him in a French shop in St. Petersburg.[9]

Ivan Lashkevych's marriage takes on particular significance if one looks closely at the way in which Acting Hetman Pavlo Polubotok and his legacy are treated in the *History of the Rus'*. At the center of the *History's* account of Polubotok is his encounter with Peter I in the SS. Peter and Paul Fortress, from which Polubotok and the entire Cossack nation emerge victorious. A story of this kind might well have emanated from surviving members of the Polubotok family. The tsar's visit to Polubotok on the eve of his death and the hetman's "rehabilitation" by virtue of that visit might have served their interests even better than the interests of the nation for which Polubotok had died. If indeed the story emanated from

---

[9] *Liubetskii arkhiv grafa Miloradovicha*, pp. 122–43; Modzalevskii, *Malorossiiskii rodoslovnik*, III: 32, 37–38. For copies of Ivan Lashkevych's marriage certificate and his will, see Russian State Library, Manuscript Division, fond 510, no. 58.

the Polubotok family, then it might well have reached the pages of the *History* through the intermediacy of Ivan Lashkevych, who was extremely close to Grandmother Polubotok, the last bearer of the family tradition.

The case for Lashkevych's involvement in the production of the *History* grows stronger if we consider other episodes of the *History* that bear directly on members of his own family. Like all the other particular episodes of the *History* discussed above, these are to be found in the post-1708 part of the narrative. Besides Polubotok, the most important figures that link Ivan Lashkevych to the *History of the Rus'* are the colonels of Pryluky, Hnat Halahan and his son, Hryhorii. The Halahans are mentioned in the *History* on four occasions, more than in any other historiographic text of the period. All these references are either neutral or positive, and some are so rich in detail as to raise suspicions about the involvement of Halahan family members or people close to them. Hnat Halahan (d. 1748) was among the first Cossack officers to switch allegiance in 1708 from Ivan Mazepa to Peter I. He was also among those who signed the petition of 1723 in defense of Hetmanate autonomy that cost Pavlo Polubotok his life. He served as colonel of Pryluky for a quarter century (1714–39), after which he resigned to make way for his son, Hryhorii (1716–77). The younger Halahan headed the regiment for another quarter century (1739–63). He was succeeded by his own son, Ivan, who headed the regiment from 1763 to 1767 with the rank of acting colonel.[10]

Together the Halahan family ran Pryluky and the surrounding area for more than fifty years, amassing enormous wealth and making friends and connections throughout the Hetmanate, including the Starodub region. One of Colonel Hryhorii Halahan's daughters, Olena, married into the Myklashevsky family. In 1758 another daughter, Paraskeva, married Stepan Ivanovych Lashkevych, a Starodub landowner and secretary of the General Chancellery. Paraskeva Halahan would become the mother of Ivan Lashkevych, a "person of interest" in our current investigation. We happen to know the exact amount of Paraskeva's dowry (the list of items given to the young bride by her loving father was published by Oleksandr Lazarevsky in the nineteenth century). We also know from the diary kept by Stepan Lashkevych that on church holidays the family used to visit Colonel Hryhorii Halahan at his family estate of Sokyryntsi and generally maintained good and close relations with the Pryluky branch of their

---

[10] Volodymyr Kryvosheia, *Ukraïns'ka kozats'ka starshyna*, pt. 1, *Uriadnyky het'mans'koï administratsii*, 2nd edn. (Kyiv, 2005), pp. 125–26.

family. It may well be that stories shared during such visits, or remembered and later retold by Lashkevych's mother, made their way into the *History*.[11]

What were those stories? One of them deals with the role that Hnat Halahan and his regiment played in the Polish campaign of 1733, which resulted among other things in the capture of Gdańsk by the Russian imperial army. According to the *History*, Halahan was a principal hero of that campaign. "Colonel Halahan amazed everyone with his courage and initiative," wrote the anonymous author:

> Among his other distinctions relating to military acumen, he made a display in the vicinity of Slutsk, where a strong cavalry corps came out against his forces and strewed millions of iron nails for a considerable distance along his front. The nails were purposely made with heavy heads, which, falling onto the earth, naturally turned up their sharp ends. Noting this, Halahan ordered a very small part of his forces to carry out a masking maneuver before the Polish front and the nails, while he himself, with his main forces, outflanked the enemy by a concealed route, attacked him from the rear, and forced him to retreat across the nails. As the nails splintered the horses' hooves, the enemy could not escape and was completely routed.[12]

This positive treatment of Halahan in the *History*, full of interesting details, stands in contrast to the accounts of the campaign of 1733 in the Cossack chronicles of the period. The *Brief Description of Little Russia*, also known as the "Lyzohub Chronicle," focuses exclusively on the exploits of its main sponsor, General Quartermaster Yakiv Lyzohub, who was the commander-in-chief of the Cossack forces in that campaign. The version of the *Brief Description* published in 1777 by Vasyl Ruban with the participation of Oleksandr Bezborodko lists both Lyzohub and Halahan among the leaders of the Cossack troops but does not go beyond the simple assertion that both served with distinction. The mention of Halahan in the Ruban/ Bezborodko publication probably served as an invitation to the author of the *History* to introduce his own Halahan story. Still, he had to have sufficient reason to admire Halahan's exploits and dispose of sufficient information to offer the detailed account that appears in his narrative.[13]

---

[11] Lazarevskii, *Opisanie staroi Malorossii: materialy dlia istorii zaseleniia, zemlevladeniia i upravleniia*, 3 vols. (Kyiv, 1888–93), III: 52ff. Cf. *Kievskaia starina*, no. 10 (November, 1888): 466ff.; Modzalevskii, *Malorossiiskii rodoslovnik*, III: 29.

[12] *Istoriia Rusov ili Maloi Rossii. Sochinenie Georgiia Koniskago, Arkhiepiskopa Beloruskago* (Moscow, 1846), p. 237.

[13] "Kratkoe opisanie Malorossii," in *Letopis' Samovidtsa po novootkrytym spiskam*, ed. O. I. Levitskii (Kyiv, 1878), pp. 211–319, here 316–17; "Letopis' ili opisanie kratkoe," in *Sbornik letopisei, otnosiashchikhsia k istorii Iuzhnoi i Zapadnoi Rusi* (Kyiv, 1888), pp. 60–61; *Kratkaia letopis' Malyia Rossii s 1506 po 1776 god* (St. Petersburg, 1777), p. 197.

It would seem that the author's interest in the Halahans and his knowledge of their military accomplishments, deeper than that of other contemporary sources, was not limited to the 1733 campaign or to the deeds of the senior Halahan. The following episode, which deals with the exploits of Hryhorii Halahan, the maternal grandfather of Ivan Lashkevych, also indicates the author's uncommonly detailed knowledge of the campaign of 1756. "In the war that began with Prussia," wrote the author,

to assist Russia's ally, the Holy Roman Empress Maria Theresa, in 1756, five thousand Little Russian registered Cossacks were dispatched, as well as a thousand from the mercenary regiments, with considerable artillery, and the following commanders were assigned to them: General Aide-de-camp Yakiv Damianovych Yakubovych; the colonel of Pryluky, Halahan; and the regimental quartermasters Skorupa of Starodub, Solonyna of Kyiv, and other regimental and company officers, as many as required by that number of troops. This corps was commanded at various times by four sections: two of them drove 10,600 oxen to the army, while the other two brought as many as 6,000 horses rounded up in Little Russia. And these troops saw action at the Battle of [Groß-]Jägersdorf and other battles for seven years, and they returned at the end of the war with two different uniforms and armaments, some with those of the hussars and others with those of Chuhuiv.[14]

Taken together with the previous Halahan episode, the description of the 1756 campaign strengthens the hypothesis of the anonymous author's particular association with the Halahan family. So does his treatment of another Pryluky episode in which, incidentally, the Halahans are not mentioned at all. It deals with the role of the Pryluky regiment in Aleksandr Menshikov's massacre of the town of Baturyn in 1708 – according to the author of the *History*, the worst crime ever committed against his nation. Responsibility for that crime was divided between Menshikov and his informer, Colonel Ivan Nis of Pryluky. The author shares Nis's disgust with Mazepa's betrayal of his ruler, but he also considers Nis a traitor to his own people – a dichotomy that often appears in his treatment of Mazepa. Here is his description of the Nis episode:

But the colonel of Pryluky, Nis, being in the town [of Baturyn] with his regiment, also in disagreement, like other regiments, with Mazepa's enterprise and disgusted with his treachery, but confined to the town by the surveillance of the Serdiuk guards, sent an officer of his, Solomakha by name, out of the town by night and ordered him, overtaking Menshikov on the march, to tell him to

[14] *Istoriia Rusov*, p. 248.

approach the town before dawn and attack the place indicated by that officer, where the Pryluky regiment was deployed. The colonel himself would be sitting on a cannon, bound in chains as if under arrest, while his troops would lie face down by the wall, and that would be a sign or indication to spare those traitors during the general massacre of the inhabitants.[15]

Oleksander Ohloblyn was the first to suggest the Pryluky origins of this story. He also pointed out that not only Nis but also Solomakha may have been an actual historical character, as there were Solomakhas in Pryluky in the latter part of the eighteenth century. Nis, who was the quartermaster of the Pryluky regiment in 1708, betrayed his colonel and relative, Dmytro Horlenko, who sided with Mazepa. He later persecuted Horlenko's family and probably left no positive memories in Pryluky. But there was another colonel besides Horlenko who may have had reason to be unhappy with Nis, namely Hnat Halahan, who replaced Nis as colonel of Pryluky in 1714. Halahan proved his loyalty to the tsar by pacifying the Zaporozhian Sich. For his services he was appointed colonel of Chyhyryn in Right-Bank Ukraine, but after the retreat of the Cossacks and Russian imperial troops from the right bank of the Dnieper River, he had to find himself a new post in the Left-Bank Hetmanate. He chose Pryluky, where he finally replaced Ivan Nis in 1714. Given the circumstances of Halahan's arrival in Pryluky, it is unlikely that relations between the old and new colonels were good. Singling out Colonel Nis as the main Ukrainian perpetrator of the Baturyn massacre would make a good deal of sense to an author whose knowledge of the subject was informed by the Halahans and their family tradition.[16]

The Halahan and Pryluky connections of Ivan Lashkevych would help explain the interest shown by the author of the *History* in a number of episodes of the Hetmanate's eighteenth-century history that affected the Pryluky regiment in one way or another. Those events included the Pikemen's Revolt of 1769–70, which shook the neighboring regiments of Lubny, Myrhorod, and Poltava and received significant attention in the *History*. The same connection could help explain the linguistic peculiarities of the *History* noted by George Y. Shevelov. Analyzing the dialectal features of Ukrainian words used by the author, Shevelov reached the conclusion that he may have come from the area north of Pryluky. Ivan Lashkevych's mother, Paraskeva Halahan, had grown up in the Pryluky

---

[15] *Ibid.*, p. 206.

[16] O. P. Ohloblyn, *Do pytannia pro avtora "Istorii Rusov"* (Kyiv, 1998), pp. 83–85; Kryvosheia, *Ukraïns'ka kozats'ka starshyna*, pp. 125–26.

region, and Ivan himself visited his grandfather's estate there, so he might easily have picked up more than a few local colloquialisms.[17]

Apart from the Lashkevyches, another Starodub noble family with links to the *History* is that of the Haletskys. They were an established Cossack officer family with deep Starodub roots that also extended to the Hadiach and Myrhorod regiments in the central and southern parts of the Hetmanate. Semen Yakovych Haletsky, a prominent personage in the *History*, began his service in 1702 as a fellow of the Cossack Host in the Starodub regiment under Colonel Mykhailo Andriiovych Myklashevsky. He moved rather quickly through the ranks, often serving as acting colonel of the regiment. His career trajectory took a sudden dive in December 1723, when he was arrested in connection with the case of Acting Hetman Pavlo Polubotok. As a captain of the Novhorod-Siverskyi company, Haletsky brought to St. Petersburg Cossack officer petitions supporting Polubotok's demands for the restoration of the hetmancy and other rights and privileges taken away by Peter I. After returning home, he was arrested and sent back to St. Petersburg, where he joined Polubotok and other officers jailed in the SS. Peter and Paul Fortress in the heart of the imperial capital. While Polubotok died in imprisonment, Semen Haletsky survived the ordeal and was released after the death of Peter I. Reinstated as acting colonel of Starodub, he was promoted in May 1734 to the post of general standard-bearer.[18]

Semen Haletsky figures prominently in the *History*'s detailed description of the battle waged by the Cossacks against the Tatars at the Haiman Valley in southern Ukraine in 1738. There are confusing parts of the story that can be attributed to its origins in the oral tradition rather than in historical documentation. Among these is the reference to Semen Haletsky as colonel of Hadiach, a title he never held. On the other hand, the anonymous author is perfectly accurate in recording that Haletsky was killed in the battle, which resulted in a Cossack defeat and numerous casualties. Although the author treats Semen Haletsky with respect, he also blames him for the disastrous outcome of the battle. According to the *History*, Haletsky, "given all his many merits, was particularly renowned as a courageous, enterprising, and efficient man ... But excessive ambition, the usual companion of complex individuals, led him into a fatal abyss that damaged the fine reputation of the whole army subordinate to

---

[17] *Istoriia Rusov*, pp. 252–53; Iurii Shevel'ov, "*Istoriia Rusov* ochyma movoznavtsia," in *Zbirnyk na poshanu prof. d-ra Oleksandra Ohloblyna*, ed. Vasyl' Omel'chenko (New York, 1977).
[18] Modzalevskii, *Malorossiiskii rodoslovnik*, 1: 235–37.

him. He was making a path for himself to the hetmancy of Little Russia, in place of the recently deceased [Danylo] Apostol, and thought to gain glory by means of deliberate feats of arms." He allegedly mistook a major Tatar army, led by the khan himself, for a small contingent and attacked it without proper preparation. The result was a major defeat.[19]

According to the author of the *History*, Colonel Semen Haletsky had a son who served in the Starodub regiment. "Haletsky, having summoned his son, Petro, who was the captain of Pohar in the Starodub regiment," wrote the anonymous author of the *History*, "allowed him, as a young man, to save himself by all available means, saying of himself that he would not do so because of his oath of obligation and his rank as commander. And so those troops were completely routed by the over-whelming Tatar forces, and Commandant Haletsky was cut to pieces, while his son and a few hundred Cossacks and dragoons saved themselves under cover of darkness among the corpses and empty trenches." Petro Semenovych Haletsky was indeed a captain in the Starodub regiment from 1734 to 1738. He later became colonel of Hadiach (hence the author's erroneous attribution of that title to Semen Haletsky) and died in that office in 1754. Some of his sons and grandsons returned to Starodub, while others remained in the south, making careers there.[20]

The Haletskys were related by marriage to two families that are particularly important with regard to the *History of the Rus'*. The first of them is the Bezborodko family. Petro Petrovych Haletsky, a grandson of General Standard-Bearer Semen Haletsky and a son of Colonel Petro Haletsky of Hadiach, married Oleksandr Bezborodko's sister, Hanna. He served as judge of the Myrhorod regiment, acquiring the rank of court councillor, one step above the level required to attain personal nobility. Oleksandr Bezborodko was most supportive of his brother-in-law with regard to the sensitive issue of a Cossack officer's noble status. "From the point of view of breeding, he can show himself anywhere without shame," wrote Bezborodko about his relative to one of his St. Petersburg contacts. "Apart from the fact that his family springs from the old Polish aristocracy, it has already been in service in Little Russia for about a hundred years."[21]

The Haletskys, who are portrayed in the *History* with sympathy and respect but not in exclusively positive terms, were part of a tight circle of

---

[19] *Istoriia Rusov*, pp. 239–41; Ohloblyn, *Liudy staroï Ukraïny*, pp. 178–79.
[20] *Istoriia Rusov*, pp. 239–41.
[21] Modzalevskii, *Malorossiiskii rodoslovnik*, 1: 234–35; David Saunders, *The Ukrainian Impact on Russian Culture, 1750–1850* (Edmonton, 1985), p. 79.

relatives and neighbors who included the Bezborodkos, Hudovyches, and Myklashevskys. Two of the Haletskys, Mykhailo Ivanovych and Petro Ivanovych, held office in Starodub in the first two decades of the nineteenth century. They may well have been the sources of the detailed but romanticized and not very accurate information about the tragic battle that two of their ancestors fought in the Haiman Valley in 1738.

One more Starodub-area noble family that made it into the *History of the Rus'* were the Skorupas. In prominence and career achievements they were no match for the aristocratic families mentioned above, but then, neither is the attention paid to the Skorupas in the *History*. Like Vasyl Hudovych and the Haletskys, father and son, a representative of the Skorupa family makes his appearance in the last, post-1708 part of the *History*. Indeed, he figures in the same episode of the Prussian campaign of 1757 that involves Lashkevych's maternal grandfather, Colonel Hryhorii Halahan. The Starodub quartermaster Pavlo Skorupa is mentioned there along with officers ranking high above him, which is interesting in itself. Of even greater interest are details about the campaign that must have come from one of its participants. The author of the *History* was eager to blame the numerous deaths among the Little Russian recruits on the arrogance of the Great Russian officers. "This came about," he says about the many deaths of his countrymen from infectious diseases, "not because of the climate or the air, which is particularly healthy in Germany and Prussia, but because of the poor maintenance of these people by their commanders or, rather, by their inspectorate, which, considering them to be on a par with the Lapps [Eastern Sami] and Kamchadals [Itelmen], drove them into tuberculosis or hypochondria because of their dialect alone."[22]

Who was the regimental quartermaster Skorupa mentioned in the *History*? His full name was Pavlo Hryhorovych Skorupa, and he spent most of his active life pursuing the office of colonel of Starodub. Skorupa began his career as a secretary in the Field Chancellery of the Hetmanate in 1738 and soon became known to Cossack officers all over the Hetmanate, as he often visited the regiments to enforce the decrees of the supreme authorities. In 1741, using his connections in high places, Skorupa got himself appointed to the post of Starodub quartermaster, but he had to wait sixteen years for that office to become vacant. He finally took office in 1757 and held it for fifteen years. As he commanded his regiment in the campaigns of the Seven Years War, Skorupa distinguished himself as a

---

[22] *Istoriia Rusov*, p. 248.

brave and resourceful commander and was promoted to the rank of colonel of the army but never became colonel of Starodub, an office that came with administrative responsibilities and significant financial benefits. He retired in 1772, his last Starodub colonel being a member of the Myklashevsky clan, Mykhailo Andriiovych Myklashevsky, Jr.[23]

There were quite a few heirs and relatives of Pavlo Skorupa living in the vicinity of Starodub in the late eighteenth and early nineteenth centuries. Perhaps the most prominent of them was Mykhailo Oleksandrovych Skorupa, who served as marshal of Mhlyn county north of Starodub from 1809 to 1815. According to Khanenko, Skorupa "initially served in some post at court and was one of the progressive individuals of the time." What exactly Skorupa's progressive views (and, by extension, the views of some of his friends and relatives) may have been can be detected from the memoirs of de la Flise. The French doctor found Mykhailo Skorupa living in "quite a beautiful" house in Mhlyn. As the marshal of the Mhlyn county nobility, Skorupa held elective office, serving at the same time as the supreme representative of the central government in the area. Given Skorupa's title and the respect his name commanded, de la Flise originally thought that he was being summoned to a marshal of the army. He was introduced instead to "a man of thirty-five, tall in stature and of noble appearance, but clad in a black tailcoat." Skorupa spoke a bit of French and invited the doctor to stay at his home – his younger brother was ill at the time. "After my examination of the patient," wrote de la Flise, "Mr. Skorupa took me to his study and offered me a pipe. A servant gave me a pipe with a long stem and an amber mouthpiece. My host questioned me in considerable detail about Napoleon and our retreat, saying that he sympathized with the French and had such regard for me that he would like me to settle permanently in his home."[24]

Skorupa's sympathy for the French was not limited to his interest in the professional skills of the doctor, which turned out be quite useful in the province. He was also considerate of the other French prisoners of war. "As the official in charge of all the prisoners of war in Mhlyn," recalled de la Flise, "he showed himself to be a kind man. On his orders, all useful arrangements were made for the prisoners." Mykhailo Skorupa was a gentleman, and he abhorred the xenophobia of his peasants, who were only too happy to kill off the hungry, frozen, and disoriented French soldiers wandering in the region after the retreat of the Grande Armée.

[23] Modzalevskii, *Malorossiiskii rodoslovnik*, III: 482–83; IV: 681–82.
[24] Dominik de lia Fliz, "Pokhod velikoi armii v Rossiiu v 1812 g.," *Russkaia starina* (1892), LXXIII: 343.

Like the peasants of the early eighteenth century who, according to the *History of the Rus'*, mistreated Swedish soldiers because they ate meat on Fridays, the Mhlyn-area peasants, by de la Flise's account, had no sympathy for the French POWs, as they did not observe Lent according to the Julian calendar (in 1812 it was twelve days behind the Gregorian one).

Mykhailo Skorupa's interest in Napoleon and sympathy toward the French may well have been informed by his interest in or attraction to the ideals of the French Revolution. But there was at least one aspect of the revolution that Skorupa decisively rejected – the execution of a monarch. Impressed by Skorupa's sympathetic treatment of the French POWs, de la Flise was puzzled by the contempt that Skorupa showed for the most senior of them, Colonel Escudié. "I did not dare to ask him the reason," wrote de la Flise,

but he himself admitted his antipathy to that soldier. He said that he had read in some French publication that a member of the Convention named Escudié, like the colonel, had voted for the execution of Louis XVI. In his view, this must have been the same man, as he was more than fifty years old. I could neither refute nor confirm that conjecture; perhaps it was accurate. The marshal added that according to his feelings, a man guilty of the death of his sovereign filled him with loathing, although there was no need to express that feeling here.[25]

Skorupa's thoughts and views are significant for everyone attempting to reconstruct the mood in Starodub society of the early nineteenth century. According to de la Flise, Skorupa's house in Mhlyn was a center where the local notables gathered for receptions, and the Skorupa brothers in turn were welcome at the homes of their much more prominent neighbors, including the Zavadovskys and Hudovyches.

We know nothing about the possible involvement of either the Skorupas or the Haletskys in any writing endeavors. They could certainly have been "consultants" to the project, sharing family stories and opinions with the author, but probably no more. Their ancestors were either mentioned in passing (Skorupa) or received not entirely positive coverage (Haletskys) in the *History*. Ivan Lashkevych's chances of direct involvement in the production of the *History* are much higher. Two of his ancestors/relatives received extremely positive coverage in the text. Moreover, he was associated with the *History of the Rus'* by geography and family history; he was also involved in literary activity. There is a good deal in his life and career that tells in his favor as a possible author or coauthor of the *History*.

[25] *Ibid.*, p. 348.

Ivan Lashkevych was of the right age – he was born in 1765 and died in 1822, just after the *History* began its triumphal march through the libraries of the local nobility. He was also of the right social background, coming from a noble family with deep Cossack roots. Lashkevych lived in the right neighborhood and had reason to dislike Old Believers, who were among his immediate neighbors (his son, Stepan, even wrote a study of Old Believer settlements in Ukraine). Ivan Lashkevych also mingled with the right kind of people, including Stepan Shyrai. He had appropriate family connections. As a grandson of Hryhorii Halahan and a beloved grandson-in-law of Grandmother Polubotok, Lashkevych had good reason and sufficient knowledge to speak positively and in significant detail about the exploits of both the Halahans and Pavlo Polubotok. Finally, it appears that he may have had the right "southern" accent. But the strongest argument in favor of Ivan Lashkevych's authorship of the *History* is that he was one of the very few individuals of his generation and background to be educated in one of the imperial capitals, where he would have been exposed to the Enlightenment ideas so dear to the author of the *History*. Lashkevych was also one of very few published authors in the Starodub region, and the only one of his generation.

The problem is that the strongest argument in favor of Lashkevych, his education and his authorship of a published work, can also be used against him in more than one way. First of all, there is nothing in Lashkevych's writings (and these, unfortunately, are limited to his Russian translation of an English novel and his numerous letters) to indicate an interest in the history of Ukraine or any other interests shared with the author of the *History*. Thus the parallels that one might draw between Lashkevych's education and family connections and certain features of the *History* find no support in his known writings. Given the nature of those texts (Lashkevych's letters deal largely with family, legal, and household matters), this is not a sufficient reason to reject his candidacy. The language of his writings, however, can provide such a reason. Lashkevych's writings show him to have been entirely at home with the Russian language of the Moscow literary salons and much less comfortable with the Russian of the military commanders and imperial administrators that influenced the author of the *History*. Lashkevych's language is almost devoid of Ukrainisms, which are very common in the *History*. All this presents a serious obstacle to anyone who would like to end the search for the author of the *History* by nominating Ivan Lashkevych. Still, that does not exclude him from the list of potential editors or coauthors of the *History*.[26]

---

[26] Modzalevskii, *Malorossiiskii rodoslovnik*, III: 38; *Liubetskii arkhiv grafa Miloradovicha*, pp. 122–59.

CHAPTER 14

A history teacher

Few Russian buildings are as well known to the general public in Russia and abroad as that of the State Historical Museum in Moscow. Constructed in the years 1875–81, it is built of red brick in the Russian Revival style and has the most prestigious address in the country – Red Square, no. 1. Today it is a commanding presence on the edge of Russia's main square, next to the Kremlin and opposite the Cathedral of Basil the Holy Fool, built to mark Ivan the Terrible's conquest of Kazan and Muscovy's ascendancy to tsardom. The building was becoming dilapidated in the last decades of the Soviet Union: during the pompous military parades and government-sponsored manifestations that took place on Red Square, its façade was often covered by huge posters celebrating Soviet power. Reconstruction began in 1986, at the dawn of Gorbachev's perestroika, and, given the economic difficulties associated with the fall of the USSR, it lasted eleven years. By 1997, when the job was done, Russia was eager to embrace its pre-Soviet heritage and identity.

The building and the museum it houses are ideal symbols of the imperial past. The museum was founded in 1872 by a group of Russian historians and antiquarians whose leading figure was Count Aleksei Uvarov, one of the first Russian archaeologists. Among the members of the group were some of the best-known Russian historians, including Sergei Soloviev and Ivan Zabelin, who took over the directorship of the museum from Uvarov in 1885. The official task of the museum was to collect artifacts associated with major events in the history of the Russian state. The Slavophiles who initiated the establishment of the museum had a broader agenda. They wanted to promote Russian history, culture, and identity in opposition to the cosmopolitan Western culture embodied in the Hermitage and other museums of St. Petersburg. Consequently, the manuscript collection of the Russian Historical Museum now houses some of the most ancient Rus' manuscripts, including Sviatoslav's Miscellanies and the Halych Gospel. Collected from all over the empire, these manuscripts embody the vision of Russian identity that was dominant in official imperial circles in the second half of the nineteenth century.[1]

Given that ethos, it is hardly surprising that one of the founders of the museum, Ivan Zabelin, included in his collection a Russian-language manuscript titled "Ruskaia istoriia" (A History of Rus'). It dealt with the history of the Ukrainian Cossacks, a subject perfectly suited to the mandate of the museum and the taste of its patron, Emperor Alexander III. An admirer of the Cossack past, the emperor made history by buying Ilia Repin's famous painting "The Reply of the Zaporozhian Cossacks" at the highest price ever paid for a painting in the Russian Empire – 35,000 rubles. According to the title page, Zabelin's manuscript came from the eighteenth century. The page reads: "A History of Rus'. Written by Yakov Radkevichev in the year 1734, January 24. Belongs to Fedor Petrovich Yatchenko since the year 1876, December 22." At the bottom of the title page there is another date and a place-name: "1874, December 22. Starodub."[2]

For more than a century, the Starodub manuscript was preserved in the collection of the Russian Historical Museum without being noticed or thoroughly studied by scholars. Given the changes in the national self-identification of Russians and Ukrainians in the course of the twentieth century and the division of labor in Soviet academic institutions, where Russian scholars studied the history of Russia and Ukrainians the history of Ukraine, the manuscript simply fell through the cracks. It was finally "rediscovered" in the early 2000s by a young Ukrainian scholar, Andrii Bovhyria, who was continuing work begun in the 1970s by the dissident historian Olena Apanovych. He undertook to track down, describe, and analyze surviving manuscripts of Cossack historical writings. In Zabelin's "History of Rus'" Bovhyria recognized a version of the *Brief Description of Little Russia*, the most popular historical manuscript in the Hetmanate during its last decades of existence.

Bovhyria was also alert to the textual parallels between the Starodub manuscript and Jean-Benoît Scherer's *Annales*. The conclusions that he reached as a result of studying the manuscript were striking indeed. He argued that Scherer most probably used a manuscript like the one from Starodub in compiling the second volume of his own work. Was Bovhyria

---

[1] Gosudarstvennyi istoricheskii muzei. Istoriia muzeia www.shm.ru/index2.html; www.shm.ru/histr_1.html.

[2] "Ruskaia istoriia," Ivan Zabelin collection, no. 617, Manuscript Division, State Historical Museum (Moscow).

right or wrong? If he was right, then we have now penetrated the secret not only of the origins of Scherer's chronicle but also of the apocryphal speech given by Pavlo Polubotok before Peter I – it came from a manuscript written by a certain Yakiv Radkevych in January 1734. What, then, becomes of the relationship between the *History of the Rus'* and Scherer's *Annales*, established by generations of scholars? Was the *History* actually based on the Starodub manuscript and not the *Annales*? One way of testing Bovhyria's hypothesis is to compare Scherer's *Annales* with the Starodub manuscript.[3]

Any reader of the Starodub manuscript is bound to be struck by the abundance of French clichés in its Russian-language narrative. This alone sets it apart from the numerous "homemade" versions and copies of the *Brief Description of Little Russia*, although it does not tell us whether the French or the Russian version came first. The answer to that question is provided by a comparison of the following passages, which serve as an introduction to Polubotok's speech to Peter I. According to Scherer, "ces députés, dis-je, s'adressèrent de rechef au czar; & Polubatok portant la parole, eut la fermeté de lui dire." In the Starodub manuscript this same passage is rendered as follows: "Sii deputaty, govoriu, otneslis' opiat' k gosudariu i Polubotok imel otvazhnost' skazat' emu" (These deputies, I say, again addressed the sovereign, and Polubotok was bold enough to say to him). The word *govoriu* (I say) is plainly a translation of *dis-je*, an expression not used in this particular context in Russian unless, of course, we are dealing with a literal translation from the French. Thus there can be little doubt that the Starodub excerpt is a Russian translation of Scherer.[4]

French clichés in the Starodub manuscript are numerous enough to substantiate the conclusion that it was based on Scherer's *Annales*, not the other way around. But what does this tell us about the relationship between Scherer and the *History of the Rus'*? Did the anonymous author borrow from the French original or from a Russian translation? The choice of Russian words used to render Scherer's French is very similar in the Starodub manuscript and the *History*, which may be an indication that the author of the *History* drew on Scherer not directly but through a Russian translation. While this deduction is not conclusive, the smoking

[3] Andrii Bovhyria, *Kozats'ke istoriopysannia v rukopysnii tradytsiï XVIII st. Spysky ta redaktsiï tvoriv* (Kyiv, 2010), pp. 124–26.
[4] "Ruskaia istoriia," fol. 54; Jean-Benoît Scherer, *Annales de la Petite-Russie, ou Histoire des Cosaques-Saporogues et des Cosaques de l'Ukraine*, 2 vols. (Paris, 1788), II: 207.

gun comes from the misspelling of the names of historical characters – a pattern that indicates borrowings on the part of the anonymous author of the *History* from a Starodub-type translation.

Here is an example. Describing the events of 1653 in Ukraine, Scherer mentions an expedition against the Cossacks led by the Polish commander Stefan Czarniecki. Scherer's rendering of the episode corresponds textually to numerous versions of the *Brief Description of Little Russia*, including the one published by Ruban. The only difference consists in the spelling of Czarniecki's name, which Scherer spells "Tschernetzi." Not surprisingly, perhaps, the author of the Starodub translation failed to recognize "Czarniecki" in "Tschernetzi" and attributed the whole episode to "Chetvertynsky" instead. He wrote: "The Polish king, having learned what was going on in Ukraine, dispatched Chetvertynsky with an army." The author of the *History*, in turn, mistook the mysterious Chetvertynsky for another figure, Prince Chetvertynsky. As a Cossack patriot, he made sure that Prince Chetvertynsky's army would be defeated by the Cossacks. To bring about the desired result, he invented an episode in which "The Polish king, having obtained news of the most recent defeat of the Polish army, which had been under the command of Prince Chetvertynsky," ordered a new expedition against Ukraine. No sources refer to Chetvertynsky as the head of a Polish army in Ukraine in 1653 except the Russian translation of Scherer and the *History of the Rus'*.[5]

We have an intriguing situation: the author of the *History* was making use of Scherer's *Annales* not directly but through a Russian translation similar to the Starodub manuscript. But who was behind its production? Scherer's *Annales* were popular in Ukraine and among those interested in Ukrainian history in the imperial capitals. The work was known, for example, to Yakiv Markevych, the author of *Zapiski o Malorossii* (Notes on Little Russia, 1798). Still, we know of only one attempt to translate the *Annales* into Russian. One such translation was produced in the early nineteenth century by Vasyl Lomykovsky (1778–1848), a descendant of a Cossack family that gave Mazepa one of his strongest supporters, General Quartermaster Ivan Lomykovsky. Vasyl Lomykovsky was a known figure on the cultural scene during the "heritage-gathering" stage of the Ukrainian national project, to use Miroslav Hroch's definition. After retiring from military service in the early nineteenth century with the rank of captain

---

[5] Scherer, *Annales*, ii: 54; "Ruskaia istoriia," fol. 15; *Istoriia Rusov ili Maloi Rosii. Sochinenie Georgiia Koniskago, Arkhiepiskopa Beloruskago* (Moscow, 1846), pp. 107–8. Cf. *Kratkaia letopis' Malyia Rossii s 1506 po 1776 god* (St. Petersburg, 1777), p. 33.

second grade, Lomykovsky settled on his estate in the former Myrhorod regiment of the Poltava gubernia – a career pattern endorsed by Catherine II and her courtiers. The former serviceman was now supposed to promote the government-sponsored Enlightenment project in the provinces. Lomykovsky fulfilled at least part of the empress's expectations, becoming involved in intellectual work and improving agricultural practices on his estate, which he called "Love of Labor Park."

As was the case with other Ukrainian "gentlemen farmers" of the period, some of Lomykovsky's activities would hardly have pleased the government. His retirement from the capital to the countryside was more an attempt to establish personal autonomy from the state than to endorse its program. First of all, he befriended such dangerous "freethinkers" as his neighbor Dmytro Troshchynsky, at whose home he met a fellow antiquarian, Andrian Chepa, and Ivan Martos, the brother of the historian Oleksandr Martos, who was an admirer of Mazepa. Ivan Martos, a Mason and a mystic, became Lomykovsky's close friend and soulmate. Lomykovsky also became engaged in the collection of Ukrainian songs long before the publication of Nikolai Tsertelev's collection in 1819. It took a while for Andrian Chepa to appreciate the importance of that undertaking of Lomykovsky's, but he eventually did so under the influence of his St. Petersburg correspondent Vasyl Anastasevych, who combined fascination with history with a growing interest in folklore. In his "retirement years," Lomykovsky continued a project he had begun while still in St. Petersburg – the collection of materials on the history of Ukraine. He produced the first volume of the manuscript "Provisions for Little Russian History" in St. Petersburg and the second and last volume after his return to Ukraine in 1812. The "Provisions" included copies of chronicles, documents, and notes that told a story very different from the one promoted by imperial officials. If the official version of Russian history featured emperors and empresses (the narrative proposed by the "scenarios of power" produced at the Russian court), Lomykovsky concentrated on Ukrainian hetmans and the rights and privileges of the Cossack estate.[6]

---

[6] On Lomykovsky, see Volodymyr Kravchenko, *Narysy z ukraïns'koï istoriohrafiï epokhy natsional'-noho Vidrodzhennia (druha polovyna XVIII–seredyna XIX st.* (Kharkiv, 1996), pp. 79–80; O. I. Zhurba, "Vasyl' Iakovych Lomykovs'kyi: istoryk chy ahronom?" *Sicheslavs'kyi almanakh* (Dnipropetrovsk, 2006), vyp. 2, pp. 153–58; Zhurba, "Predstav'te Vy sebe, kakoi zver' byl getman! Èto byli prenechestivye despoty! (Z lysta svidomoho ukraïns'koho patriota, avtonomista ta tradytsionalista XIX stolittia)," in *Dnipropetrovs'kyi istoryko-arkheohrafichnyi zbirnyk*, ed. Oleh Zhurba, no. 3 (Dnipropetrovsk, 2009), pp. 177, 195–97.

Lomykovsky's interpretation of Ukrainian history was largely shared by antiquarians of the early nineteenth century such as Vasyl Poletyka and Andrian Chepa, as well as by the author of the *History of the Rus'*. Like them, Lomykovsky complained about the destruction of the sources for Ukrainian history. "It is an incontestable fact, known to all, that in the Time of Troubles our archives were completely lost," he wrote. Like the author of the *History*, he considered the Ukrainians to be the true Russians and, again, maintained that this was common knowledge. "It is known to all," wrote Lomykovsky, "that our nation is the noble Russian nation by origin, the same nation that housed the thrones of the Russian autocrats." Some of the notes in Lomykovsky's "Provisions" reflect his dissatisfaction with Russian rule over his homeland, which was so characteristic of the mood in Little Russian society at large. Commenting on the fate of Ukraine after its takeover by Russia, Lomykovsky wrote, "When the natural daughter, Little Russia, joined her mother, Great Russia, Russia had already become a fright to all her neighbors, and only from that time did she begin to ascend to the summit of glory and greatness. Regardless of that, Russia, owing to prejudice and envy, treated her natural daughter as a stepmother would her adopted daughter."[7]

In 1809, while still in St. Petersburg, Lomykovsky undertook the translation into literary Russian of Scherer's two-volume *Annales*. He began with the first volume, but, judging by the manuscript preserved in one of the volumes of his "Provisions," never finished the project. He abandoned it before reaching the second volume of Scherer's work, which contained a French translation of the *Brief Description of Little Russia*. Is it possible that Lomykovsky actually completed his work despite the lack of evidence to that effect in his papers? That is highly unlikely. We must probably seek the author of the translation in the same place as the author of the *History*, that is, Starodub and its immediate vicinity. After all, that is where the manuscript came from, judging by its title page.[8]

Are we ready to take on another anonymous author before solving the puzzle of the first one? In the case of "A History of Rus'" we are dealing with one more Starodub manuscript that bears all the hallmarks of a historical mystification. Not only was that manuscript a mere translation of Scherer, not an original work written by Yakiv Radkevych, but it could

---

[7] "Pripasy dlia Malorossiiskoi istorii, sobrannye Vasiliem Lomikovskim," Manuscript Institute, Vernadsky Library, I, no. 54671, fol. 120ᵛ; A. Lazarevskii, *Slovar' malorusskoi stariny, sostavlennyi v 1808 g. V. Ia. Lomikovskim* (Kyiv, 1894); Bovhyria, *Kozats'ke istoriopysannia*, pp. 52–70.

[8] "Pripasy dlia Malorossiiskoi istorii, sobrannye Vasiliem Lomikovskim," Manuscript Institute, Vernadsky Library, I, no. 54663, fols. 331–66. Cf. Bovhyria, *Kozats'ke istoriopysannia*, p. 272.

not have been written at the time specified on its title page. The year 1734 on the title page of the Starodub manuscript is bogus. No translation could have been done before the publication of the original work (Scherer's *Annales*) in 1788. Moreover, the manuscript could not have been completed on January 24, 1734, as it includes a reference to the funeral of Hetman Danylo Apostol, which took place on February 5, 1734, and to the abolition of the hetmancy by decree of Empress Anna Ioannovna, which happened later that year. The title page is written in a different hand than the manuscript, and whoever composed it did a poor job on the dates. One of them, written in Church Slavonic characters, comes out as 1876; the other, written in Arabic numerals, reads December 22, 1874 (it can also be read as 1814). On the last page of the manuscript we see another date: December 22, 1878 (variant: 1818).

The confusion of dates continues in the notes at the very end of the manuscript. Of the two historical events recorded there, the copyist or owner of the manuscript got only one right – Napoleon's invasion of Russia in 1812. He wrote that the commander of the Russian forces in that war was Mikhail Kutuzov and its main "hero" Petr Bagration. (He then adds the joke that Bagration was wounded "twice, with one half, three-quarters of a quarter, and five-eighteenths of a *vershok* [an old Russian measure of length].") Under the year 1814, later corrected to 1854, reference is made to a "war with the Turks," giving General Muraviev as the Russian commander and "Dybich" as the main war hero. Hans Karl Friedrich Anton von Diebitsch, one of the Russian commanders directly involved in the suppression of the Decembrist Revolt of 1825, indeed distinguished himself in fighting the Ottomans, but he did so in the Russo-Turkish War of 1828–29, not 1814 or 1854. He died in 1831, decades before the Crimean War of 1853–56. Judging by the Church Slavonic date on the title page of the manuscript, it apparently came into the possession of Fedir Petrovych Yatchenko in 1876.[9]

Who was behind this manuscript, which was clearly much more recent than it was claimed to be? There is good reason to believe that the Yatchenko whose name appears on the title page of the "History of Rus" was the same person as Fedir Petrovych Yatchenko, listed in 1890 in the address book of the Chernihiv gubernia as an "aide to the secretary" of the Starodub regional court. He held the rank of collegiate registrar – the lowest, fourteenth, rank in the Table of Ranks of the Russian Empire. What we know about the Yatchenko family history gives some idea of

[9] "Ruskaia istoriia," title page, fols. 58, 58ᵛ, 59ᵛ.

how the "History of Rus'" could have come into the hands of a Starodub collegiate registrar. Theirs was a well-established noble family of Cossack origin that had lived for generations in Starodub and the surrounding area. In the late eighteenth and early nineteenth centuries they owned serfs in the villages of Artiushkovo, Halensk, and Kolodezek near Starodub, although they were never rich, and the number of serf households steadily diminished. Among the members of the Yatchenko family in the first decades of the nineteenth century was a certain Yefym Yatchenko who taught in the Starodub school. In 1818, one of the many dates to be found in the Starodub manuscript, he began teaching history there and may very well have been involved in the production of the manuscript. Traces of him appear in recently published documents of Mikhail Markov, the supervisor of the Chernihiv school system from 1804 to 1818 and an amateur historian whose research on Ukrainian history we have discussed earlier.

Even more intriguing is another piece of information provided by Markov's documents. They indicate that in the early nineteenth century the Starodub school employed another teacher whose name matches the one on the title page of the Starodub translation of Scherer – that of Radkevych. The Starodub teacher Radkevych mentioned by Markov had the same first name and patronymic as the alleged compiler of the eighteenth-century manuscript: Yakiv Fedorovych. What are the chances that there were two Yakiv Fedorovych Radkevyches living in Starodub at more or less the same time, given that a text allegedly composed by one of them in 1734 could not have come into existence before 1788? This is an impossible proposition. It is far more likely that there was only one individual of that name, possibly the one who taught in Starodub in the early nineteenth century. He could indeed have copied or had in his possession a copy of "A History of Rus'" that ended up with the Yatchenko family. Last but not least, if this Radkevych indeed wrote or possessed a manuscript with one fake date and author's name, could he not have produced or owned another mystification of the same kind – this one not bearing the title "A History of Rus'," like the translation of Scherer's work, but *History of the Rus'*?[10]

Where would one look for answers to these questions? We turned to the collection of the supervisor of the Chernihiv school system in the

---

[10] *Kalendar' Chernigovskoi gubernii na 1891 god* (Chernihiv, 1890), p. 233; Ekaterina Cheplianskaia, *Starodubskii uezd. Sela i zhiteli.* www.debryansk.ru/~mir17/fio_sel.htm, s.v. Artiushkovo; S. Voinov, "Mykhailo Markov: materialy do istoriï uchbovykh zakladiv chernihivs'koï dyrektsiï, 1804–1805 navchal'nyi rik," *Siverians'kyi litopys,* no. 4 (1999): 76–99, here 78, 87–91.

Chernihiv State Archives, which contains the already published documents of Mikhail Markov, and it proved to be a gold mine for our research. The Chernihiv documents make it possible to reconstruct the main stages of Radkevych's professional career and personal life in much more detail than could be done previously. According to the Starodub school reports, Yakiv Radkevych was born in 1763. He began his education at the Kyivan Academy, where he studied Latin, poetics, rhetoric, and philosophy. He then enrolled at the teachers' college in St. Petersburg, where he was trained in "all mathematical sciences, history, geography, and drawing." In February 1789 Radkevych began his teaching career as a second-grade instructor at the "main school" of Novhorod-Siverskyi, where he taught until 1796. Yatchenko, who entered the "main school" sometime around 1794, must have been one of his students there. Radkevych transferred to Starodub in 1796, a year after the establishment of the school in that town.

In Starodub, Radkevych became the teacher of the third grade – a career advance in comparison with Novhorod-Siverskyi. He seemed to be a hard worker and had connections in high places, as becomes apparent from the list of references submitted to the school authorities. If Yatchenko could produce only a letter of support from the director of the Novhorod-Siverskyi main school, Radkevych was able to furnish three letters from people of much higher standing than the director of a provincial school. In the 1804–5 academic year Radkevych had letters on file from Mikhail Golovin, professor of mathematics and physics at the St. Petersburg teachers' college and a nephew of Russia's most distinguished eighteenth-century scholar, Mikhail Lomonosov; two governors of the Novhorod-Siverskyi vicegerency, Ilia Bibikov (1785–92) and Larion Alekseev (1795–96); and the governor of the New Russia gubernia Mykhailo Myklashevsky (1802–4). The Golovin letter was, of course, the result of Radkevych's efforts as a student in St. Petersburg; Bibikov's and Alekseev's – of his good works in Novhorod-Siverskyi; and Myklashevsky's letter attested to the kind of connections he was able to make after his arrival in Starodub. Radkevych had an education, reputation, and connections that far exceeded anything his Starodub colleagues like Yatchenko could dream of.[11]

Why, then, did he end up in the Starodub county school, giving up hope of a career in the much more prestigious "main school" of Novhorod-Siverskyi? One reason was that by 1796 Novhorod-Siverskyi had ceased to be the center of a vicegerency. Paul I, eager to undo whatever

---

[11] Chernihiv State Archives, fond 229, op. 1, no. 1, fols. 3, 7ᵛ, 129–129ᵛ; no. 2, fols. 87, 142ᵛ–143; 203–203ᵛ, 339ᵛ–340.

had been done by his mother, Catherine II, abolished the vicegerencies and replaced them with gubernias, whose borders did not coincide with those of the former administrative units. Novhorod-Siverskyi suffered directly from Paul's administrative reform. Technically it was reduced to the level of Starodub, becoming a county center. People began to leave Novhorod-Siverskyi *en masse*. Bureaucrats went mainly to Chernihiv, the center of the new Little Russia gubernia, which encompassed all the former territories of the Hetmanate. Radkevych decided to go instead to Starodub, where another grade was being added to the two-grade county school.

If Paul's administrative reform was one reason for the young teacher's move, another may well have been related to his family life. Sometime in 1789, very soon after his arrival in Novhorod-Siverskyi from St. Petersburg, Radkevych married Dokiia (Yevdokiia) Ivanivna Zankovska. The bride came from a prominent Cossack officer family whose possessions and power base were in and around Starodub. Dokiia's father, Ivan Zankovsky, had served in the 1750s as an aide-de-camp in the Starodub regiment. In 1790 Dokiia gave birth to the couple's first child, a son named Andrii. Six years later the Radkevyches were blessed with a daughter, Varvara. Moving closer to Dokiia's family made good sense for a young family. Then there was the issue of property. In the 1790s Yakiv Radkevych became the owner of four households in Artiushkovo, a village in close proximity to Starodub. Most probably it was part of Dokiia's dowry.

Family, career opportunities, land, and serfs all bound Yakiv Radkevych, a recent settler in the Chernihiv region (where there were no other Radkevyches), to Starodub. Through the Zankovskys he could gain access to the best homes in the area. Dokiia's brother, Andrii Ivanovych Zankovsky, who began his career with the modest title of fellow of the standard in the Cossack service, had made a spectacular advance by the 1790s, serving "under Count O. A. Bezborodko in the postal service." He also married, although briefly, into the Myklashevsky family. After the death of his first wife, Andrii Zankovsky married Maryna Lyshen, an offspring of another Cossack officer family. Maryna's father, Andrii Lyshen, was in charge of the reorganization of the Hetmanate's archives in the 1740s. Her brother Mykhailo Lyshen married into the Shyrai family. Andrii Zankovsky eventually attained the fifth rank in the imperial Table of Ranks, becoming a state councillor. He owned twenty-three serfs in the village of Piatovsk, a mere 9 km from Starodub.[12]

[12] Chernihiv State Archives, fond 229, op. 1, no. 2, fols. 142^v–143; Vadim Modzalevskii, *Malorossiiskii rodoslovnik*, 4 vols. (Kyiv, 1908–14), II: 12; III: 158, 162; V. M. Modzalevs'kyi, *Malorosiis'kyi rodoslovnyk*, vol. v, vyp. 5 (Kyiv and St. Petersburg, 2004), p. 15; A. I. Khanenko, "Opisanie mestnostei

Starodub did not make Radkevych rich, but it turned out to be not the worst place for a young and apparently ambitious teacher when it came to career prospects. Radkevych advanced through the imperial ranks with breathtaking speed. When he began his career in Starodub, he held the fourteenth rank in the imperial table and remained at that level until 1798, but he advanced to the twelfth rank in 1799 and to the ninth rank in 1800. He reached his highest (sixth) rank of collegiate councillor in January 1821. Radkevych's superiors considered him an ideal teacher and a pillar of the Starodub educational system. One of the reports to Chernihiv characterized him as follows: "In addition to his teaching subjects, he knows poetry, rhetoric, and philosophy, all the mathematical sciences, drawing, and Latin; thanks to his exceptional diligence and zeal in the fulfillment of his duties, as well as his honesty and good behavior, he has won general praise and respect." In 1808 Radkevych received permission to add Latin as one of his teaching subjects. He would also teach German. In 1809 he submitted a collection of mathematical exercises to his superiors and was thanked for the effort. In July 1812 Radkevych reached the peak of his career as a schoolteacher and administrator. That year he was charged with the task of establishing new schools in the Starodub region, assuming the title of director of the newly opened schools.[13]

By Starodub standards, Radkevych had attained a high service rank. He also developed a reputation that extended beyond his school. In 1814, when the local officials compiled a list of Starodub nobles to be awarded a medal for services to the state during Napoleon's invasion of Russia, the court councillor (seventh rank) Radkevych was no. 17 on that hierarchically arranged list, which began with the names of such local luminaries as Mykhailo Myklashevsky and Stepan Shyrai. Altogether there were 202 Starodub noblemen who made it onto the award list: no. 17 was thus an exceptionally high standing. Radkevych's name appears on the list immediately after that of Ivan Nazarev, director of the Starodub school and his immediate superior, who also held the rank of court councillor. The nephew of Radkevych's wife, Dokiia, and a son of her influential brother, the army captain Illia Andriiovych Zankovsky, was no. 45 on the list, and Radkevych's colleague Yefym Ivanovych Yatchenko was no. 146. To be sure, official rank was not everything – origins and wealth counted as much, if not more, in

Chernigovskoi gubernii v predelakh byvshego Starodubskogo polka," *Kalendar' Chernigovskoi gubernii na 1891 god* (Chernihiv, 1890), p. 126; Cheplianskaia, *Starodubskii uezd*, s.v. Piatovsk.
[13] Chernihiv State Archives, fond 229, op. 1, no. 4, fol. 124; no. 12, fol. 142; no. 36, fol. 972ᵛ.

provincial society of the day – but it certainly helped Radkevych open doors in Starodub that would otherwise have been closed to him.[14]

From the records of the Church of St. Simeon in Starodub, to which Radkevych and his family belonged, we know that in January 1816 Radkevych buried his wife, Dokiia. We have no information about the fate of his son, but his daughter Varvara was married in 1819 to Captain Yakiv Khmelevsky, who owned the village of Khmelivka in the Starodub region. Radkevych continued to live in the Starodub house, where he was assisted by his peasant serf, Deomid Vozkrianka. He also continued to teach in the Starodub school. Radkevych is last mentioned in the Starodub school reports for the academic year 1829–30. By that time he was sixty-seven years old and probably in poor health. In the last years of Radkevych's service, the religion classes that he had taught for decades were reassigned to a local priest, his salary was reduced, and his signature disappeared from school documents – they would be signed by a secretary instead. According to church records, Yakiv Radkevych died on May 5, 1830.[15]

This is an intriguing record. It tells us that Yakiv Fedorovych Radkevych of Starodub had good reason to produce or keep in his library a Russian translation of Scherer's *Annales*. It also offers grounds to add Radkevych to our list of "unusual suspects" who might be responsible for the production of the *History of the Rus'*. Given his origins, education, professional experience, family connections, and standing in Starodub society, Radkevych seems at least as qualified as any of them. But can he pass the test that many others failed? Is there any indication that Radkevych was capable not only of reading but also of writing texts dealing with Ukrainian history? Indeed there is. According to the Chernihiv archives, in the summer of 1806 he produced a topographical description of Starodub and its county.

What was such a description, and what did its preparation involve? At the beginning of the nineteenth century, in anticipation of major progressive reforms, advisors to the new Russian emperor, Alexander I, tried to get their hands on as much information as possible about the state of the empire. "Topographical" descriptions of the empire had been prepared in the past on a fairly regular basis, but this time the process and product would be different. The new descriptions would be generated with the assistance of the freshly created network of imperial schools and teachers

---

[14] Chernihiv State Archives, fond 133, op. 1, no. 382, fol. 179ff.; fond 229, op. 1, no. 51, fols. 1260–61.
[15] Chernihiv State Archives, fond 229, op. 1, no. 51, fol. 1276–1276ᵛ; Briansk State Archives, fond 255, op. 1, no. 267, fol. 85ᵛ, 95ᵛ, 121ᵛ, 146ᵛ.

employed by them. The initiative came from Nikolai Novosiltsev, a member of Alexander's privy council, his future representative in Poland, and the drafter of a variant of the Russian constitution that met with the tsar's approval. In 1804, in his capacity as supervisor of the St. Petersburg and (temporarily) Kharkiv educational districts, Novosiltsev approached Illia Fedorovych Tymkovsky, a professor at Kharkiv University and inspector of the Kharkiv educational district, asking him to supplement his report on the condition of the school system in the Chernihiv and Poltava gubernias with topographic and statistical information on the cities, counties, land ownership, industry, agriculture, trade, movement of population, etc. in these two gubernias of the former Hetmanate. The data was to be collected through the directors and teachers of the local schools and submitted to St. Petersburg.[16]

Illia Tymkovsky in turn forwarded Novosiltsev's request to his subordinates in the two gubernias. In Chernihiv it ended up on the desk of the director of the Chernihiv school and head of the gubernia educational district, Mikhail Markov. Markov forwarded the request to the directors of elementary schools, including the one in Starodub. Although the request went to the director of the school, Ivan Nazarev, it was Yakiv Radkevych who was charged with the task. By summer of 1806 he was ready to submit his work to Markov and Tymkovsky. On July 27, 1806 Ivan Nazarev forwarded the "topographic description of Starodub county submitted by a teacher of the Starodub school, Mr. Radkevych," for the attention of Mikhail Markov. The description was received in Chernihiv on August 4. Four days later, Markov wrote to Nazarev, asking him to pass on to Radkevych his assessment of the description. On August 14 Nazarev wrote to Markov, asking him to return the topographic description.

"Your Excellency's instructions of the 8th of this month, under no. 415," wrote Nazarev, "have been conveyed by me to the teacher, Mr. Radkevych, concerning the topographic description, in response to which he expressed a keen desire to correct certain passages of it and supplement others, and for that purpose he most humbly requests that Your Excellency return it to him or, should that be impossible, then at least to delay its dispatch to the university, which I have the honor to report to Your Excellency." Markov apparently asked for more accurate information, and Radkevych

---

[16] P. M. Dobrovol'skii, "Topograficheskie opisaniia gorodov Chernigova, Nezhina i Sosnitsy s ikh povetami (rukopisi 1783 g.)," *Trudy Chernigovskoi gubernskoi arkhivnoi komissii*, ed. P. M. Dobrovol'skii (Chernihiv, 1902), vyp. 4, otd. 2, pp. 137–222, here 142–49.

obliged. He completed his corrections and additions over the next few weeks, and on October 6, 1806 Nazarev sent Markov the revised version of Radkevych's "Topographic description of the county and city of Starodub."[17]

We do not know what exactly Markov asked Radkevych to do, but we do know that a few years later Markov would embark on the project of producing not just a "topographic" but also a historical, geographic, and statistical description of Chernihiv gubernia. Drafts of individual chapters of that work have been preserved as part of Markov's papers, now housed in the manuscript collection of the Russian State Library in Moscow. They indicate Markov's deep interest in the history of the region, which was all but ignored by Novosiltsev. In 1806 Markov published his first historical work, a response to a letter sent to him by certain T. K. (probably Tymofii Kalynsky, a Chernihiv expert on issues of noble rights and Cossack history) about the early history of Chernihiv and the origins of its name. Materials collected by Markov for a historical and topographic description of Chernihiv gubernia include a historical essay on Starodub from Kyivan times on. At least part of the data for that essay may have come from Markov's Starodub subordinate, Yakiv Radkevych.[18]

In October 1806, when Radkevych completed revisions to the original version of his topographic description, Markov wasted no time in reading the manuscript. It was sent from Starodub to Chernihiv on October 6. A week later, Nazarev reported to Markov that Radkevych had been informed about Markov's "instructions ... concerning the topographic description." We do not know their content, but two weeks later, on October 26, Markov received a copy of a letter signed by Radkevych and addressed to his immediate superior, Ivan Nazarev. It read: "Requiring a leave of absence to make two visits to the village of Hryniv, to the home of His Highness Count Illia Oleksandrovych Bezborodko, and expecting to spend no more than eight days on both visits, I most humbly request His Excellency the director of schools [Mikhail Markov] to intercede on my behalf for such permission. This petition is submitted by the teacher of the third grade of the Starodub school, Yakiv Radkevych." Permission was granted, and on November 5, 1806 Radkevych was informed that he could travel to Hryniv.

---

[17] Chernihiv State Archives, fond 229, op. 1, no. 3, fols. 412, 489, 725.

[18] M. M[arkov], "Pis'mo v Chernigovskuiu gimnaziiu o drevnosti goroda Chernigova s mneniem o proizvedenii nazvaniia ego, T. K., s otvetom na sie pis'mo M. M.," *Litsei* 2 (18–26): 1; Russian State Library, Manuscript Division, fond 256, no. 271, fols. 251–68.

The Hryniv palace housed, as we know from the story of the discovery of the *History*, a good library, and Radkevych's trip to the palace soon after submitting his topographic description of Starodub might very well mean that he was going there to continue his research. It is hard to imagine any other reason for an officially approved trip by a provincial teacher to the estate of a high imperial official. Even if one assumes that Radkevych knew Illia Bezborodko through family connections, and that the count wanted to see him for whatever reason, including consultations on the founding of the Nizhyn lyceum, which was being planned at the time, it can hardly be supposed that instead of summoning Radkevych right away, Bezborodko gave him an open invitation whose timing would depend on Markov's decision. Radkevych's letter to Nazarev indicates that he knew how much time he needed to accomplish his mission but had no specific dates in mind. One of the few things that could interest a provincial teacher in Hryniv and could wait indefinitely for his arrival was the library.[19]

Whatever the reason for Radkevych's trip to Hryniv, the documents we have at our disposal establish an all-important link between one of our suspects and the place where a manuscript *History of the Rus'* was found some twenty years after Radkevych's visit. If Radkevych was a welcome guest at the estate in 1806, he may also have been there before and after November of that year. Perhaps he made use of the library to write not only his topographic description of Starodub but also a work such as the *History of the Rus'* and left a copy of it there. Or was the work commissioned by the owners of the palace? We could go on making suggestions of this kind, but they cannot be confirmed on the basis of the currently available source base, including the documents preserved in the "Radkevych files" of the Chernihiv archives. What we can do, however, is approach the problem from a different angle and return to the text of the *History* in the hope of finding specific features that fit the profile of Yakiv Radkevych. We must go once again step by step through the episodes of the *History of the Rus'* that may bear on the author's origins, upbringing, education, and circumstances attending the creation of the work.

Let us begin with his origins. All students of the *History* without exception have believed that the author came from the Cossack gentry, whose noble rights were not above reproach. We also know that he despised nobles claiming foreign origins. Does Radkevych fit this profile?

---

[19] Chernihiv State Archives, fond 229, op. 1, no. 3, fols. 725, 737, 747, 820; O. P. Ohloblyn, *Do pytannia pro avtora "Istoriï Rusiv"* (Kyiv, 1998), pp. 27–34.

We know from the Starodub school reports that he claimed noble origins and even supplied documents to establish them. But we do not have those documents, nor do we know the precise noble status to which he laid claim: the brief biographical notes preserved in the school reports are too sketchy. It is possible, however, to answer these questions on the basis of the records of the Kyivan Academy, where we know he studied before going to the St. Petersburg teachers' college in 1787. Reports on student performance for 1777 and 1780 confirm the Chernihiv data about Radkevych's age, study at the Kyivan Academy, and courses taken there, but they also contain an anomaly. Yakiv Radkevych is listed in both Kyiv reports as the son of Fedir Radkevych, a priest at the Church of the Nativity of the Theotokos in the village of Novosilky (Kyiv regiment). This is an interesting twist. What was the basis of Radkevych's claim to noble status? Data from the Kyivan Cave Monastery, to whose ecclesiastical jurisdiction the Novosilky parish belonged, show that not only Yakiv's father but also his grandfather were priests.[20]

Despite Yakiv Radkevych's priestly origins, his claim to noble status was never questioned by his Starodub superiors, meaning that he was able to provide legitimate proof of his pedigree. This could only mean that before the Radkevyches became priests, they had been Cossack officers of some importance. We know of at least one officer named Radkevych who served in the Cossack Host in its last decades of existence. A certain Andrii Radkevych was listed as acting captain of a Lubny regimental company in 1768. This was a rank that would entitle its holder to claim noble status. According to nobiliary registers of the late eighteenth century, there were numerous Radkevyches in Lubny, Pereiaslav, and Myrhorod counties. The Radkevyches of Lubny also included priests. In the 1760s one of them, Oleksandr Radkevych, attended the Kyivan Academy. He came from the village of Nekhrystovka in the Lubny region, where his father, Fedir Petrovych Radkevych, served as a priest.[21]

There is good reason to believe that while the Radkevyches were new to the Chernihiv and Kyiv regions, they were well established as a noble

[20] Chernihiv State Archives, fond 229, op. 1, no. 1, fol. 603; no. 2, fols. 37, 175^v, 228^v–229, 299^v–300, 339^v–40; no. 3, fols. 239–40; Central State Historical Archives of Ukraine (Kyiv), fond 127, op. 1043, no. 18, fol. 20^v; op. 1020, no. 4950, fol. 14; State Archives of the City of Kyiv, fond 314 (Kyievo-Pechers'ke dukhovne pravlinnia, op. 1, no. 326, fol. 9^v).

[21] Volodymyr Kryvosheia, *Ukraïns'ka kozats'ka starshyna*, pt. 1, *Uridnyky het'mans'koï administratsii*, 2nd edn. (Kyiv, 2005), p. 222; Chernihiv State Archives, fond 133, op. 2, no. 1, fols. 185, 215, 781^v; no. 8, fol. 298^v; *Opysy Livoberezhnoï Ukraïny kintsia XVIII–pochatku XIX st.*, comp. T. B. Anan'ieva (Kyiv, 1997), pp. 139, 267; *Akty i dokumenty, otnosiashchiesia k istorii Kievskoi Akademii*, otd. 2, vol. III, ed. N. I. Petrov (Kyiv, 1906), p. 290.

family in the southern part of the former Hetmanate. Noble status and the priestly profession went hand in hand among some members of the family. But if Yakiv Radkevych was indeed the author of the *History of the Rus'*, should not this close connection between priesthood and noble status derived from Cossack service find reflection in the text of the work? In fact it does. The author of the *History* was opposed to the clergy joining the nobility, but he had no compunction about nobles joining the ranks of the clergy. "The nobility, according to the example of all peoples and states," wrote the anonymous author, "naturally consisted of deserving and eminent clans in the land, and in Rus' it was always known as the knighthood ... The clergy, coming from the knighthood by election of deserving individuals, was distinguished from it only for service to God, and enjoyed the same rights with regard to civic affairs."[22]

While the Radkevyches came from the ranks of Cossack officers who later claimed noble status, their lineage by no means resembled that of the Cossack aristocracy, which included hetmans, officers of the general staff, and colonels. The Radkevyches never rose above the level of company officers – a status dangerously close to rank-and-file Cossack for anyone aspiring to recognition as a noble. It was this very stratum of Cossack descendants that battled the Heraldry Office for such recognition in the early nineteenth century. The author of the *History of the Rus'*, whoever he may have been, seems to have had nothing against enhancing the historical record of the Radkevych family. In the pages of the *History* we encounter an entirely fictitious general aide-de-camp called Rodak, in whom it is tempting to recognize a mythical founder of the Radkevych clan. Adding the compounded suffixes "ev" and "ych" to "Rodak," one easily gets the surname "Rodkevych," which means "son of Rodak" and differs from "Radkevych" by a mere letter. The Ukrainian noun *rodak*, which means "kinsman" and is derived from *rid*, meaning lineage, descent, or pedigree, would be a perfect starting point for anyone seeking to enhance his family origins.

In the pages of the *History*, Rodak's fate is closely associated with that of the alleged founder of the Khudorba family, Colonel Kindrat Khudorbai. When Bohdan Khmelnytsky allegedly sent Khudorbai to Siveria, Rodak and two other colonels made their way to the Prypiat River, heading for the borders of the Grand Duchy of Lithuania. Later Khudorbai joined Rodak, who led an army in pursuit of Janusz Radziwiłł's Lithuanian troops. They caught up with them near the town of Horodnia and

---

[22] *Istoriia Rusov*, pp. 7–8.

defeated them. After that, according to the *History*, "Rodak's corps set off with Khudorbai for Novhorod-Siverskyi." Rodak is portrayed as a figure more important than Khudorbai. Not only does he outrank Khudorbai, but he is also closer to Khmelnytsky and distinguishes himself in a region of prime importance to the author of the *History*, allegedly taking Novhorod-Siverskyi, Chernihiv, and Starodub from the Poles. "Rodak, encountering neither assistance nor opposition from the burghers because of their small numbers," wrote the author of the *History* about the Cossack siege of Novhorod-Siverskyi, "calmly approached the town and, making camp near the Yaroslav streams, or brooks, led an attack on the town from the Zubriv ravine, named after the princely menagerie that used to be there and the animals, known as bison (*zubry*), that used to be kept there." The importance of Rodak was not lost on readers of the *History*. Mykola Kostomarov turned him and other alleged participants in the siege of Novhorod-Siverskyi, as described in the *History*, into a character in his poem "The Honest Truth." He appears there under the name "Radan."[23]

Having attempted to match Radkevych's origins with those of the author of the *History*, let us try to do the same with their educational backgrounds and experiences. Are there any indications that the anonymous author studied at the Kyivan Academy and the St. Petersburg teachers' college, as Radkevych did? Yes, there are. Some passages of the *History* betray its author's familiarity with the Kyivan Academy as it existed in the late eighteenth and early nineteenth centuries. For example, in describing the accomplishments of Hetman Petro Konashevych-Sahaidachny, who died in 1622, the anonymous author claims that he restored the Kyivan Academy in the Kyiv Brotherhood Monastery. That was indeed the relationship between the academy and the monastery in the second half of the eighteenth century, but not in the seventeenth. The author's detailed description of the greetings offered by students of the academy to Empress Elizaveta Petrovna in 1744 (soon after she visited Kozelets, the home town of her partner, Oleksii Rozumovsky) reveals his good knowledge of Kyiv topography, especially the Podil quarter, where the academy was located. The author mentions, for example, that before the reception prepared for Elizabeth by the Kyivans, an actor impersonating the founder of the city, Prince Kyi, met the empress "at the end of the bridge on the bank of the Dnieper." No further explanation follows: the author simply assumes that

---

[23] *Ibid.*, pp. 68, 74–77; Mykhailo Vozniak, *Psevdo-Konys'kyi i Psevdo-Poletyka* (Istoriia Rusov u literaturi ta nautsi) (Lviv and Kyiv, 1939), p. 27.

everyone knows the location he has in mind. Indeed, most of the references to Kyiv in the *History* pertain either to the academy or to the Podil.[24]

Ironically, it is precisely in his discussion of the academy's history that the anonymous author betrays his familiarity with other institutions of higher learning. On the first page of the *History* there is a reference to the "History of the Venerable Nestor of the Caves and his successors and predecessors who wrote that history, all of whom were members of the academy or of that main school established among the Slavs in the city of Kyiv by the Greek philosopher Cyril soon after the Christian religion had been instituted there." The author then mentions "the elective prince or hetman of Rus', [Petro] Sahaidachny, and the metropolitan of Kyiv, Petro Mohyla, who restored the ancient academy." Moving the origins of the Kyivan Academy back to princely times and referring to it as the "main school" got the anonymous author into trouble with some of his nineteenth-century critics, who questioned the accuracy of his account. But this anachronistic statement can also give us an indication of the particular period in which the *History* was written and offer clues about the author's educational background.

The term "main school" (*glavnoe uchilishche*) was derived, in all probability, from the name of the Main Public School (*glavnoe narodnoe uchilishche*) established in St. Petersburg in 1783. For three years, until 1786, it included a teachers' college that was then separated from it. The professors at the Main Public School and the teachers' college were closely associated with the St. Petersburg Imperial Academy of Sciences – in other words, they were "academics" (*akademiki*), as on the first page of the *History*. That applied to Radkevych's mentor, Mikhail Golovin, who was an adjunct and then honorary member of the Imperial Academy of Sciences. Also associated with the academy was the director of the teachers' college and the "main school," Fedor Ivanovich de Mirievo (Janković Mirijewski), who wrote the first textbook of Russian history since the *Synopsis* of 1674. He became a member of the academy in 1783. Although it was no secret that the professors of the "main school" were also "academicians," this was not a fact that people unfamiliar with St. Petersburg educational institutions could readily be expected to know.[25]

---

[24] *Istoriia Rusov*, pp. i–ii, 48, 244.
[25] *Ibid.*, p. 1; A. Voronov, *Fedor Ivanovich Iankovich de-Mirievo ili narodnye uchilishcha v Rossii pri imperatritse Ekaterine II* (St. Petersburg, 1858); N. V. Sedova, "Istoriia pedagogicheskogo obrazovaniia v Rossii," pp. 260–73, here 266–68, http://ideashistory.org.ru/pdfs/33sedova.pdf; "Mikhail Evseevich Golovin," www.edu.delfa.net/cabinet/history/perv.html.

There are also indications that the author of the *History* was familiar with the topography of St. Petersburg. In his discussion of the arrest of Acting Hetman Pavlo Polubotok and his associates in the imperial capital, the anonymous author writes that the authorities placed "a secure guard around their quarters, which were at the Trinity wharf by the coffee-house." This could only have been written by an author who had been to St. Petersburg. It should be noted that, aside from Novhorod-Siverskyi, Kyiv, and Chernihiv, St. Petersburg is the only city in which the author of the *History* identifies a very specific location. He does not do so in references to Moscow. The author's familiarity with both Kyiv and St. Petersburg, his interest in the history of the Kyivan Academy, and his readiness to use the term "main school" to denote institutions of higher learning all point to Radkevych as a possible author of the *History*.[26]

There are also interesting connections to be made between the author and people with whom Radkevych studied in St. Petersburg. For two years, from December 1786 to December 1788, he attended the same classes as Maksym Berlynsky, the likely opponent of the author of the *History of the Rus'*, and himself a writer of numerous texts on the history of Kyiv and Ukraine. Berlynsky, who was born in 1764 and enrolled at the Kyivan Academy at the age of twelve, was a student of theology when he was sent to St. Petersburg along with his brother, Matvii. In 1788, after two years of study, he returned to Kyiv to teach in a local school. Kyiv was then the center of a vicegerency. So was Novhorod-Siverskyi, where Radkevych began his teaching career in February 1789. Thus the careers of the two men initially developed in unison. Their paths diverged with the abolition of the Novhorod-Siverskyi vicegerency and Radkevych's move to Starodub. Berlynsky stayed in Kyiv and became a published author; Radkevych never published anything. Were they friends or perhaps rivals in Kyiv and St. Petersburg? They were certainly acquainted during their student years and probably followed each other's careers after their return to Ukraine.[27]

There is no lack of episodes in Radkevych's life after his graduation from the St. Petersburg teachers' college that would support the hypothesis of his authorship of the *History*. For eight years, from 1789 to 1796, Radkevych lived and taught in Novhorod-Siverskyi, the topography of which was so well known to the author of the *History*. During that period

---

[26] *Istoriia Rusov*, pp. 39, 228.
[27] *Akty i dokumenty, otnosiashchiesia k istorii Kievskoi Akademii*, otd. 2, vol. v, pp. 167–75; *Istoriia Rusov*, pp. 31, 214, 222.

he had ample opportunity not only to become familiar with the urban landscape but also to make the acquaintance of numerous representatives of the Khudorba family who lived in the town and its environs. He might also have come to know the manuscript of the Khudorba History – an important *sine qua non* for any candidate author of the *History of the Rus'*. Radkevych's move to Starodub led to his taking on history as a teaching subject, which he continued to do until 1818, and religion, which he taught until the late 1820s. Starodub was a perfect location for acquainting oneself with the legends associated with the Balykino icon of the Mother of God: the anonymous author wrote about them in connection with Mazepa's revolt. According to materials collected by Mikhail Markov in the early nineteenth century, the Balykino icon was on display in one of the Starodub churches.[28]

Radkevych's teaching position at the Starodub school can also explain a number of other mysteries surrounding the *History*. As argued earlier, there is good reason to believe that its author was familiar with *Ukrainskii vestnik*, published between 1816 and 1819 by professors of Kharkiv University and delivered to the Starodub school by subscription. An important article that appeared in the periodical in 1816 and may have influenced the author of the *History of the Rus'* dealt with the origins of the term "Ukraine." It was written by none other than Radkevych's superior in Chernihiv, Mikhail Markov, who claimed that the term had come into use after the Polish authorities resettled the Rus' population to the lower reaches of the Dnieper, Buh, and Dnister rivers. This belief was shared at the time by other historians of Ukraine, including Maksym Berlynsky, who was most probably the object of the anonymous author's protest, but Markov's article, with its presentation of a similar viewpoint, might well have triggered the author's outburst.[29]

Given Markov's position on the origins of the term "Ukraine" and the anonymous author's stand on the question, it is not too difficult to imagine why the author, if he was indeed Radkevych, would be reluctant to disseminate his work under his own name and prefer to hide behind the names of Heorhii Konysky and Hryhorii Poletyka. Unlike Markov, the author of the *History of the Rus'* had never broken into the world of academic scholarship. His narrative was highly engaging, but the growing

---

[28] Russian State Library, Manuscript Division, fond 256, no. 271, fol. 254ᵛ.

[29] Mikhail Markov, "Zamechanie na stat'iu o Malorossii, pomeshchennuiu vo 2-i i 3-i knizhkakh *Ukrainskogo vestnika,*" *Ukrainskii vestnik*, no. 8 (1816): 128–37; Oleh Zhurba, *Stanovlennia ukraïns'koï arkheohrafiï: liudy, ideï, instytutsiï* (Dnipropetrovsk, 2003), pp. 147–49; *Istoriia Rusov*, pp. iii–iv.

professionalization of historical writing had little impact on him. He was prepared to recreate the past on the basis of common sense, popular memory, and a relatively limited number of narrative sources. Taking a position contrary to the one maintained by Markov, Berlynsky, and other experts in the field, the author would have done well to conceal his identity; otherwise he could have been exposed and perhaps even have lost his job. It is worth noting in this regard that the *History of the Rus'*, whose first dated manuscript comes from 1818, began its rise to prominence only after Markov's death, which occurred unexpectedly in the summer of 1819.

Radkevych's familiarity with *Ukrainskii vestnik* and his employment by the school system, which was supervised by people with close ties to the publishers of the journal, may also explain how it came about that *Ukrainskii vestnik* was probably the first publication to have printed a story borrowed from the *History of the Rus'*. As noted by Volodymyr Kravchenko, one of the most insightful present-day scholars of the *History*, in 1819 Petro Hulak-Artemovsky, an activist on the Kharkiv cultural scene, published a short story from the times of Hetman Demian Mnohohrishny in *Ukrainskii vestnik*. It displayed clear textual parallels with the *History of the Rus'*. Whether Hulak, like Ryleev after him, took the story from the manuscript (there is no indication that he was familiar with other parts of the *History*), or both he and the anonymous author used the same source, the same conclusion obtains: there had to be some connection between the author and the publishers of *Vestnik*.[30]

Such a connection is readily available in the person of the inspector of the Kharkiv school system, Professor Illia Tymkovsky of Kharkiv University. It was through him that Radkevych submitted a collection of mathematical exercises to the administration of the Kharkiv educational district in 1809. We also know that, aside from his interest in mathematics and physics, Tymkovsky collected historiographic materials. These included some of the works of the Kharkiv amateur historian Illia Kvitka, whose essays eventually made it into *Ukrainskii vestnik*. Thus Radkevych not only had access to the journal but also contacts with people involved in its publication.[31]

Have we finally tracked down our man? Let us summarize the circumstantial evidence supporting the hypothesis that Yakiv Radkevych was the

---

[30] Kravchenko, *Narysy*, p. 101; Kravchenko, "*Istoriia Rusiv* u suchasnykh interpretatsiiakh," in *Synopsis: A Collection of Essays in Honour of Zenon E. Kohut*, ed. Serhii Plokhy and Frank E. Sysyn (Edmonton, 2005), pp. 275–94.

[31] Chernihiv State Archives, fond 229, op. 1, d. 5, fol. 155; Oleksander Ohloblyn, *Liudy staroï Ukraïny* (Munich, 1959), pp. 262–69; Zhurba, *Stanovlennia*, pp. 120–37.

author or coauthor of the *History*. There is much in Radkevych's origins, upbringing, education, and career to make him a prime suspect in the case. Coming from a priestly family that claimed noble status and had close links to the Cossack officer stratum, he had the right social qualifications for the job. His years of study at the Kyivan Academy and the St. Petersburg teachers' college gave him the right kind of education, as well as familiarity with two important centers of the empire whose topography was well known to the author of the *History*. Radkevych's teaching career, first in Novhorod-Siverskyi and then in Starodub, acquainted him with two other localities that feature prominently in the *History*. It also placed him in the center of the region where the *History* was produced and began its general dissemination.

Radkevych's teaching career also put him in touch with people who were (or may have been) directly involved in the production of the *History*. In Novhorod-Siverskyi those people may have included the Khudorbas. In Starodub and environs, they included Mykhailo Myklashevsky and, possibly, Illia Bezborodko. Another important circle with which Radkevych maintained close contact was centered on the leadership of the Kharkiv educational district and publishers of *Ukrainskii vestnik*, who arguably were the first intellectuals to get their hands on the *History*. Radkevych's access to both these circles, his record of writing on Starodub topics, his travel to the Hryniv estate with its library, and his ownership of a copy of the Russian translation of Scherer, which was known to the anonymous author of the *History*, make him a particularly important suspect in our eyes – probably the most important so far.

Radkevych certainly did not belong to the established, well-to-do stratum of the Ukrainian nobility – a characteristic often attributed to the author of the *History*. But one does not have to belong to a particular circle in order to express its opinions, and Radkevych's acquaintance with people such as Bibikov, Alekseev, Myklashevsky, and Bezborodko is a matter of record. A similar assumption concerns the author's military background, as evidenced by his penchant for battle scenes and his familiarity with southern Ukraine, the theater of military operations in the Russo-Turkish wars. But it would be hard to claim on the basis of the *History* that the author's knowledge of military tactics surpassed that of an average writer of the period, in which newspapers and journals avidly covered wars and military campaigns, and salons were full of retired generals and officers only too happy to recount their war stories.

There are, however, authorial statements in the *History* that raise serious questions about Radkevych's authorship of the text. One of them occurs in the introduction, where the author dismisses the work of his opponent (most probably Berlynsky) as a "paltry little history textbook." He actually uses this term twice. It is quite difficult to imagine a teacher dismissing a textbook written by a colleague, even an opponent, with such condescension. Nor would it have been in character for a lifelong teacher such as Radkevych to accuse an opponent of never having gone beyond the walls of his school. It is equally difficult to imagine a teacher of history making daily use of a textbook produced by one of his former professors and not being influenced by it. Yet there is no textual connection between the *History of the Rus'* and the textbook of Russian history written by Fedor de Mirievo, the founder and director of the St. Petersburg teachers' college attended by Radkevych. His textbook, which was widely used in the schools of the empire in the late eighteenth and early nineteenth centuries, would have been known to any teacher of history. Then there is the problem of the absence of obvious textual parallels between the *History of the Rus'* and the only text of Radkevych's authorship in our possession. At the Starodub school graduation ceremony in 1818, Radkevych delivered a speech whose text was forwarded to Chernihiv school authorities and preserved in the local archives. The speech contains more than enough evidence that Radkevych shared many elements of Enlightenment ideology with the author of the *History*, including its emphasis on education, the common good, and laws of social development. But the Russian language of the speech seems too polished for the author of the *History*. Nor do we find any specific characteristics that would allow us to link the speech to the *History of the Rus'*.[32]

We seemed so close to cracking the case! Perhaps we still are, but for the time being it is best to be cautious. If Radkevych was indeed the author of the *History* – and many elements of our analysis show that he may have been – he would have needed a coauthor or editor. As with our previous "unusual suspects," we have no choice but temporarily to close the "Radkevych case." We shall return to it, as well as to other cold cases of ours, as more evidence is turned up by our ongoing investigation. We are about to embark on its most critical phase.

---

[32] F. I. de Mirievo, *Kratkaia Rossiiskaia istoriia* (multiple editions); Stephen Velychenko, *National History as Cultural Process* (Edmonton, 1992), pp. 90–91. For the text of Radkevych's speech, see Chernihiv State Archives, fond 229, op. 1, no. 13, fols. 666–68ᵛ.

PART V

A family circle

CHAPTER 15

A missing name

Ukrainian admirers of the Cossack past and devotees of Cossack tradition got a strong boost in December 2004 with the victory of the democratic Orange Revolution. The newly elected president of Ukraine, Viktor Yushchenko, was a collector of Ukrainian antiques and a history buff. He was convinced that Ukrainians lacked a strong national identity and believed that promoting pride in the country's history was the best way to deal with the deficiencies of its postcolonial heritage. Cossack history had a special appeal to President Yushchenko. On the day before his inauguration, Yushchenko was elected to the honorific office of hetman of Ukraine by the Great Council of Ukrainian Cossacks assembled on St. Sophia Square in downtown Kyiv. In his speech to the council, Yushchenko proudly noted his Cossack roots: he later claimed that the mother of Hetman Ivan Mazepa came from his native village of Khoruzhivka in the Siverian region of Ukraine.

During the first year of his presidency, Yushchenko created a special Baturyn Fund to support reconstruction of the palace of the last hetman of Ukraine, Kyrylo Rozumovsky, in the former Cossack stronghold of Baturyn. The initiative had strong political and cultural undertones. The town of Baturyn has a rich and tragic history. It was the seat of Ivan Mazepa, and in the fall of 1708, when the hetman switched sides and joined the advancing army of Charles XII, Baturyn was captured by Aleksandr Menshikov on the orders of Peter I. Cossack chroniclers reported that after taking the town, Menshikov massacred its entire population. The author of the *History of the Rus'* devoted some of the most memorable pages of his work to a description of the Baturyn massacre. Archaeologists who began their work there in the mid 1990s found numerous skeletons of young and old victims of the massacre, both male and female. Estimates of their number range from ten to fourteen thousand. Rumor has it that in the summer of 2009, when Russian officials proposed that President Yushchenko and Prime Minister

Vladimir Putin of Russia take part in a ceremony commemorating the tricentenary of the Battle of Poltava (1709), Yushchenko agreed, but on condition that they first go to Baturyn to honor the victims of the sack of the city in 1708. The Russian side refused.[1]

The Baturyn Fund created by President Yushchenko helped continue the excavations of the former Cossack capital. Since 2000 they have been conducted by a joint Ukrainian–Canadian team led by two enthusiasts, Volodymyr Kovalenko of Chernihiv University and Volodymyr Mezentsev of the University of Toronto. Mezentsev and his colleagues became particularly excited when they began the excavation of Ivan Mazepa's palace in Honcharivka near Baturyn. What attracted their attention was a mixture of West European and local Ukrainian elements in the architecture and ornamentation of the palace. "The Western ornamentation of the palace was supplemented with elements of the Kyivan architectural school of the seventeenth and eighteenth centuries," read the press release issued by the archaeologists. "Its entablature friezes were adorned with circular ceramic tiles featuring multicolored glazed relief rosettes. This is an exclusive feature of early modern masonry structures in Kyiv and the Middle Dnieper region. The floors of Mazepa's palace were paved with figured terracotta and blue-green glazed tiles. The heating stoves were revetted with fine tiles (*kakhli*) decorated with floral relief patterns and images of angels with extended wings. This particular representation of angels (*putti*), popular in Cossack art, was adopted from Western Renaissance or baroque painting and sculpture."[2]

The fine decorated tiles found by Mezentsev and his team in Mazepa's palace at Honcharivka were popular features of interior decoration in Cossack Ukraine. They were locally produced and almost standard in Cossack officers' houses throughout the eighteenth century. In their press release, the archaeologists were eager to stress those elements of the palace decoration that linked Ukraine with Western and Central Europe and separated it from Russia. The fine tiles were one such element, and, judging by the text of the *History of the Rus'*, the authors of the press

[1] Andrij Makuch and Volodymyr Mezentsev, "Baturyn," *Encyclopedia of Ukraine* (online version) www.encyclopediaofukraine.com/pages/B/A/Baturyn.htm. "Press Release of the Embassy of Ukraine to the Republic of Estonia," January 21, 2005, http://home.uninet.ee/~embkura/Press-10. htm; "Yushchenko Researches His Genealogy and Connects It with Family of Ivan Mazepa," www. unian.net/eng/news/news-350793.html; "Na prazdnovanie 300-letiia poltavskoi bitvy mozhet priekhat' Putin," http://gazeta.ua/index.php?id=293825&lang=ru.
[2] Volodymyr Mezentsev, "Archeological and Architectural Research Continues in Baturyn," *The Ukrainian Weekly*, April 25, 2010, p. 12.

release got it right. A tile from a heating stove featuring the image of an eagle rather than a winged angel, as in Mazepa's palace, found its way into the pages of the *History*. The episode involving this decorative tile took place in the town of Horsk southwest of Starodub.

An army officer named Yakinf Chekatunov, who was passing through that town and was not treated satisfactorily by its owner [wrote the author of the *History*], happened to see an eagle design painted by a craftsman on the tiles of a stove in one of the rooms of his house. He immediately ordered the arrest of that owner and delivered him to the ministerial office with the denunciation that he was putting flames to the sovereign's coat of arms on his stoves for reasons unknown. The ministerial office, considering this denunciation semitreasonous, interrogated the landowner about his reason for having the sovereign's coat of arms on his stove and putting flames to it. The landowner, bringing in witnesses and swearing an oath by way of evidence, excused himself by saying that he had bought the stove in the small free town of Horodnia from a local potter, Sydir Perepilka. Among a plethora of figures made for the embellishment of stoves, Perepilka had, among animate beings, people's faces, and among birds he had eagles, but it never entered the landowner's head that these might be sacred and restricted, and he bought all the stoves, including the one that had given offense, for the one and only purpose of heating his rooms in winter. Nevertheless, for all the landowner's excuses, the eagles cost him a fine herd of horses and cows, as well as a sum of money.[3]

The Horsk episode, which underlines differences of political and domestic culture between Ukrainian landowners and Russian military officers and administrators, was brought into the *History* in order to condemn the abuses visited upon loyal Cossack officers by the Secret Chancellery, an imperial institution charged with investigating accusations of high treason and cases involving the "word and deed of the sovereign." The episode made a strong impression on readers of the *History*, and not only in Ukraine. The renowned nineteenth-century Russian writer Pavel Melnikov-Pechersky turned Yakinf Chekatunov into a character in one of his short stories, *Old Wives' Tales* (1858). "I see him as if he were before me now," wrote Melnikov-Pechersky. "He was a gray and cunning little old man, to be sure . . . In his youth, back in the days of Empress Anna Ivanovna, he was an army officer and, so they say, treated *khokhly* [derogatory term for Ukrainians] very severely when he was in the Little Russian Privy Chancellery in cases of arrears."[4]

[3] *Istoriia Rusov ili Maloi Rosii. Sochinenie Georgiia Koniskago, Arkhiepiskopa Beloruskago* (Moscow, 1846), pp. 238–39.
[4] Pavel Mel'nikov-Pecherskii, "Babushkiny rosskazni," in *Sobranie sochinenii v 6-ti tomakh*, vol. 1 (Moscow, 1963), pp. 195–240; O. P. Ohloblyn, *Do pytannia pro avtora "Istoriia Rusov"* (Kyiv, 1998), pp. 62–64.

While the name of the perpetrator Chekatunov made such a career in Russian literature, the victim's name remained unknown to the public at large. That was the doing of the anonymous author of the *History*, who would not divulge the name of the mysterious owner of Horsk. How was it that he attracted so much attention and sympathy on the part of the author but remained anonymous to readers of the work? The question is not easy to answer. Oleksander Ohloblyn already pointed out that everyone in the area was aware of the identity of the owner of Horsk. For generations the town belonged to the Borozdnas, a well-established family of Cossack officers whose members included two general standard-bearers of the Hetmanate. Ohloblyn conjectured that the author might have been related to the Borozdnas and therefore refrained from mentioning their names so as to preserve his own anonymity. The scholar had in mind one of the Khanenkos, who were indeed interrelated with the Borozdnas, but his observation has broader significance. If that was indeed the case, then the author may have avoided detection in his day while leaving an important piece of evidence for later scholars.

Whose name is missing from the text of the *History*, and can it help us make progress in finding its author? The first part of the question is relatively easy to answer. The anonymous protagonist of the Horsk story is none other than Ivan Lavrentiiovych Borozdna. In 1708, at the time of Mazepa's revolt, Ivan Lavrentiiovych was a fellow of the standard in the Starodub regiment. In early February 1709 he received Tsar Peter's patent for the village of Medvediv (Medvedovo), half of Horsk, and other possessions, which tells us that whatever he may have been doing during the first stage of Mazepa's rebellion in the fall of 1708, by the end of the winter he had decided to join the tsar's side and was rewarded for doing so. He made a spectacular career, serving first as captain of the Starodub company and then as acting colonel of Starodub. But it all came crashing down in April 1725, when Ivan Borozdna was denounced by his subordinate Yakym Yanzhul, captain of the Topal company.

The denunciation was probably the result of a conflict over the Starodub colonelcy, temporarily held by Borozdna, but the accusation itself was political – a charge of high treason. Yanzhul claimed that when he responded to Borozdna's question, "To whom do you belong?" with the words, "To His Imperial Majesty," Borozdna told him: "He is dead, and the devil take you." The conversation must have taken place after the death of Peter I, and Yanzhul allegedly responded: "But we have Her Highness the Empress," to which Borozdna retorted: "And your mother with her." Both Yanzhul and Borozdna were arrested, taken to the prison of the Little Russian College in Hlukhiv, and tortured. As Borozdna refused to confess, while Yanzhul would not retract his accusation, both were sent to Siberia but then pardoned and allowed to return home. The locals never forgave Yanzhul, and as late as 1734 he petitioned the authorities, asking for a letter prohibiting anyone from accusing him of having denounced Borozdna. The Horsk story, somewhat revised and embellished with new details, was alive and well in the Starodub region, although the name of the perpetrator was changed from Yanzhul to Chekatunov, the name of the victim dropped, and the cursing of the empress replaced with the story about the tsar's eagle.[5]

Could there be a connection between Ivan Borozdna and other members of his family, who lived in the region in the early nineteenth century, and the anonymous author's unexpected silence about the name of the main character in the Horsk episode? The author of the *History* did not shy away from mentioning the Borozdna family name. It comes up once in connection with the appointment of Ivan Vladyslavovych Borozdna to the post of general standard-bearer in 1729. But that episode neither compromised the Borozdnas nor threatened to reveal the real name of the author: it was taken directly from the part of the *Brief Chronicle of Little Russia* composed by Oleksandr Bezborodko and published by Vasyl Ruban in 1777. The Horsk episode was different. Whether the author was protective of the Borozdnas or of himself, one way or another his silence must have resulted from his special consideration for that particular Cossack clan. The head of the Borozdna clan in the early nineteenth century was Petro Ivanovych Borozdna. If we want to learn more about the Borozdnas and their possible relation to the *History of the Rus'*, we would do well to take a closer look at their patriarch.[6]

Petro Borozdna, born in 1765, was a great-grandson of the victim of the Horsk episode, the Starodub captain and acting colonel Ivan Lavrentiiovych Borozdna. The colonel's son and Petro's grandfather, Ivan Ivanovych Borozdna, not only managed to maintain and extend the family possessions after the exile and subsequent death of Ivan Lavrentiiovych but also made a brilliant career in the Cossack Host. He began his service in 1735 as a fellow of the standard, took part in the Russo-Turkish War of 1735–39, and was one of the Starodub officers who signed instructions to

[5] Vadim Modzalevskii, *Malorossiiskii rodoslovnik*, 4 vols. (Kyiv, 1908–14), 1: 66–67; Mykola Horban', *Slovo i dilo* (Kharkiv, 1930; repr. Kyiv, 1993), pp. 77–82.
[6] *Istoriia Rusov*, p. 234. Cf. *Kratkaia letopis' Malyia Rossii s 1506 po 1776 god* (St. Petersburg, 1777), p. 192. On the Privy Chancellery, see *Istoriia Rusov*, pp. 228, 238–39, 243.

Catherine's Legislative Commission in 1767. Ivan Ivanovych Borozdna retired from the Cossack service in 1762 with the title of general standard-bearer. He was spectacularly rich by local standards, owning more than three thousand serfs. He also married into one of the richest and most influential local families, that of the Myklashevskys.[7]

Ivan Ivanovych Borozdna and Anastasiia Myklashevska had only one child, Ivan Ivanovych Jr. He died young, leaving to his parents' care his only son, Petro. At the age of fifteen, Petro was sent to St. Petersburg to join the guards. He wrote later: "remaining after my grandfather, the late general standard-bearer Ivan [Ivanovich] Borozdna, I entered the service in 1780 as a guardsman, a sergeant in the Preobrazhenskoe regiment." In 1786, the twenty-year-old Petro Borozdna was transferred from the guards to the regular army, ending up in the Starodub carabineer regiment. He retired from the regiment and the army in May 1787 with the rank of major around the same time as another officer of the regiment, Arkhyp Khudorba. Petro Borozdna cited ill health as a reason for his retirement, but the fact that he retired in the same month as some other Starodub-area officers suggests other reasons as well. Since war with the Ottomans was in the offing, the regiment was likely to be relocated from the Starodub area. Borozdna, who had left St. Petersburg to return to his native region, was apparently ready to quit his military career and take charge of his family's large landholdings. Thanks to his two marriages and subsequent purchases of serfs and land, his possessions now exceeded those of his famous grandfather. If Ivan Ivanovych Borozdna had 1,663 male serfs, his grandson, Petro Ivanovych, was the owner of 2,876 male "souls."[8]

Petro Borozdna's family connections and wealth helped start the retired major's civic career. In 1788 he was elected to represent the nobility of Surazh county; by 1791 he was its marshal. In 1794, at the age of twenty-eight, Borozdna was elected marshal of the nobility of the entire Novhorod-Siverskyi vicegerency. In 1797 he traveled to St. Petersburg as a member of the delegation sent by the local nobility to Catherine II to thank her for granting privileges to the noble stratum. In the early

---

[7] Modzalevskii, *Malorossiiskii rodoslovnik*, I: 69–70; G. A. Miloradovich, *Rodoslovnaia kniga Chernigovskogo dvorianstva*, vol. II (St. Petersburg, 1902); Boris Petrov, "Poèt pushkinskoi pory," in Ivan Petrovich Borozdna, *Pisano v Sele Medvedovo*... (Klintsy, 2004), pp. 15–18.

[8] Modzalevskii, *Malorossiiskii rodoslovnik*, I: 72–74; A. M. Lazarevskii, "O pomeshchikakh Borozdnakh. Ocherki stareishikh dvorianskikh rodov Chernigovskoi gubernii," *Zapiski Chernigovskogo gubernskogo statisticheskogo komiteta*, vol. II (Chernihiv, 1868), pp. 54–98, here 95; A. Martynov, *Istoriia 12-go dragunskogo Starodubovskogo polka* (St. Petersburg, [1909]), p. 54.

nineteenth century Petro Borozdna served in elective positions in Starodub and Nove Misto (Novoe Mesto) and Novozybkiv (Novozybkov) counties. Between 1802 and 1815, he was marshal of Novozybkiv county and in that capacity helped mobilize local resources during the Napoleonic invasion. "In 1812," he later wrote, "immediately after the Sovereign's appeal for the defense of the Fatherland, when the enemy had invaded Russia and was making his approach from the Mogilev [Mahilioŭ] gubernia to Novozybkiv county, which was on the border, in the shortest order I mustered [every] fifteenth man from the census rolls for the defense, armed them with full provisions, and, on the authorities' orders, posted them along the border of the Mogilev gubernia." For his efforts Borozdna was awarded a special memorial medal. In 1818 he was promoted to collegiate councillor, the sixth rank in the imperial Table of Ranks. He was also decorated with the orders of St. Vladimir (third class) and St. Anne (second class).[9]

Petro Borozdna was a pillar of the local nobility. In 1813, when he was accused of corruption with regard to procurements for the Russian army, his superior, the marshal of the Chernihiv nobility, Mykhailo Storozhenko, rejected the accusations and characterized him as "one of the most respectable members of the noble order, who has justified the trust placed in him with unimpeachable honesty for twenty-four years." Borozdna was married twice. He outlived his wives, both of whom increased his wealth with substantial dowries in serfs and land. Both came from well-established and wealthy Cossack families. Iryna Zhoravka died young, leaving Petro with Uliana, the only daughter born to them (in 1786). In 1790 Petro again became a father: his new wife, Kateryna Kuliabka-Koretska, gave him a second daughter, Anna. With Kateryna, Petro fathered eight daughters and three sons – Vasyl, Ivan, and Mykola. Kateryna died on December 27, 1817 (January 8, 1818). Petro Borozdna passed away two years later, on January 14 (26), 1820. He was fifty-four years old. By that time, quite a few of Borozdna's daughters were already married and had started their own families. Two of his sons were already published authors. Ivan went on to become a poet renowned throughout the empire. Mykola, still in school at the time of his father's death, would go on to make a brilliant career in the civil service, becoming governor of Smolensk.[10]

[9] Lazarevskii, "O pomeshchikakh Borozdnakh," p. 95.
[10] Modzalevskii, *Malorossiiskii rodoslovnik*, 1: 74–78.

What we know about Petro Borozdna apart from his family connections, his service record, and the number of serfs in his possession is that, like his sons, he was no stranger to the world of letters. Some of the books that once belonged to him are now to be found in the Library of Congress. Petro Borozdna's library included numerous eighteenth-century publications in European languages dealing with the arts, poetry, history, and mathematics. Volumes formerly owned by Borozdna in the Library of Congress collection include the *Historia Philippicae* by Marcus Junianus Justinus, published in Berlin in 1734, and a German translation of orations by Tacitus, Demosthenes, Cicero, and Marcus Julius published in Leipzig in 1729. One of those volumes, the *Poetische Schriften* of Friedrich Wilhelm von Zachariä, published in Amsterdam in 1767, bears a bookplate indicating that it came from the library of "Jean Borozdna," as well as an inscription in Cyrillic identifying the original owner, Petro Borozdna. The eighteenth-century books in his library indicate that Petro Borozdna may have known German, French, and Latin, and that he had an interest in history and literature. That interest apparently went beyond classical Roman oratory and the dramas of August von Kotzebue – German-language works that once belonged to the Borozdnas – to take in Ukrainian history and Russian literature.[11]

We find evidence of this outside Borozdna's library, on the pages of one of the most prestigious Russian journals of the time, *Vestnik Evropy*. In the spring of 1809 the readers of *Vestnik Evropy*, then published by one of Russia's best poets, Vasilii Zhukovsky, were regaled with a letter to Empress Catherine II from the former governor general of Little Russia, Petr Rumiantsev (1725–96). He had written it soon after the death of Grigorii Potemkin, which took place in October 1791. Responding to Catherine's offer to come out of retirement and take command of one of the Russian armies, Rumiantsev declined, citing his old age: "However moved I am and however appreciative of the worth of your Monarchical favors, nevertheless, Most Gracious Sovereign, I am also overcome with regret that stress in my life and weakness in spirit have rendered me unable to unsheath this gleaming blade to the glory and praise of the Sovereign and to the dread of the enemy." There was more to Rumiantsev's letter than met the eye. A few years earlier Catherine had dismissed him as governor general of Little Russia, and this was an occasion to pay back the

---

[11] Among Borozdna's books in the Library of Congress one can find Friedrich Wilhelm von Zachariä's *Poetische Schriften* (Amsterdam, 1767), http://lccn.loc.gov/90156887. Cf. http://catalog.loc.gov/cgi-in/Pwebrecon.cgi?Search%5FArg=Borozdna.

empress in her own coin. Rumiantsev, who had presided over the abolition of the Hetmanate in the 1760s and 1770s, became the darling of Ukrainian autonomists when he sided with them in the 1780s against Grigorii Potemkin. Rumiantsev had a mansion in Velyka Topal near Starodub. He died at one of his Ukrainian estates in December 1796 and was buried in the Kyivan Cave Monastery. Even in death he was regarded as a hero and a celebrity by the Ukrainian nobility, especially families associated with the Bezborodkos and Zavadovskys, Rumiantsev's protégés at court.[12]

It is hardly surprising that such a letter was submitted for publication by one of the Ukrainian readers of *Vestnik*. What is more surprising is that the reader was none other than Petro Borozdna. "The letter," wrote Vasilii Zhukovsky, "was dispatched from Little Russia by the esteemed Petr Ivanovich Borozdna, who promises to supply other most valuable manuscripts of this great Commander for publication in *Vestnik*." He then added: "The editor is duty-bound to render thanks to him." Unfortunately, no further documents of this kind appeared in the journal, and we do not know whether Borozdna ever submitted any new material or whether Zhukovsky found it insufficiently interesting to publish. It is quite clear, however, that Petro Borozdna had an interest in Ukrainian history, collected historical sources, and was particularly drawn to those that contained elements of oppositional thinking.[13]

The letter published in *Vestnik Evropy* must have had particular significance for the Ukrainian nobility, as it embodied the spirit of protest that imperial policies had evoked in the region in the early nineteenth century. Petr Rumiantsev was not only a hero to Petro Borozdna but also one of the favorite characters of the author of the *History of the Rus'*. He wrote that in 1765, upon the abolition of the Hetmanate, the Little Russian College headed by Rumiantsev "entered upon its rule like dew on a pasture or frost on fleece, that is, in perfect silence and meekness." He then added: "The Little Russian people was especially gratified by its governor general . . . and he truly justified the people's expectations with his patriotic actions to promote its welfare." This positive treatment of an official who had put an end to the Hetmanate was quite a statement on the part of the anonymous author.[14]

---

[12] Oleksander Ohloblyn, "Ukrainian Autonomists of the 1780's and 1790's and Count P. A. Rumyantsev-Zadunaysky," *Annals of the Ukrainian Academy of Sciences in the US* 6, nos. 3–4 (1958).

[13] "Pis'mo grafa Petra Aleksandrovicha Zadunaiskogo k Ekaterine II," *Vestnik Evropy* 44 (March 15, 1809): 27–29.

[14] *Istoriia Rusov*, p. 255.

Borozdna's submission to *Vestnik Evropy* shows that he was a reader of the journal and probably shared the interests and at least some of the ideas expressed by other contributors. Occasionally one even comes upon direct links between material published in *Vestnik* and the *History of the Rus'*. One such link is a legendary character called Rogdai. The anonymous author of the *History* brings him into his narrative under the year 1401, listing Rogdai among the commanders of the fictitious Rus' prince and Cossack hetman Ventseslav. Rogdai emerges as one of the best and most ferocious Rus' warriors against the Teutonic Knights. His infantry "broke into the center of the Knights' camp, bore down on their rear and in every direction with its Rus' lances, and threw them into confusion; then the surrounding forces attacked them from all sides and inflicted a decisive defeat on them, so that their dead and prisoners numbered as many as fifty thousand." As George Shevelov already noted in his linguistic study of the *History*, Rogdai first appears in this particular spelling in Vasilii Zhukovsky's short novel "Maria's Grove." There he also figures as a powerful and ruthless Rus' warrior, who was "terrible and implacable in vengeance; neither wails nor the smile of an innocent child penetrated his impregnable soul." The most intriguing element of this textual parallelism is that Zhukovsky first published "Maria's Grove" in 1809, in the January issue of *Vestnik Evropy*. Petro Borozdna, who contributed Rumiantsev's letter and saw it published in one of the March issues of the journal, must have read "Maria's Grove" along with other texts in *Vestnik* that year.[15]

Vestnik had quite a few loyal readers in Ukraine in the first decade of the nineteenth century. Ivan Hurzhiiev, a resident of Zinkiv in the Poltava gubernia, was the author of a "Letter from Little Russia" that appeared in the same issue of *Vestnik* as the Rumiantsev document. Hurzhiiev wrote: "I consider it a most pleasant duty to inform you, kind Sir, that your publication is read avidly among us." In the pages of *Vestnik Evropy* Ukrainian readers could find considerable material that would have appealed to the author of the *History of the Rus'*. This included articles on the Time of Troubles in Muscovy, to which the author of the *History* paid special attention; an essay about the Privy Chancellery, which he so detested; and a review of Voltaire's history of Peter I. Readers of *Vestnik Evropy* were also introduced to the works of two Ukrainian luminaries, Archbishop Heorhii Konysky and the son of Heorhii Poletyka, Vasyl. *Vestnik* published the text of a speech delivered by Konysky in 1765 to

---

[15] *Istoriia Rusov*, pp. 9–10; Vasilii Zhukovskii, "Mar'ina roshcha," *Vestnik Evropy*, vol. 43 (January 31, 1809): 109–28, here 120; continuation, *ibid.*, vol. 43 (February 15, 1809): 211–32.

King Stanisław August and four speeches given by Vasyl Poletyka on different occasions during the first decade of the nineteenth century. Although there are no textual parallels between the *History* and articles published in *Vestnik*, it is hard to dispel the impression that the author of the *History* and his readers would have taken great interest in many of the articles that appeared in the journal at the time.[16]

Could Petro Borozdna have been the author or coauthor of the *History*? Apart from the elements of his biography given above, his evident interest in the history of Ukraine and his familiarity with the materials published in *Vestnik Evropy*, there are other factors that point in his direction or suggest another member of the Borozdna family. One such factor is the negative attitude of the author of the *History of the Rus'* to those Ukrainian nobles who traced their origins back to the Polish nobility. Given the wealth, status, and connections of the Borozdna family, the question for its members was not whether they would be accepted into the Russian nobility but which category they would join. The Borozdnas tried to claim noble status on the basis of a genealogical table that traced their family roots to Volhynia. As a family with "Polish" noble status they could gain entry to the prestigious fourth section of the registry of the Russian nobility, but their claim to descent from the Polish nobility was not recognized by the authorities, and they had to settle for the sixth section of the register, reserved for ancient noble families of undocumented status.[17]

Another factor making Petro Borozdna or one of his siblings a strong suspect is the negative attitude of the author of the *History* to the Old Believers. Dissatisfaction with the Old Believers was common in the Starodub region, but probably no other Cossack family was more closely involved with Old Believer settlers than the Borozdnas. Ivan

---

[16] Ivan Gurzheev, "Pis'mo iz Malorossii," *Vestnik Europy*, vol. 44 (March 15, 1809): 36–38; U. F., "O tainoi kantseliarii," *ibid.*, vol. 8 (March 31, 1803): 122–31; "Rechi Romenskogo poveta marshala Vasiliia Poletiki, proiznesennye im v sobranii dvorianstva v Poltave," *ibid.*, vol. 10 (July 15, 1803): 39–45; "Rech' pol'skomu koroliu, Stanislavu Avgustu, v zashchishchenie Greko-Rossiiskoi tserkvi, v to vremia gonimoi poliakami, govorennaia Belorusskim episkopom Georgiem v Varshave 1765 goda iiulia 27-go dnia," *ibid.*, vol. 16 (July 31, 1804): 119–24; "Dve rechi, proiznesennye Romenskogo poveta marshalom, g-m Poletikoiu, po sluchaiu dvorianskikh vyborov v nyneshnem godu," *ibid.*, vol. 24 (December 15, 1805): 191–94; "Ob osvobozhdenii Moskvy ot poliakov," *ibid.*, vol. 35 (September 15, 1807): 34–54; "Rech', proiznesennaia v Poltave marshalom Malorossiiskoi Poltavskoi gubernii, Romenskogo poveta, Vasiliem Poletikoiu, v sobranii dvorianstva sei gubernii, 11 ianvaria 1809 goda," *ibid.*, vol. 43 (February 28, 1809): 262–66; K[achenovskii], review of "Istoriia Rossiiskoi imperii v tsarstvovanie Petra Velikogo. Sochinennaia Vol'terom. Chast' pervaia," *ibid.*, vol. 48 (November 15, 1809): 61–68.

[17] Modzalevskii, *Malorossiiskii rodoslovnik*, 1: 69–70; G. A. Miloradovich, *Rodoslovnaia kniga Chernigovskogo dvorianstva*, vol. 11 (St. Petersburg, 1902); Petrov, "Poèt pushkinskoi pory," pp. 15–18.

Lavrentiiovych Borozdna, the owner of Horsk and the protagonist of the Yanzhul/Chekatunov story, first invited Old Believers to settle on his property near the village of Stodola in 1707. He exempted future settlers from taxes, creating a new freehold (*sloboda*) and appointing an Old Believer called Vasilii Klintsov to serve as its elder and settlement organizer. This was a common policy at the time, as landowners usually had more land than serfs to work it and used tax holidays to attract new settlers.

Then came the tsar's circular of 1715, which placed the Old Believers under the direct jurisdiction of the government and turned the lands they settled into state properties. Ivan Lavrentiiovych Borozdna and other landowners, who expected that after the tax-free period the Old Believers would start paying their dues to the proprietors, lost not only their prospective serfs but their lands as well. Borozdna's freehold near the village of Stodola became known as Klintsy, after the name of the Old Believer who served as settlement organizer. The conflict over land ownership between the Borozdnas and the Old Believers lasted well into the eighteenth century. In the 1770s, the Old Believers of Klintsy allegedly attacked one of the homesteads belonging to the Borozdnas – the court proceedings lasted from 1772 to 1776. If one were to make a list of Starodub nobles who had reason to be unhappy with the Old Believers, the Borozdnas would almost certainly head it.[18]

Thus Petro Borozdna had the right background, education, and intellectual interests to be the author of the *History*, as well as good reason to be unhappy with former Polish nobles and Old Believer settlers. But so did some other members of his family, and he was not the only Borozdna who knew how to write. In 1818, the year in which the first dated manuscript of the *History of the Rus'* came to light, another Borozdna was in residence at Medvediv, busying himself with literary work. His name was Vasyl Borozdna, and he was Petro's eldest son.

Vasyl Borozdna was born in Medvediv on February 18, 1793 and was Petro Borozdna's second child with Kateryna Kuliabka-Koretska. Petro Borozdna enrolled his eldest son in the civil service at the age of six, enlisting him as his assistant in the Starodub district court (Petro was then the judge of Starodub county). In 1802, when Petro Borozdna became marshal of the Novozybkiv nobility, he transferred his nine-year-old son

---

[18] I. Perekrestov, "K voprosu o zakonnom ili samovol'nom zaselenii slobody Klintsy," *Klintsovskii letopisets*, vol. 1 (Klintsy, 2004), pp. 28–34; Petrov, "Poèt pushkinskoi pory," pp. 10–11; Iurii Voloshyn, *Rozkol'nyts'ki slobody na terytoriï Het'manshchyny u XVIII stolitti* (Poltava, 2005), pp. 47–81.

as well. In 1805 Vasyl Borozdna attained the rank of collegiate registrar, and in 1808 he moved up a step, becoming gubernia secretary. But in September 1813, when Vasyl was twenty, his career took a sudden turn. He resigned from his position in his father's office and headed for St. Petersburg to join the College of Foreign Affairs. In July 1814 he entered the imperial foreign service, and two years later he was assigned as a secretary to the Russian mission to Persia. The mission, which took place in 1817, was led by one of the most controversial figures in Russian history, a friend of the Decembrists and the conqueror of the Caucasus, General Aleksei Yermolov (1777–1861).

Vasyl Borozdna did well on his assignment, returning with a Persian Order of the Lion and the Sun on his chest. This was soon followed by a Russian Order of St. Anne, and in July 1818 he was promoted to collegiate assessor, advancing five ranks in four years, from thirteenth to eighth. Vasyl Borozdna resigned from the diplomatic service as unexpectedly as he joined it. By the fall of 1818 he was already home in Medvediv, probably because of urgent family business. Vasyl's mother had died in early 1818, while he was in Persia. His father, Petro, would soon follow her to the grave; he was probably already ailing in 1818. As the eldest son, Vasyl had to take care of his aging father and the huge family estate. Service in the capital would have to wait. Vasyl Borozdna confined himself to Medvediv, but he was not idle there. Apart from family affairs, he spent his time recording his impressions of Persia and drafted the first complete description of Yermolov's mission to the land of the shahs.

The idea of producing such a description was not Vasyl's alone. During the mission to Persia, he was surrounded by some of the best and most progressive minds in the empire. Among the members of Yermolov's embassy to Persia were a number of future Decembrists, including Nikolai Voeikov, but the most influential figure among the officers of the mission was Captain (Second Grade) Nikolai Nikolaevich Muraviev (1794–1866), the founder of the clandestine Sacred Society, which served as a model for the future Decembrist organizations. Muraviev's absence from St. Petersburg (he spent years in the Caucasus and Central Asia) saved him from persecution in the aftermath of the Decembrist Uprising. He made a spectacular career in the Russian military administration of the borderlands, becoming viceroy of the Caucasus in 1854. During the Yermolov mission to Persia, Muraviev organized an association in Tbilisi that was devoted to the enlightenment of its members and vaguely based on the St. Petersburg Sacred Society. The initiative had Yermolov's blessing but was only partly successful. "Our meetings in the Sultanate continued for a time," wrote Muraviev in his memoirs. "All the articles were read, but because we returned shortly afterwards, the gentlemen members gradually began to fall away and finally forgot all about the enterprise, no matter how much I shouted." It would appear, however, that at least some members of the society took Muraviev's initiative quite seriously.[19]

Vasyl Borozdna was one of the two members of Muraviev's circle who began, upon the embassy's return to Tbilisi, to work on an article about Persia. By that time Borozdna already had some experience as a writer, although of a different kind of literature. In 1814, after resigning his post in the Starodub region, and apparently before joining the foreign service, Borozdna published in Moscow a five-page pamphlet entitled *The Vision of an Aged Siberian Pagan Priest during the Battle of the Nations at Leipzig.* Borozdna's subject was the Russian army's campaign against Napoleon and the battle of October 1813 that saw the French emperor defeated, changing the course of European history. The article commissioned by Muraviev was a much more substantial undertaking. The article apparently served as a preparatory piece for a much larger project that Borozdna undertook upon his return to Medvediv. There he wrote a longer book in the style of a traveler's account entitled *A Brief Description of the Journey of the Russian Imperial Mission to Persia in 1817.* It was published in St. Petersburg in 1821. Most of the writing was apparently done in Medvediv. Vasyl was there, for example, in December 1819, when he was entered in the records of the local Orthodox church as godfather to Petro Nemyrovych-Danchenko, the son of his younger sister, Hanna Borozdna. Vasyl probably stayed in the vicinity after his father's death in early 1820. As the eldest son, he must have been a key figure in the division of property with his brothers and sisters.[20]

The Medvediv estate and Petro Borozdna's rich library were eventually inherited by Ivan Borozdna, but Vasyl must have had full access to the library during his work on the description of the Persian embassy. It appears he also collected books and manuscripts on his own. One such manuscript has been preserved in the Volodymyr Vernadsky Library of the National Academy of Sciences of Ukraine in the collection of

---

[19] "Zapiski N. P. Murav'eva," *Russkii arkhiv*, no. 4 (1866): 5, 19–20, 456, 475; A. P. Berzhe, "Posol'stvo A. P. Ermolova v Persiiu," *Russkaia starina* 6 (1877): 257–58; Moshe Gammer, "Proconsul of the Caucasus: A Re-examination of Yermolov," *Social Evolution & History* 2, no. 1 (March 2003): 177–94.

[20] Vasilii Borozdna, *Videnie prestarelogo sibirskogo zhretsa vo vremia narodnoi bitvy pri Leiptsige* (Moscow, 1814); Borozdna, *Kratkoe opisanie puteshestviia Rossiisko-Imperatorskogo posol'stva v Persiiu v 1817 g.* (St. Petersburg, 1821); Modzalevskii, *Malorossiiskii rodoslovnik*, III: 646–48.

Oleksandr Lazarevsky. The title of the manuscript is "A Chronicle of Little Russia, or An Abridged History of the Cossack Hetmans and of All Noteworthy Events in Ukraine." An inscription on the last folio of the manuscript gives the date of its creation: "Copied in September 1813." A note written on the manuscript by Lazarevsky relates how he came into possession of it: "This copy of the chronicle presented to me as a gift in June 1884 by Pavel Aleksandrovich Abaleshev from the former library of Vasyl Petrovych Borozdna. Aleksandr Lashkevich." Pavel Abaleshev was a grandson of Vasyl Borozdna who lived on his estate of Turosna, where part of the family archive was apparently preserved. Oleksandr Lashkevych, a grandson of Ivan Lashkevych, was the publisher of the Ukrainophile journal *Kievskaia starina* (Kyivan Antiquity) in 1888–89. A collector of Ukrainian antiquities, he acquired a portion of the Borozdna family archive housed in Turosna, formerly the estate of Vasyl Borozdna. During the Revolution of 1917, Pavel Abaleshev was shot by the Bolshevik secret police, the Cheka. The mansion was pillaged, but, by a stroke of luck, the manuscript survived.[21]

The "Chronicle of Little Russia" was first brought to the attention of scholars in the early 1980s by Olena Apanovych, an accomplished historian of the Cossack era and a government expert on the Polubotok treasure who was purged from the Academy of Sciences' Institute of Ukrainian History during the campaign against Ukrainian nationalism in 1972. She was lucky to find a job in the manuscript division of the library. There she managed to return to the study of her beloved early modern period, which the authorities considered "nationalistic." Under constant surveillance, she did a pioneering job of cataloguing and describing the manuscript collection of Ukrainian chronicles of the early modern period. The "Chronicle of Little Russia" was one of many manuscripts that passed through Apanovych's hands in the late 1970s and early 1980s. In her book on the Ukrainian chronicles, published in 1983, Apanovych identified the Borozdna manuscript as a version of the *Brief Description of Little Russia*, the most popular Ukrainian short chronicle of the eighteenth century. Noting parallels between some parts of the "Chronicle of Little Russia" and the *History of the Rus'*, she suggested that the author of the Borozdna

---

[21] "Letopisets o Maloi Rossii ili sokrashchennaia istoriia o kazach'ikh getmanakh i o vsem sluchivshemsia, primechaniia dostoinogo v Ukraine," Volodymyr Vernadsky Library of the National Academy of Sciences of Ukraine (Kyiv), Manuscript Institute, I, no. 6699; "Lashkevych, Oleksander," *Encyclopedia of Ukraine*, ed. Danylo Husar Struk, vol. III (Toronto, Buffalo, and London, 1993), pp. 50–51; Aleksandr Lazarevskii, "Opis' imenii Borozden, 1638," *Kievskaia starina* 27, no. 12 (1889): 622–28; V. S. Ikonnikov, *Opyt russkoi istoriografii*, p. 1230.

manuscript must have known the *History* and used it as his source. Apanovych was certainly on the right track here. The manuscript is indeed a version of the *Brief Description of Little Russia*, but its relation to that text is quite complicated. The Borozdna manuscript was in fact a version of the Russian translation of the second volume of Jean-Benoît Scherer's *Annales*, whose text was almost identical to the Yakiv Radkevych manuscript owned by the Yatchenko family.[22]

Thus, Borozdna had in his library, perhaps as early as September 1813, a copy of a Russian translation of Scherer's work, which, as we established earlier, was used by the author of the *History of the Rus'*. But where did it come from? Vasyl Borozdna may have inherited it from his father, but it is also possible that he himself added it to the family library. In September 1813 Vasyl Borozdna was twenty years old. That month he was released from his duties in the office of the marshal of the Novozybkiv nobility. He would not join the College of Foreign Affairs for another year. Judging by the publication of his first literary work in Moscow in 1814, it was approximately at this time that the young Vasyl Borozdna was trying his hand at belles lettres. He may also have been interested in the history of his homeland. Could Vasyl Borozdna have translated the text himself? That is highly unlikely, partly because we know nothing of him as a translator, and partly because he was not the only one of his contemporaries to possess a manuscript containing Russian translations of various parts of Scherer's work.

The Borozdna manuscript is almost identical to the Starodub translation of Scherer's *Annales* that bears the names of Radkevych and Yatchenko. The differences are minor. Some of them consist of added words that are not to be found either in the French original or in the Starodub translation but make sense from the viewpoint of Russian style, which may suggest that the Radkevych manuscript (or its original) is of earlier provenance than the one owned by Borozdna. What is special about the Borozdna manuscript is that it can easily be dated on the basis of the note giving September 1813 as the time of its production. It would appear that around that time Russian translations of Scherer's *Annales* became quite popular among connoisseurs of Cossack history in Starodub and its environs. Two of the three copies of the Russian translation of Scherer's chronicle known today come from the Starodub region, while the

---

[22] Olena Apanovych, *Rukopisnaia svetskaia kniga XVIII v. na Ukraine: Istoricheskie sborniki* (Kyiv, 1983), pp. 199–200. Cf. Ivan Dzyra, "Vplyv *Litopysu Malorosiï* Zhana-Benua Sherera na *Istoriiu Rusiv*," in *Problemy istoriï Ukraïny XIX–pochatku XX st.*, no. 6 (2003): 424.

provenance of the third copy, made in 1842 and now preserved in the Volodymyr Korolenko Library in Kharkiv, is unknown.[23]

We know that in December 1806, probably soon after his trip to the Hryniv estate of Count Illia Bezborodko, Yakiv Radkevych was authorized to take possession of the house donated by Petro Ivanovych Borozdna to the Starodub-area school system. Could the two have discussed not only the business transaction and the prospects of education in the region but also historical matters of common interest? Could they have exchanged manuscripts in their possession? That is quite possible. The presence of the Russian translation of Scherer in Borozdna's library is conclusive evidence that Vasyl Borozdna, a man of letters acquainted with some of the best minds of the Russian Empire during his service in St. Petersburg and his mission to Persia, was in possession of one of the unique handwritten sources of the *History of the Rus'*. Coupled with the facts that Borozdna's name was specifically omitted from the text of the *History*, and that representatives of his family were closely associated with the finders and distributors of the text, such as Myklashevsky and Shyrai, and were related to many of the Starodub families mentioned in the *History*, this conclusion must be considered an important step forward in our search for the author of the *History*. Could Vasyl Borozdna have been the author of the mysterious text? Nothing said about him to this point contradicts such a possibility.[24]

Yet there is a problem with such an identification. Comparing Vasyl Borozdna's *Brief Description of the Journey of the Russian Imperial Mission to Persia*, published in St. Petersburg in 1821, with the *History of the Rus'*, one would be hard pressed to find any parallels in style or ideas. Furthermore, Vasyl Borozdna or his St. Petersburg editors seem to have known better and more idiomatic Russian than did the author of the *History*. The mysterious manuscript is written in a language corresponding closely to that of the Cossack officers who joined the imperial service in the last decades of the eighteenth century and learned Russian as part of their military and/or administrative careers. Does this disqualify Vasyl Borozdna as a possible contributor to the creation of the *History*? Probably not or, rather, not entirely. The author of the *History* incorporated into his text many sources that were indeed written in the language of the

---

[23] "Ruskaia istoriia," Ivan Zabelin collection, no. 617, Manuscript Division, State Historical Museum (Moscow); Andrii Bovhyria, *Kozats'ke istoriopysannia v rukopysnii tradytsii XVIII stolittia. Spysky ta redaktsii tvoriv* (Kyiv, 2010), pp. 124–26.

[24] Chernihiv State Archives, Fond 229, op. 1, no. 3, fol. 851.

Cossack elites of the eighteenth and even seventeenth centuries. This could not but affect the style of the work. It should also be borne in mind that Borozdna may have been an editor rather than an original author of the *History*. In fact, he seems more plausible in such a role, since the author of the *History* clearly had many life experiences that do not match Vasyl's biography. The young Borozdna would have been in a position to contribute, in one way or another, to the writing or editing of the *History* between September 1813, when the Russian translation of Scherer was copied, and August 1814, when he entered the imperial diplomatic service. The period after his return from Persia in August 1818 works even better.

Whose editor or coauthor might Vasyl Borozdna have been? The man of greatest literary talent among the Borozdnas, Vasyl's younger brother Ivan, was born in 1804, making him too young to have been involved in the production of the *History*. But Vasyl might well have been the editor of a text produced by his father, Petro, who had the right kind of experience, both military and civic, and the right background to account not only for the language used by the author of the *History of the Rus'*, but also for the range of attitudes and political views expressed in the work. As noted above, Petro Borozdna had been enrolled in a St. Petersburg guards regiment as a child, which would have given him an opportunity to gain some command of standard Russian and mingle with the educated classes of imperial society. He served together with Arkhyp Khudorba and was closely related to the Myklashevskys.

Petro and Vasyl Borozdna are much stronger candidates for authorship than the duo of Hryhorii and Vasyl Poletyka. Were they indeed the authors? Before we answer this question, we must deal with a factor that undermines the case for the Borozdnas' authorship of the *History*. One of the most negative characters in the work – more specifically, in its final, post-1708 section – was a close relative of the Borozdnas. In fact, he was the maternal grandfather of Petro Borozdna, and his name was Antin Kryzhanovsky. The anonymous author gives the following characterization of Borozdna's grandfather and his actions:

[T]he colonel of Hadiach, Kryzhanovsky, a Jew by birth and a recent convert, who had attained riches and the rank of colonel by his constant leaseholds and farming of revenues, on seeing the unusual success in the recruitment of soldiers for Holstein service, immediately seized upon a contract and addressed the sovereign concerning it, promising to furnish an entire mounted regiment of them at his own expense. The sovereign, taking note of Kryzhanovsky's enthusiasm but unaware of his computations, in which, according to Jewish conscience, he always quadrupled the actual cost of every item, appointed Kryzhanovsky a brigadier to begin with. And he indeed formed a regiment, the so-called Podtsaboltsy regiment, from the lesser Cossacks of his own regiment, as well as from herdsmen and shepherds, from factory workers and all kinds of other riff-raff. But just as everything quick and impetuous ends the same way, the Holstein and Podtsabolsk troops were similarly afflicted: from June 1762, that is, after the death of the sovereign, they were disbanded and sent off to their homes. They shuffled down every road to Little Russia, and, according to the way they had acted during their triumphal march to St. Petersburg, all along their return path they met with the contempt of the inhabitants, who loathed them.[25]

The historical background to this episode was the recruitment by Emperor Peter III of *podtsabol'tsy*, soldiers for new units of the imperial army who were regarded with great hostility in the Hetmanate. The most obvious feature of the author's attack on Kryzhanovsky was his aggressive anti-Semitism. Anti-Jewish sentiment was nothing new in the lands of the former Cossack state, but the attack on Kryzhanovsky was also marked by the new era, in which ethnicity, not religion, defined people's primary identity. In this new world, conversion to Orthodoxy was not sufficient to turn anyone into a true Rus' native, whether that person was originally an ethnic Jew or an ethnic Pole as, according to the author of the *History*, was the case with Ivan Vyhovsky and Ivan Mazepa. Still, anti-Semitism was most likely only part of the reason for the *History*'s attack on Kryzhanovsky. His story of making it big in the Hetmanate was intriguing but by no means unique: quite a few Jewish converts enjoyed great success in the Cossack state. Their families became part and parcel of the Hetmanate elite. The most prominent of them were not the Kryzhanovskys but the Hertsyks and Markovyches. Three members of the Hertsyk family followed Hetman Ivan Mazepa into emigration, while Anastasiia Markovych became the wife of Mazepa's successor, Hetman Ivan Skoropadsky. The Kryzhanovskys were simply the most recent additions to the secular and ecclesiastical elite of the Hetmanate.[26]

The attack on Kryzhanovsky may well have been motivated by personal grievances of the author's and directed against Kryzhanovsky's heirs and

[25] *Istoriia Rusov*, p. 251; Zenon E. Kohut, "The Image of Jews in Ukrainian Intellectual Tradition: The Role of *Istoriia Rusov*," *Harvard Ukrainian Studies* 22 (1998): 343–58.

[26] Aleksandr Lazarevskii, "Liudi staroi Malorossii. 8. Kryzhanovskie," *Kievskaia starina*, no. 5 (May 1885): 7–13; Volodymyr Kryvosheia, *Ukraïns'ka kozats'ka starshyna*, pt. 1, *Uriadnyky het'mans'koï administratsii*, 2nd edn. (Kyiv, 2005), pp. 202, 229; Zenon E. Kohut, *Russian Centralism and Ukrainian Autonomy: Imperial Absorption of the Hetmanate, 1760s–1830s* (Cambridge, Mass., 1988), p. 134; Valerii Tomazov, "Oni sluzhili Ukraine. Iz istorii kazatskikh rodov evreiskogo proiskhozhdeniia," http://berkovich-zametki.com/AStarina/Nomer1/Tomazov1.htm.

relatives. Even if that was not the case, it certainly reflected negatively on the members of Kryzhanovsky's extended family at a time when racially based anti-Semitism was on the rise in the Russian Empire and in Europe generally. The highly negative treatment of Petro Borozdna's maternal grandfather, Antin Kryzhanovsky, by the author of the *History of the Rus'* raises serious doubts about the Borozdnas' possible authorship of the mysterious text. We have devoted considerable space to the numerous associations – biographic, intellectual, textual, and other – between the Borozdnas and the *History*, but now a closer look at their matrimonial ties has put the whole argument into question. Nevertheless, considered in the context of other evidence, the Kryzhanovsky episode indicates that the Borozdnas were indeed very close to the author of the *History* or, possibly, to its main sponsor – close enough, perhaps, to provoke him to an attack on the entire family.

CHAPTER 16

A son-in-law

In February 2005, students of the department of human anatomy at the Smolensk State Medical Academy were treated to an unusual presentation. One of their professors, Aleksandr Vasilievich Litvinov, delivered a paper entitled "In Search of the National Idea." What does human anatomy have to do with the national idea? The two were linked in Litvinov's presentation by the figure of Mykola (Nikolai) Borozdna (1809–80), a son of Petro Ivanovych Borozdna and a younger brother of Vasyl and Ivan Borozdna. Between 1863 and 1871 Mykola served as governor of the Smolensk gubernia and became one of the first honorary citizens of Smolensk; hence interest in him in that city was not entirely unexpected. But what does all this have to do with nationality and anatomy? An article on the Smolensk Medical Academy website explained the puzzle as follows: "A. V. Litvinov, a guardian of the finest traditions of honoring the history of our Motherland and the memory of our ancestors, is grievously offended that his countryman, a honorary citizen of the city of Smolensk and one of its best governors, has not, to this very day, been interred according to Christian custom, as he deserves. For that purpose an expedition will be organized in the summer months under the leadership of Aleksandr Vasilievich, with the participation of Smolensk archaeologists and the Department of Human Anatomy of the Academy."[1]

The grave of Mykola Borozdna, the youngest and most prominent of Petro Borozdna's sons in the imperial service, was destroyed during the Soviet era. In post-Soviet Russia the search for his grave became part of the larger project of reclaiming the prerevolutionary past, and thus the Russian national idea and identity. A few years earlier, in the fall of 2001, teachers and students of the secondary school in the village of Medvediv found next to their school fence, hidden in the dirt and waiting decades to

[1] A. Mezhov and Iu. Kuchuk, "Nravstvennoe samosovershenstvovanie. Vozvrashchenie legendy," www.smolensk.ru/user/sgma/publish/period/vivat/vivat_academia!-ssma-express-030305.htm.

be unearthed, scattered parts of four tombstones. They belonged to Petro and Kateryna Borozdna, their son, Ivan, and his wife, Nadezhda – two generations of former owners of the village. The earliest tombstone, that of Kateryna Borozdna, dated from 1818; the latest, that of Ivan Borozdna, from 1858. The burials were part of the cemetery of the local Orthodox church, which had been destroyed in the 1960s. Most of the tombstones had been heaped together and used to build a monument to villagers who fought and died in the Second World War, but those of the Borozdnas miraculously survived.[2]

Professor Litvinov's search for the remains of Mykola Borozdna was partly driven by a gruesome story that he had heard as a child from his grandfather in his native village of Kivai. The village, hard hit by fallout from the Chernobyl nuclear disaster, was a former possession of the Borozdna family and the residence of Mykola Borozdna. According to the story, workers who were demolishing the local Orthodox church in 1930 in order to use its bricks for the construction of a village school stumbled upon a large stone slab beneath the floor. The demolition workers instantly turned into treasure hunters. The destruction of the old order and the construction of a new one went hand in hand with dispossession of the old ruling class. By the 1930s that class was gone, but its graves remained. The workers removed the slab, beneath which they found two corpses, one of a man in a gold-braided general's uniform, the other of a woman in a blue dress. The workers were looking for gold and were bitterly disappointed to find none in the grave. Having taken the general's decorations and saber, they left the church cursing the exploiters who had left nothing to the exploited. Local inhabitants would later fill the grave with crushed stone. Legend has it that they refused to bury the robbers, after their demise, in the village cemetery.

Professor Litvinov was determined to do justice to those interred in the Kivai church by excavating their remains and giving the former owners of his village a proper Christian burial. He believed that the man in the general's uniform was none other than Mykola Borozdna, and that the woman in blue was his wife, Yelysaveta Mykhailivna Myklashevska. We do not know the outcome of Professor Litvinov's initiative, as the websites of the Smolensk Medical Academy and the Smolensk regional administration (the latter has a short biography of Borozdna as a governor of the region) provide no information in that regard. But there is no

---

[2] Boris Petrov, "Poèt pushkinskoi pory," in Ivan Petrovich Borozdna, *Pisano v sele Medvedovo …* (Klintsy, 2004), pp. 83–86.

reason to doubt his identification. His rediscovery of the Kivai burial, along with the reconstruction of the Borozdna necropolis in Medvediv by local history enthusiasts, reminds one of the close connections between the Borozdnas and their numerous neighbors who were directly or indirectly associated with the public appearance and dissemination of the *History*. This suggests a number of important questions about the changing patterns of intermarriage in the former Hetmanate and, last but not least, contributes to our search for the author of the *History*. As we have noted, he may have been close to the family while harboring serious reservations about some of its members.[3]

Marriages were not a matter of whim in the lands of the former Hetmanate. They were rarely driven by the wishes of the bride and groom, and in such exceptional cases they might lead to major family upheavals entailing protracted lawsuits, as was the case with Ivan Lashkevych's marriage to Anastasiia Myloradovych. More often than not, marriages between teenage brides and much older grooms were not love matches but concerned the acquisition of property and the reinforcement of ties between families already long associated by previous marriages. There were family clusters in the Hetmanate that had existed for generations. The Borozdnas were no exception. For generations they had belonged to a clan or a family cluster that included the Myklashevskys, Shyrais, Nemyrovych-Danchenkos, and Kuliabka-Koretskys, among others. Those clans were quite stable. Family ties and property-based matrimonial relations led, however, not only to love and friendship between family members but also to conflict and hatred driven by personal antipathy and by disputes over inheritance and the division of property.

The Borozdna graves tell an interesting story of social and cultural change in the Starodub region in the early nineteenth century. If Petro Borozdna was buried next to his wife, Kateryna Kuliabko-Koretska, who like his first wife, Iryna Zhoravka, was a descendant of the Cossack officer elite, his son Ivan was buried next to a woman who was born far from the Hetmanate, Nadezhda Nikiforova, the daughter of a Russian noble family in the Tver gubernia. Ivan Borozdna's second wife, Liubov Stromilova, also came from Central Russia – her family possessions were in the Tula

---

[3] Mezhov and Kuchuk, "Nravstvennoe samosovershenstvovanie. Vozvrashchenie legendy"; "Borozdna, Nikolai Petrovich," www.admcity.smolensk.ru/info/best_people/borozdna.html; *Manmade and Natural Radioactivity in Environmental Pollution and Radiochronology*, ed. Richard Tykva and Dieter Berg (Dordrecht, 2004), p. 126.

and Vladimir gubernias. Ivan Borozdna belonged to the first generation of landholders in the former Hetmanate who began to marry outside the usual circle of the former Cossack officer elite. Ivan's brother Vasyl was married to Liubov Ugriumova, whose name also suggests Russian origins. The old, relatively closed world of the generation of Petro Borozdna was crumbling, adding to the sense of uncertainty among the elite of the former Hetmanate.[4]

Change was in the air, but not everything had changed overnight in Starodub and its environs. The prevailing pattern remained that of marriage within the old familiar circle of the Starodub elite, and the case of Petro Borozdna's youngest son, Mykola, fits that pattern. He was married to and buried next to Yelysaveta Myklashevska, the daughter of the Borozdnas' neighbor and owner of Ponurivka, Mykhailo Myklashevsky. This marriage, which fits the Borozdna family's standard pattern of marital ties, is of particular interest to our search for the author of the *History of the Rus'*. Mykola Borozdna was born in Medvediv in October 1808. He graduated from Moscow University in April 1826 and began his career as a civil servant, stationed first in Riazan and then in Simferopol. In 1830 he retired from the civil service, returned to the Starodub region, and married Yelysaveta Myklashevska. The owner of Kivai soon began to climb the nobiliary service ladder. He was elected marshal of the Novozybkiv nobility, then of the nobility of the entire Chernihiv gubernia. In the wake of the 1861 land reform and the emancipation of the peasantry, he was appointed governor of Smolensk. Borozdna turned out to be effective in his post and was generally admired by his subordinates. Mykola Borozdna died in 1878 or 1880. His wife, Yelysaveta Myklashevska, lived until 1886. It was then that the two were buried on their family estate of Kivai.[5]

The Borozdnas and Myklashevskys had been linked by matrimonial ties at least since the eighteenth century. Anastasiia Myklashevska was the wife of General Standard-Bearer Ivan Ivanovych Borozdna and a grandmother of Petro Ivanovych Borozdna. Mykola's marriage into Myklashevsky's family, which took place after Petro Borozdna's death, strengthened those traditional ties, which also survived Mykhailo Myklashevsky. When the aged owner of Ponurivka died in August 1847, his obituary in *Moskovskie vedomosti* (Moscow News) was written by none other than Mykola's

---

[4] Vadim Modzalevskii, *Malorossiiskii rodoslovnik*, 4 vols. (Kyiv, 1908–14), I: 74–77.
[5] *Ibid.*, I: 77–78; II: 498–99.

brother, Ivan Borozdna. In 1857, when after decades of exile Aleksandr von Brigen, the husband of Yelysaveta Myklashevska's sister Sofiia and the "discoverer" of the *History*, visited his wife's estate for the first time since his arrest in January 1826, Mykola Borozdna was a member of the welcoming party. Von Brigen was particularly impressed by the younger Borozdna. "I liked them all, and I can say that they all looked after me,' he wrote from Ponurivka in August 1857. "Nastasia Yakov[levna], Varvara Vas[ilievna], and Nik[olai] Pet[rovich] Borozdna are distinguished from the rest in that regard . . . I have met few people as well-mannered and pleasant as he."[6]

The Borozdna–Myklashevsky connection may well explain how the *History of the Rus'*, if it was indeed written by the Borozdnas, reached the Myklashevskys' estate of Ponurivka, but it does not help resolve the "Kryzhanovsky problem" presented in the previous chapter. Perhaps other matrimonial connections of the Borozdnas may prove more helpful? One such connection to consider is that between the Borozdnas and the Shyrais, especially given that the retired Major General Stepan Mykhailovych Shyrai, the "finder" of the *History of the Rus'* at the Hryniv estate of the Bezborodkos, was a son-in-law of Petro Borozdna. What do we know about his relations with the Borozdnas, and what exactly was his role in the second discovery of the *History* known to us? We shall begin with the first part of the question.

The wedding of Stepan Shyrai and Petro Borozdna's first-born daughter, Uliana, took place on January 20, 1801. The Borozdnas and the Shyrais were close neighbors: Medvediv is only 18 km from Starodub, and only a little farther away from Solova, the family estate of the Shyrais. Now they became close relatives. The marriage was probably facilitated by Petro Borozdna's and Stepan Shyrai's joint service in the Starodub carabineer regiment in the 1780s. The two men were of the same generation: in fact, the son-in-law was four years older than his father-in-law. Stepan Shyrai was born in 1761. His parents were Mykhailo Shyrai, the marshal of the Starodub nobility and a wealthy scion of an established Cossack family, and his wife, Mariia Vasylivna Hudovych, a daughter of the general treasurer of the Hetmanate and a sister of one of the most distinguished commanders of the Russian Empire, Count Ivan Hudovych. On May 10, 1771, Mykhailo Shyrai enlisted his teenage son Stepan in the military with the Cossack rank of fellow of the standard. The regulations introduced by Peter I in the early eighteenth century obliged the children of

---

[6] I. P. Borozdna, "Nekrologiia tainogo sovetnika i kavalera M. P. Miklashevskogo," *Moskovskie vedomosti*, 1847, no. 131; A. F. Brigen, *Pis'ma. Istoricheskie sochineniia* (Irkutsk, 1986), pp. 376–77.

the nobility to start at the bottom of the Table of Ranks, and the nobles tried to beat the system by starting their children's formal careers as early as possible. In April 1785, Stepan Shyrai joined the Starodub carabineer regiment with the rank of premier major. He was transferred to the Little Russian grenadier regiment and took part in Russian military campaigns first in Poland and then against the Ottomans in southern Ukraine and Moldavia. He would return to the Starodub regiment in 1792, a decorated and battle-scarred colonel who had taken part in major battles of the Russo-Turkish war of 1787–92. He fought in the Battle of Rymnik and participated in the capture of Izmail (1790).

During the war, Shyrai served on the staff of Aleksandr Suvorov. At one point Shyrai acted as a courier between Suvorov and a rising star in the Russian military establishment, Mikhail Kutuzov. If one trusts an apocryphal story, Suvorov once sent a handsome young officer as a messenger to Empress Catherine II, who loved to meet young officers – some of those messengers even became her favorites at court. Shyrai apparently did not make it into the empress's bed, but he must have made a good impression. He was decorated and promoted through the ranks. Shyrai's spectacular career was aided by his connections (through his cousin Hanna Shyrai) with Illia Bezborodko. Oleksandr Bezborodko knew Shyrai as a young officer and at least on one occasion used him to pass a letter to his father, residing in Ukraine. In 1791 Bezborodko included Shyrai in the Russian delegation to the Iaşi peace conference with the Ottomans. Upon the conclusion of the peace talks, Shyrai hand-delivered a congratulatory letter from the Russian authorities to the grand vizier of the Ottoman Empire. His service as an honorary courier did not end there. He was also sent to St. Petersburg to deliver the signed peace treaty to Empress Catherine II and is mentioned in one of her letters to Bezborodko. This mission may have been the basis for the apocryphal story involving Suvorov.[7]

Shyrai ended his military career with the rank of major general. In 1797, Emperor Paul I dismissed him as commander of the Riga cuirassier regiment for the mutiny of his subordinates. Shyrai returned to his home estate of Solova in the neighborhood of Starodub. At the age of

[7] See "Shyrai, Stepan Mikhailovich," in *Russkii biograficheskii slovar' v 25 tt.*, ed. A. A. Polovtsov, vol. XXIII (St. Petersburg, 1911), pp. 300–1; V. L. Modzalevs'kyi, *Malorosiis'kyi rodoslovnyk*, vol. v, vyp. 5 (Kyiv and St. Petersburg, 2004), pp. 15–16; S. I. Ushakov, *Deianiia rossiiskikh polkovodtsev i generalov* (Moscow, 1822), vol. i, pp. 96–97; N. I. Grigorovich, *Kantsler kniaz' A. Bezborod'ko v sviazi s sobytiiami ego vremeni*, 2 vols. (St. Petersburg, 1879–81), pp. 172, 208, 217, 639; Oleksander Ohloblyn, *Liudy staroï Ukraïny* (Munich, 1959), pp. 155–56.

thirty-seven, he was a desirable match for many Starodub families with daughters of marriageable age. He chose Petro Borozdna's teenage daughter, Uliana. In 1801, the year of her marriage, she was fifteen, while he turned forty. There seem to have been no marital problems at first. Uliana gave birth to two sons and two daughters. But as time passed, dark clouds appeared on the family's horizon. Shyrai's relations with his young wife deteriorated, leading to a dispute over control of Uliana's significant dowry in which her father became involved. As a result, relations between the younger father-in-law and the older and more powerful son-in-law were damaged beyond repair, setting the stage for a family feud that continued for decades after Petro Borozdna's death in 1820.

The origins of the conflict go back to the first years of Stepan Shyrai's marriage. In June 1802, a year and a half after her marriage to Shyrai, the sixteen-year-old Uliana signed papers according to which she transferred her dowry to her husband but retained the right to change that decision subsequently. Seven years later, in August 1809, she signed a different statement according to which she gave her dowry to her children, while making her husband the actual manager of her property. There was no provision in the statement allowing Uliana to take back her property if something went wrong with her marriage, which was already showing many signs of strain. The transfer of control over the dowry to Shyrai was opposed by the Borozdnas, especially the family patriarch and Uliana's father, Petro Borozdna. In all likelihood the father-in-law and son-in-law clashed over the matter as early as 1809, although we have no direct proof of that.

We do, however, have a letter sent in 1811 by Stepan Shyrai to Mykola Ivanovych Nemyrovych-Danchenko, who was married to Uliana's sister, making him another son-in-law of Petro Borozdna. The Nemyrovych-Danchenkos, a family that produced one of the best-known Russian theater directors of all time, Vladimir Nemirovich-Danchenko (1858–1943), were closely associated with the Borozdnas by numerous intermarriages, and Mykola Ivanovych Nemyrovych-Danchenko seemed especially close to Petro Borozdna. Stepan Shyrai decided to make use of that closeness and asked Mykola to serve as an intermediary between him and Petro Borozdna. He also told Mykola his side of the story, which was extremely disturbing. It turns out that Shyrai had not only taken control of Uliana's dowry but also abandoned her, moving out of his family estate of Solova and settling permanently in Starodub.

How to explain such behavior? Shyrai claimed that he was not a perpetrator but a victim of Uliana's actions. He could no longer live under the same roof with his estranged wife. "Civil law prohibits me from seeing her," wrote Shyrai to Nemyrovych-Danchenko. "Living in the same house means suffering and taking many precautions, for newly intercepted correspondence is all about wishes for my death, about the theft of property and animal lust. I swear by almighty God that I bear no hatred for all that has been done to me, considering all of it to be the work of evil spirits. A pathological inclination, and an insatiable one at that, to all sorts of abominations; disturbances at home at every hour; scoundrels coming in from every direction; the corruption of domestics; exposing oneself to constant danger – all this would long ago have compelled me to take other measures if I did not respect human rights and fear divine wrath, for there is no crime where involuntary impulse is concerned." The retired general claimed that he had no ulterior motives in taking control of Uliana's dowry: "It is only envy that makes the property under my control appear to be huge, but my own exceeds it twice over; it is not for the sake of caprice or vanity but for the welfare of my children that I must preserve and safeguard it from all illegitimate pretensions."[8]

What did Stepan Shyrai have in mind? Many relatives and neighbors of the Shyrais knew Uliana as an "intelligent, gentle, and virtuous" woman of "quiet, modest, noble character." But some of them also remembered a different Uliana Shyrai. In the 1840s, after Uliana's death (which came in 1839), one of the Shyrais' neighbors, a certain Zhyvotkevych, told court officials investigating the Shyrai family feud that Uliana "was modest in character but fiery in temperament." He elaborated as follows: "Uliana Shyrai would have seizures resembling insanity, and then she would make presents to anyone of whatever came to hand, and in forgetfulness she would exceed the bounds of decency with regard to the male sex. During the blessing of the house at Solova, when Shyrai lived there with his wife, at Shyrai's request the right reverend [Archbishop Mikhail Desnitsky] of Chernihiv instructed Uliana Shyrai in a separate room concerning marital fidelity."

Count Hudovych, a relative of Stepan Shyrai, presented a more balanced picture, but he also drew attention to Uliana's illness. He told the court officials that "he rarely had occasion to see Shyrai's wife, but it always seemed to him that when free of seizures she was modest, gentle, and cordial in behavior." Another neighbor, Actual State Councillor Iskrytsky, stated that he "had heard from his relatives who visited Uliana Shyrai that when she was in a diseased state, she preferred conversation

---

[8] "Pamiatnoe delo," *Osnova* (July 1861): 41–74, here 60–64.

and occupations not customary to her, liked to live in the servants' wing and not in the house, and she was insufficiently careful of her dress." Doctor Kuzminsky, who treated Uliana Shyrai during the last years of her life, testified that she "had general derangement that sometimes lasted a week, with symptoms of insomnia and loquaciousness or taciturnity and sullenness."[9]

These testimonies leave little doubt that Uliana Shyrai suffered from mental illness, and that Shyrai was probably sincere when he claimed in his letter to Nemyrovych-Danchenko that he had no choice but to take control of Uliana's dowry for the benefit of their children. He was probably no less sincere when he wrote that he feared for his own life. These could be legitimate concerns, given what we know about Uliana's mental state. But Uliana's family apparently did not see it that way. Petro Borozdna was concerned about the fate of the possessions that he had given as a dowry. In all likelihood, he did not want the separation of Shyrai and his daughter to become public knowledge. Moreover, the family heard rumors that after Shyrai left Solova for Starodub in December 1811, Uliana was not well treated by Shyrai's servants there. She was neglected by the estate manager and always under the control of serfs who would not allow her to leave the village. Relations between the two families went from bad to worse in November 1818, when Uliana gave birth to her third son, Oleksandr: Stepan Shyrai, who claimed that he was not living in wedlock, refused to recognize him as his child. When Oleksandr turned four, Shyrai ordered him to be taken away from Uliana and given to peasants in one of his villages to be raised.

Stepan Shyrai's decision to take away Uliana's child left her heart-broken and more desperate than ever before. Her only hope was her eldest son, Mykhailo Shyrai (1802–33), a student of Moscow University and the only member of the family who could act independently of the old Shyrai. Uliana made Mykhailo promise her that he would act as a father to Oleksandr, and he kept his word. He first placed Oleksandr with the family of a priest in Novhorod-Siverskyi and then took him to Moscow, where he was left under the name Oleksandr Zabotin in the custody of Anna Vasilievna Kubareva, the mother of Mykhailo's friend, Professor Aleksei Kubarev of the University of Moscow. She was supposed to supervise Oleksandr's preparation for enrollment at the university. But Oleksandr's fate took a turn for the worse when his only protector, Mykhailo Shyrai, died in the early 1830s. Mrs. Kubareva had little choice

---

[9] *Ibid.*, pp. 52–53.

but to place Oleksandr in an orphanage, where he learned trades. Uliana Shyrai never recovered from the loss of Oleksandr and the death of Mykhailo. She passed away after a debilitating illness in 1839.

Stepan Shyrai would live another two years. After the death of his wife, he took measures to ensure that Oleksandr would never be recognized as his son and that all of his and Uliana's property would go to their two surviving daughters. On Shyrai's orders, church books containing the registration of Oleksandr's birth in 1818 were doctored and incriminating pages replaced with forged ones. The fraud was uncovered after Stepan Shyrai's death, when Oleksandr, with the help of his mother's brothers, Ivan and Mykola Borozdna, filed a lawsuit claiming his part of the inheritance. Shyrai's two daughters challenged the claim. The court procedures dragged on for years, turning the Shyrai dispute into a "memorable case" that served as an endless source of gossip among the Starodub notables. The courts eventually decided in favor of Oleksandr Zabotin and the Borozdna family, which supported him. He was allowed not only to resume the use of his original surname but also to take possession of Stepan Shyrai's estate of Solova.[10]

The Shyrai–Borozdna feud eventually faded into the past, but not without leaving deep scars on the lives and memories of its participants and numerous traces in the historical sources of the era. It seems plausible that those sources may include not only the court records but also the *History of the Rus'*, which may well bear traces of the Shyrai–Borozdna feud and Stepan Shyrai's unhappiness with his in-laws. The Kryzhanovsky episode, to the degree that it might have been directed against the Borozdnas, would certainly fit the bill. The same applies to the Horsk episode, in which the name of the Borozdnas is not mentioned at all. In the latter case, the author may well have passed over the family name not in order to protect the Borozdnas but, on the contrary, to avoid mentioning their name in a context that might produce sympathy toward them on the part of the reader.

What do we know about Stepan Shyrai's involvement with the *History?* According to a story told by a Starodub nobleman and amateur historian, Oleksandr Khanenko (1816–95), and recorded by Oleksandr Lazarevsky, the first manuscript of the *History of the Rus'* to become known to the general public was found in 1828 on the Hryniv estate of Count Illia Bezborodko (1756–1815). It was discovered in the library of the palace built

---

[10] "Pamiatnoe delo," *Osnova* (September 1861): 110–34; Modzalevs'kyi, *Malorosiis'kyi rodoslovnyk*, vol. v, vyp. 5, pp. 19–20.

for the count in the early nineteenth century – a huge two-story building with a six-column portico. Rumor had it that the building had been designed by the famous imperial architect Giacomo Quarenghi, who had built numerous palaces in St. Petersburg. Although the rumor proved false, the palace was a jewel of local architecture. Count G. G. Kushelev, a relative of the Bezborokos, writing in September 1825 claimed that the palace at the Hryniv estate was superior to some of the family palaces in the capital, "spacious and ten times more splendid than that of St. Petersburg, hung with French tapestries, [and] articles that have been brought there, paintings."[11]

The Hryniv estate was located approximately 17 km east of Starodub and a bit more than 25 km north of Mykhailo Myklashevsky's estate of Ponurivka. When Aleksandr von Brigen visited Ponurivka in the fall of 1825, the estate had just passed from Illia Bezborodko's wife, Hanna Shyrai, who had died the previous year, to Bezborodko's daughter Kleopatra. The Hryniv manuscript was allegedly found three years later, during the transfer of the estate from Kleopatra to Prince Sergei Golitsyn, a hero of the Napoleonic Wars who bought Hryniv from the cash-strapped Kleopatra in 1828. The finders of the manuscript were Stepan Laikevych and Oleksandr Hamaliia, two clerks of the Starodub court who catalogued the library. They reported their find to the highest noble official in the area, Stepan Shyrai, a retired general, wealthy landowner, and marshal of the nobility of the Chernihiv gubernia. He allegedly ordered a copy to be made.

Ohloblyn considered the story apocryphal and questioned not only the date of the first appearance of the *History* but also that of the transfer of the Hryniv estate to Golitsyn. His skepticism was somewhat excessive. Important elements of the story are corroborated by other sources. Golitsyn did indeed purchase the estate in 1828, and it was also around that time that the manuscript became known to a broader public. The historian Dmitrii Bantysh-Kamensky was one of the beneficiaries of Shyrai's initiative. But Ohloblyn's criticism was not completely unfounded. The *History* was indeed well known in the Starodub region even before the "discovery" of 1828. One proof of that comes directly from von Brigen's letter, written in the fall of 1825. Another involves none other than Stepan Shyrai. It comes from a diary entry dating from the summer

[11] "Grinevo," *Delovoi Briansk*, no. 1 (2003), http://pogar-ray.land.ru/hist/7.htm; O. P. Ohloblyn, *Do pytannia pro avtora "Istoriï Rusov"* (Kyiv, 1998), p. 30.

of 1821, seven years before the Hryniv discovery and four years prior to von Brigen's letter from Ponurivka.[12]

On June 3, 1822, Mikhail Pogodin (1800–75), then a 22-year-old student at Moscow University, later a prominent Russian historian and one of the leaders of the Slavophile movement, recorded in his diary a conversation he had that day on the prevailing moods in "Little Russia" – the former Cossack lands of Ukraine. "Not a shadow of their former rights remains among them now. The Little Russians call themselves the true Russians and the others Muscovites (*moskali*). They do not entirely like them. Thus Muscovy was something apart. They also call the Old Believers Muscovites. They love Mazepa. Earlier they did not supply recruits but [Cossack] regiments. Thus there were regiments from Chernihiv, [Novhorod]-Siverskyi, and so on. That was much better: they were all from one region and therefore more comradely, more in agreement. But now someone from Irkutsk stands next to a Kyivan; a man from Arkhangelsk next to one from Astrakhan. What is the sense of it?"[13]

Pogodin was an interesting and controversial figure in the history of Russo-Ukrainian relations. A friend of Mykhailo Maksymovych, he was originally a strong supporter of the nascent Ukrainian intellectual movement but turned against it after the arrest of members of the Brotherhood of SS. Cyril and Methodius. Regarding the *History of the Rus'*, he followed the path of other students of the monument, his original excitement giving way to a more critical approach. He welcomed Bodiansky's publication of the *History* in 1846, noting in his diary: "I read Konysky with satisfaction – the horrors that our heroes and Peter allow themselves there." Later Pogodin was much more reserved. In 1869 he wrote to Maksymovych: "Is there data about Konysky's original? Did someone fix up his language, perhaps? . . . Is there not patriotic woolgathering here? Is Bodiansky's edition a good one?" Pogodin may well have been more qualified to answer these questions than any of his correspondents, including Maksymovych. His diary entries for June 1822 indicate that he may have been closer to the circle of the author of the *History* than any other student of its text.[14]

[12] Aleksandr Lazarevskii, *Ocherki, zametki i dokumenty*, vol. 1 (Kyiv, 1892), p. 48; Ohloblyn, *Do pytannia*, pp. 27–34.
[13] Diary of Mikhail Pogodin, Russian State Library, Manuscript Division, fond 231/I, K. 30, no. 1, entry for June 3, 1822. Cf. Nikolai Barsukov, *Zhizn' i trudy M. P. Pogodina*, vol. 1 (St. Petersburg, 1888), p. 153.
[14] Mykhailo Vozniak, *Psevdo-Konys'kyi i Psevdo-Poletyka (Istoria Rusov u literaturi ta nautsi)* (Lviv and Kyiv, 1939), pp. 35–36, 45.

Pogodin's entry for June 3 concerning Ukrainian grievances and aspirations came out of a discussion with Aleksei Kubarev, his mentor at Moscow University, and with his and Kubarev's close friend Mykhailo Shyrai, a son of Stepan Shyrai. It was from the younger Shyrai, then also a student at Moscow University and Pogodin's rival in the dissertation competition for the university's gold medal, that Pogodin took the information on Ukrainian moods and entered it in his diary. The rest of the conversation, as summarized by Pogodin, focused on "a certain Sudiienko, who, holding no civic office, governed the whole town merely by the respect that he commanded," and "Metropolitan Mikhail [of St. Petersburg]," who was "idolized in Chernihiv." The impressions recorded by Pogodin came from Shyrai's family circle in Ukraine. The Sudiienkos were related to the Shyrais, and Mykhailo Shyrai's father, Stepan, was closely associated with Metropolitan Mikhail Desnitsky of St. Petersburg, formerly archbishop of Chernihiv, who had visited his family estate in Solova and tried to influence the behavior of Uliana Shyrai.[15]

On the one hand, Pogodin's diary entry confirms Ohloblyn's insistence, now shared by all students of the *History*, that the finding of the text in Hryniv was not in fact its first discovery. On the other hand, it makes General Shyrai, one of the leading figures in a story all but dismissed by Ohloblyn, much more important and interesting than previously assumed. Pogodin's entry leaves little doubt that Stepan Shyrai and/or some members of his family shared some of the essential ideas expressed in the *History of the Rus'* long before the old general began to distribute copies of the manuscript. There can be only two explanations for this fact: either the Shyrais had already read the *History* before the summer of 1822, or the author of the *History* came from circles close to the Shyrais. Both suppositions find some support in the historical sources. As Ohloblyn pointed out, Shyrai's connection to the Hryniv estate was not limited to his high office of marshal of the Chernihiv nobility. The estate belonged to the Shyrai family in the eighteenth century and passed to the Bezborodkos only as part of the dowry of Illia Bezborodko's fourteen-year-old bride, Hanna Shyrai, a cousin of Stepan Shyrai. She owned the estate after Illia's death in 1815 and kept it among her possessions until her own death in 1824. Stepan Shyrai was thus no outsider in Hryniv and could have had access to his cousin's library long before her death. He might have read the *History* if it was already in the library or even placed it there himself.

---

[15] Diary of Mikhail Pogodin, vol. 1, entry for June 3, 1822. Cf. Barsukov, *Zhizn' i trudy M. P. Pogodina*, 1: 153; Ohloblyn, *Liudy staroï Ukraïny*, pp. 155–57.

The entry in Pogodin's diary raises important questions about Shyrai's circle of friends and relatives, who may have shared the views communicated to Pogodin by Mykhailo Shyrai and Aleksei Kubarev. Who were they? It is quite possible that the circle included the author of the *History* or people involved in one way or another in the production of the manuscript. We shall attempt to reconstruct the Shyrai circle, starting with a close look at Stepan Shyrai himself.

When Shyrai retired in 1797 to his family estate of Solova, he was still full of energy and eager to serve. According to one apocryphal story, Shyrai, disappointed by the poor performance of the local governor, offered his services as governor of Little Russia to Emperor Paul. That proved a *faux pas*. The emperor had never forgiven Shyrai the mutiny in his regiment, and by that time the all-powerful Oleksandr Bezborodko was gone (he died in 1799). Emperor Paul's response to Shyrai was published in the second half of the nineteenth century by A. V. Sheremetev. He wrote: "On Emperor Paul's accession to the throne, he [Shyrai] wrote him a letter describing how incompetently and absurdly Little Russia was being ruled by the appointed governors, and then proposed himself as governor general, as one with a perfect knowledge of the Little Russian people. On receipt of that letter, Emperor Paul answered him as follows: 'Mr. State Councillor Shyrai, The attainment of the highest honors in the empire is permitted to all; your desire to be governor general of Little Russia is praiseworthy, but your desire alone is insufficient for it – my consent is also indispensable for that purpose, and I do not deign to grant it to you. Paul.'"[16]

Whether the emperor's letter was authentic or not, it served as the basis of one of the many stories circulating all over the empire about Stepan Shyrai, who was known for his wit and was regarded as a "great eccentric." Anecdotes about Shyrai's lenient treatment of his corrupt estate managers became especially popular. "Shyrai was once told that his estate manager was a thief; that he had already built himself a house in Starodub," went one of them. "And he was advised to get another manager. 'But has he already built that house?' asked Shyrai. 'He has.' 'If I take another one, he will just start building a house,' coolly observed Shyrai." Another story was no less colorful. "Another time Shyrai, having learned of the thievery of one of the estate managers, ordered that his pockets be sewn up and that he be brought to him. 'Put your hands in your pockets!' ordered

---

[16] A. Sheremet'ev, "Pis'mo imperatora Pavla Shiraiu," *Russkaia starina* 12, no. 4 (1875): 820. Cf. Mikhail Pyliaev, *Zamechatel'nye chudaki i originaly* (Moscow, 2003), pp. 268–70.

Shyrai. The manager tried to do so but could not. 'Where will you put your stolen goods, you thief?' asked Shyrai. The manager was flustered. 'What, are you ashamed? Ah, you thief, you thief! Get out of here!' muttered Shyrai and let the thief go scot-free."[17]

By the standards of his day, Shyrai was apparently lenient not only toward his managers but also toward his serfs, of whom he owned more than two thousand. Judging by the stories told by his son, Mykhailo, to Mikhail Pogodin, the retired general tried to improve the lot of the peasants. On one occasion Pogodin noted in his diary: "I visited [Mykhailo] Shyrai; we went to the Kremlin, took a walk there, recalled old times, enjoyed the view, and spoke about the condition of Russia." He then turned to the peasant question: "It seems that it [emancipation] should not be introduced among us now, at least in certain gubernias. The proof is obvious. State peasants live no better than those of landowners. The people cannot yet make use of liberty as they should. Mykh[ailo] St[epanovych] [Shyrai] assured me that his father's peasants made a great many complaints about him for having built them new cottages. They would have preferred to sit in their old smoke-filled ones. This matter should be addressed gradually, restricting the rights of the landowners and defining the obligations of the peasants."[18]

Stepan Shyrai was known to his neighbors, relatives, and friends not only for his idiosyncrasies. He was also apparently a gold mine of memories about the good old days. Mikhail Pogodin was happy to record in his diary numerous anecdotes from the life of Aleksandr Suvorov recounted by Stepan Shyrai to Aleksei Kubarev. During the summer vacation of 1821 Kubarev, who served as a mentor to Mykhailo Shyrai during his studies at Moscow University, visited the Shyrais. The old Shyrai shared with him some of his anecdotes and personal stories, which left no doubt that he, like his former commander, Suvorov, had a low opinion of Emperor Paul. According to one apocryphal story heard from Shyrai, "Suvorov ... said to a general who brought him some piece of news from Paul: 'Tell the Sovereign from me, if you can, that my life is in his hands, but my glory is above him.'" Suvorov once wrote to Paul concerning his former subordinates who got into trouble with the law: "Suv[orov] wrote: my head was often exposed to death under your mother's rule. If it is also required now in order to save these unfortunate ones, it is ready." Most of the stories came from the age of Catherine. One

---

[17] "Istoricheskie anekdoty i smeshnye istorii," www.funspot.ru/vorovstvo/29.html.
[18] Diary of Mikhail Pogodin, vol. 1, entry for August 29, 1820.

of them concerned Shyrai's visit to Suvorov soon after the death of Catherine II had been announced. The distressed Suvorov allegedly greeted Shyrai with the following words: "Ah, those damned rhymesters, those scoundrels, how can one believe them? They said that Catherine was immortal, but now she has died."[19]

Shyrai clearly cherished his memories of the good old days, and, when it came to his own career, better days than those of Catherine's rule could hardly be imagined. When in 1826, in connection with the coronation of Emperor Nicholas I, Shyrai was awarded the Order of St. Vladimir, third class, he refused it. Acceptance would have meant surrendering the Order of St. Vladimir, fourth class, which he had received personally from Catherine II. When Suvorov asked, "What is this award supposed to mean?" Shyrai, who matched Suvorov himself in wit, gave a reply that became known throughout the army: "It means that I am brave, but not too brave (*khrabr da ne vel'mi*)." Shyrai's point was that truly brave soldiers were being decorated with the Order of St. George. Now he would not surrender the "not too brave" order. Had Shyrai's case been a standard one, he would have been compelled to accept the Order of St. Vladimir, since it was up to his superiors to decide on the appropriate level of award. But Shyrai approached a powerful friend in St. Petersburg, and in September 1826, instead of the Order of St. Vladimir, third class, he was awarded the Order of St. Anne, first class. He was extremely proud of the award. The only portrait of the retired major general known today depicts him with the star and the broad ribbon of the Order of St. Anne. Shyrai's contemporaries recalled his lavish receptions, "at which he appeared in a nankeen frock-coat with the Star of St. Anne." It has been claimed that he "wished to immortalize the receipt of this award, and on his family estate he built a magnificent palace that was to bear witness to his descendants, from generation to generation, of the honor once merited by its builder. The palace was built in the form of the Cross of St. Anne: at its center was a round salon like the circle at the center of the Cross of St. Anne, and on the cupola was an image of St. Anne corresponding to the one depicted on the cross."[20]

The reference was probably to Shyrai's house in Pantusiv (Pantusovo), a village in close proximity to Starodub. In late 1811 he moved from his

---

[19] Diary of Mikhail Pogodin, vol. 1, entries for October 3, 1821, and February 19, 1822; Barsukov, *Zhizn' i trudy M. P. Pogodina*, 1: 134–36.

[20] I. S. Listovskii, "Rasskazy iz nedavnei stariny," *Russkii arkhiv*, no. 3 (1878): 507–21, here 519–20; Pyliaev, *Zamechatelnye chudaki i originaly*, pp. 268–70; *Chernigovskie gubernskie vedomosti*, no. 632 (1895): 1.

ancestral village of Solova to the town of Starodub, and in the latter half of the 1820s he traded his Starodub home for a new estate in the village of Pantusiv, 6 km to the north. Shyrai bought that estate from the Budlianskys, an old Cossack family related to the last hetman of Ukraine, Kyrylo Rozumovsky. It was an impressive estate. At the turn of the nineteenth century it was visited by a Russian writer, Prince K. P. Shalikov, who was so impressed by the garden and park that he compared it to the Sheremetev family estate in the village of Kuskovo near Moscow. Shalikov described Pantusiv as a "village with a large old house and an old regular orchard adjoined by a great wild grove. In general, it has a wonderful location and picturesque views all around that you enjoy from the windows of the house, the prospects of the lanes, and the shade of the pavilions," wrote the guest from Moscow. "At every moment," he concluded his description, "Pantusovo reminds us of Kuskovo."[21]

Shyrai spent the rest of his life in that Starodub Kuskovo. Between 1818 and 1828, when he was marshal of the Chernihiv nobility, the retired general would regularly travel to Chernihiv, but the town of Starodub, where he owned numerous properties, and then Pantusiv remained the center of his activities through all those years. He was popular in the neighborhood, known for his "lavish balls and receptions." According to Oleksandr Khanenko – the same Khanenko who related to Oleksandr Lazarevsky the story of how the *History of the Rus'* was found at Illia Bezborodko's Hryniv estate – the Shyrai residence "brought together all the best people of the Siverian districts at the time." Khanenko, who was born in 1816, was referring to the situation in the 1820s, recent enough for him to remember if not from his own childhood, then from the recollections of his relatives. Shyrai's family connections, his meteoric military career and his later role as marshal of the Chernihiv gubernia nobility, coupled with his independent character and wealth, made him a leading force in Starodub society.[22]

Who were Shyrai's "best people"? Judging by what we can deduce from the Pogodin diary, Shyrai was especially close to relatives and neighbors who shared the same imperial experiences as he. One of them was Osyp Sudiienko, whom Aleksei Kubarev, Pogodin's mentor at Moscow University, visited along with the younger Shyrai in the summer of 1821, and

[21] K. P. Shalikov, *Puteshestvie v Malorossiiu* (Moscow, 1803), pp. 176–78. Cf. Valentin Korovin, *Landshaft moikh voobrazhenii. Stranitsy prozy russkogo sentimentalizma* (Moscow, 1990), p. 556; Cheplianskaia, *Starodubskii uezd.*

[22] N. O. Herasymenko, "Nevydani lysty O. I. Khanenka do O. M. Lazarevs'koho," *Ukraïns'kyi istorychnyi zhurnal,* no. 3 (2009): 92–108.

whose talents as a charismatic leader he praised. The Sudiienkos were related to the Shyrais. Osyp Sudiienko's maternal grandfather was Stepan Spyrydonovych Shyrai, a grandfather of Stepan Shyrai. Sudiienko was a trusted assistant of Oleksandr Bezborodko during his years in St. Petersburg and the manager of his and Illia Bezborodko's estates in Ukraine. Awarded titles and estates by his patrons, he further enriched himself by managing their properties. In St. Petersburg his rise to wealth and power was regarded as an example of the corruption rife among "Little Russians." In Ukraine, however, visitors to his palace in the village of Ochkynia (now Ochkino in Russia) were awed by his power and the lavish decoration of his palace – they had seen nothing like it outside the capital. Sudiienko was also a generous donor to local cultural and historical initiatives. In 1809, at the behest of the local governor, he donated a large sum (50,000 rubles) for the construction of a church on the Poltava battlefield to commemorate the Russian soldiers who had fallen there. The donation was a bribe in all but form: Sudiienko wanted the emperor to recognize his son Mykhailo, born out of wedlock, as his legitimate heir. Upon receiving a personal letter of thanks from Emperor Alexander I, Osyp Sudiienko doubled his donation. Mykhailo Sudiienko, a friend of Pushkin, later became president of the Kyiv Commission for the Study of Ancient Documents and showed special interest in Cossack historical writing.[23]

According to Pogodin's diary, a special place in Shyrai's recollections about the good old days was reserved for an imperial luminary with Starodub roots, Count Petro Zavadovsky. The Zavadovskys were related to the Shyrais: Petro Zavadovsky's mother came from that influential Starodub family, and the young Petro was raised by his maternal grandfather, Mykhailo Shyrai. In his St. Petersburg years he loved to reminisce about his Shyrai relations back in Ukraine. They were in fact his closest relatives. In his diary Pogodin recorded the following story, which originated with Shyrai, about Zavadovsky's palace: "In his village of Lialychi he [Zavadovsky] built a palace huge enough for a tsar, as well as ancillary buildings, surrounded the forest with a stone wall twenty versts long, and gave a splendid ball. Shyr[ai] did not go for supper and, remaining with him, asked: 'Tell me, Count Pet[ro] Vas[ylyovych], why did you do all this? Did you have your

[23] Volodymyr Chukhno, "Osyp Stepanovych Sudiienko i ioho blahodiini spravy," *Siverians'kyi litopys*, no. 4 (2009): 96–107.

descendants in mind?' 'No, I wanted to live just as I pleased for three days; now I have been doing so for three months and am content.'"[24]

Zavadovsky's mansion in Lialychi made an unforgettable impression on everyone who visited it. Prince Shalikov, who stopped by at the turn of the nineteenth century, described it in a chapter of his travel log titled "The Gift of Catherine." He wrote: "When you survey the artless bounty of nature and the magnificent urban house here, you imagine him as a guest, a foreigner who wandered in from Milionnaia Street in St. Petersburg." Shalikov was also impressed by the English garden, which featured "a grand white pavilion shaded on three sides by a thick growth of tall trees." "You approach it, and in the center of the colonnade you see his Trans-Danubian Achilles – a life-size statue on a rough-hewn marble pedestal," wrote Shalikov. This was a monument erected by Zavadovsky to his patron, the former ruler of Little Russia and chief integrator of the Hetmanate into the Russian Empire, Prince Petr Rumiantsev-Zadunaisky, who received the honorary title "Zadunaisky" [Trans-Danubian] for his victories over the Ottomans in the Danube region. "He is shown, as usual, in Roman dress," as Shalikov described the monument, "his head bare, his helmet hanging from the knot of a stump on which the hero is taking a brief rest to recover from the immortal accomplishment of his labor; in one hand he holds his field marshal's baton, with which he touches the coat of arms on his shield, which stands by his left leg and bears the following motto: *non solum armis* (not by arms alone)." Remarkably, the cult of Petr Rumiantsev among the Ukrainian nobility of the early nineteenth century served as a symbol of both loyalty and opposition to the empire.[25]

If one trusts Pogodin's diary, the general leitmotif of Ukrainian complaints was dissatisfaction with the treatment meted out by the imperial authorities to the former Hetmanate. There were plenty of reasons for that attitude, rooted not only in the careers of high-flying imperial officials like Shyrai but also less prominent members of the former Cossack elite in their native Ukraine. Not surprisingly, then, the circle of Shyrai's relatives, neighbors, and friends includes most of our "unusual suspects." Shyrai was at the center of the group that we defined as closely related to him, either as sources of information, writers, or possible editors of the mysterious manuscript.

---

[24] Priscilla Roosevelt, *Life on the Russian Country Estate: A Social and Cultural History* (New Haven, Conn., 1995), p. 47; Diary of Mikhail Pogodin, vol. 1, entries for October 3, 1821; February 19, 1822. Cf. Barsukov, *Zhizn' i trudy M. P. Pogodina*, 1: 134–36.

[25] Shalikov, "Puteshestvie v Malorossiiu," in *Landshaft moikh voobrazhenii*, pp. 562–63.

A person specifically mentioned by Khanenko as part of Shyrai's circle was Mykhailo Skorupa, who regularly visited at his home. These two prominent Starodub figures were linked by more than friendship: Mykhailo Skorupa's father, who was a nephew of Pavlo Skorupa, was raised by his close relatives, the Shyrais. Generation after generation, these two Starodub families were associated in a variety of ways, including marriage. Pavlo Skorupa's brother Hryhorii married into the Shyrai family as early as the second decade of the eighteenth century. Another close acquaintance of Shyrai was Ivan Lashkevych, who lived in Brakhliv, a mere 12 km southeast of the Shyrai family estate of Solova. It was through Shyrai that Lashkevych sent one of his letters home from St. Petersburg. "I now dispatch this [letter] through my neighbor and friend Stepan Mykhailovych Shyrai in the hope that it will reach you quickly through Brakhlovo," wrote Lashkevych to Nastasia in June 1790, amid the court battle with his in-laws. Lashkevych was only four years younger than Shyrai, and the two had probably known each other since childhood. It is tempting to assume that, given the friendship attested by Lashkevych in his letter, he was also a welcome guest at Shyrai's home in the early nineteenth century, when the retired major general returned to his home estate.[26]

Then there was a circle of close relatives. They included Shyrai's nephews, the Haletskys, who held a number of positions in the nobiliary administration of Starodub in the early nineteenth century. Relations between the two families went as far back as the first half of the eighteenth century, when General Standard-Bearer Semen Haletsky married into that clan. His grandson, Ivan Petrovych Haletsky, followed what appears to have become a family tradition and married Hanna Mykhailivna Shyrai, a sister of Stepan Shyrai. The Myklashevskys were another Starodub family that had close links to the Shyrais. One of the heroes of the *History*, the Starodub colonel Mykhailo Andriiovych Myklashevsky, was Stepan Shyrai's maternal grandfather. Even closer family relations existed between the Hudovyches and the Shyrais. Vasyl Hudovych, a much more prominent figure in the *History* than Colonel Myklashevsky, was Stepan Shyrai's maternal grandfather. His daughter, Mariia Hudovych, was Stepan Shyrai's mother, and her numerous brothers, including Andrii and Ivan, were Stepan Shyrai's uncles. Shyrai is known to have maintained good relations with

---

[26] Herasymenko, "Nevydani lysty O. I. Khanenka do O. M. Lazarevs'koho," p. 103; *Liubetskii arkhiv grafa Miloradovicha*, p. 131; Modzalevskii, *Malorossiiskii rodoslovnik*, III: 32.

members of the Hudovych family well into the nineteenth century. Finally, Shyrai was both close to the Borozdnas and separated from them.[27]

What else do we know about Shyrai's personal life and his circle of friends? He was an unsurpassed storyteller. Pogodin recorded only episodes directly related to major figures of Russian imperial history, but Shyrai's stories about eighteenth-century Ukraine must have been no less informative and colorful. We know, for example, that in his circle he recounted the story of Catherine II's visit to Novhorod-Siverskyi in 1787 and her conversation with Vasyl Khanenko, the former first adjutant of Emperor Peter III. It is tempting to assume that at least some of those anecdotes found their way into the *History of the Rus'*, whose author paid so much attention to the family stories of Starodub-area notables. Stepan Mykhailovych Shyrai died in Pantusiv in 1841 at the age of 80 – ancient by the standards of the mid nineteenth century. He was remembered as "ambitious and proud, highly indulgent with his peasants and servants; severe with children." His neighbors gave him the following characterization: "philanthropic, firm, decisive, noble, kind, good-humored, loved company, hospitable, severe, reticent, unyielding, willful, proud, ambitious, remembered insults done to him." Shyrai left a lasting memory – an obtrusive skeleton in his family closet and the unresolved mystery of the *History* manuscript that he distributed.[28]

Was Stepan Mykhailovych Shyrai more than a mere promoter of the mysterious text? Is it possible that he also sponsored and perhaps co-authored it?

[27] Modzalevskii, *Malorossiiskii rodoslovnik*, I: 234–35; III: 475–79, 489–90; David Saunders, *The Ukrainian Impact on Russian Culture, 1750–1850* (Edmonton, 1985), p. 79; "Pamiatnoe delo," *Osnova* (July 1861), pp. 50–52.
[28] "Pamiatnoe delo," *Osnova* (July 1861): 52; Ohloblyn, *Do pytannia pro avtora "Istoriï Rusov,"* p. 121.

CHAPTER 17

The rivals

In June 2000 the mother superior of the Hustynia Trinity Monastery in the Chernihiv region of Ukraine received a telegram from a most unexpected place – Paris. The sender was Prince Mikhail Repnin, a descendant of Nikolai Repnin-Volkonsky, an early nineteenth-century governor of Little Russia who was buried in that monastery. The Paris Repnin was sending his best regards to the nuns on the occasion of the quadricentennial of the monastery. The fact that the monastery had managed to remain in existence so long was a miracle in itself. It was founded in 1600, during the Cossack era, and was one of the best-known Orthodox sanctuaries in the Hetmanate. Cossack officers were proud to add their names to the ranks of the monastery's benefactors, and Hetman Ivan Mazepa funded the construction of one of its churches. The abolition of the Hetmanate left Hustynia with few donors, making it vulnerable to closure. It was shut down on orders from St. Petersburg in 1793 as part of the government's seizure of monastic landholdings.

Hustynia was revived thanks to local donations fifty years later. It resumed its activities in 1844, just in time to become the burial place of Nikolai Repnin, who died in January 1845. It was shut down again after the Revolution of 1917. The tombs were desecrated, the graves robbed and left open. The real miracle was that the monastery was not blown up by demolition teams of the early 1930s that were preparing the country for the advent of communism. The new religion turned out to be false. Communism did not arrive, and sixty years later the Soviet Union fell, taking with it the practice of eradicating religion and destroying ecclesiastical monuments. The Hustynia Monastery opened its gates to a new generation of nuns in December 1993. It took no small effort to revive and rebuild the monastery once again, this time in conditions of a post-Soviet economic collapse. The nuns had much to celebrate and be grateful for in June 2000. The telegram from Paris was a token of recognition of their efforts and of the link to the past that they were eager to restore and build on.[1]

Today the Hustynia Monastery is a major tourist attraction. It has put the nearby town of Pryluky on the cultural map of Ukraine and is one of the feature destinations on tours of the "emerald necklace of Chernihiv." Promotional materials issued by tourist agencies present the revived monastery to the general public not only as a major religious center but also as an important historical and cultural monument. In that regard, visitors are invited to admire the Cossack baroque architecture of the monastery's churches. They are also informed that in the seventeenth century the monks of Hustynia edited and sent out into the larger world arguably one of the most important chronicles of the Cossack era. Known to the scholarly community as the *Hustynia Chronicle*, it reestablished the historical link between the Ukraine of the Cossacks and the medieval Rus' of the Kyivan princes – a link that remains crucial for present-day Ukrainian identity. The fact that Taras Shevchenko, a Romantic poet and the spiritual father of modern Ukraine, whose interest in the *History of the Rus'* we discussed earlier, visited Hustynia and painted watercolor images of its churches is another selling point of the tourist booklets. And, last but not least, they present Hustynia as the location of the tombs of quite a few famous Ukrainian families.

First among them is the tomb of the Repnins – Prince Nikolai Repnin and his wife, Varvara Rozumovska. There are also family tombs of representatives of two local Cossack officer families with deep roots in the Pryluky regiment – the Horlenkos and the Markevyches. Among the latter is the tomb of Mykola Markevych, the author of a five-volume *History of Little Russia* published in 1842–43. Markevych's *History* was inspired by the *History of the Rus'* and therefore regarded by many as an alternative to the four-volume history of Ukraine sponsored by Nikolai Repnin and written by Dmitrii Bantysh-Kamensky. For those familiar with Ukrainian history, this is one of the most intriguing paradoxes of Hustynia that the tour books pass over in silence – the monastery was not only the site of the copying and dissemination of the *Hustynia Chronicle*, one of the defining texts of early modern Ukrainian historiography, but also became the last resting place of the promoters of two different visions of Ukrainian history, one sponsored by Repnin, the other written by

[1] "Prazdnovanie 400-letiia so dnia osnovaniia Gustynskogo Sviato-Troitskogo Monastyria," http://gustynia.kiev.ua/2009/03/22/400-%d0%bb%d0%b5%d1%82%d0%b8%d0%b5/; "Sviato-Troitskii zhenskii monastyr'," http://old.orthodox.com.ua/?menu=7&submenu=2.

Markevych. The first strove to incorporate Little Russia into the empire; the second helped turn it into modern Ukraine.[2]

Tour guides present Governor Nikolai Repnin as one of the most prominent figures of nineteenth-century Ukraine who did a great deal for the country and was loved by the local people. The Hustynia tour guides do not lie – not only in the sense that this is exactly what they have been reading in the specialized literature on the subject, but also with regard to "history as it was." Nikolai Repnin died revered by the local nobility and by the peasants, whom he helped protect from the abuses of their masters. But that is only part of the story. The true history of Nikolai Repnin's life and relations with Ukrainian society is more complex.

Nikolai Repnin was born Nikolai Volkonsky in 1778 to a Russian aristocratic family and began his service to the empire in the Izmailovskoe guards regiment at the age of fourteen. His maternal grandfather was Field Marshal Nikolai Vasilievich Repnin (1734–1801), Catherine's ruthless ambassador in Warsaw on the eve of the first partition of Poland and a comrade-in-arms of Petr Rumiantsev and Aleksandr Suvorov. Together, on behalf of the empire, they handled Polish and Ottoman affairs, of which the Ukrainian question was a major part. The old field marshal played matchmaker for his grandson, arranging his marriage to Varvara Rozumovska, a granddaughter of the last hetman of Ukraine, Kyrylo Rozumovsky (1728–1803). The wedding took place in September 1802 in Baturyn, the Hetmanate's last capital and the location of Rozumovsky's magnificent palace, whose reconstruction became one of the architectural legacies of Viktor Yushchenko's presidency. Kyrylo Rozumovsky, who was present at the wedding, would die a few months later, on January 1, 1803. By the time the wedding took place, Nikolai Volkonsky was already officially known as Nikolai Repnin-Volkonsky. Alexander I gave him the right to that name after Prince Nikolai Vasilievich Repnin died in May 1801, leaving no male heir to inherit the family name. Nikolai Repnin-Volkonsky has been remembered by history simply as Nikolai Repnin.

Nikolai Repnin's first rendezvous with destiny took place on the battlefield of Austerlitz in November 1805. Repnin led his men in an attack described in the first part of Leo Tolstoy's *War and Peace*. There

---

[2] "Gustynia. Tury v Gustynskii monastyr': izumrudnoe ozherel'e Chernigovshchiny, 1 den'," www.dinaitour.com/tourism/article/?tour=23&sub=142&col=244; Nikolai Markevich, *Istoriia Malorossii*, 5 vols. (Moscow, 1842–43).

Prince Andrei Bolkonsky (a character partly based on Repnin) picks up a banner from the hands of a fallen lieutenant and leads his men against the advancing French. He is wounded and lies on the battlefield, looking up at the vast sky above him. Tolstoy renders that iconic episode of the novel as follows: "Above him was nothing, nothing but the sky – the lofty sky, not clear sky, but still infinitely lofty, with gray clouds creeping gently across. 'It's so quiet, peaceful and solemn; not like me rushing about,' thought Prince Andrei." In *War and Peace*, Napoleon, visiting the battle-field after the fighting, spots the wounded and shell-shocked Bolkonsky lying on the ground and tells his men: "Pick him up, this young man and have him taken to a dressing station." This scene was also based on Repnin's experience. After being wounded, he attracted Napoleon's notice and received special treatment in French captivity. His wife, Varvara Rozumovska, was allowed to join him and care for him in one of the local monasteries. Napoleon offered Repnin freedom on condition that he promise never again to take up arms against France. Repnin refused, citing his oath of allegiance to the emperor of Russia, but was released nevertheless. He did not live to regret his decision.[3]

In 1812, when Napoleon invaded the Russian Empire, Repnin, having served a brief stint as a diplomat, rejoined the army and helped lead Russian troops first in their retreat to Moscow and then in their pursuit of the retreating Napoleon into the heart of Europe. In February 1813, Repnin's men were the first to enter Berlin. In the fall of that year he was appointed governor general of Saxony. He enjoyed the job, but with the war over, he was relieved of that duty in the autumn of the following year. In September 1816 the former governor general of Saxony was appointed governor general of Little Russia, which included the Chernihiv and Poltava gubernias. These provinces had civil governors of their own but were under the overall supervision of the governor general, headquartered in Poltava. In a way, it seemed as if Repnin was moving from one occupied territory to another: by 1816, the local Ukrainian nobility was in open opposition to Repnin's predecessor, Yakov Lobanov-Rostovsky. His removal and Repnin's appointment was a victory for the local Cossack aristocracy – Mykhailo Myklashevsky, among others, welcomed the new governor general. Count Oleksandr Zavadovsky, a son of Catherine's one-time lover, the Cossack officer and later imperial minister Petro Zavadovsky, said: "I would like to honor him [Repnin] in Little Russia as much as in Saxony."

---

[3] Leo Tolstoy, *War and Peace*, trans. Anthony Briggs (New York, 2005), pp. 299, 311.

The new governor general was an energetic and determined leader. As he introduced imperial policies in the region, he was solicitous of its economic development and the welfare of its inhabitants. An ideal imperial administrator, Repnin emerged as a strong defender of the interests of his provinces in St. Petersburg. To begin with, he supported the demands of the local nobility for recognition of the noble status of the heirs of Cossack officeholders. It was Repnin's petitions of 1820 and 1827 that made a real difference in the capital and obliged the authorities to examine the question again and again. Repnin also did his best to soften the impact of heavy-handed imperial measures in his two gubernias. He opposed St. Petersburg on the question of the Cossack right to sell ancestral lands. In 1830–31, during the Polish uprising, Repnin spearheaded the formation of Cossack regiments, reviving the most cherished dream of descendants of the Hetmanate's Cossack stratum. He was no less active in defending the Ukrainian peasantry's economic rights and protecting serfs against arbitrary abuse by their masters. Last but not least, he did his best to counteract the effects of natural disasters – the drought of 1820 and the famine that struck Ukraine in 1833, a century before Stalin's man-made famine of 1932–33.

Most of the big issues that Repnin tackled as governor of Little Russia were deeply rooted in the Cossack history of the region. The governor's memoranda to St. Petersburg were full of historical references; some of them were historical briefs with background information on the legal and institutional traditions of the Hetmanate. But the governor's interest in the past was not only utilitarian. Soon after taking office, Repnin commissioned a comprehensive multivolume history of the region. His choice for official historiographer of Ukraine was Dmitrii Bantysh-Kamensky, a son of Mykola (Nikolai) Bantysh-Kamensky, a native of the Hetmanate and long-time director of the Moscow Archive of the College of Foreign Affairs. Repnin brought the young Bantysh-Kamensky to Poltava, first as officer for special assignments and then as the head of his chancellery. Repnin spared no effort to help his subordinate in his historiographic endeavor. He sent numerous letters to governors, church hierarchs, and amateur antiquarians, encouraging them to share their historical treasures with his appointee. The work was finished in record time: it appeared in print in 1822. Bantysh-Kamensky wrote a foreword to the first volume: "I undertook this work at the behest of the military governor of Little Russia, who also administers civil affairs in the Chernihiv and Poltava gubernias, Prince Nikolai Grigorievich Repnin. I am obliged to this esteemed superior of mine for many sources and for direct participation in the first volume. The description of the Battle of Berestechko is the work of his pen."[4]

The governor took the task of writing the history so seriously that he himself drafted the chapter on the battle fought by Hetman Bohdan Khmelnytsky at Berestechko in 1651. It was not as substantial as Oleksandr Bezborodko's addition to Ruban's *Brief Chronicle of Little Russia*, but it was done much more professionally. The pattern was unmistakable: Repnin was following in the footsteps of Prince Bezborodko, taking up the symbolic leadership of the country and providing a new account of Ukrainian history. In Poltava, Repnin also patronized a group of local intellectuals who shared his concern for the well-being of Little Russia, the study of its history, and the development of culture. Apart from Bantysh-Kamensky, they included Ivan Kotliarevsky, the author of *Eneïda* (1798), the first work of modern Ukrainian literature, who wrote in Ukrainian, and Vasyl Kapnist, the celebrated author of the freethinking *Ode on the Elimination of Slavery in Russia* (1786), who wrote in Russian. Repnin and his wife, Varvara, founded and supported a number of educational and philanthropic institutions in Poltava. While representing the capital in the two former Cossack gubernias, and doing his best to integrate them more fully into the empire, Repnin, through his defense of the economic interests of the region and his support of cultural initiatives, won the trust of the local Ukrainian intelligentsia to a degree that none of his predecessors had ever managed.

When Nikolai Repnin left the governor's office in 1834, his departure was regretted by many. The nobility of Pryluky county, where Repnin's estate of Yahotyn was located, even considered placing a bust of him in the building of the nobiliary assembly. When Repnin died in 1845, he was mourned not only by his noble clients but by people in all walks of life. Repnin's daughter, Varvara, wrote about her father's death to her secret and platonic love, the serf-born poet Taras Shevchenko:

My good and melancholy singer! ... Weep out a song in memory of a man whom you so knew how to respect and love! ... My good father is no longer among us! ... After a lengthy and oppressive illness, exhausted by heavy suffering, he gave up his soul to God on January 7. You will understand the emptiness of Yahotyn. I had begun to write on the road to Pryluky, where we took his holy remains, that is, to the Hustynia Monastery. That was his wish. O Taras Hryhorovych! My good friend! ... How to convey to you all those endless minutes through which we passed during those days! ... I wanted to tell

---

[4] Dmitrii Bantysh-Kamenskii, *Istoriia Maloi Rossii*, vol. 1 (Moscow, 1822), p. v.

you how your countrymen showed themselves all along the route; how in Pryluky good people unharnessed the horses and, in a terrible snowstorm, pulled the sleigh bearing the coffin through the whole town . . . .

A few months later Shevchenko visited Hustynia and painted his famous watercolors of the monastery.[5]

Repnin left a strong imprint on Ukrainian history of the first half of the nineteenth century. He has been remembered as a highly positive figure in both the Russian imperial and the Ukrainian national historical traditions. But this is not the image of the governor general that would have been recognized by many leaders of the Ukrainian gentry. This holds particularly for the gentry of the Chernihiv gubernia, where Repnin's popularity was never high, and where he was hated by many until the very end of his long tenure. Few residents of the former Hetmanate had more difficult relations with Repnin and greater reason to dislike him than the marshal of the Chernihiv nobility from 1818 to 1828, Stepan Mykhailovych Shyrai.

From the perspective of many Chernihiv landowners, Repnin's rule in Ukraine was nothing short of a disaster. The gentry's claim to noble status was one of the rare issues on which Repnin and the local marshals worked together. Repnin believed, not without foundation, that the poor government of the region was a direct outcome of the corruption that marred the nobiliary electoral system, in which the key offices were traditionally divided among members of a few hereditary clans. He was determined to break the power of the clans – a task that he accomplished only in part. His other concern was the welfare of the Cossacks and peasants. Improving their social and economic status meant limiting the arbitrary power of the local nobility. Cruel treatment of serfs by their masters was the norm, not the exception, and peasants occasionally struck back by killing landowners. Repnin made a name for himself throughout the empire as a proponent of more humane treatment of the serfs. Whether he did so out of his liberal convictions, his duty as governor, or his Christian commitment, he made many enemies among the local nobility. The high-minded nobles failed to make a connection between their own liberties and the basic rights of their serfs.

[5] "Repnin-Volkonskii, kniaz' Nikolai Grigor'evich," in *Russkii biograficheskii slovar'*, ed. A. A. Polovtsev, 25 vols. (Moscow, 1896–1918), xxii: 118–24; Valentyna Shandra, "Malorosiis'ke heneral-hubernatorstvo u period uriaduvannia M. P. Repnina (1816–34)," *Ukraïns'kyi istorychnyi zhurnal*, no. 4 (2000): 79–90; I. F. Pavlovskii, *Poltavtsy: ierarkhi, gosudarstvennye i obshchestvennye deiateli i blagotvoriteli* (Poltava, 1914), pp. 38–45; David Saunders, *The Ukrainian Impact on Russian Culture, 1750–1850* (Edmonton, 1985), pp. 182–83.

The governor general was continuously in conflict with the gentry, which used its right to elect marshals – the highest noble officials in the regions – to empower individuals who would defend their interests against the growing power of the imperial center. Repnin did not hesitate to employ harsh measures against the unruly nobles, including arrest and the rejection of candidates for marshal whom he considered too loyal to their constituency. In 1817, his first full year in office, Repnin refused to confirm the election of Dmytro Troshchynsky, the former minister of justice, as marshal of the Poltava nobility. Troshchynsky had been among those who welcomed Repnin's appointment, but the honeymoon soon came to an end. He later became a leading figure among the local "liberals," who included future participants in the Decembrist revolt.

The trajectory of Stepan Shyrai's relations with Repnin was not unlike that of Troshchynsky's. Originally Shyrai must have enjoyed a period of good relations with Repnin, who confirmed his election as marshal of the Chernihiv nobility at least three times. But this, too, came to an abrupt end in 1826, when Repnin arrested a number of Chernihiv-area nobles for taking part in a minor conflict during the nobiliary elections. The case was reported to Emperor Nicholas I, who found Repnin overzealous. Repnin in turn decided to make Shyrai, who had been absent during the incident, pay the price for his humiliation. He removed the major general from office, citing "old age and episodes of illness that made it difficult for him to appear as required at the call of his superiors." This was most probably a mere pretext, as there were other disagreements between the two men. Shyrai is known to have been very critical of the existing system whereby serfs owned by local nobles were recruited into the imperial army. As noted in the diary of Mikhail Pogodin, this was one of the sources of discontent among the Little Russian nobles. Many of them still remembered the halcyon days when military service was the prerogative of Cossacks and did not undermine the economic interests of the serf-owning nobility. Shyrai petitioned St. Petersburg in that regard, circumventing Repnin and openly challenging his authority.

Repnin would not forgive that insubordination. He barred Shyrai from election in 1828, and then again in 1829. When Shyrai arrived in Chernihiv for the elections of 1829, Repnin sent the civil governor of the Chernihiv gubernia a message in which he wrote:

Reports have reached me that S. M. Shyrai has come to Chernihiv and wishes to take up the post of gubernia marshal at the imminent elections. After the complaint that he made to the Sovereign Emperor about me, I am not inclined to admit him to that post for the current three-year term; however, if the gentry elects him in the future and he changes his behavior, I shall be glad to confirm him in it. Wherefore I most humbly request Your Excellency to inform me of this for consideration prior to my arrival in Chernihiv; indeed, I shall be most grateful if Your Excellency should find an opportunity to let him apprehend this.[6]

Repnin succeeded, and Shyrai was barred from standing for the next term. But Shyrai was not the kind to surrender without a fight. Decades after the conflict, he would be remembered for his determined opposition to the governor general of Little Russia. According to one apocryphal story, Shyrai, "a very intelligent man, but a great eccentric ... took particular pleasure in quarreling with all the Little Russian governors general and in noting all their administrative blunders. They were terribly afraid of his sarcastic remarks, which were immediately relayed in comical form to his countrymen Troshchynsky and Kochubei in St. Petersburg." But this time high connections were of no avail. By the 1820s Dmytro Troshchynsky was out of power, and Viktor Pavlovych Kochubei (1768–1834), the former protégé of Oleksandr Bezborodko and then minister of the interior, had to be particularly careful, for his own nephew was deeply involved in the conflict over Shyrai's reelection as marshal of the Chernihiv nobility.[7]

The nephew was Demian Kochubei. For quite a while, Repnin was in conflict with the younger Kochubei over his bootlegging activities in the Great Russian gubernias. When the nobility, realizing that Repnin would block the election of Shyrai, decided to replace him with Demian Kochubei, who had originally agitated for Shyrai, Repnin used his power to derail that plan as well. Viktor Kochubei in St. Petersburg was alarmed and took extra precautions to shield himself from accusations of nepotism and lobbying on behalf of a relative. He wrote a highly circumspect letter to Repnin in which he said: "I think only of what is general, of what may be useful *en masse*." For all his caution, Kochubei was no friend of Repnin and privately was very critical of his rule. Viktor Kochubei welcomed the transfer of his son-in-law, who had worked for a while as civil governor of Chernihiv, to St. Petersburg, away from the irascible Repnin. "Here [in Ukraine]," he wrote on one occasion, "everything goes against common sense, and abuses are innumerable. The governor general eats and drinks in his country home, while the gubernias are administered by bureaucratic officials who use every opportunity to make money." The accusation was hardly fair. Repnin was indeed known for his lavish way of life and spent

---

[6] Pavlovskii, *Poltavtsy*, pp. 38–45.
[7] A. Sheremet'ev, "Pis'mo imperatora Pavla Shiraiu," *Russkaia starina* 12, no. 4 (1815): 820.

much time at his Yahotyn estate near Pryluky, but he was also an efficient governor. Certainly he was efficient enough to stand his ground in a confrontation with a powerful St. Petersburg official.[8]

Stepan Shyrai had to step down. There would be no new election for the old major general, who was already pushing seventy. But it is unlikely that he learned his lesson and "changed his behavior," as Repnin hoped. Long after leaving office, Shyrai remained a highly respected figure in the Chernihiv gubernia and the leader of nobiliary opposition to government encroachment on local privileges. When in December 1840 Vasyl Liubomyrsky, the marshal of the Chernihiv nobility, received proposals for the elimination of the Lithuanian Statute – the last vestige of the Hetmanate's legacy in the empire – he sent a copy of them for evaluation not only to all county marshals of the gubernia but also to the long-retired Stepan Shyrai. "Your experience," wrote Liubomyrsky, "and the trust that all the nobility reposes in you guarantee that your conclusion will be infallible." Shyrai responded in the following month that the Lithuanian Statute "not only is not subject to annulment according to spurious prejudices of some kind but, possessing its full clarity and presenting no obstacle to the efficacy of other laws, still constitutes an indispensable necessity for the benefit, welfare, and jurisprudence of the inhabitants of the Chernihiv and Poltava gubernias." Most marshals of the Chernihiv gubernia were of the same opinion, including the younger generation of Shyrai's extended family: Mykola Borozdna in Novozybkiv, Mykhailo Sudiienko in Novhorod-Siverskyi, and Petro Shyrai in Surazh. The Lithuanian Statute, which was abolished in the western provinces of the empire in 1840, remained in force in the Hetmanate for another few years.[9]

Stepan Shyrai began to distribute copies of the *History of the Rus'* some time prior to the start of his conflict with the governor general. One of the copies reached Repnin's protégé Dmitrii Bantysh-Kamensky, the author of the *History of Little Russia*, who in March 1825 was appointed civil governor of Tobolsk. In the revised edition of his book that appeared in 1830, Bantysh-Kamensky used the *History of the Rus'* as one of his sources and acknowledged receipt of the manuscript from

---

[8] Saunders, *The Ukrainian Impact*, p. 111; Pavlovskii, *Poltavtsy*; Shandra, "Malorosiis'ke heneralhubernatorstvo"; Volodymyr Sverbyhuz, *Starosvits'ke panstvo* (Warsaw, 1999), pp. 122–24.

[9] Mykola Vasylenko, "Iak skasovano Lytovs'koho statuta," in *Vybrani tvory u tr'okh tomakh*, vol. II: *Iurydychni pratsi* (Kyiv, 2006), pp. 284–353, here 326–29.

"the marshal of the Chernihiv gubernia, Stepan Mykhailovych Shyrai."
Bantysh-Kamensky probably received the manuscript before his departure from Ukraine, as it is quoted in the memorandum on the rights of
the Cossacks signed by Nikolai Repnin in the fall of 1824. The rivalry
between the governor general of Little Russia and the marshal of
the Chernihiv nobility began in the sphere of historiography even
before it entered that of politics. If Repnin had sponsored Bantysh-
Kamensky's *History of Little Russia*, Shyrai had his own historical
project to support.[10]

As the broad dissemination of the *History* in manuscript form attests, it
resonated exceptionally well with the nobility of the former Hetmanate. It
continued the long tradition of the production and dissemination of
historical knowledge in manuscript form. That tradition included not
only the well-known Cossack annals of the first half of the eighteenth
century, such as the chronicles of Samiilo Velychko and Hryhorii
Hrabianka, but also local Starodub-area writings – chronicles composed
by Roman Rakushka-Romanovsky (the Eyewitness), Hryhorii Pokas
of Pochep, Fedir Mankivsky of Sheptaky, and [Arkhyp] Khudorba of
Pohrebky near Novhorod-Siverskyi.[11]

Nikolai Repnin's memorandum of 1824 indicates that not only
Bantysh-Kamensky but also Repnin himself were familiar with and influenced by the *History*. The *History of the Rus'*, however, was a gentry version
of the Ukrainian past to a degree that Bantysh-Kamensky's history was
not and could not be. We find an indication of this in Mikhail Pogodin's
diary, which was so crucial to our efforts to link the author of the *History*
with the family of Pogodin's friend Mykhailo Shyrai. On May 25, 1822, a
few weeks before Pogodin sat down to record the concerns of Little
Russian society, which mirrored those of the author of the *History*
himself, he made another extremely interesting diary entry about his
visit to Konstantin Kalaidovich, one of the leading students of the
Russian chronicles. Pogodin wrote: "I took pleasure in conversing with
him on various historical topics, including the *History of Little Russia*
that is being published by Kamensky. [Viktor Pavlovich] Kochubei does
not want any mention there of the wife of Colonel Kochubei of Peter's

[10] Bantysh-Kamenskii, *Istoriia Maloi Rossii*, vol. 1 (Moscow, 1830), p. x; Leontii Diachuk, "Zapyska
pro malorosiis'kych Kozakiv Mykoly Repnina-Volkons koho," in *Chetverta akademiia pam'iati
profesora Volodymyra Antonovycha* (Kyiv, 1999), pp. 117–40.
[11] Andrii Bovhyria, *Kozats'ke istoriopysannia v rukopysnii tradytsii XVIII stolittia. Spysky ta redaktsiï
tvoriv* (Kyiv, 2010), pp. 136–48, 250, 257, 263, 278, 287, 296.

time who had ties with Mazepa, nor of the latter's letter in which Koch [ubei] is reproached with having been the son of a peasant .... Ah, blockheads – what are they ashamed of?" Pogodin's final comment had to do with the allegedly low origins of the Kochubeis. Born a serf, Pogodin could not resist the urge to make fun of the nobiliary pride of one of the leading aristocrats of the empire. Even more interesting to us, however, is the information that Viktor Kochubei tried to intervene in the editing of the *History of Little Russia* so that his family would be presented in the best possible light.

We know that Kochubei corresponded with both Repnin and Bantysh-Kamensky about the *History of Little Russia*. He was the one who informed the author that his work had been presented to the emperor himself, had met with his approval, and had earned him the title of state councillor. But neither the author nor his sponsor, Nikolai Repnin, did anything to accommodate Kochubei's requests. Bantysh-Kamensky had to delete from his work some statements regarding Little Russia's lost rights and freedoms that the censor found too inflammatory, but he did not change the parts of the narrative dealing with Kochubei's ancestors. The *History* tells a long story about the relations between Hetman Ivan Mazepa and Motria Kochubei, a young daughter of his one-time friend, General Judge Vasyl Kochubei. The offended father denounced Mazepa to the tsar, accusing him of treason. The tsar did not believe the accusations and turned over Vasyl Kochubei, along with his relative and accomplice, Colonel Ivan Iskra of Poltava, to Mazepa for execution. There was nothing wrong, in the context of the early nineteenth century, with having one's ancestors dying to show their loyalty to the tsar, but a record of intimate relations between an anathematized hetman and an ancestor could hardly reflect well on descendants of that family.

If the Repnin-sponsored *History of Little Russia* did not take Kochubei's concerns into account, the Shyrai-sponsored *History of the Rus'* did. Its author explained Kochubei and Iskra's denunciation of Mazepa by "jealousy toward Iskra's wife, who had suspicious relations with the hetman." By this account, then, it was a member of Iskra's family, not Kochubei's, who was involved with Mazepa! The claim was dubious at best, as no other source says anything about an amorous relationship between Mazepa and any female member of the Iskra clan. In order to cover his tracks, the author of the *History* attributed this information to "folk legend." One way or another, as far as the *History* was concerned, Viktor Kochubei's name and that of his family was cleared of any dubious association with the anathematized Mazepa. We do not know how Kalaidovich learned of Kochubei's dissatisfaction with Bantysh-Kamensky's *History*, but what is striking is that Pogodin, referring to "the wife of Colonel Kochubei," introduced into the Mazepa story the subject of "the colonel's wife," which finds no parallel in any text other than the *History of the Rus'*. The usual references are to the daughter of General Judge Kochubei. Did the reference to the colonel's wife come from Kochubei via Kalaidovich, or could Pogodin have heard it from Mykhailo Shyrai? We do not know the answer to this question, but it is certainly difficult if not impossible to make sense of the note in Pogodin's diary without bringing in the Shyrais and their relations in Ukraine, Moscow, and St. Petersburg.[12]

The story of the colonel's wife and the complex relations (to say the least) between Viktor Kochubei and Nikolai Repnin may have had a sequel that influenced the way in which Nikolai Repnin ended his career and, indeed, his life. After Repnin's dismissal as governor general of Little Russia, the administration of the region was eventually entrusted to Viktor Kochubei's son-in-law, Count Aleksandr Stroganov. It was on his watch that an investigation was launched into the alleged embezzlement of state funds by the former governor general. It was claimed that Repnin had misappropriated 200,000 rubles during the construction of the Institute for Noble Girls in Poltava. In the midst of the investigation, Repnin resigned from the State Council in St. Petersburg and went abroad with his family. Most of his estates were confiscated to pay for the losses incurred by the state treasury. The investigation did not incriminate him: it turned out that Repnin had indeed directed funds intended for other purposes to the construction of the institute, but he did not embezzle them, and in fact contributed 65,000 rubles of his own money to the project. But the inquiry was not closed until after Repnin's death and probably not only poisoned but also shortened his life. When in 1842 Repnin returned from abroad and settled on his estate at Yahotyn – the only possession not seized by the investigators – he was a financially broken man. He still contributed generously to the reconstruction of the Hustynia Monastery, where he was buried in January 1845.

---

[12] Volodymyr Kravchenko, *Narysy z istoriï ukraïns'koï istoriohrafiï epokhy natsional'noho Vidrodzhennia (druha polovyna XVIII–seredyna XIX st.)* (Kharkiv, 1996), pp. 169, 177; Saunders, *The Ukrainian Impact*, pp. 183, 311; *Istoriia Rusov ili Maloi Rosii. Sochinenie Georgiia Koniskago, Arkhiepiskopa Beloruskago* (Moscow, 1846), p. 201; cf. Bantysh-Kamenskii, *Istoriia Maloi Rossii* (Moscow, 1903), pp. 373, 574–77.

It is not clear whether it was pure accident that the investigation of Repnin was launched by a son-in-law of Viktor Kochubei (it is known that Repnin was also in conflict with the imperial minister of finance, Count Dmitrii Guriev, whose son, Aleksandr, replaced Repnin as governor general of Little Russia in 1834), but it is hard to avoid the impression that toward the end of his life the long-serving governor of Little Russia was forced to pay a price for interfering with powerful Ukrainian nobles and their relatives and protectors in St. Petersburg. Nikolai Repnin outlived Stepan Shyrai by less than two years. The rivalry between the two towering figures of Little Russian politics of the 1820s was finally over. But the competition between their opposing visions of Ukraine and its past was only entering its most interesting stage.[13]

Thus, Repnin and Shyrai were rivals. Each of them saw the interests of Little Russia differently, and they were involved in promoting different historical visions of Ukraine as well. This conclusion provides us with a new background against which to consider the appearance and initial dissemination of the *History of the Rus'*. It also allows us to return to Stepan Shyrai as someone who might have been involved not only in the dissemination of the manuscript but also in its production. There seems to be enough evidence to suggest that he was involved in both.

A factor that told in favor of Shyrai's involvement in the production of the text earlier and continues to do so now is that of his origins. In this respect, he fits the profile of the author or coauthor of the *History* in more than one way. His Cossack/noble origins are appropriate to the attitude manifested by the anonymous author toward the role of the Cossacks and the nobility in Ukrainian history. Shyrai's career as a military officer, especially his partici-pation in the wars with the Ottomans and the partitions of Poland, can explain the anonymous author's love of battle scenes and his knowledge of the geography of southern Ukraine, where most of those battles, real and imagined, took place. He also owned properties in Yelysavethrad and Olviopol counties of southern Ukraine. In the course of his military career, Shyrai met or became aware of a number of personalities important to the

[13] Valentyna Shandra, "Creating an Imperial Elite: Prince Nikolai Repnin – Military Governor-General of Little Russia," *Den'* (Kyiv), no. 42 (December 26, 2006); no. 1 (January 16, 2007). On the office of governor in the nineteenth-century Russian Empire and governors' relations with the center, see essays by Alsu Biktasheva, "Mekhanizm naznacheniia gubernatorov v Rossii v pervoi polovine XIX veka," *Otechestvennaia istoriia*, no. 6 (2006): 31–41; Biktasheva, "Nadzor nad gubernatorami v Rossii v pervoi polovine XIX veka," *Voprosy istorii*, no. 9 (2007): 97–105. I am grateful to John LeDonne for information on the Repnin–Guriev rivalry.

author of the *History*. One of them was Arkhyp Khudorba, the likely author of one of the most important sources of the *History of the Rus'* – the Khudorba History. Khudorba served together with Shyrai in the Starodub carabineer regiment in 1785–86. Another was General Aleksei Melgunov, the governor general of New Russia in 1764 and the anti-hero of the *History*'s account of the Pikemen's Revolt in southern Ukraine. Like Shyrai's uncles Andrii and Ivan Hudovych, General Melgunov was close to Emperor Peter III. Like Shyrai himself, he served briefly (in 1762) as commander of the Riga dragoon regiment. Shyrai's origins, age, and military experience can also explain some peculiarities of the language of the *History* – a mixture of Russian abounding in military and bureaucratic terminology and dialectal Ukrainian.

The most interesting and by far the strongest arguments in favor of Shyrai's involvement in either writing or editing the *History* come not from his military and diplomatic experiences but from his "retirement years," which he spent in the Starodub region. His properties adjoined settlements of Old Believers, which may well explain the anonymous author's preoccupation with their religion and ethnic origin – as late as the first decades of the twentieth century, they were referred to locally as Muscovites. Also essential to our argument is the role that Shyrai played in Starodub and environs in the first decades of the nineteenth century. He served as marshal of the Chernihiv nobility at a time when the elite of the former Hetmanate was fighting hard for recognition of noble status on behalf of descendants of Cossack officers who had held relatively low ranks. From the very beginning, the Chernihiv nobles were at the forefront of that struggle, relying heavily on historical arguments and presenting their efforts to gain noble status as a contest for the honor and historical rights of the whole Little Russian nation. Stepan Shyrai must have shared that attitude.

In 1818, the year in which Shyrai became marshal of the Chernihiv nobility, the case for recognition of the noble status of the descendants of Cossack officers took a turn for the worse. In December 1818 the Heraldry Office ruled: "Little Russian ranks lower than eighth class not substantiated by hetmans' proclamations granting real estate to their ancestors . . . are not recognized by the Heraldry Office as conferring noble status." The nobility of the Chernihiv and Poltava gubernias was up in arms. Ten years later, in 1828, the Chernihiv and Poltava nobility once again joined forces to demand the restoration of Little Russian rights and privileges and recognition of the noble status of Little Russian ranks. "The nobility of the Chernihiv gubernia insistently repeats its previous petitions for the settlement of the matter and granting of favor so that Little Russian ranks be recognized as proof of nobility, if anyone's ancestors held them, and that, pending settlement of the matter, contrary decisions on the part of the Heraldry Office be suspended," read a statement from Shyrai's office.[14]

Through all these years, Shyrai was at the hub of local politics and society, and his home in Starodub served as a meeting ground for the "best people" of the Siverian region. The core of that circle was made up of Shyrai's close relatives, whose family stories made their way into the *History*. What the Myklashevskys, Hudovyches, and Haletskys all had in common, apart from the depiction of their ancestors in the final section of the *History*, was their close family ties with Stepan Shyrai. He and his family stood at the center of the web of matrimonial ties that linked those families and connected the Starodub aristocrats with the St. Petersburg world of the Zavadovskys and Bezborodkos – also relatives of Stepan Shyrai. Whether one believes in Shyrai's involvement in the production of the *History* or not, the manuscript miraculously reflects not only his likes but also his dislikes with regard to his personal and family links and contacts. The more closely Starodub families were related to Shyrai, the more prominently they figured in the pages of the *History*.

At the top of the list was Vasyl Hudovych, the mouthpiece for the ideas of the author himself and the maternal grandfather of Stepan Shyrai. Less attention is given to the colonel of Starodub, Mykhailo Andriiovych Myklashevsky, a maternal ancestor of Stepan Shyrai removed from him by a couple of generations. Shyrai's other relations, the Haletskys, are singled out for consideration, not always in a positive light. But not everything depended on ties between families: relations within the family were also important, as is well attested by Shyrai's breakup with his wife, Uliana, and his difficult relations with her family, the Borozdnas. Not only are the Borozdnas not mentioned by name in the *History* when the author retells one of their family stories, but one of Petro Borozdna's ancestors, Colonel Antin Kryzhanovsky of Hadiach, is singled out as the object of the author's most vicious attack. Beyond question, the text of the *History* that Stepan Shyrai distributed in the 1820s represented his views on which ancestors of the Starodub elite of the early nineteenth century deserved to be noted in Ukrainian history and which did not.

---

[14] Quoted in Sverbyhuz, *Starosvits'ke panstvo*, pp. 172, 191, 194–97; Zenon E. Kohut, *Russian Centralism and Ukrainian Autonomy: Imperial Absorption of the Hetmanate, 1760s–1830s* (Cambridge, Mass., 1988), pp. 248–58.

This puts Shyrai in a league of his own as compared with the other Starodub candidates discussed in this book. None of them fits the profile of the author as well as he does. Of all the suspects, past and present, it is only Shyrai in whose home we know ideas similar if not identical to those presented in the *History* to have been discussed before the first sighting of the *History* in 1824 and its official discovery in 1828. Most of the Ukrainian concerns recorded in Mikhail Pogodin's diary in June 1822 mirror the main themes of the *History*. They include the claim of Cossack primacy with regard to the Rus' name and history; the dislike of ethnic Russians, referred to as Muscovites; the longing to restore lost rights and freedoms; and, last but not least, the respectful treatment if not outright adoration of Hetman Ivan Mazepa. The Pogodin diary provides a kind of evidence that can be compared to the results of a forensic test: it points to a unique intellectual and ideological DNA shared by Stepan Shyrai and the author of the *History*. It ties together and presents in a new light all the circumstantial evidence we have accumulated in the course of our investigation.

Although a great deal of circumstantial evidence points to Shyrai as the author of the *History*, his candidacy is anything but problem-free. Among the factors that discourage us from thinking of him as the sole producer of the *History* is that his family claimed descent from the Polish nobility – a practice detested by the anonymous author. Stepan Shyrai was certainly a great storyteller, but there is nothing to suggest that the retired major general was also a writer. We lack the textual DNA to link him to the *History of the Rus'*. If Stepan Shyrai was not the sole author, who was? Whodunit?

We have established the time frame for the creation of the *History*, as well as the place of its creation, and identified a number of people who could have been sponsors, authors, coauthors, or editors of the text. Apart from Shyrai, we have suggested Ivan Lashkevych, Yakiv Radkevych, and Petro and Vasyl Borozdna. They were all linked by time, space, background, and family or social connections. All of them have good credentials for participation in the project, but at this point we simply lack evidence to declare any of them a sole author of the *History*. It may be that the author was someone else, an individual close to the circle described in this book. But it is also possible that the problem lies not with the answers we get but with the questions we ask. What if there was no one author of the *History of the Rus'*?

"Much consideration of authorial work," writes Harold Love in his study of authorship, "still takes as its model the single author creating a text in solitariness – Proust's cork-lined room, Dickens's prefabricated

Swiss chalet, Mary Ward's elegant study at 'Stocks.' In doing so it restricts itself not just to a particular kind of authorship but to a particular phase of that kind of authorship." Love argues that this particular vision of authorship ignores one of its most ancient forms – collaborative authorship. It took different forms over the centuries, ranging from "precursory authorship," whereby an individual produced parts of a text that would later be used by others; to "executive authorship," involving one or more persons who actually gave the product its shape; to "revisionary authorship," which gives editors their due; and, finally, "declarative authorship," which is characteristic of works ghostwritten for political figures and celebrities.[15]

Could the *History of the Rus'* have been a product of collaborative authorship? Can the answer to the riddle of the *History of the Rus'* be akin to the one offered by Agatha Christie in her *Murder on the Orient Express*, where all twelve suspects turn out to be guilty of stabbing the victim and committing the crime? Suggestions about the collective authorship of the *History* have been made in the past, describing the manuscript as a product either of the Novhorod-Siverskyi patriotic circle or the group of Poltava Masons around the governor general of Little Russia, Nikolai Repnin. None of these hypotheses has ever been substantiated with evidence. But the concepts of precursory and collaborative authorship, which admit contributions to the text by authors of earlier Cossack chronicles, including the *Brief Description of Little Russia* and the Khudorba History, are certainly applicable to the *History of the Rus'*. Turning to the historical writing of the late eighteenth and early nineteenth centuries, it is important to remember that the famous and powerful of the era did not have to do all their research and writing alone. If we consider the examples of Oleksandr Bezborodko, who sponsored the publication of Ruban's *Brief Chronicle of Little Russia* and contributed a chapter to it, or Prince Nikolai Repnin, who sponsored Bantysh-Kamensky's *History of Little Russia* and contributed a chapter, then we must allow for the possibility that the person responsible for the production of the *History* did not write the text alone but sponsored the compilation of the work, writing or dictating anecdotes dealing with the post-1708 history of the Hetmanate, and then perhaps helping to disseminate the manuscript, with which he did not want his name associated.

This approach puts Stepan Mykhailovych Shyrai, the retired major general and marshal of the Chernihiv nobility, in an entirely new context.

---

[15] Harold Love, *Attributing Authorship. An Introduction* (Cambridge, 2002), pp. 32–50.

As noted above, he had all the qualifications required to be considered the sponsor of the book and a source of its colorful stories. Someone close to Shyrai or susceptible to his influence could have been the author or editor of the main text. His son Mykhailo was too young to contribute to the *History* prior to 1818, but from what we know about Stepan Shyrai, he was always surrounded by helpers and minions. This comes across quite clearly from the materials of the Shyrai-Zabotin court case. It is also the image of Shyrai in one of the apocryphal stories about his idiosyncrasies, according to which "Shyrai always walked the streets with a large retinue of petty landowners who carried out various domestic functions for him: one would carry his pipe, another his tobacco pouch, etc." One assumes that there may also have been people carrying pens, ink, and paper so that their patron's stories could be put down in writing under the name of a deceased Orthodox archbishop. Shyrai himself had no problem with forging documents: on his orders, the church books recording Oleksandr Shyrai's birth were doctored so as to make that record disappear.[16]

Our discussion of the *History*'s narrative as related to the family lives of major figures in Starodub noble society, including Mykhailo Myklashevsky and Petro Borozdna, as well as local authors such as Ivan Lashkevych, Yakiv Radkevych, and Vasyl Borozdna permits the suggestion that the authorship of the *History* may also have been collaborative in a more traditional way. Some, if not all, of the above-mentioned individuals may indeed have contributed to the creation of the *History*, either by telling their family stories or by sharing their knowledge of history and literature with the primary author; perhaps by helping to produce a first draft, or even taking a leading role in writing the entire text. They all had the right qualifications for the job, and, as far as we know, they shared not only family lore but also historical documents and historiographic sources. Otherwise it would be impossible to explain how the Khudorba manuscript was known not only to the Myklashevskys but also to the author of the *History*, or how a Russian translation of Scherer's *Annales*, a copy of which bears the name of Yakiv Radkevych, made its way into the Borozdnas' library. It also appears that they read the same journals – certainly *Vestnik Evropy* and perhaps *Ukrainskii vestnik*.

The *History of the Rus'* was most probably conceived in the heat of the struggle for recognition of the noble status of Cossack officeholders, which culminated in 1809 with a provisional victory for the nobiliary

---

[16] Mikhail Pyliaev, *Zamechatel'nye chudaki i originaly* (Moscow, 2001), pp. 268–70.

cause in St. Petersburg. The work apparently took final shape after the Napoleonic Wars. The Cossack units that had taken part in the defense of the empire were now disbanded, the rights of the Cossacks were under attack, and a new world order was decreed by the Congress of Vienna – an order in which the Polish enemies of the Cossacks gained rights of autonomy and privileges that had long been taken away from the Cossacks themselves. The price paid for integration into the empire seemed too high and the rewards too low. The world had to be reminded of Cossack glory, services to the empire, and sacrifices endured. The appearance of the first dated copy of the *History of the Rus'* in 1818 suggests that its author must have done most of the work required either before Shyrai's election as marshal of the Chernihiv nobility or during his first year in the office.

The efforts of Nikolai Repnin to start the collection of sources for Bantysh-Kamensky's *History of Little Russia*, which began in 1816, may very well have spurred the author and his circle to complete their version of Ukrainian history. The names of Archbishop Konysky and Hryhorii Poletyka, highly respected in Ukrainian society, were chosen as a cover and a mark of legitimacy. The circulation of the *History* would be limited to the immediate circle of friends and relatives, which included the Shyrais and the Myklashevskys. Sometime between 1822 and 1824 Shyrai began to distribute the *History* more widely. He sent a copy of the manuscript to Bantysh-Kamensky in time to influence Nikolai Repnin's memorandum on the rights of the Cossacks. It was also around that time that Kondratii Ryleev first consulted the manuscript for his epic poem *Nalyvaiko*. The Hryniv "discovery" of the *History*, if not actually staged by Shyrai, may have been a mere stimulus to the further distribution of the mysterious text.

Oleksander Ohloblyn wrote in 1942 that the main purpose of his efforts to locate the author of the *History* was to uncover the background and views of his milieu: "The name of the author of the work will make his cultural and social milieu apparent to us, just as the elucidation of his milieu, on the basis of study of the work itself, will give us a full and expressive representation of the ideology of its creator." That is also the ultimate goal of the detective work undertaken in this book. Our efforts have not resulted in the pinpointing of an exclusive author of the mysterious text; instead, we have identified a circle responsible for its production. We have also identified a person at the center of that circle. There is no doubt in our mind that this broadly defined and not always harmonious group of Starodub friends and relatives was responsible not only for the launching of the *History* but also for its production. This seems to be the most definite and probably the most enduring outcome of our journey. One can now place the *History* into its proper political, ideological, and cultural context and uncover the original meaning of the text that mesmerized generations of readers.[17]

Research on the milieu that produced the *History of the Rus'* is just getting under way, about to enter perhaps its most interesting stage. We hope that this book will help revive interest in the lives and legacies of the largely forgotten circle of Starodub patriots, caught forever between their Cossack past and the new imperial realities, between empire and nation, and ultimately between Russia and Ukraine. Starodub, which happenstance has placed on the Russian side of the Soviet-era border, needs to be reexamined as part of the world to which it once belonged – the world defined by the borders of the Hetmanate and the Russian Empire, not those of present-day Russia and Ukraine.

In September 2003, Bishop Feofilakt of the Briansk and Sevsk eparchy of the Russian Orthodox Church officially removed the anathema allegedly placed on the town of Starodub in the second half of the seventeenth century. The story of the anathema has no basis in historical sources (including the *History of the Rus'*), but the legend, which came to the fore after the disintegration of the Soviet Union, claimed that the town had been hard hit by the economic crisis because it had remained loyal to the Russian tsar in Cossack times, which led the treasonous Ukrainian hetman to have it anathematized. With the removal of the anathema, divine blessings were restored to Starodub, its loyalty to the Russian state rewarded, and a harsh chapter of its history closed. Indeed, precious little remains today of the lives lived by the Starodub notables not only in the seventeenth and eighteenth centuries but even in the nineteenth.[18]

The Bezborodko palace in Hryniv still stands, but it is in a state of utter disrepair. Zavadovsky's spectacular mansion in Lialychi is in ruins. Apart from the shell of a church, nothing remains of Myklashevsky's estate of Ponurivka. The graves of the Borozdnas were restored thanks to the efforts of local enthusiasts, but the burial place of Mykhailo Myklashevsky still awaits discovery. There is little to remind one of Shyrai's house in Solova.

[17] O. P. Ohloblyn, *Do pytannia pro avtora "Istoriï Rusov"* (Kyiv, 1998), p. 18.

[18] V. M. Pus', "Starodubskie legendy," http://starburg.ru/starodubskie_legendy/index.html; "Ocherk o Starodube. Istoriia odnoi komandirovki," http://starburg.ru/ocherk_o_starodube/index.html.

We do not even know where Shyrai was buried: was it in Pantusiv, where he lived the last years of his life, or in Solova, where he built the family Church of the Archangel Michael in 1785? The Moscow poet Boris Romanov could not find Shyrai's grave near the dilapidated and vandalized church. With a sense of loss and despair, he asked in his *Ode to the Village of Solova*:

> When did the dread Archangel Michael
> Ring for the last time over the unforgettable cemetery?
> Where does Stepan Shyrai sleep in it?
> What band rode roughshod here?
> When did the Cossack land forget Suvorov's adjutant?[19]

There is no hope that anyone will ever find the grave of Shyrai's uncle, General Field Marshal Ivan Hudovych. His portrait is displayed on the website of the Moscow city government among the portraits of past administrators of the Russian capital, but his remains were scattered on the grounds of the Cave Monastery in Kyiv. The conqueror of the Caucasus stated in his will that he was to be buried at the St. Sophia Cathedral in Kyiv, but his heirs changed his will and buried him in the Dormition Cathedral of the Cave Monastery. In the fall of 1941, during the German occupation of the Ukrainian capital, the eleventh-century cathedral was blown up either by Soviet agents or by their Nazi nemesis. If the Soviet agents were behind it, then they missed their target – the ruler of Slovakia, Jozef Tiso – who wanted to visit the monastery. The cathedral was rebuilt in 2000, but the remains of Hudovych are still unaccounted for.[20]

Hardly better was the posthumous fate of Prince Nikolai Repnin and his wife, Varvara, who died in Moscow but was buried along with her husband at Hustynia. In the 1930s their graves were opened and robbed. What remains today is the Repnin family tomb beneath the Resurrection Church of the monastery, which may or may not contain the remains of Prince Repnin and his wife. To be sure, there is a new addition to the tomb that holds the remains of Orest Makarenko, a son of the Ukrainian architect Mykola Makarenko, who is credited with saving Hustynia and a

[19] Boris Romanov, "Oda selu Solova," http://forum.vgd.ru/206/25801/; "Solova. Tserkov' Mikhaila Arkhangela," *Narodnyi katalog pravoslavnoi arkhitektury*, http://sobory.ru/article/index.html?object=01631; E. A. Cheplianskaia, "Starodubskii uezd. Solova" www.debryansk.ru/~mir17/fio_sel9.htm.

[20] "Graf Gudovich, Ivan Vasil'evich, Ofitsial'nyi server Pravitel'stvo Moskvy," www.google.com/imgres?imgurl=http://www.mos.ru/wps/PA_1b9e2384/; "Pokoritel' Khadzhibeia," *Fokus* http://focus.ua/history/896; Ievhen Kabanets', *Zahybel' Uspens'koho soboru: mify i diisnist'. Dokumental'-ne rozsliduvannia* (Kyiv, 2011).

number of Kyivan architectural monuments from demolition in the
1930s. Orest died while helping his father research the monastery's architectural treasures. Also desecrated was the tomb of the Markevyches,
including the author of the *History of Little Russia,* Mykola Markevych,
beneath the main church of the monastery, that of the Holy Trinity.[21]

Few present-day visitors to the Hustynia Monastery are sufficiently
informed to appreciate the paradox that the Hustynia necropolis offers
those better versed in Ukrainian and Russian history. Buried there, in the
nave of a church built by Ivan Mazepa, is Nikolai Repnin, a Great Russian
governor general of Little Russia, next to the graves of descendants of
Ukrainian noble families whom he fought for a good part of his life.
While Repnin's tomb became an object of pilgrimage in the years
following the collapse of the Soviet Union, we know nothing about
the location of the burial place of his political opponent, the defender
of gentry rights Stepan Shyrai. His ancestral possessions, and most probably his grave as well, are now located on the territory of the Russian
Federation. If one of the participants in the great debate over the national
identity of the Eastern Slavs is remembered and revered by Russians and
Ukrainians alike, the other is completely forgotten and, in more ways than
one, remains unaccounted for.

The historical ideas they helped promote are a different matter. Today's
world, defined by exclusive national identities, is very much a creation of
Stepan Shyrai and his Starodub friends and collaborators, who sparked the
formation of a modern nation, irrespective of their own wishes and
intentions. The national ideology that the *History of the Rus'* helped
formulate and promote nationalized the masses on both sides of the
current Russo-Ukrainian border. In the environs of Starodub, the villages
of the Old Believers, who were hated by the local nobility, overwhelmed
former Cossack lands and turned them into a province of modern Russia.
The Ukrainian peasants whom Prince Repnin tried to protect from their
Ukrainian landowners appropriated the national ideology of their exploiters. Surprisingly, they also turned the grave of the Great Russian governor
general at the Hustynia monastery into a milestone of their quest for a
modern national identity. It is one of the many ironies of the situation
that this particular quest began with the *History of the Rus'.*

---

[21] "Sviato-Troitskii zhenskii monastyr'" http://old.orthodox.com.ua/?menu=7&submenu=2;
Stanislav Vlasenko, "Eshche odna taina Gustynskikh monakhin'," http://blog.turmir.com/
blog_13656.html.

Epilogue

On May 10, 2009, passengers on the Moscow-bound train that stopped for passport inspection in Briansk, the capital of the Russian province that includes Starodub, witnessed a disturbing scene. A modestly dressed man in his early fifties was removed from the train by the Russian border guards. His passport was taken away. The man was then declared *persona non grata* and banned from entering Russia, where he had lived for almost fifty years. No reason was given, but some time earlier an article had appeared on a website closely associated with the Russian authorities accusing a Moscow librarian, Yurii Kononenko, of anti-state activities. These included smuggling subversive literature into Russia and launching an audio book in Moscow based on the *History of the Rus'*.[1]

On the latter count, Yurii Kononenko, the individual removed from a Moscow-bound train in May 2009, was indeed guilty as charged. He was an organizer of an event that took place on October 6, 2007 in the Library of Ukrainian Literature near the Riga station immediately outside the central ring line of the Moscow subway system. The audio book was produced by Viktor Marchenko, a professor of physics at one of the Moscow universities. The producer and organizers of the launch had every reason to be proud of their accomplishment. After being reprinted in 1991 in Kyiv and then posted on the Kyiv-based Izbornyk website, both in the original and in Ivan Drach's Ukrainian translation, the *History of the Rus'* was finally taking on its true, not virtual, voice. The launch was announced on the Moscow-based Kobza website, and few of those who gathered on that rainy afternoon of October 2007 to listen to the text of

---

[1] "Ukraïntsiam zaboroniaiut' v'ïzd u Rosiiu," http://upi.org.ua/news/2009–05–15–7037; Elena Marinicheva, "Pochemu Iuru Kononenko ne pustili v Moskvu?" http://emarinicheva.livejournal. com/81399.html.

the *History* thought that they were involved in anything illegal or subversive. They were wrong.[2]

A few days after the launch, Yurii Kononenko was fired from his position at the Library of Ukrainian Literature. In the media frenzy that followed, the launch of the audio book was cited as an example of Kononenko's subversive activities. Roman Manekin, a native of Ukraine who took Russian citizenship after the disintegration of the USSR and established himself as one of the leading Russian commentators on Ukraine and Russo-Ukrainian relations, accused Kononenko of inciting ethnic hatred, with particular reference to his role in the audio book launch. Citing Nikolai Ulianov's *Origins of Ukrainian Separatism* (1966), Manekin claimed that the *History of the Rus'* was nothing but a manifesto of Ukrainian nationalism. "All that Cossackdom asserted and shouted at its councils during the hundred years of the hetman regime; all that it wrote in its 'letters' and proclamations did not fall into oblivion," wrote Manekin, quoting Ulianov. He continued the quotation: "one of those apocrypha has long since become prominent, gaining absolutely exclusive significance and playing the role of a Koran in the history of the separatist movement . . . I am speaking of the well-known *History of the Rus'*."[3]

Despite numerous protests, Yurii Kononenko was not reinstated in his position at the Ukrainian library. Nor can he return to his family in Moscow. Is he being barred from Russia for illegitimate reasons? Does he really constitute a threat to the Russian state and its stability? At least in part, the answer to these questions depends on whether one considers the author (or a group of collaborative authors) of the *History of the Rus'* a promoter of Ukrainian nationalism and a Russia-hater, as claimed by those who inspired the media campaign against Kononenko. As has been demonstrated in this book, that certainly was not the case. The short version of the answer is as follows: the author of the *History* was neither a Ukrainian nationalist nor a hater of Russia. Modern Ukrainian nationalism did not yet exist. As our analysis of the text of the *History* and our study of the lives and career patterns of the members of the Shyrai circle

[2] "Istoriia Rusov, Moscow, 1846," "Istoriia Rusiv, tr. Ivan Drach," Izbornyk. Istoriia Ukraïny IX–XVIII stolit'. Dzherela ta interpretatsiia http://litopys.org.ua/; Bohdan Bezpal'ko, "U subotu 15-ho zhovtnia u Bibliotetsi ukraïns'koï literatury u Moskvi," http://kobza.com.ua/content/blogcategory/51/86/50/50/.

[3] Roman Manekin, "Biblioteka ukrainskoi literatury v Moskve – filial ukrainskikh natsionalistov?" October 22, 2007, Kreml.org Politicheskaia ekspertnaia set', www.kreml.org/opinions/163555553?mode=print. Cf. N. Ul'ianov, *Proiskhozhdenie ukrainskogo separatizma* (New York, 1966), p. 104; Iurii Kononenko, "Zhanr politychnoho donosu zhyvyi," http://kobza.com.ua/content/view/1888/76/.

have shown, the producers and readers of the *History* were trying to negotiate the best deal possible for their nation of Cossack notables within the Russian Empire, not outside it. The long answer is much more complex and nuanced. I shall try to account for its complexity by putting the *History of the Rus'* into a number of broader contexts. One of them is that of modern nation-building; another is the history of empires and imperial borderlands; and yet another is the role of historical mythologies in the formation and maintenance of national ideology.

The *History of the Rus'* is complex in its composition and multiplicity of meanings, but it also fits some of the classic schemas of modern national development very well. The *History* made its first appearance around the time when, according to Miroslav Hroch's three-stage model of the growth of national movements, the Ukrainian national project embarked on its first, heritage-gathering stage. The year 1818, which appears on the title page of the first dated manuscript of the *History of the Rus'*, turned out to be crucial for Ukrainian national development. In that year Oleksii Pavlovsky published the first grammar of the modern Ukrainian language. In the following year Nikolai Tsertelev issued the first collection of Ukrainian songs, and Ivan Kotliarevsky, the author of *Eneïda* (1798), a Ukrainian-language poetic travesty of Virgil's *Aeneid*, wrote the first theatrical plays in Ukrainian. With these major literary works in the local vernacular, the grammar of that vernacular, and a collection of folklore all completed within a two-year period, it would be hard to imagine a more appropriate time for the appearance of the *History of the Rus'*. The *History* added an all-important historical component to the literary, linguistic, and folkloric elements of the Ukrainian national "awakening."[4]

Timing is not the only feature of the *History* that makes it fit comfortably into the first stage of the Ukrainian national revival. Its genre is also appropriate. The author makes no secret of his intention to produce a national history – a narrative that will glorify his nation and its accomplishments. He refers to the object of his work as the Rus', Little Russian or, alternatively, the Cossack nation. This multiplicity of names helps

---

[4] See Aleksei Pavlovskii, *Grammatika malorossiiskogo narechiia* (St. Petersburg, 1818); Nikolai Tsertelev, *Opyt sobraniia starinnykh malorossiiskikh pesnei* (St. Petersburg, 1819); Ivan Kotliarevs'kyi, *Eneida. Na malorossiiskii iazyk perelitsiovannaia I. Kotliarevskim* (St. Petersburg, 1798); Boris Kirdan (Borys Kyrdan), *Sobirateli narodnoi poèzii. Iz istorii ukrainskoi fol'kloristiki XIX v.* (Moscow, 1974); Hryhorii Hrabovych (George Grabowicz), *Do istoriï ukraïns'koï literatury* (*Toward a History of Ukrainian Literature*) (Kyiv, 1997), pp. 316–32; Orest Subtelny, *Ukraine: A History*, 4th edn. (Toronto, 2009), pp. 224–32.

turn the history of the Cossacks as a corporate estate and a political entity, referred to as the Hetmanate, Ukraine, or Little Russia, into the story of a nation. The author of the *History* did not accomplish this on his own: the eighteenth-century Cossack chroniclers had already written about the "Cossack Little Russian nation." What was new in the *History* was its emphasis on the national elements of the narrative, as well as the identification of the nation with the ethnic group, which was counterposed to its numerous "others." In the early nineteenth century, the nobles of the northern parts of the former Hetmanate found themselves confronted as never before by competitors defined in ethnic terms. To the Great Russian Old Believers, who had been in the region since the early eighteenth century, the partitions of Poland added Polish nobles, with whom the former Cossack elite came into contact in the neighboring Mahiliŏu gubernia, and Jewish merchants, who moved into the area in the early nineteenth century. With his references to "native-born" (*prirodnye*) Little Russians, Great Russians, Poles, and Jews, the author of the *History* asserted the ethnicity of his own nation to a degree unmatched by his predecessors. As a result, he produced a classic national narrative that attributed his nation's victories to the heroic deeds of native-born Little Russians and explained its defeats by the evil deeds of "non-natives."

Even so, the Starodub author was anything but a modern nationalist. On the one hand, he made a considerable advance on such predecessors as Semen Divovych, the author of the *Conversation between Great Russia and Little Russia* (1762), when he treated Great and Little Russia as separate nations, not only different administrative and legal divisions of the Russian Empire. On the other hand, his transition from an estate-based to an ethnically based concept of the nation was far from complete. In social terms, the Rus' nation of the *History* was that of the Cossack officers and their noble descendants, and only occasionally was membership extended to the popular masses. The author of the *History* was dismissive of people of low social status and critical of the actions of uneducated peasants. He was prepared to include them as part of the nation only if that furthered his argument, as in the case of peasant revolts against the Swedish army on the eve of the Battle of Poltava. The author of the *History* was the first in a long line of Ukrainian intellectuals who struggled with the religious and ethnic affinity of Russians and Ukrainians even as he treated them as distinct nations. He turned that affinity into his principal weapon, claiming that the Cossacks took precedence over the Great Russians as the first Rus' nation and trying to shame them into granting equal rights to their Little Russian brethren.

The phenomenal popularity of the *History of the Rus'*, whose admirers included such literary giants as Kondratii Ryleev, Alexander Pushkin, Nikolai Gogol, and Taras Shevchenko, should be attributed to two of its important features – the promotion of patriotism and the virtues of struggle against foreign oppression, which was open to various interpretations, and a historiographic style that emphasized the heroic deeds of ancestors, thereby appealing to the sensibilities of the Romantic age. No other historical work of the period managed to combine these two features, which made the popularity of the *History* not only possible but almost inevitable. The claim that the *History* had been written by generations of monks and edited by such prominent figures as Konysky and Poletyka, and thus ought to be authentic and reliable, added to the appeal of the text. The genre of historical mystification also gave the author an advantage over his competitors, who included Nikolai Karamzin, the first volumes of whose *History of the Russian State* appeared in print in 1818, and Dmitrii Bantysh-Kamensky, whose four-volume *History of Little Russia* was published in 1822. Not only were their works devoid of "freedom-loving ideas," but they also lacked the drama and detail of the *History*, whose author was not hampered by the dearth of historical sources. While maintaining the image of authenticity, he could add information, introduce new characters, and enhance the record of existing ones. He also concocted long speeches for his characters to deliver, incorporating politically and ideologically risky statements for which he bore no direct responsibility.

The Starodub author's model of historical narrative did not come from Mikhail Lomonosov, Vasilii Tatishchev, Mikhail Shcherbatov, or Ivan Boltin, whose histories of Russia relied heavily on the dry chronicle record and were thus difficult for readers of the Romantic age to digest. His model came largely from non-Russian sources. Among them were the early eighteenth-century Cossack chronicles, whose authors followed the humanist historiographic tradition in their love for stories of heroes and battles and in their reliance on speeches allegedly delivered by their protagonists to explain their motives and feelings. If humanist models were largely abandoned in Western Europe by the end of the seventeenth century, they survived in Europe's eastern borderlands and were brought back just at the time when Romanticism revived interest in heroic deeds and passionate speeches. Among the more recent influences was French historiography of the Enlightenment and early Romanticism. The author of the *History* knew Voltaire, whom he quoted on more than one occasion, and he was very well acquainted with Jean-Benoît Scherer's history of the Cossacks. The Russian translation of Scherer's *Annales de la Petite-Russie* was a precursor of the *History* with regard to its Russian language, literary style, treatment of events and, last but not least, some of its political ideas.

It was not only through the works of Western authors that the ideas and tropes of the Enlightenment and early Romanticism made their way into the *History*. The author was familiar with Russian political and literary discourse of the period, which was heavily influenced by the ideas of the French *philosophes*, and he knew the writings of Russia's first Romantics, including Gavriil Kamenev's *Gromval* and Vasilii Zhukovsky's *Maria's Grove*. Western influences were reinforced by native sources that emphasized the virtues of patriotism and estate rights and freedoms. Together they helped turn the *History of the Rus'* into a text that emphasized such themes as the struggle for national freedom, resistance to tyranny, the importance of lawful rule, and belief in reason as the guiding principle of historical development. The prominence of the nation in the *History* is a good example of how the ideas of prerevolutionary French historiography were complemented by the local tradition of Cossack chronicle writing. Scherer's *Annales* were the history of a nation rather than of a social order or a political entity. But so was Petro Symonovsky's *Brief Description of the Cossack Little Russian Nation* (1765). And so, in the *History of the Rus'*, the old nation of Cossack officers was transformed into a nation of Little Russian nobles fully conversant not only with the latest Western trends but also with the deeply rooted intellectual traditions of their homeland.[5]

Apart from the history of modern nation-building, another useful context for understanding the *History of the Rus'* and its era is the imperial one. It helps explain those features of the *History* that are overlooked, marginalized, or completely misunderstood in nation-driven narratives of

---

[5] On the humanist tradition in European historiography, see Anthony Grafton, *What Was History? The Art of History in Early Modern Europe* (Cambridge, 2007), pp. 189–25. On the development of early modern Ukrainian historiography, see Zenon E. Kohut, *The Question of Russo-Ukrainian Unity and Ukrainian Distinctiveness in Early Modern Ukrainian Thought and Culture* (Washington, D.C., 2001); Kohut, "Origins of the Unity Paradigm: Ukraine and the Construction of Russian National History (1620–1860)," *Eighteenth-Century Studies* 35, no. 1 (2001): 70–76; Serhii Plokhy, *The Origins of the Slavic Nations: Premodern Identities in Russia, Ukraine and Belarus* (Cambridge, 2006), pp. 161–202, 299–353; Plokhy, *Ukraine and Russia: Representations of the Past* (Toronto, 2008), pp. 4–48; Frank Sysyn, "The Cossack Chronicles and the Development of Modern Ukrainian Culture and National Identity," *Harvard Ukrainian Studies* 14, nos. 3–4 (1990): 593–607; Sysyn, "The Image of Russia and Russian–Ukrainian Relations in Ukrainian Historiography of the Late Seventeenth and Early Eighteenth Centuries," in *Culture, Nation and Identity: The Ukrainian–Russian Encounter, 1600–1945* (Edmonton and Toronto, 2003), pp. 108–43.

Ukrainian and Russian history. As we have seen, the *History of the Rus'* was produced in a milieu of elite hereditary Cossacks who were well integrated into the Russian Empire. That elite was largely concerned with the loss of its traditional rights and privileges and wanted to improve the conditions of its integration into the imperial political and social space. As the empire expanded, turning former frontierlands into the imperial core and tearing down old internal boundaries, the Enlightenment project of centralization and standardization called for eliminating special rights and privileges granted to particular corporate estates and territories. Resistance to that project was at the core of the argument presented in the *History of the Rus'*. Both sides in this dispute spoke the language of the Enlightenment but used it differently, to emphasize either rationality and imperial centralization or, contrariwise, the rights and freedoms of former subjects now turned citizens.

The immediate political, social, and cultural ethos of the centralizing empire could not help but influence a number of important features of the *History of the Rus'*. One of them was the language in which it was written, that is, the Russian used by the Ukrainian elite of the late eighteenth and early nineteenth centuries. This was by no means the language of the literary salons of the imperial capitals, and it was strongly influenced by the military and bureaucratic terminology of the period (the hallmark of the Cossack elite's imperial experience), as well as by the Ukrainian vernacular (spoken in their milieu and used in their historiographic tradition). The increasing influence of Russian manifested by the *History of the Rus'* gave evidence of the new cultural situation in the Hetmanate, which had all the hallmarks of a colonial setting. The Russian language of the *History* (unlike the Ukrainian language of Kotliarevsky's *Eneïda*) linked the hereditary Cossack elite with the Russian imperial core but separated it from its own people. It ideally suited the elite's political and cultural agenda of integrating itself into the empire. While the Russian language made possible the spectacular success of the *History* among the Little Russian nobility and Russian readers alike, these two groups interpreted the *History* differently. If the first understood and embraced its national message, the second initially saw it as an important historical resource in the struggle for the liberalization of Russia's autocratic regime.

It is also difficult, if not impossible, to understand the main historical argument of the *History* outside the imperial setting. The author advanced his nation's claim to the core of the empire's historical identity – the name and heritage of Rus'. Not only did he refer to the Cossacks as the nation of

Rus', but he also set out to narrate the history of his homeland, called Little Russia in the title of the work, as part of all-Russian history. This approach was spelled out in the introduction to the *History*, and the trend that it represented remained dominant in Ukrainian historiography for the rest of the nineteenth century. Its practitioners, from Dmitrii Bantysh-Kamensky to Mykola Markevych and Mykola Kostomarov, tried to fit the history of Ukraine into an all-Russian context. The anonymous author's rejection of the term "Ukraine" and his emphasis on the Rus' origins and Rus' primogeniture of the Cossacks was an attempt to end the subordination of Little Russia to Great Russia. By claiming the history of Kyivan Rus' for his nation and stressing that the Rus' name and history had been stolen from the Cossacks, the author was not undermining the imperial narrative but rearranging it in order to bring his people closer to its center.

Thus Cossack Rus' emerged in the *History* as not only historically superior to Great Russia but also more Russian than the Russians themselves. This argument not only promoted the political and social agenda of the hereditary Cossack elite but was also congruent with the dominant trend in the Russian historical imagination of the period, which saw Kyiv and Dnieper Ukraine as the cradle of the Russian state and nation and considered the inhabitants of that region the only true exemplars of Russianness, uncorrupted by time and foreign influence. The presentation of the Ukrainian Cossacks as true Russians puzzled subsequent generations of readers, who lived in an age of exclusive national identities and struggled to reconcile the author's Rus' terminology with his emphasis on the distinct character of the Cossack nation. The *History* thus became the starting point for a number of historiographic excursions that led to separate national narratives. It worked fairly well in both imperial (all-Russian and Little Russian) and Ukrainian national historiographic contexts, depending on the features of the text stressed by individual scholars. The anonymous author's attack on the Poles was considered proof of his true Russianness, and his rejection of the name "Ukraine" was taken to demonstrate his belief in the unity of the Rus' nation; conversely, his glorification of the Cossacks and vilification of the tsar's Great Russian subjects was embraced as a hallmark of his Ukrainian identity.

As we see from the text of the *History* and our discussion of the Starodub group of "unusual suspects," the author of the *History* was hardly a principled enemy of empires or imperial rule *per se*. He did his best to maintain his loyalty to the ruling dynasty while defending the rights and privileges of the Cossack nation. Telling in that regard is his choice of heroes and villains. By far the most positive character in the

History is Hetman Bohdan Khmelnytsky. The object of a cult revived by the Cossack elite in the wake of the Poltava debacle of 1709, Khmelnytsky served as an ideal symbol of both loyalty to the empire and the inviolability of the rights and privileges granted to the Cossack polity by the Russian tsars. Hetman Ivan Vyhovsky, who rebelled against the tsar soon after Khmelnytsky's death, by contrast, emerges as one of the most negative Cossack characters of the narrative. The rights and privileges secured by Vyhovsky from the Polish state are treated with respect verging on admiration, but the hetman himself is condemned. As for Ivan Mazepa, the author was reluctant either to embrace him as a hero or to reject him as a traitor. He found a solution to his dilemma in the story of Hetman Pavlo Polubotok, who died defending the rights of his nation even as he refused to rebel against the tsar. Mazepa's call for Ukrainian independence is never fully developed as a historiographic or political theme and remains a latent threat to the empire. The author's immediate purpose was to secure the best deal possible with the imperial authorities. Thus Russian rulers such as Peter I and Catherine II were shielded from direct criticism, which was directed against such imperial advisers as the butcher of Baturyn, Aleksandr Menshikov.[6]

If the Starodub author, or a group of coauthors, were indeed loyal to the empire and simply wanted a better deal for their nation, why did he/ they decide to hide behind the names of two Ukrainian luminaries of the previous century? Traditional answers to this question include references to the "freedom-loving" bent of the narrative, which was in conflict with prevailing ideological trends in the empire, its negative portrayal of representatives of the dominant Great Russian nation, its lenient treatment of traitors to the empire such as Ivan Mazepa, and its ambiguous attitude toward Russian rulers. All that may be true, but we are dealing

---

[6] On major trends in nineteenth-century Ukrainian historiography, see Taras Koznarsky, "Izmail Sreznevsky's *Zaporozhian Antiquity* as a Memory Project," *Eighteenth-Century Studies* 35, no. 1 (2001): 92–100; Volodymyr Kravchenko, *Narysy z ukraïns'koï istoriohrafiï epokhy natsional'noho Vidrodzhennia (druha polovyna XVIII–seredyna XIX st.)* (Kharkiv, 1996); Serhii Plokhy, *Unmaking Imperial Russia: Mykhailo Hrushevsky and the Writing of Ukrainian History* (Toronto, 2005), pp. 17–212; Oleksii Tolochko, "Kyievo-Rus'ka spadshchyna v istorychnii dumtsi Ukraïny pochatku XIX st.," in V. F. Verstiuk, V. M. Horobets', and O. P. Tolochko, *Ukraïna i Rosiia v istorychnii retrospektyvi*, vol. I: *Ukraïns'ki proekty v Rosiis'kii imperiï* (Kyiv, 2004), pp. 250–350; Stephen Velychenko, *National History as Cultural Process: A Survey of the Interpretations of Ukraine's Past in Polish, Russian and Ukrainian Historical Writing from the Earliest Times to 1914* (Edmonton, 1992), pp. 165–213; Velychenko, "Rival Grand Narratives of National History: Russian/Soviet, Polish and Ukrainian Accounts of Ukraine's Past (1772–1991)," *Österreichische Osthefte* 42 (2000): 139–60; Oleh Zhurba, *Stanovlennia ukraïns'koï arkheohrafiï: liudy, ideï, instytutsiï* (Dnipropetrovsk, 2003).

here with much more than the attempt of a politically threatened or insecure author to hide his real name. The *History* was a work of mystification in which the author used the story about the monastic origins of the manuscript and its editing by Archbishop Konysky not merely to cover his tracks but to authenticate the forgery and endow the manuscript with an authority that his own name could hardly provide. This was a relatively common practice in the early Romantic era, which was rich in forged historical and literary texts. In the context of growing tensions between imperial and national identities, they served as a means of renegotiating historical space dominated by empires. The old art of mystification became one of the few available ways to enhance the prestige of nations lacking states of their own in conflict with their much more established imperial competitors.

The *History of the Rus'* bears all the hallmarks of the national mystifications of the period and has been justly compared to such classic examples of that genre as James Macpherson's Ossianic poetry of the 1760s and the historical forgeries of Václav Hanka, which surfaced in Habsburg Bohemia in the early nineteenth century. The decision of the author of the *History* to write his work in the imperial language reflected not only the colonial status of Ukrainian culture in the Russian Empire but also general European practice in the production of national mystifications. Macpherson published his Ossianic poetry in English, claiming that it was a translation from the Gaelic. He produced the reverse translation into Gaelic only after the authenticity of his texts was challenged. Hanka published his "findings" both in the language of the "original" and in German "translation." In all three cases, the argument was addressed to the English-, German-, and Russian-speaking elites and readers in the core territory of the empire. The choice of language initially confused the imperial readership. Not only did Russian readers admire the *History* before its anti-Russian bias was pointed out, but Englishmen praised Ossianic poetry before they uncovered its Scottish message.

The content of the message was basically identical in all three cases. The Scottish, Czech, and Cossack Rus' nations were portrayed as culturally and historically equal or even superior to the dominant imperial nations. But this superiority was limited almost exclusively to the cultural sphere. It raised no political challenge to the integrity of the empire. In his historical works, Macpherson showed support for the union of England and Scotland (1701). The writings of Václav Hanka were equally devoid of a specific anti-imperial agenda. These authors did not strive for national independence but sought to reinterpret the past and renegotiate cultural relationships in order to claim a more advantageous place for their respective national elites in the pecking order of the empire.

Like the works of Macpherson and Hanka, the *History* came into existence at a time of cultural upheaval and growing interest in the collection of historical artifacts and preservation of local heritage. The mystifications of the era were desperate responses to a longing for (invariably glorious) local tradition, which was considered lost beyond recovery by any other means. The Ukrainian antiquarians of the 1810s, like their Scottish counterparts of the 1760s, complained of a lack of historical sources and pined for lost manuscript treasures. They hoped for a miracle, a recovery of a national Homer, and a sort of a miracle did indeed take place. It came in the form of "reconstructive forgeries" – freshly created literary and historical texts that recovered parts of the otherwise lost national narrative. The "signatures" of Ossian in Scotland and Konysky in Ukraine gave these works an authority and appeal they would otherwise have lacked. Few were willing to challenge the legitimacy of mystifications unless they belonged to nations that had nothing to gain from such "reconstructive forgeries." English and Irish authors exposed Macpherson as an impostor before his "crime of writing" was admitted by the Scots, and in the Ukrainian case it was Russian authors who first declared the *History* an unreliable historical source.[7]

Romanticism made the appearance of "reconstructive forgeries" not only possible but also welcome and to some degree legitimate. The terms "forgery" and "forgers," which are attractive to readers and often appear in the titles of books devoted to the mystifications of the late eighteenth and early nineteenth centuries, are liable to misrepresent the cultural significance of this phenomenon, if used without qualifiers. All over Europe there was not just a demand for "impostures" but active support for their production. The Edinburgh friends and financial backers of Macpherson funded his expedition to the Highlands to collect more "Scottish" folklore. Václav Hanka, who published his *Manuscripts of Dvůr Králové and of Zelená Hora* in 1818 (incidentally, the year that appears on the first dated

---

[7] On the history of mystifications, along with the works cited in the introduction to this book, see Paul Baines, *The House of Forgery in Eighteenth-Century Britain* (Burlington, 1999); Margaret Russett, *Fictions and Fakes: Forging Romantic Authenticity, 1760–1845* (Cambridge, 2006). For the impact of Macpherson's poetry on the rise of the Romantic movement, see Howard Gaskill, ed., *The Reception of Ossian in Europe* (Cardiff, 2004). On the reception of Ossian in the Russian Empire, see Iurii Levin, *Ossian v russkoi literature: konets XVIII–pervaia tret' XIX veka* (Leningrad, 1980). On the function of historical forgeries in East Central Europe and Ukraine, see Hryhorii Hrabovych, "Slidamy natsional'nykh mistyfikatsii," *Krytyka* (Kyiv) 5, no. 6 (June 2001): 14–23.

manuscript of the *History*), found a perfect institutional home in the Prague National Museum, which was established by Czech aristocrats. The estates of rich Starodub landowners who were spotted disseminating manuscripts of the *History* served as launching pads for the spectacular literary career of that imposture. Not surprisingly, the authors of mystifications were sensitive not only to the cultural needs of their peoples but also to the historical interests and proclivities of their sponsors. Macpherson created impressive (and, needless to say, fake) genealogies for some of his Scottish backers. František Palacký, another beneficiary of the generosity of Bohemian aristocrats and the father of Czech national historiography, "proved" beyond reasonable doubt the Bohemian origins of his benefactor, Count Kaspar Maria Sternberg. In this context, the episodes of the *History* dealing with the invented genealogy of the Khudorbas and the anonymous author's differential treatment of the family histories of Starodub notables do not seem out of place.

Taking a closer look at the noble backers of national mystifications, it is hard to ignore the striking parallels between the Starodub notables who helped produce and disseminate the *History* and the Bohemian aristocrats whose involvement in cultural affairs helped create conditions for the emergence of Václav Hanka's forgeries. Both groups were among the victims of imperial reforms launched by "enlightened despots" of the eighteenth century and continued by their successors. In the Czech case, these were the reforms of Empress Maria Theresa and her son, Joseph II; in the Ukrainian case, they were the reforms of Catherine II, Paul I, and Alexander I. Both imperial governments were not only abolishing the old regional rights and privileges of the landowning elites but also undermining their socioeconomic base by trying to improve the lot of peasant serfs. Insult was added to injury when the Czech and Ukrainian elites, once very influential at court, lost their commanding positions in Vienna and St. Petersburg to rival groups. At the Habsburg court the Bohemians were replaced by Italians in the first half of the eighteenth century. The Ukrainians lost most of their influence at the Russian court with the death of Prince Bezborodko in 1799. The losers were forced to return home and forge an alliance with local patriots, who had opposed imperial centralization all along.

Of course, there were also significant differences between these two elites. The Bohemian aristocrats were much better established, far richer, and began their nation-building activities before the Cossacks did. They built numerous institutions (some of which still exist) that laid the academic and cultural foundations for the modern Czech nation. The

Cossack aristocracy was weaker by far, and its contribution to nation-building, at least originally, was much more limited. The local notables built no institutions and never employed people of the caliber of Palacký as librarians or archivists on their estates, since they looked to the empire to do that for them. They did, however, take advantage of the incompleteness of centralization in Russia. If in the Habsburg Empire local administration was taken away from the aristocracy and handed over to imperial officials, in the Russian Empire the notables continued to control local centers of power and used them to resist the encroachments of St. Petersburg. It was from the home of a marshal of the local nobility that the *History of the Rus'* began its triumphal march into the broader literary world.[8]

What seems especially important for our discussion is that the Czech and Ukrainian nobilities were as one in their fascination with local history – in the Czech case with the Kingdom of Bohemia, and in the Ukrainian case with the Cossack Hetmanate. Both groups had to rely, though not exclusively, on invented histories, and both thus contributed to the rise of modern national identities. The turn to a new identity took place in both cases, but most particularly in the Hetmanate, against the background of a crisis of the old estate-based group identity. As Liah Greenfeld remarks with regard to the rise of Russian national identity, "[n]ationality elevated every member of the nation and offered an absolute guarantee from the loss of status beyond a certain – high – level. One could be stripped of nobility, but ... not of nationality. There was in nationalism the assurance of a modicum of unassailable dignity, dignity that was one's to keep." The former Cossack officeholders, whose noble status was questioned or revoked by the imperial authorities, indeed had nowhere to turn in their quest for dignity but the national narrative embodied in the *History of the Rus'*. Unlike their Czech counterparts, the Cossack notables did not have to reconcile their corporate estate identity with their national one: both were Cossack, and both were rooted in the glorious past that had to be recovered. In the *History of the Rus'*, both the cult of reason promoted by the Enlightenment and the power of the imagination released by Romanticism were put into the service of that ambitious project.[9]

---

[8] On the Czech cultural revival and the role of the nobility in its burgeoning, see Hugh LeCaine Agnew, *Origins of the Czech National Renaissance* (Pittsburgh, Pa., 1993); Rita Krueger, *Czech, German and Noble: Status and National Identity in Habsburg Bohemia* (New York, 2009); David L. Cooper, *Creating the Nation: Identity and Aesthetics in Early Nineteenth-Century Russia and Bohemia* (DeKalb, Ill., 2010).

[9] Liah Greenfeld, *Nationalism: Five Roads to Modernity* (Cambridge, Mass., 1992), pp. 220, 253.

The national mystifications of the late eighteenth and early nineteenth centuries gave a powerful stimulus to the creation of modern national ideologies. Like burned-out stages of rockets (to develop an image used by Ivan Drach with reference to the *History of the Rus'*), the mystifications could be dropped once they had fulfilled their function. The rocket continued its flight, its trajectory no longer defined by the hopes and expectations of those who produced the first stage.

Whatever the authors of historical mystifications thought of empires, the national mythologies launched with their help eventually served to undermine and destroy imperial rule. The dissemination and reception of the *History of the Rus'* typifies the formation, reconstruction, and modification of national mythologies. The *History* helped nationalize the Cossack myth, whose origins can be traced back to the early seventeenth century, when the Orthodox churchmen of the Polish-Lithuanian Commonwealth sought to enlist the Cossacks in their struggle against the Rome-sponsored and Polish-backed church union. They hailed the Cossacks as descendants of the Kyivan princes, fighters against the Ottoman menace, and loyal sons of the Orthodox Church. By the eighteenth century, the Cossack myth had acquired new characteristics. In chronicles now written not by Orthodox monks but by Cossack secretaries of the Hetmanate's chancellery, emphasis was placed on Cossack resistance to Polish rule and on their voluntary submission to the Muscovite tsars. After the Cossack officers completed their transition from a military elite to a corporate estate, they needed the Cossack myth to protect the rights and freedoms once given to the Cossack Host by the tsars. Unless they kept the Cossack name and memory alive, they had no legal or historical basis for maintaining their privileges.

The *History of the Rus'* brought together both these strands of the Cossack myth. The Cossacks emerge from the ages of the *History* both as heirs of the Kyivan Rus' princes and as glorious fighters against Polish oppression who deserved special treatment by the Russian state because of their voluntary submission to tsarist rule and their military service to the empire. The purpose behind this treatment of the old myth, as we have seen, was to obtain the best possible terms for the integration of the Cossack elite into the Russian Empire. To that end, the treatment of the Cossacks as a separate nation, already present in the eighteenth-century chronicles, was further enhanced; the first steps were taken to rehabilitate the Ukrainian record before and after Poltava; and the ethnic and cultural affinity of the Rus' nation of the Cossacks and the Great Russian nation of the tsars was emphasized. In its new form, the Cossack myth served the demands of the moment rather well: it raised the specter of Mazepa as a threat of potential rebellion against the empire even as it tried to shame the imperial authorities into recognizing the noble status of descendants of the Cossack elite.

The *History* also made the Cossack myth available to a new generation of Ukrainian intellectuals, but it could not control their interpretation of it for very long. The members of the Brotherhood of SS. Cyril and Methodius, who originally embraced the Cossack myth as presented in the *History of the Rus'*, soon redefined it in their own terms. Mykola Kostomarov, Panteleimon Kulish, and Taras Shevchenko were eager to stress the egalitarianism of the Cossacks. Some of these intellectuals rejected the elitist attitude of the *History of the Rus'* as a product of the conservatism of the landowning classes. The next generation of Ukrainian activists rehabilitated the *History* as a monument of Ukrainian political thought, but they also further modified the Cossack myth embodied in it. Mykhailo Drahomanov, who regarded the *History* as the first manifestation of Ukrainian liberal ideology, thought of Cossackdom as characterized by adherence to democratic institutions and practices, which linked Ukraine with Europe and distinguished it from authoritarian Russia.

The Russian Revolution of 1917 gave new meaning to the old historical myth. The Cossack myth made a dramatic entrance into Ukrainian politics in 1918, when Hetman Pavlo Skoropadsky, elected by a congress of Ukrainian landowners, used Cossack symbols and traditions to legitimize his rule over Ukraine. The elitist version of the Cossack myth, as presented in the *History of the Rus'*, briefly triumphed over its egalitarian variant. But the socialist leaders of the Ukrainian Revolution were not prepared to surrender the Cossack myth to their class enemies. When they overthrew Hetman Skoropadsky in late 1918, they did so under the leadership of Symon Petliura, a former newspaper editor whom they now called the Supreme Otaman – an office and term that harked back to the Cossack military tradition. Even the Bolsheviks bought into the myth, creating their own detachments of Red Cossacks, although their endorsement of Cossackdom was to be short-lived.

The Soviet authorities regarded the Cossacks and their history with suspicion, seeing in them representatives of the well-to-do Russian peasantry that resisted Stalin's collectivization of agriculture and, in the Ukrainian case, symbols of Ukrainian nationalism. In the late 1930s they rehabilitated Bohdan Khmelnytsky, originally treated as a hostile representative of the ruling classes, because of his anti-Polish record and contribution to what became known as the "reunification" of Ukraine and Russia. But the rest of Cossack mythology was suppressed in the Soviet historical narrative. In the early 1970s, research and writing on Cossack history was virtually outlawed in Soviet Ukraine as Petro Shelest, the independent-minded Ukrainian party boss, was removed from his post on allegations of national deviation and idealization of the Cossack past. In 1990, when the Cossack myth made a spectacular return to the Ukrainian public sphere, with pro-independence marches commemorating five hundred years of Ukrainian Cossackdom, it seemed only natural that the *History of the Rus'* should make its return as well. Since 1991 it has been published several times, both in its Russian-language original text and in modern Ukrainian translation, contributing to the revival of Cossack mythology among the broad masses of the Ukrainian population.

Despite the fierce historical debates that continue to rock Ukrainian society, the Cossack myth is the only feature of historical memory that remains unchallenged at the level of mass identity. In political terms, the Cossack myth in present-day Ukraine has relatively little to do with its representation in the *History of the Rus'*. It now serves to assert Ukraine's historical uniqueness and independence. Accordingly, it stresses elements of the Cossack past different from those emphasized in the *History*. In its current incarnation, the Cossack myth drops its anti-Polish and anti-Jewish themes and has little interest in close cultural affinity with Russia. Still, many elements of the traditional mythology remain the same, as attested by the continuing popularity of Bohdan Khmelnytsky and the glorification of other Cossack leaders, including Ivan Pidkova and Severyn Nalyvaiko. The Cossack myth, which the Ukrainian nation-building project took from the *History of the Rus'* in the early nineteenth century, remains an important component of Ukrainian historical and national identity. It also continues to cause problems for the ethnic identification of those inhabiting the former Cossack territories of Starodub and Kuban, now in the Russian Federation.[10]

The development and modification of Cossack mythology makes it quite obvious that not all national traditions were "invented" by nineteenth-century nation builders. The historical myths, as Anthony Smith has pointed out, can be adapted to different circumstances and

---

[10] On the development of Cossack mythology in Ukraine and Russia, see John A. Armstrong, "Myth and History in the Evolution of Ukrainian Consciousness"; Serhii Plokhy, *Tsars and Cossacks: A Study in Iconography* (Cambridge, Mass., 2002); Plokhy, *Ukraine and Russia*, pp. 165–81, 196–212; Frank E. Sysyn, "The Reemergence of the Ukrainian Nation and Cossack Mythology," *Social Research* 58, no. 4 (Winter 1991): 845–64; Laura Olson, *Performing Russia: Folk Revival and Russian Identity* (London, 2004), pp. 160–75.

acquire new meanings in different contexts. They can also successfully cross the imagined boundaries between nations formed in the early modern period and those constituted more recently. The Cossack myth, first created and promoted in the interest of the Orthodox Church and the Ruthenian nation of the seventeenth century, was transformed into the founding myth of the Little Russian nation in the eighteenth century and then made a successful passage into the era of modern nationalism. The role played in this process by the *History of the Rus'*, a transitional text between premodern and modern nationalism, indicates that there is no revolutionary change from one to the other when it comes to historical narrative. The transition takes time and occurs gradually.[11]

In closing, let us return to the case of Yurii Kononenko. It is certainly anachronistic to regard the *History of the Rus'* as a manifestation of modern Ukrainian nationalism or to consider Kononenko's involvement in the popularization of that book a threat to the stability of the Russian state. The Russian authorities, however, clearly thought otherwise. In the fall of 2010 they moved to ban the Federal Ukrainian Cultural Autonomy in Russia, an umbrella organization for Ukrainian communities throughout the Russian Federation of which Kononenko remained vice president. In the closing days of that year, the Moscow authorities shut down the Library of Ukrainian Literature, although the Ukrainian embassy in Moscow stated that the library contained no books considered hateful or subversive by the Russian authorities. It may be assumed that what truly concerned the Russian authorities was the spread in Russia of the ideas of the Ukrainian Orange Revolution of 2004 and the possibility that Ukrainians in the Russian Federation, who number three million, might assert an exclusivist Ukrainian identity and develop a primary loyalty to independent Ukraine. As was the case throughout most of the nineteenth and twentieth centuries, at the beginning of the new millennium the *History of the Rus'* continued to be associated (rightly or wrongly) with the ideas of civic freedom and the rise of Ukrainian assertiveness and identity.[12]

[11] Anthony D. Smith, *The Ethnic Origins of Nations* (Oxford and New York, 1986), pp. 174–208. On the "invention of national tradition" paradigm, see Hugh Trevor-Roper, "The Invention of Tradition: The Highland Tradition in Scotland," in *The Invention of Tradition*, ed. Eric Hobsbawm and Terence Ranger (Cambridge, 1997), pp. 15–41. On national historical narratives in Western and Central Europe, see Stefan Berger, Mark Donovan, and Kevin Passmore, "Apologias for the Nation-State in Western Europe since 1800," in Berger *et al.*, *Writing National Histories: Western Europe since 1800* (London and New York, 1999), pp. 3–14.

[12] Paul Goble, "Moscow Seeks to Shut Down Ukrainian Cultural Autonomy Groups in Russia," *Kyiv Post*, March 22, 2010, www.kyivpost.com/blogs/blogger/469/post/5230/; "Pislia druho obshuku

As the Russian authorities contended with the alleged threat posed by the Ukrainian Cossack myth, they were faced with a related domestic challenge. On the eve of the Russian population census in the fall of 2010, a group of local patriots in Rostov on the Don, the historical capital of the Don Cossacks, issued a video clip with a song that called on the inhabitants of the region to report their nationality as "Cossack." The lyrics of the rap song released by the group stress the unique role of the Cossacks on Russia's southern frontier, glorify the mythologized Cossack past, emphasize the linguistic peculiarities of the Cossacks, and lament their disappearance as a distinct cultural group. "We are respected in the Caucasus and in central Russia," sang the representatives of the new Cossack nation. "Forces were lost in the era of the Red Terror. Of millions of Cossacks, hundreds of thousands remain. We are being reborn from the ashes; graves are creaking . . . Our right to call ourselves a nation was taken away from us. They de-Cossackized us, burned us, robbed us of our glory. In place of our thousand-year history, they gave us [the history of] peasants . . . Our seagoing exploits were reduced to nothing. Who knows that [Semen] Dezhnev was a Cossack, and Yermak and [Vitus] Bering along with him? . . . Whoever feels Cossack blood seething in his veins – your nationality is Cossack! . . . Our national language is *balachka* [Ukrainian colloquialism for "talk"] and *gutor* [Russian colloquialism for "talk"] . . . . Europe was enraptured by our people's culture."[13]

Is the birth of a new Cossack nation indeed in the offing? It is at least clear that the singers have their mythology right, and there are other nation-building movements that can serve them as inspiration. In the year 2000 Paul Robert Magocsi, a professor of Ukrainian studies at the University of Toronto and an intellectual leader of the Rusyn movement, which claims that the people of Ukrainian Transcarpathia and neighboring regions of Poland and Slovakia are not part of the Ukrainian nation but constitute a separate Rusyn nationality, published a collection of essays entitled *Of the Making of Nationalities There Is No End.* It would appear that there is indeed no end in sight to imagining new nationalities, be they Rus', Rusyn, or Cossack. And if that is so, then this book may be not only about the past but also about the future.[14]

---

ukraïns'ku biblioteku v Moskvi zakryly," Informatsiine ahentstvo UNIAN, December 26, 2010, www.unian.net/ukr/news/news-413409.html.

[13] "Natsional'nost': kazak," www.youtube.com/watch?v=I6XSJKUwTpc&feature=player_embedded.

[14] Paul Robert Magocsi, *Of the Making of Nationalities There Is No End,* 2nd edn. (Boulder, Col., 2000).

Cossack family networks

BEZBORODKOS

The Grand Chancellor of the Russian Empire, Oleksandr Bezborodko (1747–99), had many family connections in the former Hetmanate. He was an uncle of Count Viktor Kochubei, the imperial minister of the interior (1819–25), and of Nastasia Bakurynska, the wife of Mykhailo Myklashevsky. His brother, Illia Bezborodko, was married to Hanna Shyrai. It was on their estate in Hryniv that one of the first copies of the *History of the Rus'* was found in the 1820s.

BOROZDNAS

Petro Borozdna (1765–1820), a retired major, marshal of the nobility of Novozybkiv county, and contributor to *Vestnik Evropy*, was a great-grandson of Ivan Borozdna and a grandson of Antin Kryzhanovsky, two eighteenth-century Cossack notables whose stories are featured in the *History of the Rus'*. Petro Borozdna's sons Vasyl and Ivan were published authors. Another son, Mykola, a future governor of Smolensk, married into the Myklashevsky family. Petro Borozdna's daughter, Uliana, was the wife of Stepan Shyrai.

LASHKEVYCHES

Ivan Lashkevych (1765–1822), a retired second major, alumnus of Moscow University, and a published translator from English, was a great-grandson of Hnat Halahan and a grandson of Hryhorii Halahan, colonels of the Pryluky regiment whose exploits are described in the *History of the Rus'*. His wife, Nastasia Myloradovych, was a great-granddaughter of Pavlo Polubotok, one of the most prominent characters in the *History*. Lashkevych was a neighbor of the Myklashevskys and the Shyrais.

MYKLASHEVSKYS

Mykhailo Myklashevsky (1757–1847), a retired imperial governor and senator, was a great-grandson of Colonel Mykhailo Myklashevsky of Starodub, who is treated with particular respect in the *History*. It was on his estate that Aleksandr von Brigen discovered the manuscript of the *History* in the fall of 1825 and collected information about the Khudorba History. The Myklashevskys intermarried with the Bezborodkos, Borozdnas, and Shyrais.

RADKEVYCHES

Yakiv Radkevych (1763–1830), a history teacher at the Starodub school and owner of a copy of Jean-Benoît Scherer's *Annales* in Russian translation used by the author of the *History of the Rus'*, was an acquaintance of Mykhailo Myklashevsky and Petro Borozdna. He married into the Zankovsky family, which had extensive connections in the Starodub regiment. Radkevych's brother-in-law, Andrii Zankovsky, served under Oleksandr Bezborodko and married into the Myklashevsky family. A brother of Zankovsky's second wife, Mykhailo Lyshen, married into the Shyrai family.

SHYRAIS

Stepan Shyrai (1761–1841), a retired general and the marshal of the Chernihiv nobility, became the most ardent promoter of the *History* after a copy of it was discovered on the Hryniv estate. Shyrai was a grandson of Vasyl Hudovych, who is very positively depicted in the *History*. He was also related to the Myklashevskys, Haletskys, and Skorupas, whose ancestors are discussed in the *History*. Shyrai was related to the Bezborodkos through a cousin, Hanna Shyrai-Bezborodko. He was a son-in-law of Petro Borozdna.

Acknowledgments

This book is the result of a project that spanned more than a quarter of a century. My fascination, sometimes bordering on obsession, with the *History of the Rus'* and the question of its authorship began soon after Oleksa Myshanych published excerpts from the work in an anthology of eighteenth-century Ukrainian literature in 1983. My first essay on the topic appeared in 1989. After that, no matter what my current project, the *History* would always be lingering in the background, an unsolved puzzle that simply refused to go away. It always demanded more study, more research, and more help from my friends and colleagues, whose advice, assistance, and sincere interest in the project helped me keep going when I was all but prepared to give up. I would like to take this opportunity to thank all those who helped me complete my research and produce this book.

I was fortunate enough to meet some of the scholars of the *History* and of Cossack historical writing in general who appear in the pages of this book, and whose devotion to their subject inspired me in my own research. Among them were Olena Apanovych, Yaroslav Dzyra, Oleksa Myshanych, Fedir Shevchenko, Yurii Shevelov, and Volodymyr Zamlynsky. All of them are gone now, but their scholarly legacy lives on, and not only in this book. For the stories they shared with me and their advice I will always be grateful. I would also like to thank the following friends and colleagues, dispersed across two continents.

At the University of Dnipropetrovsk in Ukraine, I am especially grateful to Fr. Yurii Mytsyk, who introduced me to the world of Cossack historical writing, and Liudmila Shvarts, the coauthor of my first article on the *History of the Rus'*. In Ukraine I also benefited from the advice of the late Anatolii Boiko, Andrii Bovhyria, Volodymyr Kravchenko, Volodymyr Kryvosheia, Oleksii Tolochko, Maksym Yaremenko, and Oleh Zhurba. Yaroslav Fedoruk and Natalia Yakovenko impressed upon me the importance of carrying on and concluding this study. Natalia

371

Yakovenko and Oleksii Tolochko also read the entire manuscript and suggested ways of improving it. Zenon Kohut, Oleh Ilnytzkyj, Frank Sysyn, and Myroslav Yurkevich at the University of Alberta, and Taras Koznarsky of the University of Toronto in Canada, provided excellent advice on how I could improve the drafts of my essays and conference papers dealing with the *History*. Especially useful were the comments of Frank Sysyn, who often did not agree with my reading of the *History* and its message, and Myroslav Yurkevich, who edited my prose and provided thoughtful suggestions on how it could be improved. At Harvard, I would like to thank Michael Flier, George Grabowicz, John LeDonne, Terry Martin, and Roman Szporluk for their advice and interest in the project. Phil Bodrock read and commented on the final draft of the manuscript. I especially value the encouragement I received from the late Ihor Ševčenko, whose masterful interpretation of texts and unique ability to place them in the broadest possible cultural contexts served as an example and inspiration for my own research.

I also owe a debt of gratitude to those who helped me find my way through the labyrinths of archival and library collections pertaining to the lands of the former Hetmanate. I am especially grateful for the support and assistance offered me by Hennadii Boriak, Liubov Dubrovina, Ekaterina Cheplianskaia, Mariia Masukova, Anna Morozova, Tatiana Oparina, Ihor Skochylias, Oleh Turii, and Volodymyr Kulyk. Serhy Yekelchyk and Hiroaki Kuromiya read parts of the book and gave me excellent advice on how it could be improved. My graduate student Oksana Mykhed helped me track down bibliographic rarities and decipher nineteenth-century handwriting. At Harvard my research on this project was supported by the George O'Neill senior faculty research grant from the Davis Center for Russian and Eurasian Studies and a faculty research grant from the Ukrainian Research Institute. I would like to thank Lis Tarlow and Maria Altamore at the Davis Center, Tymish Holowinsky and M. J. Scott at the Ukrainian Institute, and Cory Paulsen in the Department of History at Harvard for their assistance in securing funding for this seemingly endless project.

My special thanks go to my agent, Steve Wasserman, for helping to negotiate the contract for the publication of this book. Chris Chappell at Palgrave Macmillan and Michael Watson at Cambridge University Press helped me revise my original proposal. I am also grateful for the advice I received from anonymous reviewers whom they persuaded to read selected chapters of the manuscript. The readers not only provided extremely important feedback but also endorsed the manuscript while

I was still working on some of its most challenging parts. I hope they will not be disappointed with the final result. At Cambridge University Press, my thanks go to Anna Zaranko, Chloe Howell, Sarah Roberts, and Radhika Venkatesen for their excellent work in copy-editing the manuscript and guiding it through the production process. Finally, I would like to thank the person most responsible for the appearance of this book. Many of my friends and colleagues urged me to put every other project aside and write it. But there has been no more enthusiastic supporter of this enterprise and no more interested and critical reader of the manuscript than my wife. I dedicate this book to her.

Index